Rationalism in Politics

RATIONALISM
IN POLITICS

and other essays

Michael Oakeshott

METHUEN

LONDON and NEW YORK

First published in 1962 by
Methuen & Co. Ltd
11 New Fetter Lane, London EC4P 4EE
Reprinted twice
Reprinted 1984

First published as a University Paperback in 1967
Reprinted 1981

Published in the USA by
Methuen & Co.
in association with Methuen, Inc.
733 Third Avenue, New York, NY 10017

© *1962 Michael Oakeshott*

Printed in Great Britain by
J. W. Arrowsmith Ltd, Bristol

British Library Cataloguing in Publication Data
Oakeshott, Michael
Rationalism in politics and other essays.
1. Political science
I. Title
320'.08   *JA*66   80–42279

ISBN 0–416–69950–2 (*University paperbacks; 225*)

Contents

Preface   *page* vii

Rationalism in Politics   1

The Political Economy of Freedom   37

The Tower of Babel   59

Rational Conduct   80

Political Education   111

The Activity of being an Historian   137

On being Conservative   168

The Voice of Poetry in the
    Conversation of Mankind   197

The Moral Life in the Writings of
    Thomas Hobbes   248

The Study of 'Politics' in a University   301

To C. S.

Preface

Of these essays, composed during the last twelve years, seven were first published elsewhere. Each was written for a different occasion, but they seem to me to go together well enough to be put together. They are all concerned with doing, understanding and explaining; with different modes of these activities and with their relations to one another. And, although they do not compose a settled doctrine, they disclose a consistent style or disposition of thought. The essay on poetry is a belated retraction of a foolish sentence in *Experience and its Modes*.

1962   M. O.

Rationalism in Politics

Les grands hommes, en apprenant aux faibles à réfléchir, les ont mis
sur la route de l'erreur. VAUVENARGUES, *Maxims et Réflexions*, 221

I

The object of this essay is to consider the character and pedigree of
the most remarkable intellectual fashion of post-Renaissance Europe.
The Rationalism with which I am concerned is modern Rationalism.
No doubt its surface reflects the light of rationalisms of a more distant past, but in its depth there is a quality exclusively its own, and it
is this quality that I propose to consider, and to consider mainly in
its impact upon European politics. What I call Rationalism in politics
is not, of course, the only (and it is certainly not the most fruitful)
fashion in modern European political thinking. But it is a strong and
a lively manner of thinking which, finding support in its filiation
with so much else that is strong in the intellectual composition of
contemporary Europe, has come to colour the ideas, not merely of
one, but of all political persuasions, and to flow over every party line.
By one road or another, by conviction, by its supposed inevitability,
by its alleged success, or even quite unreflectively, almost all politics
today have become Rationalist or near-Rationalist.

The general character and disposition of the Rationalist are, I
think, not difficult to identify. At bottom he stands (he always
stands) for independence of mind on all occasions, for thought free
from obligation to any authority save the authority of 'reason'. His
circumstances in the modern world have made him contentious: he
is the *enemy* of authority, of prejudice, of the merely traditional,
customary or habitual. His mental attitude is at once sceptical and
optimistic: sceptical, because there is no opinion, no habit, no belief,
nothing so firmly rooted or so widely held that he hesitates to question it and to judge it by what he calls his 'reason'; optimistic,
because the Rationalist never doubts the power of his 'reason' (when
properly applied) to determine the worth of a thing, the truth of an

opinion or the propriety of an action. Moreover, he is fortified by a belief in a 'reason' common to all mankind, a common power of rational consideration, which is the ground and inspiration of argument: set up on his door is the precept of Parmenides – judge by rational argument. But besides this, which gives the Rationalist a touch of intellectual equalitarianism, he is something also of an individualist, finding it difficult to believe that anyone who can think honestly and clearly will think differently from himself.

But it is an error to attribute to him an excessive concern with *a priori* argument. He does not neglect experience, but he often appears to do so because he insists always upon it being his own experience (wanting to begin everything *de novo*), and because of the rapidity with which he reduces the tangle and variety of experience to a set of principles which he will then attack or defend only upon rational grounds. He has no sense of the cumulation of experience, only of the readiness of experience when it has been converted into a formula: the past is significant to him only as an encumbrance. He has none of that *negative capability* (which Keats attributed to Shakespeare), the power of accepting the mysteries and uncertainties of experience without any irritable search for order and distinctness, only the capability of subjugating experience; he has no aptitude for that close and detailed appreciation of what actually presents itself which Lichtenberg called *negative enthusiasm*, but only the power of recognizing the large outline which a general theory imposes upon events. His cast of mind is gnostic, and the sagacity of Ruhnken's rule, *Oportet quaedam nescire*, is lost upon him. There are some minds which give us the sense that they have passed through an elaborate education which was designed to initiate them into the traditions and achievements of their civilization; the immediate impression we have of them is an impression of cultivation, of the enjoyment of an inheritance. But this is not so with the mind of the Rationalist, which impresses us as, at best, a finely-tempered, neutral instrument, as a well-trained rather than as an educated mind. Intellectually, his ambition is not so much to share the experience of the race as to be demonstrably a self-made man. And this gives to his intellectual and practical activities an almost preternatural deliberateness and self-consciousness, depriving them of any element of passivity, removing from them all sense of rhythm and continuity and dissolving them into a succession of climacterics, each to be surmounted by a *tour de raison*. His mind has no atmosphere, no changes of season and temperature; his intellectual processes, so far as possible, are insulated from all external influence and go on in the void. And having cut himself off from the traditional knowledge of his society, and denied the value of any education more extensive than a training in a technique of analysis, he is apt to attribute to mankind a necessary inexperience in all the critical moments of life, and if he were more self-critical he might begin to wonder how the race had ever succeeded in surviving. With an almost poetic fancy, he strives to live each day as if it were his first, and he believes that to form a habit is to fail. And if, with as yet no thought of analysis, we glance below the surface, we may, perhaps, see in the temperament, if not in the character, of the Rationalist, a deep distrust of time, an impatient hunger for eternity and an irritable nervousness in the face of everything topical and transitory.

Now, of all worlds, the world of politics might seem the least amenable to rationalist treatment – politics, always so deeply veined with both the traditional, the circumstantial and the transitory. And, indeed, some convinced Rationalists have admitted defeat here: Clemenceau, intellectually a child of the modern Rationalist tradition (in his treatment of morals and religion, for example), was anything but a Rationalist in politics. But not all have admitted defeat. If we except religion, the greatest apparent victories of Rationalism have been in politics: it is not to be expected that whoever is prepared to carry his rationalism into the conduct of life will hesitate to carry it into the conduct of public affairs.[1]

But what is important to observe in such a man (for it is characteristic) is not the decisions and actions he is inspired to make, but the source of his inspiration, his idea (and with him it will be a deliberate and conscious idea) of political activity. He believes, of course, in the open mind, the mind free from prejudice and its relic, habit. He believes that the unhindered human 'reason' (if only it can

---

[1] A faithful account of the politics of rationalism (with all its confusions and ambivalences) is to be found in J. H. Blackham, *Political Discipline in a Free Society*.

be brought to bear) is an infallible guide in political activity. Further, he believes in argument as the technique and operation of 'reason'; the truth of an opinion and the 'rational' ground (not the use) of an institution is all that matters to him. Consequently, much of his political activity consists in bringing the social, political, legal and institutional inheritance of his society before the tribunal of his intellect; and the rest is rational administration, 'reason' exercising an uncontrolled jurisdiction over the circumstances of the case. To the Rationalist, nothing is of value merely because it exists (and certainly not because it has existed for many generations), familiarity has no worth, and nothing is to be left standing for want of scrutiny. And his disposition makes both destruction and creation easier for him to understand and engage in, than acceptance or reform. To patch up, to repair (that is, to do anything which requires a patient knowledge of the material), he regards as waste of time; and he always prefers the invention of a new device to making use of a current and well-tried expedient. He does not recognize change unless it is a self-consciously induced change, and consequently he falls easily into the error of identifying the customary and the traditional with the changeless. This is aptly illustrated by the rationalist attitude towards a tradition of ideas. There is, of course, no question either of retaining or improving such a tradition, for both these involve an attitude of submission. It must be destroyed. And to fill its place the Rationalist puts something of his own making – an ideology, the formalized abridgment of the supposed substratum of rational truth contained in the tradition.

The conduct of affairs, for the Rationalist, is a matter of solving problems, and in this no man can hope to be successful whose reason has become inflexible by surrender to habit or is clouded by the fumes of tradition. In this activity the character which the Rationalist claims for himself is the character of the engineer, whose mind (it is supposed) is controlled throughout by the appropriate technique and whose first step is to dismiss from his attention everything not directly related to his specific intentions. This assimilation of politics to engineering is, indeed, what may be called the myth of rationalist politics. And it is, of course, a recurring theme in the literature of Rationalism. The politics it inspires may be called the politics of the felt need; for the Rationalist, politics are always charged with the feeling of the moment. He waits upon circumstance to provide him with his problems, but rejects its aid in their solution. That anything should be allowed to stand between a society and the satisfaction of the felt needs of each moment in its history must appear to the Rationalist a piece of mysticism and nonsense. And his politics are, in fact, the rational solution of those practical conundrums which the recognition of the sovereignty of the felt need perpetually creates in the life of a society. Thus, political life is resolved into a succession of crises, each to be surmounted by the application of 'reason'. Each generation, indeed, each administration, should see unrolled before it the blank sheet of infinite possibility. And if by chance this *tabula rasa* has been defaced by the irrational scribblings of tradition-ridden ancestors, then the first task of the Rationalist must be to scrub it clean; as Voltaire remarked, the only way to have good laws is to burn all existing laws and to start afresh.[1]

Two other general characteristics of rationalist politics may be observed. They are the politics of perfection, and they are the politics of uniformity; either of these characteristics without the other denotes a different style of politics, the essence of rationalism is their combination. The evanescence of imperfection may be said to be the first item of the creed of the Rationalist. He is not devoid of humility; he can imagine a problem which would remain impervious to the onslaught of his own reason. But what he cannot imagine is politics which do not consist in solving problems, or a political problem of which there is no 'rational' solution at all. Such a problem must be counterfeit. And the 'rational' solution of any problem is, in its nature, the perfect solution. There is no place in his scheme for a 'best in the circumstances', only a place for 'the best'; because the function of reason is precisely to surmount circumstances. Of course, the Rationalist is not always a perfectionist in general, his mind governed in each occasion by a comprehensive Utopia; but invariably he is a perfectionist in detail. And from this politics of perfection

---

[1] Cf. Plato, *Republic*, 501A. The idea that you can get rid of a law by burning it is characteristic of the Rationalist, who can think of a law only as something written down.

springs the politics of uniformity; a scheme which does not recognize circumstance can have no place for variety. 'There must in the nature of things be one best form of government which all intellects, sufficiently roused from the slumber of savage ignorance, will be irresistibly incited to approve,' writes Godwin. This intrepid Rationalist states in general what a more modest believer might prefer to assert only in detail; but the principle holds – there may not be one universal remedy for all political ills, but the remedy for any particular ill is as universal in its application as it is rational in its conception. If the rational solution for one of the problems of a society has been determined, to permit any relevant part of the society to escape from the solution is, *ex hypothesi*, to countenance irrationality. There can be no place for preference that is not rational preference, and all rational preferences necessarily coincide. Political activity is recognized as the imposition of a uniform condition of perfection upon human conduct.

The modern history of Europe is littered with the projects of the politics of Rationalism. The most sublime of these is, perhaps, that of Robert Owen for 'a world convention to emancipate the human race from ignorance, poverty, division, sin and misery' – so sublime that even a Rationalist (but without much justification) might think it eccentric. But not less characteristic are the diligent search of the present generation for an innocuous power which may safely be made so great as to be able to control all other powers in the human world, and the common disposition to believe that political machinery can take the place of moral and political education. The notion of founding a society, whether of individuals or of States, upon a Declaration of the Rights of Man is a creature of the rationalist brain, so also are 'national' or racial self-determination when elevated into universal principles. The project of the so-called Re-union of the Christian Churches, of open diplomacy, of a single tax, of a civil service whose members 'have no qualifications other than their personal abilities', of a self-consciously planned society, the Beveridge Report, the Education Act of 1944, Federalism, Nationalism, Votes for Women, the Catering Wages Act, the destruction of the Austro-Hungarian Empire, the World State (of H. G. Wells or anyone else), and the revival of Gaelic as the official language of

Eire, are alike the progeny of Rationalism. The odd generation of rationalism in politics is by sovereign power out of romanticism.

2

The placid lake of Rationalism lies before us in the character and disposition of the Rationalist, its surface familiar and not unconvincing, its waters fed by many visible tributaries. But in its depths there flows a hidden spring, which, though it was not the original fountain from which the lake grew, is perhaps the pre-eminent source of its endurance. This spring is a doctrine about human knowledge. That some such fountain lies at the heart of Rationalism will not surprise even those who know only its surface; the superiority of the unencumbered intellect lay precisely in the fact that it could reach more, and more certain, knowledge about man and society than was otherwise possible; the superiority of the ideology over the tradition lay in its greater precision and its alleged demonstrability. Nevertheless, it is not, properly speaking, a philosophical theory of knowledge, and it can be explained with agreeable informality.

Every science, every art, every practical activity requiring skill of any sort, indeed every human activity whatsoever, involves knowledge. And, universally, this knowledge is of two sorts, both of which are always involved in any actual activity. It is not, I think, making too much of it to call them two sorts of knowledge, because (though in fact they do not exist separately) there are certain important differences between them. The first sort of knowledge I will call technical knowledge or knowledge of technique. In every art and science, and in every practical activity, a technique is involved. In many activities this technical knowledge is formulated into rules which are, or may be, deliberately learned, remembered, and, as we say, put into practice; but whether or not it is, or has been, precisely formulated, its chief characteristic is that it is susceptible of precise formulation, although special skill and insight may be required to give it that formulation.[1] The technique (or part of it) of driving a motor car on English roads is to be found in the Highway Code, the technique of cookery is contained in the cookery book, and the

[1] G. Polya, *How To Solve It*.

technique of discovery in natural science or in history is in their rules of research, of observation and verification. The second sort of knowledge I will call practical, because it exists only in use, is not reflective and (unlike technique) cannot be formulated in rules. This does not mean, however, that it is an esoteric sort of knowledge. It means only that the method by which it may be shared and becomes common knowledge is not the method of formulated doctrine. And if we consider it from this point of view, it would not, I think, be misleading to speak of it as traditional knowledge. In every activity this sort of knowledge is also involved; the mastery of any skill, the pursuit of any concrete activity is impossible without it.

These two sorts of knowledge, then, distinguishable but insep-arable, are the twin components of the knowledge involved in every concrete human activity. In a practical art, such as cookery, nobody supposes that the knowledge that belongs to the good cook is con-fined to what is or may be written down in the cookery book; tech-nique and what I have called practical knowledge combine to make skill in cookery wherever it exists. And the same is true of the fine arts, of painting, of music, of poetry; a high degree of technical knowledge, even where it is both subtle and ready, is one thing; the ability to create a work of art, the ability to compose something with real musical qualities, the ability to write a great sonnet, is another, and requires, in addition to technique, this other sort of knowledge. Again, these two sorts of knowledge are involved in any genuinely scientific activity.[1] The natural scientist will certainly make use of the rules of observation and verification that belong to his tech-nique, but these rules remain only one of the components of his knowledge; advance in scientific discovery was never achieved merely by following the rules.[2] The same situation may be observed also in religion. It would, I think, be excessively liberal to call a man a Christian who was wholly ignorant of the technical side of Christ-ianity, who knew nothing of creed or formulary, but it would be

[1] Some excellent observations on this topic are to be found in M. Polanyi, *Science, Faith and Society*.

[2] Polya, for example, in spite of the fact that his book is concerned with heuristic, suggests that the root conditions of success in scientific research are, first, 'to have brains and good luck', and secondly, 'to sit tight and wait till you get a bright idea', neither of which are technical rules.

even more absurd to maintain that even the readiest knowledge of creed and catechism ever constituted the whole of the knowledge that belongs to a Christian. And what is true of cookery, of painting, of natural science and of religion, is no less true of politics: the knowledge involved in political activity is both technical and practical.[1] Indeed, as in all arts which have men as their plastic material, arts such as medicine, industrial management, diplomacy, and the art of military command, the knowledge involved in political activity is pre-eminently of this dual character. Nor, in these arts, is it correct to say that whereas technique will tell a man (for example, a doctor) *what* to do, it is practice which tells him *how* to do it – the 'bed-side manner', the appreciation of the individual with whom he has to deal. Even in the *what*, and above all in diagnosis, there lies already this dualism of technique and practice: there is no knowledge which is not 'know how'. Nor, again, does the distinction between technical and practical knowledge coincide with the distinction between a knowledge of means and a knowledge of ends, though on occasion it may appear to do so. In short, nowhere, and pre-eminently not in political activity, can technical knowledge be separated from practical knowledge, and nowhere can they be considered identical with one another or able to take the place of one another.[2]

[1] Thucydides puts an appreciation of this truth into the mouth of Pericles. To be a politician and to refuse the guidance of technical knowledge is, for Pericles, a piece of folly. And yet the main theme of the Funeral Oration is not the value of technique in politics, but the value of practical and traditional knowledge. ii, 40.

[2] Duke Huan of Ch'i was reading a book at the upper end of the hall; the wheelwright was making a wheel at the lower end. Putting aside his mallet and chisel, he called to the Duke and asked him what book he was reading. 'One that records the words of the Sages,' answered the Duke. 'Are those Sages alive?' asked the wheelwright. 'Oh, no,' said the Duke, 'they are dead.' 'In that case,' said the wheelwright, 'what you are reading can be nothing but the lees and scum of bygone men.' 'How dare you, a wheelwright, find fault with the book I am reading. If you can explain your statement, I will let it pass. If not, you shall die.' 'Speaking as a wheelwright,' he replied, 'I look at the matter in this way; when I am making a wheel, if my stroke is too slow, then it bites deep but is not steady; if my stroke is too fast, then it is steady, but it does not go deep. The right pace, neither slow nor fast, cannot get into the hand unless it comes from the heart. It is a thing that cannot be put into words [rules]; there is an art in it that I cannot explain to my son. That is

Now, what concerns us are the differences between these two sorts of knowledge; and the important differences are those which manifest themselves in the divergent ways in which these sorts of knowledge can be expressed and in the divergent ways in which they can be learned or acquired.

Technical knowledge, we have seen, is susceptible of formulation in rules, principles, directions, maxims – comprehensively, in propositions. It is possible to write down technical knowledge in a book. Consequently, it does not surprise us that when an artist writes about his art, he writes only about the technique of his art. This is so, not because he is ignorant of what may be called the aesthetic element, or thinks it unimportant, but because what he has to say about *that* he has said already (if he is a painter) in his pictures, and he knows no other way of saying it. And the same is true when a religious man writes about his religion[1] or a cook about cookery. And it may be observed that this character of being susceptible of precise formulation gives to technical knowledge at least the appearance of certainty: it appears to be possible to be certain about a technique. On the other hand, it is a characteristic of practical knowledge that it is not susceptible of formulation of this kind. Its normal expression is in a customary or traditional way of doing things, or, simply, in practice. And this gives it the appearance of imprecision and consequently of uncertainty, of being a matter of opinion, of probability rather than truth. It is, indeed, a knowledge that is expressed in taste or connoisseurship, lacking rigidity and ready for the impress of the mind of the learner.

Technical knowledge can be learned from a book; it can be learned in a correspondence course. Moreover, much of it can be learned by heart, repeated by rote, and applied mechanically: the logic of the syllogism is a technique of this kind. Technical know-

---

why it is impossible for me to let him take over my work, and here I am at the age of seventy still making wheels. In my opinion it must have been the same with the men of old. All that was worth handing on, died with them; the rest, they put in their books. That is why I said that what you were reading was the lees and scum of bygone men.' *Chuang Tʒu*.

[1] St Francois de Sales was a devout man, but when he writes it is about the technique of piety.

ledge, in short, can be both taught and learned in the simplest mean-
ings of these words. On the other hand, practical knowledge can
neither be taught nor learned, but only imparted and acquired. It
exists only in practice, and the only way to acquire it is by apprenticeship to a master – not because the master can teach it (he cannot),
but because it can be acquired only by continuous contact with one
who is perpetually practising it. In the arts and in natural science what
normally happens is that the pupil, in being taught and in learning
the technique from his master, discovers himself to have acquired
also another sort of knowledge than merely technical knowledge,
without it ever having been precisely imparted and often without
being able to say precisely what it is. Thus a pianist acquires artis-
try as well as technique, a chess-player style and insight into the
game as well as a knowledge of the moves, and a scientist acquires
(among other things) the sort of judgement which tells him when
his technique is leading him astray and the connoisseurship which
enables him to distinguish the profitable from the unprofitable
directions to explore.

Now, as I understand it, Rationalism is the assertion that what I
have called practical knowledge is not knowledge at all, the assertion
that, properly speaking, there is no knowledge which is not technical knowledge. The Rationalist holds that the only element of
knowledge involved in any human activity is technical knowledge,
and that what I have called practical knowledge is really only a sort
of nescience which would be negligible if it were not positively mischievous. The sovereignty of 'reason', for the Rationalist, means the
sovereignty of technique.

The heart of the matter is the pre-occupation of the Rationalist
with certainty. Technique and certainty are, for him, inseparably
joined because certain knowledge is, for him, knowledge which does
not require to look beyond itself for its certainty; knowledge, that
is, which not only ends with certainty but begins with certainty and
is certain throughout. And this is precisely what technical knowledge
appears to be. It seems to be a self-complete sort of knowledge
because it seems to range between an identifiable initial point (where
it breaks in upon sheer ignorance) and an identifiable terminal point,
where it is complete, as in learning the rules of a new game. It has

the aspect of knowledge that can be contained wholly between the two covers of a book, whose application is, as nearly as possible, purely mechanical, and which does not assume a knowledge not itself provided in the technique. For example, the superiority of an ideology over a tradition of thought lies in its appearance of being self-contained. It can be taught best to those whose minds are empty; and if it is to be taught to one who already believes something, the first step of the teacher must be to administer a purge, to make certain that all prejudices and preconceptions are removed, to lay his foundation upon the unshakable rock of absolute ignorance. In short, technical knowledge appears to be the only kind of knowledge which satisfies the standard of certainty which the Rationalist has chosen.

Now, I have suggested that the knowledge involved in every concrete activity is never solely technical knowledge. If this is true, it would appear that the error of the Rationalist is of a simple sort – the error of mistaking a part for the whole, of endowing a part with the qualities of the whole. But the error of the Rationalist does not stop there. If his great illusion is the sovereignty of technique, he is no less deceived by the apparent certainty of technical knowledge. The superiority of technical knowledge lay in its appearance of springing from pure ignorance and ending in certain and complete knowledge, its appearance of both beginning and ending with certainty. But, in fact, this is an illusion. As with every other sort of knowledge, learning a technique does not consist in getting rid of pure ignorance, but in reforming knowledge which is already there. Nothing, not even the most nearly self-contained technique (the rules of a game), can in fact be imparted to an empty mind; and what is imparted is nourished by what is already there. A man who knows the rules of one game will, on this account, rapidly learn the rules of another game; and a man altogether unfamiliar with 'rules' of any kind (if such can be imagined) would be a most unpromising pupil. And just as the self-made man is never literally *self*-made, but depends upon a certain kind of society and upon a large unrecognized inheritance, so technical knowledge is never, in fact, self-complete, and can be made to appear so only if we forget the hypotheses with which it begins. And if its self-completeness is illusory, the certainty which was attributed to it on account of its self-completeness is also an illusion.

But my object is not to refute Rationalism; its errors are interesting only in so far as they reveal its character. We are considering not merely the truth of a doctrine, but the significance of an intellectual fashion in the history of post-Renaissance Europe. And the questions we must try to answer are: What is the generation of this belief in the sovereignty of technique? Whence springs this supreme confidence in human 'reason' thus interpreted? What is the provenance, the context of this intellectual character? And in what circumstances and with what effect did it come to invade European politics?

3

The appearance of a new intellectual character is like the appearance of a new architectural style; it emerges almost imperceptibly, under the pressure of a great variety of influences, and it is a misdirection of inquiry to seek its origins. Indeed, there are no origins; all that can be discerned are the slowly mediated changes, the shuffling and reshuffling, the flow and ebb of the tides of inspiration, which issue finally in a shape identifiably new. The ambition of the historian is to escape that gross abridgment of the process which gives the new shape a too early or too late and a too precise definition, and to avoid the false emphasis which springs from being over-impressed by the moment of unmistakable emergence. Yet that moment must have a dominating interest for those whose ambitions are not pitched so high. And I propose to foreshorten my account of the emergence of modern Rationalism, the intellectual character and disposition of the Rationalist, by beginning it at the moment when it shows itself unmistakably, and by considering only one element in the context of its emergence. This moment is the early seventeenth century, and it was connected, *inter alia*, with the condition of knowledge – knowledge of both the natural and the civilized world – at that time.

The state of European knowledge at the beginning of the seventeenth century was peculiar. Remarkable advances had already been achieved, the tide of inquiry flowed as strongly as at any other period in our history, and the fruitfulness of the presuppositions which inspired this inquiry showed no sign of exhaustion. And yet to intelligent observers it appeared that something of supreme importance was lacking. 'The state of knowledge,' wrote Bacon, 'is not prosperous nor greatly advancing.'[1] And this want of prosperity was not attributable to the survival of a disposition of mind hostile to the sort of inquiry that was on foot; it was observed as a hindrance suffered by minds already fully emancipated from the presuppositions (though not, of course, from some of the details) of Aristotelian science. What appeared to be lacking was not inspiration or even methodical habits of inquiry, but a consciously formulated technique of research, an art of interpretation, a method whose rules had been written down. And the project of making good this want was the occasion of the unmistakable emergence of the new intellectual character I have called the Rationalist. The dominating figures in the early history of this project are, of course, Bacon and Descartes, and we may find in their writings intimations of what later became the Rationalist character.

Bacon's ambition was to equip the intellect with what appeared to him necessary if certain and demonstrable knowledge of the world in which we live is to be attained. Such knowledge is not possible for 'natural reason', which is capable of only 'petty and probable conjectures', not of certainty.[2] And this imperfection is reflected in the want of prosperity of the state of knowledge. The *Novum Organum* begins with a diagnosis of the intellectual situation. What is lacking is a clear perception of the nature of certainty and an adequate means of achieving it. 'There remains,' says Bacon, 'but one course for the recovery of a sound and healthy condition – namely, that the entire work of understanding be commenced afresh, and the mind itself be from the very outset not left to take its own course, but guided at every step.'[3] What is required is a 'sure plan', a new 'way' of understanding, an 'art' or 'method' of inquiry, an 'instrument' which (like the mechanical aids men use to increase the effectiveness of their natural strength) shall supplement the weakness of the natural reason: in short, what is required is a formulated technique of inquiry.[4] He recognizes that this technique will appear

[1] Bacon, *Novum Organum* (Fowler), p. 157.
[2] *Ibid.*, p. 184.   [3] *Ibid.*, p. 182.   [4] *Ibid.*, p. 157.

as a kind of hindrance to the natural reason, not supplying it with wings but hanging weights upon it in order to control its exuberance;[1] but it will be a hindrance of hindrances to certainty, because it is lack of discipline which stands between the natural reason and certain knowledge of the world. And Bacon compares this technique of research with the technique of the syllogism, the one being appropriate to the discovery of the truth of things while the other is appropriate only to the discovery of the truth of opinions.[2]

The art of research which Bacon recommends has three main characteristics. First, it is a set of rules; it is a true technique in that it can be formulated as a precise set of directions which can be learned by heart.[3] Secondly, it is a set of rules whose application is purely mechanical; it is a true technique because it does not require for its use any knowledge or intelligence not given in the technique itself. Bacon is explicit on this point. The business of interpreting nature is 'to be done as if by machinery',[4] 'the strength and excellence of the wit (of the inquirer) has little to do with the matter',[5] the new method 'places all wits and understandings nearly on a level'.[6] Thirdly, it is a set of rules of universal application; it is a true technique in that it is an instrument of inquiry indifferent to the subject-matter of the inquiry.

Now, what is significant in this project is not the precise character of the rules of inquiry, both positive and negative, but the notion that a technique of this sort is even possible. For what is proposed – infallible rules of discovery – is something very remarkable, a sort of philosopher's stone, a key to open all doors, a 'master science'. Bacon is humble enough about the details of this method, he does not think he has given it a final formulation; but his belief in the possibility of such a 'method' in general is unbounded.[7] From our point of view, the first of his rules is the most important, the precept that we must lay aside received opinion, that we must 'begin anew from the very foundations'.[8] Genuine knowledge must begin with a purge of the mind, because it must begin as well as end in certainty and must be complete in itself. Knowledge and opinion are separated

---

[1] Bacon, *Novum Organum* (Fowler), p. 295.   [2] *Ibid.*, p. 168.
[3] *Ibid.*, p. 168.   [4] *Ibid.*, p. 182.   [5] *Ibid.*, p. 162.
[6] *Ibid.*, p. 233.   [7] *Ibid.*, p. 331.   [8] *Ibid.*, p. 295.

absolutely; there is no question of ever winning true knowledge out of 'the childish notions we at first imbibed'. And this, it may be remarked, is what distinguishes both Platonic and Scholastic from modern Rationalism: Plato is a rationalist, but the dialectic is not a technique, and the method of Scholasticism always had before it a limited aim.

The doctrine of the *Novum Organum* may be summed up, from our point of view, as the sovereignty of technique. It represents, not merely a preoccupation with technique combined with a recognition that technical knowledge is never the whole of knowledge, but the assertion that technique and some material for it to work upon are all that matters. Nevertheless, this is not itself the beginning of the new intellectual fashion, it is only an early and unmistakable intimation of it: the fashion itself may be said to have sprung from the exaggeration of Bacon's hopes rather than from the character of his beliefs.

Descartes, like Bacon, derived inspiration from what appeared to be the defects of contemporary inquiry; he also perceived the lack of a consciously and precisely formulated technique of inquiry. And the method propounded in the *Discours de la Méthode* and the *Regulae* corresponds closely to that of the *Novum Organum*. For Descartes, no less than for Bacon, the aim is certainty. Certain knowledge can spring up only in an emptied mind; the technique of research begins with an intellectual purge. The first principle of Descartes is 'de ne reçevoir jamais aucune chose pour vraie que je ne la connusse évidemment être telle, c'est-à-dire d'éviter soigneusement la précipitation et la prévention', 'de bâtir dans un fonds qui est tout à moi'; and the inquirer is said to be 'comme un homme qui marche seul et dans les ténèbres'.[1] Further, the technique of inquiry is formulated in a set of rules which, ideally, compose an infallible method whose application is mechanical and universal. And thirdly, there are no grades in knowledge, what is not certain is mere nescience. Descartes, however, is distinguished from Bacon in respect of the thoroughness of his education in the Scholastic philosophy and in the profound impression that geometrical demonstration had upon his mind, and the effect of these differences in education and

[1] *Discours de la Méthode*, ii.

inspiration is to make his formulation of the technique of inquiry more precise and in consequence more critical. His mind is oriented towards the project of an infallible and universal method or research, but since the method he propounds is modelled on that of geometry, its limitation when applied, not to possibilities but to things, is easily apparent. Descartes is more thorough than Bacon in doing his scepticism for himself and, in the end, he recognizes it to be an error to suppose that the method can ever be the sole means of inquiry.[1] The sovereignty of technique turns out to be a dream and not a reality. Nevertheless, the lesson his successors believed themselves to have learned from Descartes was the sovereignty of technique and not his doubtfulness about the possibility of an infallible method.

By a pardonable abridgment of history, the Rationalist character may be seen springing from the exaggeration of Bacon's hopes and the neglect of the scepticism of Descartes; modern Rationalism is what commonplace minds made out of the inspiration of men of discrimination and genius. *Les grands hommes, en apprenant aux faibles à réfléchir, les ont mis sur la route de l'erreur.* But the history of Rationalism is not only the history of the gradual emergence and definition of this new intellectual character; it is, also, the history of the invasion of every department of intellectual activity by the doctrine of the sovereignty of technique. Descartes never became a Cartesian; but, as Bouillier says of the seventeenth century, 'le cartésianisme a triomphé; il s'est emparé du grand siècle tout entier, il a pénétré de son esprit, non seulement la philosophie, mais les sciences et les lettres ellesmêmes'.[2] It is common knowledge that, at this time, in poetry and in drama, there was a remarkable concentration on technique, on rules of composition, on the observance of the *bienséances* of literature, which continued unabated for nearly two centuries. A stream of books flowed from the presses on the 'art of poetry', the 'art of living', the 'art of thinking'. Neither religion, nor natural science, nor education, nor the conduct of life itself escaped from the influence of the new Rationalism; no activity was immune, no society untouched.[3]

---

[1] *Discours de la Méthode*, vi. [2] *Histoire de la philosophie cartésienne*, i, 486.
[3] One important aspect of the history of the emergence of Rationalism is the changing connotation of the word 'reason'. The 'reason' to which the

The slowly mediated changes by which the Rationalist of the seventeenth century became the Rationalist as we know him today, are a long and complicated story which I do not propose even to abridge. It is important only to observe that, with every step it has taken away from the true sources of its inspiration, the Rationalist character has become cruder and more vulgar. What in the seventeenth century was '*L'art de penser*' has now become *Your mind and how to use it, a plan by world-famous experts for developing a trained mind at a fraction of the usual cost.* What was the *Art of Living* has become the *Technique of Success*, and the early and more modest incursions of the sovereignty of technique into education have blossomed into *Pelmanism.*

The deeper motivations which encouraged and developed this intellectual fashion are, not unnaturally, obscure; they are hidden in the recesses of European society. But among its other connections, it is certainly closely allied with a decline in the belief in Providence: a beneficient and infallible technique replaced a beneficient and infallible God; and where Providence was not available to correct the mistakes of men it was all the more necessary to prevent such mistakes. Certainly, also, its provenance is a society or a generation which thinks what it has discovered for itself is more important than what it has inherited,[1] an age over-impressed with its own accomplishment and liable to those illusions of intellectual grandeur which are the characteristic lunacy of post-Renaissance Europe, an age

---

Rationalist appeals is not, for example, the Reason of Hooker, which belongs still to the tradition of Stoicism and of Aquinas. It is a faculty of calculation by which men conclude one thing from another and discover fit means of attaining given ends not themselves subject to the criticism of reason, a faculty by which a world believed to be a machine could be disclosed. Much of the plausibility of Rationalism lies in the tacit attribution to the new 'reason' of the qualities which belong properly to the Reason of the older intellectual tradition. And this ambiguity, the emergence of the new connotation out of the old, may be observed in many of the writers of the early seventeenth century – in, for example, the poetry of Malherbe, an older contemporary of Descartes, and one of the great progenitors of the sovereignty of technique in literature.

[1] This was certainly true of the age of Bacon. And Professor Bernal now tells us that more has been found out at large and in detail about nature and man in the thirty years after 1915 than in the whole of history.

never mentally at peace with itself because never reconciled with its past. And the vision of a technique which puts all minds on the same level provided just that short cut which would attract men in a hurry to appear educated but incapable of appreciating the concrete detail of their total inheritance. And, partly under the influence of Rationalism itself, the number of such men has been steadily growing since the seventeenth century.[1] Indeed it may be said that all, or almost all, the influences which in its early days served to encourage the emergence of the Rationalist character have subsequently become more influential in our civilization.

Now, it is not to be thought that Rationalism established itself easily and without opposition. It was suspect as a novelty, and some fields of human activity – literature, for example – on which at first its hold was strong, subsequently freed themselves from its grasp. Indeed, at all levels and in all fields there have been continuous criticism of the resistance to the teachings of Rationalism. And the significance of the doctrine of the sovereignty of technique becomes clearer when we consider what one of its first and profoundest critics has to say about it. Pascal is a judicious critic of Descartes, not opposing him at all points, but opposing him nevertheless, on points that are fundamental.[2] He perceived, first, that the Cartesian desire for certain knowledge was based upon a false criterion of certainty.

---

[1] Not so very long ago, I suppose, the spectators at horse-races were mostly men and women who knew something at first-hand about horses, and who (in this respect) were genuinely educated people. This has ceased to be so, except perhaps in Ireland. And the ignorant spectator, with no ability, inclination or opportunity to educate himself, and seeking a short cut out of his predicament, demands *a book*. (The twentieth century vogue in cookery books derives, no doubt, from a similar situation.) The authors of one such book, *A Guide to the Classics, or how to pick the Derby winner*, aware of the difference between technical and complete knowledge, were at pains to point out that there was a limit beyond which there were no precise rules for picking the winner, and that some intelligence (not supplied by the rules themselves) was necessary. But some of its greedy, rationalistic readers, on the look-out for an infallible method, which (like Bacon's) would place their small wits on a level with men of genuine education, thought they had been sold a pup – which only goes to show how much better they would have spent their time if they had read St Augustine or Hegel instead of Descartes: *je ne puis pardonner à Descartes*.

[2] *Pensées* (Brunschvicg), i, 76.

Descartes must begin with something so sure that it cannot be doubted, and was led, as a consequence, to believe that all genuine knowledge is technical knowledge. Pascal avoided this conclusion by his doctrine of probability: the only knowledge that is certain is certain on account of its partiality; the paradox that probable knowledge has more of the whole truth than certain knowledge. Secondly, Pascal perceived that the Cartesian *raisonnement* is never in fact the whole source of the knowledge involved in any concrete activity. The human mind, he asserts, is not wholly dependent for its successful working upon a conscious and formulated technique; and even where a technique is involved, the mind observes the technique 'tacitement, naturellement et sans art'. The precise formulation of rules of inquiry endangers the success of the inquiry by exaggerating the importance of method. Pascal was followed by others, and indeed much of the history of modern philosophy revolves round this question. But, though later writers were often more elaborate in their criticism, few detected more surely than Pascal that the significance of Rationalism is not its recognition of technical knowledge, but its failure to recognize any other: its philosophical error lies in the certainty it attributes to technique and in its doctrine of the sovereignty of technique; its practical error lies in its belief that nothing but benefit can come from making conduct self-conscious.

4

It was, of course, improbable that politics should altogether escape the impress of so strong and energetic an intellectual style as that of the new Rationalism. But what, at first sight, is remarkable is that politics should have been earlier and more fully engulfed by the tidal wave than any other human activity. The hold of Rationalism upon most departments of life has varied in its firmness during the last four centuries but in politics it has steadily increased and is stronger now than at any earlier time. We have considered already the general intellectual disposition of the Rationalist when he turns to politics; what remains to be considered are the circumstances in which European politics came to surrender almost completely to the Rationalist and the results of the surrender.

That all contemporary politics are deeply infected with Rationalism will be denied only by those who choose to give the infection another name. Not only are our political vices rationalistic, but so also are our political virtues. Our projects are, in the main, rationalist in purpose and character; but, what is more significant, our whole attitude of mind in politics is similarly determined. And those traditional elements, particularly in English politics, which might have been expected to continue some resistance to the pressure of Rationalism, have now almost completely conformed to the prevailing intellectual temper, and even represent this conformity to be a sign of their vitality, their ability to move with the times. Rationalism has ceased to be merely one style in politics and has become the stylistic criterion of all respectable politics.

How deeply the rationalist disposition of mind has invaded our political thought and practice is illustrated by the extent to which traditions of behaviour have given place to ideologies, the extent to which the politics of destruction and creation have been substituted for the politics of repair, the consciously planned and deliberately executed being considered (for that reason) better than what has grown up and established itself unselfconsciously over a period of time. This conversion of habits of behaviour, adaptable and never quite fixed or finished, into comparatively rigid systems of abstract ideas, is not, of course, new; so far as England is concerned it was begun in the seventeenth century, in the dawn of rationalist politics. But, while formerly it was tacitly resisted and retarded by, for example, the informality of English politics (which enabled us to escape, for a long time, putting too high a value on political action and placing too high a hope in political achievement – to escape, in politics at least, the illusion of the evanescence of imperfection), that resistance has now itself been converted into an ideology.[1] This is, perhaps, the main significance of Hayek's *Road to Serfdom* – not the cogency of his doctrine, but the fact that it is a doctrine. A plan to resist all planning may be better than its opposite, but it belongs to the same style of politics. And only in a society already deeply infected with Rationalism will the conversion of the traditional resources of resistance to the tyranny of Rationalism into a self-

---

[1] A tentative, and therefore not a fundamentally damaging, conversion of this sort was attempted by the first Lord Halifax.

conscious ideology be considered a strengthening of those resources. It seems that now, in order to participate in politics and expect a hearing, it is necessary to have, in the strict sense, a doctrine; not to have a doctrine appears frivolous, even disreputable. And the sanctity, which in some societies was the property of a politics piously attached to traditional ways, has now come to belong exclusively to rationalist politics.

Rationalist politics, I have said, are the politics of the felt need, the felt need not qualified by a genuine, concrete knowledge of the permanent interests and direction of movement of a society, but interpreted by 'reason' and satisfied according to the technique of an ideology: they are the politics of the book. And this also is characteristic of almost all contemporary politics: not to have a book is to be without the one thing necessary, and not to observe meticulously what is written in the book is to be a disreputable politician. Indeed, so necessary is it to have a book, that those who have hitherto thought it possible to get on without one, have had, rather late in the day, to set about composing one for their own use. This is a symptom of the triumph of technique which we have seen to be the root of modern Rationalism; for what the book contains is only what it is possible to put into a book – rules of a technique. And, book in hand (because, though a technique can be learned by rote, they have not always learned their lesson well), the politicians of Europe pore over the simmering banquet they are preparing for the future; but, like jumped-up kitchen-porters deputizing for an absent cook, their knowledge does not extend beyond the written word which they read mechanically – it generates ideas in their heads but no tastes in their mouths.

Among the other evidences of Rationalism in contemporary politics, may be counted the commonly admitted claim of the 'scientist' as such (the chemist, the physicist, the economist or the psychologist) to be heard in politics; because, though the knowledge involved in a science is always more than technical knowledge, what it has to offer to politics is never more than a technique. And under this influence, the intellect in politics ceases to be the critic of political habit and becomes a substitute for habit, and the life of a society loses its rhythm and continuity and is resolved into a succession of problems and crises. Folk-lore, because it is not technique, is identified with nescience, and all sense of what Burke called the partnership between present and past is lost.[1]

There is, however, no need to labour the point that the most characteristic thing about contemporary politics is their rationalist inspiration; the prevailing belief that politics are easy is, by itself, evidence enough. And if a precise example is required we need look no further for it than the proposals we have been offered for the control of the manufacture and use of atomic energy. The rationalist faith in the sovereignty of technique is the presupposition both of the notion that some over-all scheme of mechanized control is possible and of the details of every scheme that has so far been projected: it is understood as what is called an 'administrative' problem. But, if Rationalism now reigns almost unopposed, the question which concerns us is, What are the circumstances that promoted this state of affairs? For the significance of the triumph lies not merely in itself, but in its context.

Briefly, the answer to this question is that the politics of Rationalism are the politics of the politically inexperienced, and that the outstanding characteristic of European politics in the last four centuries is that they have suffered the incursion of at least three types of political inexperience – that of the new ruler, of the new ruling class, and of the new political society – to say nothing of the incursion of a new sex, lately provided for by Mr Shaw. How appropriate rationalist politics are to the man who, not brought up or educated to their exercise, finds himself in a position to exert political initiative and authority, requires no emphasis. His need of it is so great that he will have no incentive to be sceptical about the possibility of a magic technique of politics which will remove the handicap of his lack of political education. The offer of such a technique will seem to him the offer of salvation itself; to be told that the necessary knowledge is to be found, complete and self-contained, in a book, and to be told that this knowledge is of a sort that can be learned by heart quickly and applied mechanically, will seem, like salvation, something almost too good to be true. And yet it was this, or something

[1] A poetic image of the politics of Rationalism is to be found in Rex Warner's book, *The Aerodrome*.

near enough to be mistaken for it, which he understood Bacon and Descartes to be offering him. For, though neither of these writers ventures upon the detailed application of his method to politics, the intimations of rationalist politics are present in both, qualified only by a scepticism which could easily be ignored. Nor had he to wait for Bacon and Descartes (to wait, that is, for a general doctrine of Rationalism); the first of these needy adventurers into the field of politics was provided for on his appearance a century earlier by Machiavelli.

It has been said that the project of Machiavelli was to expound a *science* of politics, but this, I think, misses the significant point. A science, we have seen, is concrete knowledge and consequently neither its conclusions, nor the means by which they were reached, can ever, as a whole, be written down in a book. Neither an art nor a science can be imparted in a set of directions; to acquire a mastery in either is to acquire an appropriate connoisseurship. But what can be imparted in this way is a technique, and it is with the technique of politics that Machiavelli, as a writer, is concerned. He recognized that the technique of governing a republic was somewhat different from that appropriate to a principality, and he was concerned with both. But in writing about the government of principalities he wrote for the *new* prince of his day, and this for two reasons, one of principle and the other personal. The well-established hereditary ruler, educated in a tradition and heir to a long family experience, seemed to be well enough equipped for the position he occupied; his politics might be improved by a correspondence course in technique, but in general he knew how to behave. But with the new ruler, who brought to his task only the qualities which had enabled him to gain political power and who learnt nothing easily but the vices of his office, the *caprice de prince*, the position was different. Lacking education (except in the habits of ambition), and requiring some short-cut to the appearance of education, he required a book. But he required a book of a certain sort; he needed a crib: his inexperience prevented him from tackling the affairs of State unseen. Now, the character of a crib is that its author must have an educated man's knowledge of the language, that he must prostitute his genius (if he has any) as a translator, and that it is powerless to save the ignorant reader from all possibility of mistake. The project of Machiavelli was, then, to provide a crib to politics, a political training in default of a political education, a technique for the ruler who had no tradition. He supplied a demand of his time; and he was personally and temperamentally interested in supplying the demand because he felt the 'fascination of what is difficult'. The new ruler was more interesting because he was far more likely than the educated hereditary ruler to get himself into a tricky situation and to need the help of advice. But, like the great progenitors of Rationalism in general (Bacon and Descartes), Machiavelli was aware of the limitations of technical knowledge; it was not Machiavelli himself, but his followers, who believed in the sovereignty of technique, who believed that government was nothing more than 'public administration' and could be learned from a book. And to the new prince he offered not only his book, but also, what would make up for the inevitable deficiencies of his book – himself: he never lost the sense that politics, after all, are diplomacy, not the application of a technique.

The new and politically inexperienced social classes which, during the last four centuries, have risen to the exercise of political initiative and authority, have been provided for in the same sort of way as Machiavelli provided for the new prince of the sixteenth century. None of these classes had time to acquire a political education before it came to power; each needed a crib, a political doctrine, to take the place of a habit of political behaviour. Some of these writings are genuine works of political vulgarization; they do not altogether deny the existence or worth of a political tradition (they are written by men of real political education), but they are abridgements of a tradition, rationalizations purporting to elicit the 'truth' of a tradition and to exhibit it in a set of abstract principles, but from which, nevertheless, the full significance of the tradition inevitably escapes. This is pre-eminently so of Locke's *Second Treatise of Civil Government*, which was as popular, as long-lived and as valuable a political crib as that greatest of all cribs to a religion, Paley's *Evidences of Christianity*. But there are other writers, like Bentham or Godwin, who, pursuing the common project of providing for the political inexperience of succeeding generations, cover up all trace of the political habit and tradition of their society with a purely speculative idea:

these belong to the strictest sect of Rationalism. But, so far as authority is concerned, nothing in this field can compare with the work of Marx and Engels. European politics without these writers would still have been deeply involved in Rationalism, but beyond question they are the authors of the most stupendous of our political rationalisms – as well they might be, for it was composed for the instruction of a less politically educated class than any other that has ever come to have the illusion of exercising political power. And no fault can be found with the mechanical manner in which this greatest of all political cribs has been learned and used by those for whom it was written. No other technique has so imposed itself upon the world as if it were concrete knowledge; none has created so vast an intellectual proletariat, with nothing but its technique to lose.[1]

The early history of the United States of America is an instructive chapter in the history of the politics of Rationalism. The situation of a society called upon without much notice to exercise political initiative on its own account is similiar to that of an individual or a social class rising not fully prepared to the exercise of political power; in general, its needs are the same as theirs. And the similarity is even closer when the independence of the society concerned begins with an admitted illegality, a specific and express rejection of a tradition, which consequently can be defended only by an appeal to something which is itself thought not to depend upon tradition. Nor, in the case of the American colonists, was this the whole of the pressure which forced their revolution into the pattern of Rationalism. The founders of American independence had both a tradition of European thought and a native political habit and experience to draw upon. But, as it happened, the intellectual gifts of Europe to America (both in philosophy and religion) had, from the beginning, been predominantly rationalistic: and the native political habit, the product of the circumstances of colonisation, was what may be

---

[1] By casting his technique in the form of a view of the course of events (past, present and future), and not of 'human nature', Marx thought he had escaped from Rationalism; but since he had taken the precaution of first turning the course of events into a doctrine, the escape was an illusion. Like Midas, the Rationalist is always in the unfortunate position of not being able to touch anything, without transforming it into an abstraction; he can never get a square meal of experience.

called a kind of natural and unsophisticated rationalism. A plain and unpretending people, not given over-much to reflection upon the habits of behaviour they had in fact inherited, who, in frontier communities, had constantly the experience of setting up law and order for themselves by mutual agreement, were not likely to think of their arrangements except as the creation of their own unaided initiative; they seemed to begin with nothing, and to owe to themselves all that they had come to possess. A civilization of pioneers is, almost unavoidably, a civilization of self-consciously self-made men, Rationalists by circumstance and not by reflection, who need no persuasion that knowledge begins with a *tabula rasa* and who regard the free mind, not even as the result of some artificial Cartesian purge, but as the gift of Almighty God, as Jefferson said.

Long before the Revolution, then, the disposition of mind of the American colonists, the prevailing intellectual character and habit of politics, were rationalistic. And this is clearly reflected in the constitutional documents and history of the individual colonies. And when these colonies came 'to dissolve the political bands which had connected them with one another', and to declare their independence, the only fresh inspiration that this habit of politics received from the outside was one which confirmed its native character in every particular. For the inspiration of Jefferson and the other founders of American independence was the ideology which Locke had distilled from the English political tradition. They were disposed to believe, and they believed more fully than was possible for an inhabitant of the Old World, that the proper organization of a society and the conduct of its affairs were based upon abstract principles, and not upon a tradition which, as Hamilton said, had 'to be rummaged for among old parchments and musty records'. These principles were not the product of civilization; they were natural, 'written in the whole volume of human nature'.[1] They were to be discovered in

---

[1] There is no space here to elucidate the exceedingly complicated connections between the politics of 'reason' and the politics of 'nature'. But it may be observed that, since both reason and nature were opposed to civilization, they began with a common ground; and the 'rational' man, the man freed from the idols and prejudices of a tradition, could, alternatively, be called the 'natural' man. Modern Rationalism and modern Naturalism in politics, in religion and in education, are alike expressions of a general

nature by human reason, by a technique of inquiry available alike to all men and requiring no extraordinary intelligence in its use. Moreover, the age had the advantage of all earlier ages because, by the application of this technique of inquiry, these abstract principles had, for the most part recently, been discovered and written down in books. And by using these books, a newly made political society was not only not handicapped by the lack of a tradition, but had a positive superiority over older societies not yet fully emancipated from the chains of custom. What Descartes had already perceived, 'que souvent il n'y a pas tant de perfection dans les ouvrages composés de plusieurs pièces et faits de la main de divers maîtres qu'en ceux anquels un seul a travaillé', was freshly observed in 1777 by John Jay – 'The Americans are the first people whom Heaven has favoured with an opportunity of deliberating upon, and choosing the forms of government under which they should live. All other constitutions have derived their existence from violence or accidental circumstances, and are therefore probably more distant from their perfection . . .'[1] The Declaration of Independence is a characteristic product of the *saeculum rationalisticum*. It represents the politics of the felt need interpreted with the aid of an ideology. And it is not surprising that it should have become one of the sacred documents of the politics of Rationalism, and, together with the similar documents of the French Revolution, the inspiration and pattern of many later adventures in the rationalist reconstruction of society.

The view I am maintaining is that the ordinary practical politics of European nations have become fixed in a vice of Rationalism, that much of their failure (which is often attributed to other and more immediate causes[2]) springs in fact from the defects of the Rationalist character when it is in control of affairs, and that (since the rationalist disposition of mind is not a fashion which sprang up only yesterday)

---

presumption against all human achievement more than about a generation old.

[1] Of course both 'violence' and 'accidental circumstances' were there, but being present in an unfamiliar form they were unrecognized.

[2] War, for example. War is a disease to which a rationalist society has little resistance; it springs easily from the kind of incompetence inherent in rationalist politics. But it has certainly increased the hold of the Rationalist disposition of mind on politics, and one of the disasters of war has been the now customary application to politics of its essentially rationalist vocabulary.

we must not expect a speedy release from our predicament. It is always depressing for a patient to be told that his disease is almost as old as himself and that consequently there is no quick cure for it, but (except for the infections of childhood) this is usually the case. So long as the circumstances which promoted the emergence of rationalist politics remain, so long must we expect our politics to be rationalist in disposition.

I do not think that any or all of the writers whom I have mentioned are responsible for our predicament. They are the servants of circumstances which they have helped to perpetuate (on occasion they may be observed giving another turn to the screw), but which they did not create. And it is not to be supposed that they would always have approved of the use made of their books. Nor, again, am I concerned with genuinely philosophical writing about politics; in so far as that has either promoted or retarded the tendency to Rationalism in politics, it has always been through a misunderstanding of its design, which is not to recommend conduct but to explain it. To explore the relations between politics and eternity is one thing; it is something different, and less commendable, for a practical politician to find the intricacy of the world of time and contingency so unmanageable that he is bewitched by the offer of a quick escape into the bogus eternity of an ideology. Nor, finally, do I think we owe our predicament to the place which the natural sciences and the manner of thinking connected with them has come to take in our civilization. This simple diagnosis of the situation has been much put about, but I think it is mistaken. That the influence of the genuine natural scientist is not necessarily on the side of Rationalism follows from the view I have taken of the character of any kind of concrete knowledge. No doubt there are scientists deeply involved in the rationalist attitude, but they are mistaken when they think that the rationalist and the scientific points of view necessarily coincide. The trouble is that when the scientist steps outside his own field he often carries with him only his technique, and this at once allies him with the forces of Rationalism.[1] In short, I think the great prestige

[1] A celebrated scientist tells us: 'I am less interested than the average person in politics because I am convinced that all political principles today are makeshifts, and will ultimately be replaced by principles of scientific knowledge.'

of the natural sciences has, in fact, been used to fasten the rationalist disposition of mind more firmly upon us, but that this is the work, not of the genuine scientist as such, but of the scientist who is a Rationalist in spite of his science.

5

To this brief sketch of the character, and the social and intellectual context of the emergence of Rationalism in politics, may be added a few reflections. The generation of rationalist politics is by political inexperience out of political opportunity. These conditions have often existed together in European societies; they did so in the ancient world, and that world at times suffered the effects of their union. But the particular quality of Rationalism in modern politics derives from the circumstance that the modern world succeeded in inventing so plausible a method of covering up lack of political education that even those who suffered from that lack were often left ignorant that they lacked anything. Of course, this inexperience was never, in any society, universal; and it was never absolute. There have always been men of genuine political education, immune from the infection of Rationalism (and this is particularly so of England, where a political education of some sort has been much more widely spread than in some other societies); and sometimes a dim reminder of the limitations of his technique has penetrated even the mind of the Rationalist. Indeed, so impractical is a *purely* rationalist politics, that the new man, lately risen to power, will often be found throwing away his book and relying upon his general experience of the world as, for example, a business man or a trade union official. This experience is certainly a more trustworthy guide than the book – at least it is real knowledge and not a shadow – but still, it is not a knowledge of the political traditions of his society, which, in the most favourable circumstances, takes two or three generations to acquire.

Nevertheless, when he is not arrogant or sanctimonious, the Rationalist can appear a not unsympathetic character. He wants so much to be right. But unfortunately he will never quite succeed. He began too late and on the wrong foot. His knowledge will never be more than half-knowledge, and consequently he will never be more than half-right.[1] Like a foreigner or a man out of his social class, he is bewildered by a tradition and a habit of behaviour of which he knows only the surface; a butler or an observant house-maid has the advantage of him. And he conceives a contempt for what he does not understand; habit and custom appear bad in themselves, a kind of nescience of behaviour. And by some strange self-deception, he attributes to tradition (which, of course, is pre-eminently fluid) the rigidity and fixity of character which in fact belongs to ideological politics. Consequently, the Rationalist is a dangerous and expensive character to have in control of affairs, and he does most damage, not when he fails to master the situation (his politics, of course, are always in terms of mastering situations and surmounting crises), but when he appears to be successful; for the price we pay for each of his apparent successes is a firmer hold of the intellectual fashion of Rationalism upon the whole life of society.

Without alarming ourselves with imaginary evils, it may, I think, be said that there are two characteristics, in particular, of political Rationalism which make it exceptionally dangerous to a society. No sensible man will worry greatly because he cannot at once hit upon a cure for what he believes to be a crippling complaint; but if he sees the complaint to be of a kind which the passage of time must make more rather than less severe, he will have a more substantial cause for anxiety. And this unfortunately appears to be so with the disease of Rationalism.

First, Rationalism in politics, as I have interpreted it, involves an identifiable error, a misconception with regard to the nature of human knowledge, which amounts to a corruption of the mind. And consequently it is without the power to correct its own short-comings; it has no homeopathic quality; you cannot escape its errors by becoming more sincerely or more profoundly rationalistic. This, it may be observed, is one of the penalties of living by the book; it leads not only to specific mistakes, but it also dries up the mind itself: living by precept in the end generates intellectual dishonesty. And further, the Rationalist has rejected in advance the only external

---

[1] There is a reminiscence here of a passage in Henry James, whose study of Mrs Headway in *The Siege of London* is the best I know of a person in this position.

inspiration capable of correcting his error; he does not merely neglect the kind of knowledge which would save him, he begins by
destroying it. First he turns out the light and then complains that he
cannot see, that he is 'comme un homme qui marche seul et dans les
ténèbres'. In short, the Rationalist is essentially ineducable; and he
could be educated *out* of his Rationalism only by an inspiration which
he regards as the great enemy of mankind. All the Rationalist can
do when left to himself is to replace one rationalist project in which
he has failed by another in which he hopes to succeed. Indeed, this
is what contemporary politics are fast degenerating into: the political
habit and tradition, which, not long ago, was the common possession
of even extreme opponents in English politics, has been replaced by
merely a common rationalist disposition of mind.

But, secondly, a society which has embraced a rationalist idiom of
politics will soon find itself either being steered or drifting towards
an exclusively rationalist form of education. I do not mean the crude
purpose of National Socialism or Communism of allowing no
education except a training in the dominant rationalist doctrine, I
mean the more plausible project of offering no place to any form of
education which is not generally rationalistic in character.[1] And when
an exclusively rationalist form of education is fully established,
the only hope of deliverance lies in the discovery by some
neglected pedant, 'rummaging among old parchments and musty
records', of what the world was like before the millennium
overtook it.

From the earliest days of his emergence, the Rationalist has taken
an ominous interest in education. He has a respect for 'brains', a
great belief in training them, and is determined that cleverness shall
be encouraged and shall receive its reward of power. But what is this
education in which the Rationalist believes? It is certainly not an
initiation into the moral and intellectual habits and achievements of
his society, an entry into the partnership between present and past,
a sharing of concrete knowledge; for the Rationalist, all this would
be an education in nescience, both valueless and mischievous. It is a
training in technique, a training, that is, in the half of knowledge

---

[1] Something of this sort happened in France after the Revolution; but it
was not long before sanity began to break in.

which can be learnt from books when they are used as cribs. And the Rationalist's affected interest in education escapes the suspicion of being a mere subterfuge for imposing himself more firmly on society, only because it is clear that he is as deluded as his pupils. He sincerely believes that a training in technical knowledge is the only education worth while, because he is moved by the faith that there is no knowledge, in the proper sense, except technical knowledge. He believes that a training in 'public administration' is the surest defence against the flattery of a demagogue and the lies of a dictator.

Now, in a society already largely rationalist in disposition, there will be a positive demand for training of this sort. Half-knowledge (so long as it is the technical half) will have an economic value; there will be a market for the 'trained' mind which has at its disposal the latest devices. And it is only to be expected that this demand will be satisfied; books of the appropriate sort will be written and sold in large quantities, and institutions offering a training of this kind (either generally or in respect of a particular activity) will spring up.[1] And so far as our society is concerned, it is now long since the exploitation of this demand began in earnest; it was already to be observed in the early nineteenth century. But it is not very important that people should learn the piano or how to manage a farm by a correspondence course; and in any case it is unavoidable in the circumstances. What is important, however, is that the rationalist inspiration has now invaded and has begun to corrupt the genuine educational provisions and institutions of our society: some of the ways and means by which, hitherto, a genuine (as distinct from a merely technical) knowledge has been imparted have already disappeared, others are obsolescent, and others again are in process of being corrupted from the inside. The whole pressure of the circumstances of our time is in this direction. Apprenticeship, the pupil working alongside the master who in teaching a technique also

---

[1] Some people regard this as the inevitable result of an industrial civilization, but I think they have hit upon the wrong culprit. What an industrial civilization needs is genuine skill; and in so far as our industrial civilization has decided to dispense with skill and to get along with merely technical knowledge it is an industrial civilization gone to the bad.

imparts the sort of knowledge that cannot be taught, has not yet disappeared; but it is obsolescent, and its place is being taken by technical schools whose training (because it can be a training only in technique) remains insoluble until it is immersed in the acid of practice. Again, professional education is coming more and more to be regarded as the acquisition of a technique,[1] something that can be done through the post, with the result that we may look forward to a time when the professions will be stocked with clever men, but men whose skill is limited and who have never had a proper opportunity of learning the *nuances* which compose the tradition and standard of behaviour which belong to a great profession.[2] One of the ways in which this sort of knowledge has hitherto been preserved (because it is a great human achievement, and if it is not positively preserved it will be lost) and transmitted is a family tradition. But the Rationalist never understands that it takes about two generations of practice to learn a profession; indeed, he does everything he can to destroy the possibility of such an education, believing it to be mischievous. Like a man whose only language is Esperanto, he has no means of knowing that the world did not begin in the twentieth century. And the priceless treasure of great professional traditions is, not negligently but purposefully, destroyed in the destruction of so-called vested interests. But perhaps the most serious rationalist attack upon education is that directed against the Universities. The demand for technicians is now so great that the existing institutions for training them have become insufficient, and the Universities are in process of being procured to satisfy the demand. The ominous phrase, 'university trained men and women', is establishing itself, and not only in the vocabulary of the Ministry of Education.

To an opponent of Rationalism these are local, though not negligible, defeats, and, taken separately, the loss incurred in each

[1] Cf. James Boswell, *The Artist's Dilemma.*

[2] The army in wartime was a particularly good opportunity of observing the difference between a trained and an educated man; the intelligent civilian had little difficulty in acquiring the technique of military leadership and command, but (in spite of the cribs provided: *Advice to Young Officers*, etc.) he always remained at a disadvantage beside the regular officer, the man educated in the feelings and emotions as well as the practices of his profession.

may not be irreparable. At least an institution like a University has a positive power of defending itself, if it will use it. But there is a victory which the Rationalist has already won on another front from which recovery will be more difficult because, while the Rationalist knows it to be a victory, his opponent hardly recognizes it as a defeat. I mean the circumvention and appropriation by the rationalist disposition of mind of the whole field of morality and moral education. The morality of the Rationalist is the morality of the self-conscious pursuit of moral ideals, and the appropriate form of moral education is by precept, by the presentation and explanation of moral principles. This is represented as a higher morality (the morality of the free man: there is no end to the clap-trap) than that of habit, the unselfconscious following of a tradition of moral behaviour; but, in fact, it is merely morality reduced to a technique, to be acquired by training in an ideology rather than an education in behaviour. In morality, as in everything else, the Rationalist aims to begin by getting rid of inherited nescience and then to fill the blank nothingness of an open mind with the items of certain knowledge which he abstracts from his personal experience, and which he believes to be approved by the common 'reason' of mankind.[1] He will defend these principles by argument, and they will compose a coherent (though morally parsimonious) doctrine. But, unavoidably, the conduct of life, for him, is a jerky, discontinuous affair, the solution of a stream of problems, the mastery of a succession of crises. Like the politics of the Rationalist (from which, of course, it is inseparable), the morality of the Rationalist is the morality of the self-made man and of the self-made society: it is what other peoples have recognized as 'idolatry'. And it is of no consequence that the moral ideology which inspires him today (and which, if he is a politician, he preaches) is, in fact, the desiccated relic of what was once the unself-conscious moral tradition of an aristocracy who, ignorant of ideals, had acquired a habit of behaviour in relation to one another and had handed it on in a true moral education. For the Rationalist, all that matters is that he has at last separated the ore of the ideal from the dross of the habit of behaviour;

---

[1] Of this, and other excesses of Rationalism, Descartes himself was not guilty. *Discours de la Méthode*, iii.

and, for us, the deplorable consequences of his success. Moral ideals are a sediment; they have significance only so long as they are suspended in a religious or social tradition, so long as they belong to a religious or a social life.[1] The predicament of our time is that the Rationalists have been at work so long on their project of drawing off the liquid in which our moral ideals were suspended (and pouring it away as worthless) that we are left only with the dry and gritty residue which chokes us as we try to take it down. First, we do our best to destroy parental authority (because of its alleged abuse), then we sentimentally deplore the scarcity of 'good homes', and we end by creating substitutes which complete the work of destruction. And it is for this reason that, among much else that is corrupt and unhealthy, we have the spectacle of a set of sanctimonious, rationalist politicians, preaching an ideology of unselfishness and social service to a population in which they and their predecessors have done their best to destroy the only living root of moral behaviour; and opposed by another set of politicians dabbling with the project of converting us from Rationalism under the inspiration of a fresh rationalization of our political tradition.

1947

---

[1] When Confucius visited Lao Tzu he talked of goodness and duty. 'Chaff from the winnower's fan,' said Lao Tzu, 'can so blear the eyes that we do not know if we are looking north, south, east or west; at heaven or at earth. . . . All this talk of goodness and duty, these perpetual pin-pricks, unnerve and irritate the hearer; nothing, indeed, could be more destructive of inner tranquillity.' *Chuang Tzu.*

The Political Economy of Freedom

The work of the late Professor Henry C. Simons of the University of Chicago will be well known to students of economics, and they will not need their attention called to this collection of some of his more important essays.[1] To others, however, it may be supposed that his name will be unknown. But, in spite of the fact that he is neither a brilliant nor a popular writer, he has something for the general reader; and though much of what he says has the USA for its immediate background, he has something in particular for the English reader. And I propose in this review to recommend him as a writer who should not be neglected by anyone interested in the way things are going. As an economist, Simons was concerned particularly with problems of banking, currency and monetary policy, but (like his teacher and colleague at Chicago, Professor F. H. Knight,[2] who has built up so distinguished a school of economic studies at that university) he was well aware that in every discussion of a special problem and in every proposal of economic policy there lies an often undisclosed preference for a society integrated in one way rather than another. And in order to make his preferences in this matter secure against superstition, he went to some trouble to bring them out into the open and to put them in order. They do not amount to anything so elaborate as a political philosophy, indeed he claims for them only the title of 'a political credo'; there is nothing pretentious in this attempt to hold 'economics' and 'politics' together. And it is successful mainly because it is not merely one project among others but represents the permanent habit of his mind. It is true there are a couple of essays in this volume directed expressly to the investigation of political ends and means, but the bulk of them

---

[1] *Economic Policy for a Free Society*. University of Chicago Press and Cambridge University Press, 1948, 21*s*. net.
[2] F. H. Knight, *Ethics of Competition* (1935), and *Freedom and Reform* (1947).

is concerned with special economic problems and he never fails to
show how his proposed solution is related to the wider context of
the type of society he believes to be desirable. To those anxious to
find out where they stand in these matters he offers not only a lucid,
if fragmentary, account of his own preferences, but also a profound
insight into the compatibility or incompatibility of different economic expedients with different forms of social integration.

Needless to say, Simons does not pretend to invent a political
credo for himself: he is without the vanity of those who refuse to be
convinced of their own honesty of purpose until they have made a
desert of their consciousness before beginning to cultivate it for
themselves. His pride is in belonging to a tradition. He speaks of
himself as 'an old-fashioned liberal', and he allies himself with a line
of predecessors which includes Adam Smith, Bentham, Mill, Sidg-
wick as well as de Tocqueville, Burckhardt and Acton. This strikes
one as being a trifle uncritical; the historical nuance is missed. But it
is nothing to worry about. Simons was a generous-minded man
where the work of others was concerned, accepting gratefully what
was offered and providing the critical subtleties for himself. If he was
a liberal, at least he suffered from neither of the current afflictions of
liberalism – ignorance of who its true friends are, and the nervy
conscience which extends a senile and indiscriminate welcome to
everyone who claims to be on the side of 'progress'. We need not,
however, disturb ourselves unduly about the label he tied on to his
credo. He calls himself a liberal and a democrat, but he sets no great
store by the names, and is concerned to resolve the ambiguity which
has now unfortunately overtaken them. It is to be expected, then,
that much of what Simons has to say will seem at once familiar and
unpardonably out-moded. It will seem familiar, not because it has
been unduly chewed over in recent years, but because the leaders of
fashion, the intellectual dandies of the Fabian Society, preserved it in
their hastily composed syllabus of errors. And it will seem outmoded
because of the disapproval of these eccentric arbiters. The great
merit of this book, however, is the opportunity it gives to 'this
sophisticated generation', which knows all the answers but is sadly
lacking in education, to consider for itself what it has been told to
reject as mere superstition.

Simons finds in its 'emphasis on liberty' the 'distinctive feature' of the tradition with which he allies himself; he believes in liberty. And this at once will raise a presumption against him. For to be a genuine libertarian in politics is to belong to a human type now sadly out of fashion. Other loves have bewitched us; and to confess to a passion for liberty – not as something worth while in certain circumstances but as the *unum necessarium* – is to admit to a disreputable naïvety, excusable only where it masks a desire to rule. Liberty has become the emblem of frivolous or of disingenuous politics. But the damage which libertarian politics have suffered from open and from hidden enemies is not irreparable; after all, their cunning is only circuitous folly and will find them out. It is self-appointed friends who have often shown themselves more dangerous. We must be clear, they say, about what we mean by 'freedom'. First, let us define it; and when we know what it is, it will be time enough to seek it out, to love it and to die for it. What is a free society? And with this question (proposed abstractly) the door opens upon a night of endless quibble, lit only by the stars of sophistry. Like men born in prison, we are urged to dream of something we have never enjoyed (freedom from want) and to make that dream the foundation of our politics. We are instructed to distinguish between 'positive' and 'negative' freedom, between the 'old' and the 'new' freedom, between 'social', 'political', 'civil', 'economic' and 'personal' freedom; we are told that freedom is the 'recognition of necessity'; and we are taught that all that matters is 'inner freedom' and that this is to be identified with equality and with power: there is no end to the abuse we have suffered. But a generation which has stood so long on that doorstep, waiting for the dawn, that 'le silence éternel de ces espaces infinis' has begun to unnerve it, should now be ready to listen to a more homely message. And anyone who has the courage to tell it to come in and shut the door may perhaps be given a hearing. This at least is what I understand Simons to be saying to us. The freedom which he is to inquire into is neither an abstraction nor a dream. He is a libertarian, not because he begins with an abstract definition of liberty, but because he has actually enjoyed a way of living (and seen others enjoy it) which those who have enjoyed it are accustomed (on account of certain precise characteristics) to call a free way of living, and because he has found it to be good. The purpose of the inquiry is not to define a word, but to detect the secret of what we enjoy, to recognize what is hostile to it, and to discern where and how it may be enjoyed more fully. And from this inquiry will spring, not only a closer understanding of what we actually enjoy, but also a reliable criterion for judging the proposed abstract freedoms which we are urged to pursue. For a proposed freedom which manifestly could not be achieved by means of the kind of arrangements which secure to us the freedom we now enjoy will reveal itself as an illusion. Moreover, we must refuse to be jockeyed into writing 'freedom', in deference to the susceptibilities of, say, a Russian or a Turk who has never enjoyed the experience (and who, consequently, can think only in abstractions), because any other use of the English word would be misleading and eccentric. *Freedom*, in English, is a word whose political connotation springs as directly from our political experience as the connotations of ἐλευθερία, *libertas* and *liberté* spring respectively from quite different experiences.

What, then, are the characteristics of our society in respect of which we consider ourselves to enjoy freedom and in default of which we would not be free in our sense of the word? But first, it must be observed that the freedom we enjoy is not composed of a number of independent characteristics of our society which in aggregate make up our liberty. Liberties, it is true, may be distinguished, and some may be more general or more settled and mature than others, but the freedom which the English libertarian knows and values lies in a coherence of mutually supporting liberties, each of which amplifies the whole and none of which stands alone. It springs neither from the separation of church and state, nor from the rule of law, nor from private property, nor from parliamentary government, nor from the writ of *habeas corpus*, nor from the independence of the judiciary, nor from any one of the thousand other devices and arrangements characteristic of our society, but from what each signifies and represents, namely, the absence from our society of overwhelming concentrations of power. This is the most general condition of our freedom, so general that all other conditions may be seen to be comprised within it. It appears, first, in a diffusion of authority between past, present and future. Our society is ruled by none of these exclusively. And we should consider a society governed wholly by its past, or its present, or its future to suffer under a despotism of superstition which forbids freedom. The politics of our society are a conversation in which past, present and future each has a voice; and though one or other of them may on occasion properly prevail, none permanently dominates, and on this account we are free. Further, with us power is dispersed among all the multitude of interests and organizations of interest which comprise our society. We do not fear or seek to suppress diversity of interest, but we consider our freedom to be imperfect so long as the dispersal of power among them is incomplete, and to be threatened if any one interest or combination of interests, even though it may be the interest of a majority, acquires extraordinary power. Similarly, the conduct of government in our society involves a sharing of power, not only between the recognized organs of government, but also between the Administration and the Opposition. In short, we consider ourselves to be free because no one in our society is allowed unlimited power – no leader, faction, party or 'class', no majority, no government, church, corporation, trade or professional association or trade union. The secret of its freedom is that it is composed of a multitude of organizations in the constitution of the best of which is reproduced that diffusion of power which is characteristic of the whole.

Moreover, we are not unaware that the balance of such a society is always precarious. 'The history of institutions,' says Acton, 'is often a history of deception and illusions.' Arrangements which in their beginnings promoted a dispersion of power often, in the course of time, themselves become over-mighty or even absolute while still claiming the recognition and loyalty which belonged to them in respect of their first character. To further liberty we need to be clear-sighted enough to recognize such a change, and energetic enough to set on foot the remedy while the evil is still small. And what more than anything else contributes to this clear-sightedness is relief from the distraction of a rigid doctrine which fixes upon an institution a falsely permanent character, and then (when the illusion is at last recognized) calls for a revolution. The best institutions, of course, are those whose constitution is both firm and self-critical, enjoying their character as the repository of a beneficial fragment of power but refusing the inevitable invitation to absolutism. And though these are few, it is perhaps permissible to number among them the hitherto existing parties of English politics.

It might be thought (by those who have not enjoyed the experience of living in such a society, and who can therefore think of it only in the abstract) that a society of this sort could be saved from disintegration only by the existence at its head of some overwhelming power capable of holding all other powers in check. But that is not our experience. Strength we think to be a virtue in government, but we do not find our defence against disintegration either in arbitrary or in very great power. Indeed, we are inclined to see in both these the symptoms of an already advanced decay. For overwhelming power would be required only by a government which had against it a combination so extensive of the powers vested in such a variety of different individuals and interests as to convict the government of a self-interest so gross as to disqualify it for the exercise of its proper function. Normally, to perform its office (which is to prevent coercion) our government requires to wield only a power greater than that which is concentrated in any one other centre of power on any particular occasion. Consequently it is difficult to excite in us the belief that a government not possessed of overwhelming power is on that account a weak government. And we consider that our freedom depends as much upon the moderation of the power exercised by government as upon the proper and courageous use of that power when necessity arises.

But further, our experience has disclosed to us a method of government remarkably economical in the use of power and consequently peculiarly fitted to preserve freedom: it is called the rule of law. If the activity of our goverment were the continuous or sporadic interruption of the life and arrangements of our society with arbitrary corrective measures, we should consider ourselves no longer free, even though the measures were directed against concentrations of power universally recognized to be dangerous. For not only would government of this kind require extraordinary power (each of its acts being an *ad hoc* intervention), but also, in spite of this concentration of governmental power, the society would be without that known and settled protective structure which is so important a condition of freedom. But government by rule of law (that is, by means of the enforcement by prescribed methods of settled rules binding alike on governors and governed), while losing nothing in strength, is itself the emblem of that diffusion of power which it exists to promote, and is therefore peculiarly appropriate to a free society. It is the method of government most economical in the use of power; it involves a partnership between past and present and between governors and governed which leaves no room for arbitrariness; it encourages a tradition of resistance to the growth of dangerous concentrations of power which is far more effective than any promiscuous onslaught however crushing; it controls effectively, but without breaking the grand affirmative flow of things; and it gives a practical definition of the kind of limited but necessary service a society may expect from its government, restraining us from vain and dangerous expectations. Particular laws, we know, may fail to protect the freedom enjoyed in our society, and may even be destructive of some of our freedom; but we know also that the rule of law is the greatest single condition of our freedom, removing from us that great fear which has overshadowed so many communities, the fear of the power of our own government.

Of the many species of liberty which compose the freedom we enjoy, each amplifying and making more secure the whole, we have long recognized the importance of two: the freedom of association, and the freedom enjoyed in the right to own private property. A third species of liberty is often set beside these two: freedom of speech. Beyond question this is a great and elementary form of freedom; it may even be regarded as the key-stone of the arch of our liberty. But a key-stone is not itself the arch, and the current exaggeration of the importance of this form of liberty is in danger of concealing from us the loss of other liberties no less important. The major part of mankind has nothing to say; the lives of most men do not revolve round a felt necessity to speak. And it may be supposed that this extraordinary emphasis upon freedom of speech is the work of the small vocal section of our society and, in part, represents a legitimate self-interest. Nor is it an interest incapable of abuse; when it is extended to the indiscriminate right to take and publish photographs, to picket and enter private houses and cajole or blackmail defenceless people to display their emptiness in foolish utterances, and to publish innuendos in respect of those who refuse to speak, it begins to reveal itself as a menace to freedom. For most men, to be deprived of the right of voluntary association or of private property would be a far greater and more deeply felt loss of liberty than to be deprived of the right to speak freely. And it is important that this should be said just now in England because, under the influence of misguided journalists and cunning tyrants, we are too ready to believe that so long as our freedom to speak is not impaired we have lost nothing of importance – which is not so. However secure may be a man's right to speak his thoughts, he may find what is to him a much more important freedom curtailed when his house is sold over his head by a public authority, or when he is deprived of the enjoyment of his leasehold because his landlord has sold out to a development company, or when his membership of a trade union is compulsory and debars him from an employment he would otherwise take.

The freedom of association enjoyed in our society has created a vast multitude of associations so that the integration of our society may be said to be largely by means of voluntary associations; and on this account we consider our freedom extended and made more secure. They represent a diffusion of power appropriate to our notion of freedom. The right of voluntary association means the right to take the initiative in forming new associations, and the right to join or not to join or to quit associations already in existence: the right of voluntary association is also a right of voluntary dissociation. And it means also the duty of not forming or joining any association designed to deprive, or in effect depriving, others of the exercise of any of their rights, particularly that of voluntary association. This duty is not to be thought of as a limitation of the right; the right, like all rights, is without any limits except those provided by the system of rights to which it belongs and those inherent in its own character: this duty is merely the negative definition of the right. And when we consider the full nature of the right, it is clear that its exercise can be hostile to what we know as our freedom only when it leads to that which in fact denies its own character – a 'compulsory-voluntary' association. A 'compulsory-voluntary' association is a conspiracy to abolish our right of association; it is a concentration of power actually or potentially destructive of what we call freedom.

It will be agreed that, from one point of view, property is a form of power, and an institution of property is a particular way of organizing the exercise of this form of power in a society. From this point of view distinctions between different kinds of property scarcely appear; certainly all categorical distinctions are absent. Personal and real property, chattels, property in a man's own physical and mental capacities and property in the so-called means of production, are all, in different degrees, forms of power, and incidentally spring from the same sources, investment, inheritance and luck. In every society an institution of property is unavoidable. The ideally simplest kind of institution is that in which all proprietary right is vested in one person who thereby becomes despot and monopolist, his subjects being slaves. But, besides being the least complex, this institution is, to our way of thinking, the most hostile to freedom. We have, perhaps, been less successful, from the point of view of freedom, in our institution of property than in some of our other arrangements, but there is no doubt about the general character of the institution of property most friendly to freedom: it will be one which allows the widest distribution, and which discourages most effectively great and dangerous concentrations of this power. Nor is there any doubt about what this entails. It entails a right of private property – that is, an institution of property which allows to every adult member of the society an equal right to enjoy the ownership of his personal capacities and of anything else obtained by the methods of acquisition recognized in the society. This right, like every other right, is self-limiting: for example, it proscribes slavery, not arbitrarily, but because the right to own another man could never be a right enjoyed equally by every member of a society. But in so far as a society imposes external limits, arbitrarily excluding certain things from private ownership, only a modified right of private property may be said to prevail, which provides for less than the maximum diffusion of the power that springs from ownership. For what may not be owned by any individual must nevertheless be owned, and it will be owned, directly or indirectly, by the government, adding to governmental power and constituting a potential threat to freedom. Now, it may happen that a society determines to withdraw from the possibility of private ownership certain things not inherently excluded by the right of private property itself, and there may be good reason for taking this course. But it should be observed that whatever benefits may flow from such an arrangement, the increase of liberty as we understand it is not among them. The institution of property most favourable to liberty is, unquestionably, a right to private property least qualified by arbitrary limits and exclusions, for it is by this means only that the maximum diffusion of the power that springs from ownership may be achieved. This is not mere abstract speculation; it is the experience of our society, in which the greatest threats to freedom have come from the acquisition of extra-ordinary proprietary rights by the government, by great business and industrial corporations and by trade unions, all of which are to be regarded as arbitrary limitations of the right of private property. An institution of property based upon private property is not, of course, either simple or primitive; it is the most complex of all institutions of property and it can be maintained only by constant vigilance, occasional reform and the refusal to tinker. And it is instructive to observe how closely many of the private property rights which we all regard as inseparable from freedom are bound up with other private property rights which it is now the custom erroneously to consider hostile to freedom. That a man is not free unless he enjoys a proprietary right over his personal capacities and his labour is believed by everyone who uses freedom in the English sense. And yet no such right exists unless there are many potential employers of his labour. The freedom which separates a man from slavery is nothing but a freedom to choose and to move among autonomous, independent organizations, firms, purchasers of lab-our, and this implies private property in resources other than personal capacity. Wherever a means of production falls under the control of a single power, slavery in some measure follows.

With property we have already begun to consider the economic organization of society. An institution of property is, in part, a device for organizing the productive and distributive activity of the society. For the libertarian of our tradition the main question will be how to regulate the enterprise of making a living in such a way that it does not destroy the freedom he prizes. He will, of course, recognize in our institution of private property a means of organizing this enterprise wholly friendly to liberty. All monopolies, or near monopolies, he knows as impediments to that liberty, and the greatest single institution which stands between us and monopoly is private property. Concerning monopolies he will have no illusions; he will not consider them optimistically, hoping that they will not abuse their power. He will know that no individual, no group, association or union can be entrusted with much power, and that it is mere foolishness to complain when absolute power is abused. It exists to be abused. And consequently he will put his faith only in arrangements which discourage its existence. In other words, he will recognize that the only way of organizing the enterprise of getting a living so that it does not curtail the freedom he loves is by the establishment and maintenance of effective competition. He will know that effective competition is not something that springs up of its own accord, that both it and any alternative to it are creatures of law; but since he has observed the creation (often inadvertently) by law of monopolies and other impediments to freedom, he will not think it beyond the capacity of his society to build upon its already substantial tradition of creating and maintaining effective competition by law. But he will recognize that any confusion between the task of making competition effective and the task (to be performed by effective competition itself) of organizing the enterprise of getting a living and satisfying wants will at once be fatal to liberty as he knows it. For to replace by political control the integration of activity which competition (the market) provides is at once to create a monopoly and to destroy the diffusion of power inseparable from freedom. No doubt the libertarian, in this matter, will have to listen to the complaint that he has neglected to consider the efficiency with which his economic system produces the goods; how shall we reconcile the conflicting claims of freedom and efficiency? But he will have his answer ready. The only efficiency to be considered is the most economical way of supplying the things men desire to purchase. The formal circumstances in which this may be at its maximum is where enterprise is effectively competitive, for here the entrepreneur is merely the intermediary between consumers of goods and sellers of services. And below this ideal arrangement, the relevant comparison is not between the level of efficiency attainable in an improved (but not perfected) competitive economy and the efficiency of a perfectly planned economy, but between an improved competitive economy and the sort of planned economy (with all its wastefulness, frustration and corruption) which is the only practical alternative. Everything, in short, that is inimical to freedom – monopoly, near monopoly and all great concentrations of power – at the same time impedes the only efficiency worth considering.

This outline of the political faith of a libertarian in the English tradition will be thought to lack something important unless there is added to it at least a suggestion of the end or purpose which informs such a society. It belongs, however, to some other tradition to think of this purpose 'as the achievement of a premeditated utopia, as an abstract ideal (such as happiness or prosperity), or as a preordained and inevitable end. The purpose of this society (if indeed it may be said to have one) is not something put upon it from the outside, nor can it be stated in abstract terms without gross abridgment. We are not concerned with a society which sprang up yesterday, but with one which possesses already a defined character and traditions of activity. And in these circumstances social achievement is to perceive the next step dictated or suggested by the character of the society in contact with changing conditions and to take it in such a manner that the society is not disrupted and that the prerogatives of future generations are not grossly impaired. In place of a preconceived purpose, then, such a society will find its guide in a principle of *continuity* (which is a diffusion of power between past, present and future) and in a principle of *consensus* (which is a diffusion of power between the different legitimate interests of the present). We call ourselves free because our pursuit of current desires does not deprive us of a sympathy for what went before; like the wise man, we remain reconciled with our past. In the obstinate refusal to budge, in the pure pragmatism of a plebiscitary democracy, in the abridgment of tradition which consists in merely doing what was done 'last time', and in the preference for the short-cut in place of the long way round that educates at every step, we recognize, alike, the marks of slavery. We consider ourselves free because, taking a view neither short nor long, we are unwilling to sacrifice either the present to a remote and incalculable future, or the immediate and foreseeable future to a transitory present. And we find freedom once more in a preference for slow, small changes which have behind them a voluntary consensus of opinion, in our ability to resist disintegration without suppressing opposition, and in our perception that it is more important for a society to move together than for it to move either fast or far. We do not pretend that our decisions are infallible; indeed, since there is no external or absolute test of perfection, infallibility has no meaning. We find what we need in a principle of change and a principle of identity, and we are suspicious of those who offer us more; those who call upon us to make great sacrifices and those who want to impose upon us an heroic character.

Now, though none of these characteristics is fully present in our society at this time, none is wholly absent. We have experienced enough of it over a sufficiently long period of time to know what it means, and from that experience has sprung our notion of freedom. We call ourselves free because our arrangements approximate to this general condition. And the enterprise of the libertarian in politics will be to cultivate what has already been sown, and to avoid the fruitless pursuit of proposed freedoms which could not be secured by the only known method of achieving freedom. Policy will not be the imagination of some new sort of society, or the transformation of an existing society so as to make it correspond with an abstract ideal; it will be the perception of what needs doing now in order to realize more fully the intimations of our existing society. The right conduct of policy, then, involves a profound knowledge of the character of the society, which is to be cultivated, a clear perception of its present condition, and the precise formulation of a programme of legislative reform.

The present condition of our society is exceedingly complex; but, from the point of view of the libertarian, three main elements may be distinguished. There is, first, a widespread and deplorable ignorance of the nature of the libertarian tradition itself, a confusion of mind in respect of the kind of society we have inherited and the nature of its strength and weakness. With eyes focused upon distant horizons and minds clouded with foreign clap-trap, the impatient and sophisticated generation now in the saddle has dissolved its partnership with its past and is careful of everything except its liberty. Secondly, owing to the negligence of past generations, there is an accumulated mass of maladjustment, of undispersed concentrations of power, which the libertarian will wish to correct because it threatens liberty, and which others also may wish to correct for less cogent reasons. Thirdly, there is the contemporary mess, sprung from the attempts of men ignorant of the nature of their society to correct its maladjustments by means of expedients which, because they are not inspired by a love of liberty, are a threat to freedom both in failure and in success.

The two great, mutually exclusive, contemporary opponents of libertarian society as we know it are collectivism and syndicalism. Both recommend the integration of society by means of the erection and maintenance of monopolies; neither finds any virtue in the diffusion of power. But they must be considered mutually exclusive opponents of a free society because the monopoly favoured by syndicalism would make both a collective and a society of free men impossible.

Collectivism in the modern world has several synonyms; it stands for a managed society, and its other titles are communism, national socialism, socialism, economic democracy and central planning. But we will continue to call it collectivism, this being its least emotive name. And we will assume that the problem of imposing a collectivist organization upon a society which enjoys a high degree of freedom has been successfully solved – that is, we will assume that the necessary contemporary *consensus* has been achieved. This is not a tremendous assumption, because (paradoxically enough) collectivism appears most readily to us as a remedy for elements in our society which are agreed to be impediments to freedom. What the libertarian is concerned to investigate is the compatibility of collectivist organization with freedom as he knows it. To be brief, collectivism and freedom are real alternatives – if we choose one we cannot have the other. And collectivism can be imposed upon a society educated in a love of freedom with an appearance of not destroying *continuity*, only if men forget their love of liberty. This, of course, is not a new idea, it is how the matter appeared to observers, such as de Tocqueville, Burckhardt and Acton, when the character of modern collectivism was in process of being revealed.

Neglecting the more scandalous charges which may be brought against collectivism in action, let us consider only the defects (from the point of view of liberty) inherent in the system. The opposition of collectivism to freedom appears first in the collectivist rejection of the whole notion of the diffusion of power and of a society organized by means of a multitude of genuinely voluntary associations. The cure proposed for monopoly is to create more numerous and more extensive monopolies and to control them by force. The organization to be imposed upon society springs from the minds of those who compose the government. It is a comprehensive organization; loose ends, uncontrolled activities must be regarded as the product of incompetence because they unavoidably impair the structure of the whole. And great power is required for the over-all control of this organization – power sufficient not merely to break up a single over-mighty concentration of power when it makes its appearance, but to control continuously enormous concentrations of power which the collectivist has created. The government of a collectivist society can tolerate only a very limited opposition to its plans; indeed, that hard-won distinction, which is one of the elements of our liberty, between opposition and treason is rejected: what is not obedience is sabotage. Having discouraged all other means of social and industrial integration, a collectivist government must enforce its imposed order or allow the society to relapse into chaos. Or, following a tradition of economy in the use of power, it will be obliged to buy off political opposition by favouring groups able to demand favours as the price of peace. All this is, clearly, an impediment to freedom; but there is more to follow. In addition to the rule of law, and often in place of it, collectivism depends for its working upon a lavish use of discretionary authority. The organization it imposes upon society is without any inner momentum; it must be kept going by promiscuous, day-to-day interventions – controls of prices, licences to pursue activities, permissions to make and to cultivate, to buy and to sell, the perpetual readjustment of rations, and the distribution of privileges and exemptions – by the exercise, in short, of the kind of power most subject to misuse and corruption. The diffusion of power inherent in the rule of law leaves government with insufficient power to operate a collectivist society. It will be observed, further, that collectivism involves the abolition of that division of labour between competitive and political controls which belongs to our freedom. Competition may, of course, survive anomalously and vestigially, in spite of policy; but, in principle, enterprise is tolerated only if it is not competitive, that is, if it takes the form of syndicates which serve as instruments of the central authorities, or smaller businesses which a system of quotas and price controls has deprived of all elements of risk or genuine enterprise. Competition as a form of organization is first devitalized and then destroyed, and the integrating office it performs in our society is incorporated in the functions of government, thus adding to its power and involving it in every conflict of interest that may arise in the society. And with the disappearance of competition goes what we have seen to be one of the essential elements of our liberty. But of all the acquisitions of governmental power inherent in collectivism, that which comes from its monopoly of foreign trade is, perhaps, the most dangerous to liberty; for freedom of external trade is one of the most precious and most effective safeguards a community may have against excessive power. And just as the abolition of competition at home draws the government into (and thus magnifies) every conflict, so collectivist trading abroad involves the government in competitive commercial transactions and increases the occasions and the severity of international disharmony. Collectivism, then, is the mobilization of a society for unitary action. In the contemporary world it appears as a remedy for the imperfect freedom which springs from imperfect competition, but it is a remedy designed to kill. Nor is this surprising, for the real spring of collectivism is not a love of liberty, but war. The anticipation of war is the great incentive, and the conduct of war is the great collectivizing process. And large-scale collectivism is, moreover, inherently warlike; the condition of things in which it is appropriate in the end makes its appearance. It offers a double occasion for the loss of liberty – in the collectivist organization itself and in the purpose to which that organization is directed. For though collectivism may recommend itself as a means to 'welfare', the only 'welfare' it is capable of pursuing – a centralized, national 'welfare' – is hostile to freedom at home and results in organized rivalry abroad.

Collectivism is indifferent to all elements of our freedom and the enemy of some. But the real antithesis of a free manner of living, as we know it, is syndicalism. Indeed, syndicalism is not only destructive of freedom; it is destructive, also, of any kind of orderly existence. It rejects both the concentration of overwhelming power in the government (by means of which a collectivist society is always being rescued from the chaos it encourages), and it rejects the wide dispersion of power which is the basis of freedom. Syndicalism is a contrivance by means of which society is disposed for a perpetual civil war in which the parties are the organized self-interest of functional minorities and a weak central government, and for which the community as a whole pays the bill in monopoly prices and disorder. The great concentrations of power in a syndicalist society are the sellers of labour organized in functional monopoly associations. All monopolies are prejudicial to freedom, but there is good reason for supposing that labour monopolies are more dangerous than any others, and that a society in the grip of such monopolies would enjoy less freedom than any other sort of society. In the first place, labour monopolies have shown themselves more capable than enterprise monopolies of attaining really great power, economic, political and even military. Their appetite for power is insatiable and, producing nothing, they encounter none of the productional diseconomies of undue size. Once grown large, they are exceedingly difficult to dissipate and impossible to control. Appearing to spring from the lawful exercise of the right of voluntary association (though as monopolistic associations they are really a denial of that right), they win legal immunities and they enjoy popular support however scandalous their activity. Enterprise monopolies, on the other hand (not less to be deplored by the libertarian), are less dangerous because they are less powerful. They are precariously held together, they are unpopular and they are highly sensitive to legal control. Taken separately, there is no question which of the two kinds of monopoly is the more subversive of freedom. But in addition to its greater power, the labour monopoly is dangerous because it demands enterprise monopoly as its complement. There is a disastrous identity of interest between the two kinds of monopoly; each tends to foster and to strengthen the other, fighting together to maximize joint extractions from the public while also fighting each other over the division of the spoils. Indeed, the conflict of capital and labour (the struggle over the division of earnings) is merely a sham fight (often costing the public more than the participants), concealing the substantial conflict between the producer (enterprise and labour, both organized monopolistically) and the consumer. Syndicalism, then, has some claim to be considered the pre-eminent adversary of freedom, but it is not less the enemy of collectivism. A collectivist government faced with numerous functional minorities each organized monopolistically with power to disrupt the whole plan of production unless its demands are met and each (when not making large demands) keeping the civil war going by means of promiscuous little hindrances to the orderly conduct of business, would be the easy victim of blackmail. And if the collectivist government derived its political strength from highly syndicalist labour organizations, its desperate position would be that of a victim of blackmail in a society which had not made the activity an offence. Of all forms of society, a collectivist society is least able to deal with the disruptive potentialities of syndicalism.

Where collectivism and syndicalism have imposed themselves upon societies which enjoy a libertarian tradition they appear as mutually exclusive tendencies (sometimes anomalously in alliance with one another) threatening achieved freedom. But to the libertarian who still has faith in his tradition, the chief danger lies, not in the possibility that either will establish itself exclusively, but in their joint success in hindering a genuinely libertarian attack upon the accumulated maladjustments in our society and upon our real problems. That attack is certainly long overdue, and the delay must not be attributed entirely to the popularity of these pseudo-remedies. Libertarian society has not been entirely idle in the past fifty years;

liberty has been extended by the correction of many small abuses. But the general drift of reform in this country has too often been inspired by vaguely collectivist motives. Liberty has been lost inadvertently through the lack of a clearly formulated libertarian policy of reform.

However, Simons now comes forward with such a policy. He is not the first to do so, but no friend of freedom will fail to benefit by reflecting upon what he has to say. Nobody could be less complacent about the present state of liberty than Simons; and his proposals are not only libertarian, they are in many respects (as he points out) more radical than the projects of the collectivists. A planner who aims at change by means of promiscuous intervention and the use of discretionary anthority, while destroying liberty, does less for reform than a libertarian who would extend and consolidate the rule of law. Simons calls his policy a 'positive programme for *Laissez Faire*', mainly because it aims at making competition effective wherever effective competition is not demonstrably impossible, at re-establishing a diffusion of power now deeply compromised by monopolies of all sorts, and at preserving that division of labour between competitive and political controls which is the secret of our liberty. But, both in England and in America, the policy he proposed in 1934 would now in part be a programme of *laissez faire* in the historical sense – a programme of removing specific restrictions upon competition which have established themselves not by default but by the activity of collectivists. Nevertheless, his proposals have, of course, nothing whatever to do with that imaginary condition of wholly unfettered competition which is confused with *laissez faire* and ridiculed by collectivists when they have nothing better to say. As every schoolboy used to know, if effective competition is to exist it can do so only by virtue of a legal system which promotes it, and that monopoly has established itself only because the legal system has not prevented it. To know that unregulated competition is a chimera, to know that to regulate competition is not the same thing as to interfere with the operation of competitive controls, and to know the difference between these two activities, is the beginning of the political economy of freedom.

The libertarian, then, finds the general tendency towards a policy of collectivism a hindrance; but the unavoidable (and exceedingly uneconomical) collectivism which sprang up in libertarian societies engaged in a war of survival is recognized as an evil not without compensation. The believer in collectivism naturally looks upon war as an opportunity not to be missed, and the demobilization of society is no part of his programme. But to those who believe in liberty and yet remain hesitant about demobilization, Simons addresses some wise words: 'If wars are frequent, victories will probably go to those who remain mobilized . . . [But] if there are vital, creative forces to be released by demobilization – by return to a free society – the nation may thereby gain enough strength to compensate handsomely for the risks involved.' Every man, whom war took away from his chosen vocation, returned to it with pent-up energies ready to be released; and what is true of an individual may here be true also of an economy. Demobilization offered an opportunity for the springing up of a revitalized and more effectively competitive economy (an opportunity of which the collectivists deprived us), which would have made us more able to withstand future wars. There is a potential gain, if it can be harvested, for a society with a libertarian tradition, in the successive shocks of mobilization and demobilization. And just as a civilian will fight better (for he has something to fight for) if in the intervals of peace he is permitted to be a civilian (and not kept bumming around in an industrial army), so an economy which is, in peace, allowed to stretch itself and flex its limbs will be found, when it is mobilized for war, to possess superior stamina to one kept permanently mobilized.

The main principles of the policy are simple, and we have already noticed them. First, private monopoly in all its forms is to be suppressed. This means the establishment and maintenance (by means of the reform of the law which gives shape to the world of business and industry) of effective competition wherever effective competition is not demonstrably impossible: a genuine 'socialization' of enterprise in place of the spoof 'socialization' of the collectivist. The monopolies and the monopolistic practices to be destroyed are monopolies of labour. Restraint of trade must be treated as a major crime. In respect of enterprise, the absurd powers of corporations must be reduced. 'There is simply no excuse,' says Simons, 'except with a narrow and specialized class of enterprise, for allowing corporations to hold stock in other corporations – and no reasonable excuse (the utilities apart) for hundred-million-dollar corporations, no matter what form their property may take. Even if the much advertised economies of gigantic financial combinations were real, sound policy would wisely sacrifice these economies to preservation of more economic freedom and equality.' The corporation is a socially useful device for organizing ownership and control in operating companies of size sufficient to obtain the real economies of large-scale production under unified management; but the corporation law which has allowed this device to work for the impediment of freedom is long overdue for reform. In respect of labour, the problem of reducing the existing or threatened monopolies and monopoly practices is more difficult. The best one may hope, perhaps, is that labour monopolies, if not fostered and supported by the law, will cease to grow and even decline in power. And if we deal intelligently with other, easier problems, it is to be expected that this problem will become less intractable by progress in other directions.

Secondly, undertakings in which competition cannot be made to work as the agency of control must be transferred to public operation. Now the difference between this policy and that of the collectivist should be observed. There is, in the first place, a difference of emphasis. The collectivists would, in the end, take over every undertaking the 'nationalization' of which does not offer insuperable technical difficulties; the libertarian would create a government-controlled monopoly only when monopoly of some sort is unavoidable. The collectivist favours monopolies as an opportunity for the extension of political control; the libertarian would break up all destructible monopolies. And the ground of this emphasis is clear. To the libertarian all monopolies are expensive and productive of servility. While the collectivist welcomes and sees his opportunity in a society in which (owing to growth of population and changes in the technique of production) enterprise tends to become gigantic even when the law does not encourage undue size, the libertarian sees in this tendency a threat to freedom which must be warded off (and can be warded off) by the appropriate legal reforms. And from this difference of emphasis springs all the other differences: the

disinclination to create monopolies where there are none (in education, for example), the disposition to reduce and to simplify all
monopolies taken over so that they may contribute as little as possible to the power of government, the strongest legal discourage-
ment to the appearance of syndicalist tendencies within these monopolies, and the recognition that the effect of all such proposals upon
the power of government is as important as their effect upon 'society'.
In short, the political economy of freedom rests upon the clear
acknowledgment that what is being considered is not 'economics'
(not the maximization of wealth, not productivity or the standard of
life), but *politics*, that is, the custody of a manner of living; that
these arrangements have to be paid for, are a charge upon our productive capacity; and that they are worth paying for so long as the
price is not a diminution of what we have learned to recognize as
liberty.

The third object of this economic policy is a stable currency,
maintained by the application of fixed and known rules and not by
day-to-day administrative tricks. And that this belongs to the
political economy of freedom needs no argument: inflation is the
mother of servitude.

Politics is not the science of setting up a permanently impregnable
society, it is the art of knowing where to go next in the exploration
of an already existing traditional kind of society. And in a society,
such as ours, which has not yet lost the understanding of government as the prevention of coercion, as the power which holds in
check the overmighty subject, as the protector of minorities against
the power of majorities, it may well be thought that the task to
which this generation is called is not the much advertised 'reconstruction of society' but to provide against the new tyrannies which
an immense growth in population in a wantonly productivist society
are beginning to impose; and to provide against them in such a
manner that the cure is not worse than the disease.

1949

The Tower of Babel

The project of finding a short cut to heaven is as old as the human race. It is represented in the mythology of many peoples, and it is recognized always as an impious but not ignoble enterprise. The story of the Titans is, perhaps, the most complicated of the myths which portray this *folie de grandeur*, but the story of the Tower of Babel is the most profound. We may imagine the Titans drawing back after the first unsuccessful assault to hear one of their number suggest that their programme was too ambitious, that perhaps they were trying to do too much and to do it too quickly. But the builders of the Tower, whose top was to reach to heaven, were permitted no such conference; their enterprise involved them in the babblings of men who speak, but do not speak the same language. Like all profound myths, this represents a project the fascination of which is not confined to the childhood of the race, but is one which the circumstances of human life constantly suggest and one which no failure can deprive of its attraction. It indicates also the consequences of such an enterprise. I interpret it as follows.

The pursuit of perfection as the crow flies is an activity both impious and unavoidable in human life. It involves the penalties of impiety (the anger of the gods and social isolation), and its reward is not that of achievement but that of having made the attempt. It is an activity, therefore, suitable for individuals, but not for societies. For an individual who is impelled to engage in it, the reward may exceed both the penalty and the inevitable defeat. The penitent may hope, or even expect, to fall back, a wounded hero, into the arms of an understanding and forgiving society. And even the impenitent can be reconciled with himself in the powerful necessity of his impulse, though, like Prometheus, he must suffer for it. For a society, on the other hand, the penalty is a chaos of conflicting ideals, the disruption of a common life, and the reward is the renown which attaches to monumental folly. *A mesure que l'humanité se perfectionne l'homme se dégrade.* Or, to interpret the myth in a more light-hearted fashion: human life is a gamble; but while the individual must be allowed to bet according to his inclination (on the favourite or on an outsider), society should always back the field. Let us consider the matter in application to our own civilization.

The activity with which we are concerned is what is called moral activity, that is, activity which may be either good or bad. The moral life is human affection and behaviour determined, not by nature, but by art. It is conduct to which there is an alternative. This alternative need not be consciously before the mind; moral conduct does not necessarily involve the reflective choice of a particular action. Nor does it require that each occasion shall find a man without a disposition, or even without predetermination, to act in a certain way: a man's affections and conduct may be seen to spring from his character without thereby ceasing to be moral. The freedom without which moral conduct is impossible is freedom from a natural necessity which binds *all* men to act alike. This does not carry us very far. It identifies moral behaviour as the exercise of an acquired skill (though the skill need not have been self-consciously acquired), but it does not distinguish it from other kinds of art – from cookery or from carpentry. However, it carries us far enough for my purpose, which is to consider the *form* of the moral life, and in particular the form of the moral life of contemporary Western civilization.

In any manifestation of the moral life, form and content are, of course, inseparable. Nevertheless, neither can be said to determine the other; and in considering the form we shall be considering an abstraction which, in principle, is indifferent to any particular content, and indifferent also to any particular ethical theory. The practical question, What kinds of human enterprise should be designated right and wrong? and the philosophical question, What is the ultimate nature of moral criteria? are both outside what we are to consider. We are concerned only with the shape of the moral life. And our concern must be philosophical and historical, rather than practical, because neither a society nor an individual is normally given the opportunity of making an express choice of the form of a moral life.

The moral life of our society discloses a form neither simple nor homogeneous. Indeed, the form of our morality appears to be a mixture of two ideal extremes, a mixture the character of which derives from the predominance of one extreme over the other. I am not convinced of the necessary ideality of the extremes; it is perhaps possible that one, if not both, could exist as an actual form of the moral life. But even if this is doubtful, each can certainly exist with so little modification from the other that it is permissible to begin by regarding them as possible forms of morality. Let us consider the two forms which, either separately or in combination, compose the form of the moral life of the Western world.

2

In the first of these forms, the moral life is *a habit of affection and behaviour*; not a habit of reflective *thought*, but a habit of *affection* and *conduct*. The current situations of a normal life are met, not by consciously applying to ourselves a rule of behaviour, nor by conduct recognized as the expression of a moral ideal, but by acting in accordance with a certain habit of behaviour. The moral life in this form does not spring from the consciousness of possible alternative ways of behaving and a choice, determined by an opinion, a rule or an ideal, from among these alternatives; conduct is as nearly as possible without reflection. And consequently, most of the current situations of life do not appear as occasions calling for judgment, or as problems requiring solutions; there is no weighing up of alternatives or reflection on consequences, no uncertainty, no battle of scruples. There is, on the occasion, nothing more than the unreflective following of a tradition of conduct in which we have been brought up. And such moral habit will disclose itself as often in *not* doing, in the taste which dictates abstention from certain actions, as in performances. It should, of course, be understood that I am not here describing a form of the moral life which assumes the existence of a moral sense or of moral intuition, nor a form of the moral life presupposing a moral theory which attributes authority to conscience. Indeed, no specific theory of the source of authority is involved in this form of the moral life. Nor am I describing a merely primitive form of morality, that is, the morality of a society unaccustomed to reflective thought. I am describing the form which moral action takes (because it can take no other) in all the emergencies of life when time and opportunity for reflection are lacking, and I am supposing that what is true of the emergencies of life is true of most of the occasions when human conduct is free from natural necessity.

Every form of the moral life (because it is affection and behaviour determined by art) depends upon education. And the character of each form is reflected in the kind of education required to nurture and maintain it. From what sort of education will this first form of the moral life spring?

We acquire habits of conduct, not by constructing a way of living upon rules or precepts learned by heart and subsequently practised, but by living with people who habitually behave in a certain manner: we acquire habits of conduct in the same way as we acquire our native language. There is no point in a child's life at which he can be said to begin to learn the language which is habitually spoken in his hearing; and there is no point in his life at which he can be said to begin to learn habits of behaviour from the people constantly about him. No doubt, in both cases, what is learnt (or some of it) can be formulated in rules and precepts; but in neither case do we, in this kind of education, learn by learning rules and precepts. What we learn here is what may be learned without the formulation of its rules. And not only may a command of language and behaviour be achieved without our becoming aware of the rules, but also, if we have acquired a knowledge of the rules, this sort of command of language and behaviour is impossible until we have forgotten them as rules and are no longer tempted to turn speech and action into the applications of rules to a situation. Further, the education by means of which we acquire habits of affection and behaviour is not only coeval with conscious life, but it is carried on, in practice and observation, without pause in every moment of our waking life, and perhaps even in our dreams; what is begun as imitation continues as selective conformity to a rich variety of customary behaviour. This sort of education is not compulsory; it is inevitable. And lastly (if education in general is making oneself at home in the natural and civilized worlds), this is not a separable part of education. One may set apart an hour in which to learn mathematics and devote another to the Catechism, but it is impossible to engage in any activity whatever without contributing to this kind of moral education, and it is impossible to enjoy this kind of moral education in an hour set aside for its study. There are, of course, many things which cannot be learned in this sort of education. We may learn in this manner to play a game, and we may learn to play it without breaking the rules, but we cannot acquire a knowledge of the rules themselves without formulating them or having them formulated for us. And further, without a knowledge of the rules we can never know for certain whether or not we are observing them, nor shall we be able to explain why the referee has blown his whistle. Or, to change the metaphor, from this sort of education can spring the ability never to write a false line of poetry, but it will give us neither the ability to scan nor a knowledge of the names of the various metric forms.

It is not difficult, then, to understand the sort of moral education by means of which habits of affection and behaviour may be acquired; it is the sort of education which gives the power to act appropriately and without hesitation, doubt or difficulty, but which does not give the ability to explain our actions in abstract terms, or defend them as emanations of moral principles. Moreover, this education must be considered to have failed in its purpose if it provides a range of behaviour insufficient to meet all situations without the necessity of calling upon reflection, or if it does not make the habit of behaviour sufficiently compelling to remove hesitation. But it must not be considered to have failed merely because it leaves us ignorant of moral rules and moral ideals. And a man may be said to have acquired most thoroughly what this kind of moral education can teach him when his moral dispositions are inseverably connected with his *amour-propre*, when the spring of his conduct is not an attachment to an ideal or a felt duty to obey a rule, but his self-esteem, and when to act wrongly is felt as diminution of his self-esteem.

Now, it will be observed that this is a form of morality which gives remarkable stability to the moral life from the point of view either of an individual or of a society; it is not in its nature to countenance large or sudden changes in the kinds of behaviour it desiderates.

Parts of a moral life in this form may collapse, but since the habits of conduct which compose it are never recognized as a system, the collapse does not readily spread to the whole. And being without a perceived rigid framework distinct from the modes of behaviour themselves (a framework, for example, of abstract moral ideals), it is not subject to the kind of collapse which springs from the detection of some flaw or incoherence in a system of moral ideals. Intellectual error with regard to moral ideas or opinions does not compromise a moral life which is firmly based upon a habit of conduct. In short, the stability which belongs to this form of the moral life derives from its elasticity and its ability to suffer change without disruption. First, there is in it nothing that is absolutely fixed. Just as in a language there may be certain constructions which are simply bad grammar, but in all the important ranges of expression the language is malleable by the writer who uses it and he cannot go wrong unless he deserts its genius, so in this form of the moral life, the more thorough our education the more certain will be our taste and the more extensive our range of behaviour within the tradition. Custom is always adaptable and susceptible to the *nuance* of the situation. This may appear a paradoxical assertion; custom, we have been taught, is blind. It is, however, an insidious piece of misobservation; custom is not blind, it is only 'blind as a bat'. And anyone who has studied a tradition of customary behaviour (or a tradition of any other sort) knows that both rigidity and instability are foreign to its character. And secondly, this form of the moral life is capable of change as well as of local variation. Indeed, no traditional way of behaviour, no traditional skill, ever remains fixed; its history is one of continuous change. It is true that the change it admits is neither great nor sudden; but then, revolutionary change is usually the product of the eventual overthrow of an aversion from change, and is characteristic of something that has few internal resources of change. And the appearance of changelessness in a morality of traditional behaviour is an illusion which springs from the erroneous belief that the only significant change is that which is either induced by self-conscious activity or is, at least, observed on the occasion. The sort of change which belongs to this form of the moral life is analogous to the change to which a living language is subject: nothing is more habitual or customary than our ways of speech, and nothing is more continuously invaded by change. Like prices in a free market, habits of moral conduct show no revolutionary changes because they are never at rest. But it should be observed, also, that because the internal movement characteristic of this form of the moral life does not spring from reflection upon moral principles, and represents only an unselfconscious exploitation of the genius of the tradition of moral conduct, it does not amount to moral self-criticism. And, consequently, a moral life of this kind, if it degenerates into super-stition, or if crisis supervenes, has little power of recovery. Its defence is solely its resistance to the conditions productive of crisis.

One further point should, perhaps, be noticed: the place and character of the moral eccentric in this form of the moral life, when it is considered as the form of the moral life of a society. The moral eccentric is not, of course, excluded by this form of morality. (The want of moral sensibility, the hollowness of moral character, which seems often to inhere in peoples whose morality is predominantly one of custom, is improperly attributed to the customary form of their morality; its cause lies elsewhere.) We sometimes think that deviation from a customary morality must always take place under the direction of a formulated moral ideal. But this is not so. There is a freedom and inventiveness at the heart of every traditional way of life, and deviation may be an expression of that freedom, springing from a sensitiveness to the tradition itself and remaining faith-ful to the traditional form. Generally speaking, no doubt, the inspir-ation of deviation from moral habit is perfectionist, but it is not necessarily consciously perfectionist. It is not, in essence, rebellious, and may be likened to the sort of innovation introduced into a plastic art by the fortuitous appearance in an individual of a specially high degree of manual skill, or to the sort of change a great stylist may make in a language. Although in any particular instance deviation may lead the individual eccentric astray, and although it is not something that can profitably be imitated, moral eccentricity is of value to a society whose morality is one of habit of behaviour (regardless of the direction it may take) so long as it remains the activity of the individual and is not permitted to disrupt the communal life. In a morality of an habitual way of behaviour, then, the influence of the moral eccentric may be powerful but is necessarily oblique, and the attitude of society towards him is necessarily ambivalent. He is admired but not copied, reverenced but not followed, welcomed but ostracized.

3

The second form of the moral life we are to consider may be regarded as in many respects the opposite of the first. In it activity is determined, not by a habit of behaviour, but by *the reflective application of a moral criterion*. It appears in two common varieties: as *the self-conscious pursuit of moral ideals*, and as *the reflective observance of moral rules*. But it is what these varieties have in common that is important, because it is this, and not what distinguishes them from one another, which divides them from the first form of morality.

This is a form of the moral life in which a special value is attributed to self-consciousness, individual or social; not only is the rule or the ideal the product of reflective thought, but the application of the rule or the ideal to the situation is also a reflective activity. Normally the rule or the ideal is determined first and in the abstract; that is, the first task in constructing an art of behaviour in this form is to express moral aspirations in words – in a rule of life or in a system of abstract ideals. This task of verbal expression need not begin with a moral *de omnibus dubitandum*; but its aim is not only to set out the desirable ends of conduct, but also to set them out clearly and unambiguously and to reveal their relations to one another. Secondly, a man who would enjoy this form of the moral life must be certain of his ability to defend these formulated aspirations against criticism. For, having been brought into the open, they will henceforth be liable to attack. His third task will be to translate them into behaviour, to apply them to the current situations of life as they arise. In this form of the moral life, then, action will spring from a judgment concerning the rule or end to be applied and the determination to apply it. The situations of living should, ideally, appear as problems to be solved, for it is only in this form that they will receive the attention they call for. And there will be a resistance to the urgency of action; it will appear more important to have the right moral ideal, than to act. The application of a rule or an ideal to a situation can never be easy; both ideal and situation will usually require interpretation, and a rule of life (unless the life has been simplified by the drastic reduction of the variety of situations which are allowed to appear) will always be found wanting unless it is supplemented with an elaborate casuistry or hermeneutic. It is true that moral ideals and moral rules may become so familiar that they take on the character of an habitual or traditional way of *thinking* about behaviour. It is true also that long familiarity with our ideals may have enabled us to express them more concretely in a system of specific rights and duties, handy in application. And further, a moral ideal may find its expression in a type of human character – such as the character of the gentleman – and conduct become the imaginative application of the ideal character to the situation. But these qualifications carry us only part of the way: they may remove the necessity for *ad hoc* reflection on the rules and ideals themselves, but they leave us still with the problem of interpreting the situation and the task of translating the ideal, the right or the duty into behaviour. For the right or the duty is always to observe a rule or realize an end, and not to behave in a certain concrete manner. Indeed, it is not desired, in this form of the moral life, that tradition should carry us all the way; its distinctive virtue is to be subjecting behaviour to a continuous corrective analysis and criticism.

This form of the moral life, not less than the other, depends upon education, but upon an education of an appropriately different sort. In order to acquire the necessary knowledge of moral ideals or of a rule of life, we need something more than the observation and practice of behaviour itself. We require, first, an intellectual training in the detection and appreciation of the moral ideals themselves, a training in which the ideals are separated and detached from the necessarily imperfect expression they find in particular actions. We require, secondly, training in the art of the intellectual management of these ideals. And thirdly, we require training in the application of ideals to concrete situations, in the art of translation and in the art of selecting appropriate means for achieving the ends which our education has inculcated. Such an education may be made compulsory in a society, but if so it is only because it is not inevitable. It is true that, as Spinoza says,[1] a substitute for a perfectly trained moral judgment may be found in committing a rule of life to memory and following it implicitly. But, though this is as far as some pupils will get, it cannot be considered to be the aim of this moral education. If it is to achieve its purpose, this education must carry us far beyond the acquisition of a moral technique; and it must be considered to have failed in its purpose if it has not given both ability to determine behaviour by a self-conscious choice and an understanding of the ideal grounds of the choice made. Nobody can fully share this form of the moral life who is not something of a philosopher and something of a self-analyst: its aim is moral behaviour springing from the communally cultivated reflective capacities of each individual.

Now, a moral life in which everyone who shares it knows at each moment exactly what he is doing and why, should be well protected against degeneration into superstition and should, moreover, give remarkable confidence to those who practise it. Nevertheless, it has its dangers, both from the point of view of an individual and from that of a society. The confidence which belongs to it is mainly a confidence in respect of the moral ideals themselves, or of the moral rule. The education in the ideals or in the rule must be expected to be the most successful part of this moral education; the art of applying the ideals is more difficult both to teach and to learn. And together with the certainty about how to *think* about moral ideals, must be expected to go a proportionate uncertainty about how to *act*. The constant analysis of behaviour tends to undermine, not only prejudice in moral habit, but moral habit itself, and moral reflection may come to inhibit moral sensibility.

Further, a morality which takes the form of the self-conscious pursuit of moral ideals is one which, at every moment, calls upon those who practise it to determine their behaviour by reference to a vision of perfection. This is not so much the case when the guide is a moral rule, because the rule is not represented as perfection and constitutes a mediation, a cushion, between the behaviour it demands on each occasion and the complete moral response to the situation. But

[1] *Ethica*, V, x.

when the guide of conduct is a moral ideal we are never suffered to escape from perfection. Constantly, indeed on all occasions, the society is called upon to seek virtue as the crow flies. It may even be said that the moral life, in this form, demands an hyperoptic moral vision and encourages intense moral emulation among those who enjoy it, the moral eccentric being recognized, not as a vicarious sufferer for the stability of a society, but as a leader and a guide. And the unhappy society, with an ear for every call, certain always about what it ought to *think* (though it will never for long be the same thing), in action shies and plunges like a distracted animal.

Again, a morality of ideals has little power of self-modification; its stability springs from its inelasticity and its imperviousness to change. It will, of course, respond to interpretation, but the limits of that response are close and severe. It has a great capacity to resist change, but when that resistance is broken down, what takes place is not change but revolution – rejection and replacement. Moreover, every moral ideal is potentially an obsession; the pursuit of moral ideals is an idolatry in which particular objects are recognized as 'gods'. This potentiality may be held in check by more profound reflection, by an intellectual grasp of the whole system which gives place and proportion to each moral ideal; but such a grasp is rarely achieved. Too often the excessive pursuit of one ideal leads to the exclusion of others, perhaps all others; in our eagerness to realize justice we come to forget charity, and a passion for righteousness has made many a man hard and merciless. There is, indeed, no ideal the pursuit of which will not lead to disillusion; *chagrin* waits at the end for all who take this path. Every admirable ideal has its opposite, no less admirable. Liberty or order, justice or charity, spontaneity or deliberateness, principle or circumstance, self or others, these are the kinds of dilemma with which this form of the moral life is always confronting us, making us see double by directing our attention always to abstract extremes, none of which is wholly desirable. It is a form of the moral life which puts upon those who share it, not only the task of translating moral ideals into appropriate forms of con- duct, but also the distracting intellectual burden of removing the verbal conflict of ideals before moral behaviour is possible. These conflicting ideals are, of course, reconciled in all amiable characters (that is, when they no longer appear as ideals), but that is not enough; a verbal and theoretical reconciliation is required. In short, this is a form of the moral life which is dangerous in an individual and disastrous in a society. For an individual it is a gamble which may have its reward when undertaken within the limits of a society which is not itself engaged in the gamble; for a society it is mere folly.

4

This brief characterization of what appear to be two forms of the moral life, while perhaps establishing their distinction or even their opposition, will have made us more doubtful about their capability of independent existence. Neither, taken alone, recommends itself convincingly as a likely form of the moral life, in an individual or in a society; the one is all habit, the other all reflection. And the more closely we examine them, the more certain we become that they are, not forms of the moral life at all, but ideal extremes. And when we turn to consider what sort of a form of the moral life they offer in combination, we may perhaps enjoy the not illusory confidence that we are approaching more nearly to concrete possibility, or even historical reality.

In a mixture in which the first of these extremes is dominant, the moral life may be expected to be immune from a confusion between behaviour and the pursuit of an ideal. Action will retain its primacy, and, whenever it is called for, will spring from habit of behaviour. Conduct itself will never become problematical, inhibited by the hesitations of ideal speculation or the felt necessity of bringing philosophic talent and the fruits of philosophic education to bear upon the situation. The confidence in action, which belongs to the well-nurtured customary moral life, will remain unshaken. And the coherence of the moral life will not wait upon the abstract unity which the reflective relation of values can give it. But, in addition, this mixed form of the moral life may be supposed to enjoy the advantages that spring from a reflective morality – the power to criticize, to reform and to explain itself, and the power to propagate itself beyond the range of the custom of a society. It will enjoy also the appropriate intellectual confidence in its moral standards and purposes. And it will enjoy all this without the danger of moral criticism usurping the place of a habit of moral behaviour, or of moral speculation bringing disintegration to moral life. The education in moral habit will be supplemented, but not weakened, by the education in moral ideology. And in a society which enjoyed this form of the moral life, both habit and ideology might be the common possession of all its members, or moral speculation might in fact be confined to the few, while the morality of the many remained one of the habit of behaviour. But, in any case, the internal resources of movement of this form of morality would be supplied by both its components: to the potential individual eccentricity which belongs to a traditional morality would be added the more consciously rebellious eccentricity which has its roots in the more precisely followed perfectionism of a morality of ideals. In short, this form of the moral life will offer to a society advantages similar to those of a religion which has taken to itself a theology (though not necessarily a popular theology) but without losing its character as a way of living.

On the other hand, a morality whose form is a mixture in which the second of our extremes is dominant will, I think, suffer from a permanent tension between its component parts. Taking charge, the morality of the self-conscious pursuit of ideals will have a disintegrating effect upon habit of behaviour. When action is called for, speculation or criticism will supervene. Behaviour itself will tend to become problematical, seeking its self-confidence in the coherence of an ideology. The pursuit of perfection will get in the way of a stable and flexible moral tradition, the naïve coherence of which will be prized less than the unity which springs from self-conscious analysis and synthesis. It will seem more important to have an intellectually defensible moral ideology than a ready habit of moral behaviour. And it will come to be assumed that a morality which is not easily transferable to another society, which lacks an obvious universality, is (for that reason) inadequate for the needs of the society of its origin. The society will wait upon its self-appointed moral teachers, pursuing the extremes they recommend and at a loss when they are silent. The distinguished and inspiring visiting preacher, who nevertheless is a stranger to the way we live, will displace the priest, the father of his parish. In a moral life constantly or periodically suffering the ravages of the armies of conflicting ideals, or (when these for the time have passed) falling into the hands of censors and inspectors, the cultivation of a habit of moral behaviour will have as little opportunity as the cultivation of the land when the farmer is confused and distracted by academic critics and political directors. Indeed, in such a mixture (where habit of behaviour is subordinate to the pursuit of ideals) each of the components is unavoidably playing a role foreign to its character; as in a literature in which criticism has usurped the place of poetry, or in a religious life in which the pursuit of theology offers itself as an alternative to the practice of piety.

These, however, must be counted incidental, though grave, imperfections in this mixture of extremes in the moral life; the radical defect of this form is the radical defect of its dominant extreme – its denial of the poetic character of all human activity. A prosaic tradition of thought has accustomed us to the assumption that moral activity, when analysed, will be found to consist in the translation of an idea of what ought to be into a practical reality, the transformation of an ideal into a concrete existence. And we are accustomed, even, to think of poetry in these terms; first, a 'heart's desire' (an idea) and then its expression, its translation into words. Nevertheless, I think this view is mistaken; it is the superimposition upon art and moral activity generally of an inappropriate didactic form. A poem is not the translation into words of a state of mind. What the poet says and what he wants to say are not two things, the one succeeding and embodying the other, they are the same thing; he does not know what he wants to say until he has said it. And the 'corrections' he may make to his first attempt are not efforts to make words correspond more closely to an already formulated idea or to images already fully formed in his mind, they are renewed efforts to formulate the idea, to conceive the image. Nothing exists in advance of the poem itself, except perhaps the poetic passion. And what is true of poetry is true also, I think, of all human moral activity. Moral ideals are not, in the first place, the products of reflective thought, the verbal expressions of unrealized ideas, which are then translated (with varying degrees of accuracy) into human behaviour; they are the products of human behaviour, of human practical activity, to which reflective thought gives subsequent, partial and abstract expression in words. What is good, or right, or what is considered to be reasonable behaviour may exist in advance of the situation, but only in the generalized form of the possibilities of behaviour determined by art and not by nature. That is to say, the capital of moral ideals upon which a morality of the pursuit of moral ideals goes into business has always been accumulated by a morality of habitual behaviour, and appears in the form of abstract ideas only because (for the purposes of subscription) it has been transformed by reflective thought into a currency of ideas.[1] This view of the matter does not, of course, deprive moral ideals of their power as critics of human habits, it does not denigrate the activity of reflective thought in giving this verbal expression to the principles of behaviour; there is no doubt whatever that a morality in which reflection has no part is defective. But it suggests that a morality of the pursuit of moral ideals, or a morality in which this is dominant, is not what it appears at first sight to be, is not something that can stand on its own feet. In such a morality, that which has power to rescue from superstition is given the task of generating human behaviour – a task which, in fact, it cannot perform. And it is only to be expected that a morality of this sort will be subject to sudden and ignominious collapse. In the life of an individual this collapse need not necessarily be fatal; in the life of a society it is likely to be irretrievable. For a society is a common way of life; and not only is it true that a society may perish of a disease which is not necessarily fatal even to those of its members who suffer from it, but it is also true that what is corrupting in the society may not be corrupting in its members.

5

The reader, knowing as much as I about the form of the moral life

---

[1] For example, Jên (consideration for others) in the Confucian morality was an abstraction from the filial piety and respect for elders which constituted the ancient Chinese habit of moral behaviour. The activity of the Sages, who (according to Chuang Tzu) *invented* goodness, duty and the rules and ideals of moral conduct, was one in which a concrete morality of habitual behaviour was sifted and refined; but, like too critical anthologists, they threw out the imperfect approximations of their material and what remained was not the reflection of a literature but merely a collection of masterpieces.

of contemporary Christendom, will not need to be told where all this is leading. If what I have said is not wide of the mark, it may perhaps be agreed that the form of our morality is that of a mixture in which the morality of the self-conscious pursuit of moral ideals is dominant. The moral energy of our civilization has for many centuries been applied mainly (though not, of course, exclusively) to building a Tower of Babel; and in a world dizzy with moral ideals we know less about how to behave in public and in private than ever before. Like the fool, our eyes have been on the ends of the earth. Having lost the thread of Ariadne, we have put our confidence in a plan of the labyrinth, and have given our attention to interpreters of the plan. Lacking habits of moral behaviour, we have fallen back upon moral opinions as a substitute; but, as we all know, when we reflect upon what we are doing we too often conclude that it is wrong. Like lonely men who, to gain reassurance, exaggerate the talents of their few friends, we exaggerate the significance of our moral ideals to fill in the hollowness of our moral life. It is a pitiless wedding which we have celebrated with our shadowy ideal of conduct. No doubt our present moral distraction (which is now several centuries old) springs partly from doubts we have in respect of the ideals themselves; all the effort of analysis and criticism has not yet succeeded in establishing a single one of them unquestionably. But this is not the root of the matter. The truth is that a morality in this form, regardless of the quality of the ideals, breeds nothing but distraction and moral instability. Perhaps it is a partial appreciation of this which has led some societies to give an artificial stability to their moral ideals. A few of these ideals are selected, those few are turned into an authoritative canon which is then made a guide to legislation or even a ground for the violent persecution of eccentricity. A moral ideology is established and maintained because this appears the only means of winning the necessary moral stability for the society. But in fact it is no remedy; it merely covers up the corruption of consciousness, the moral distraction inherent in morality as the self-conscious pursuit of moral ideals. However, it serves to illustrate the truth that the one kind of society which must of necessity be the enemy of profitable moral eccentricity is the society whose moral organization springs from the pursuit of ideals; for the moral life of such a society is itself nothing better than an arbitrary selection of moral eccentricities.

Now, I am not contending that our morality is wholly enclosed in the form of the self-conscious pursuit of moral ideals. Indeed, my view is that this is an ideal extreme in moral form and not, by itself, a possible form of morality at all. I am suggesting that the form of our moral life is dominated by this extreme, and that our moral life consequently suffers the internal tension inherent in this form. Certainly we possess habits of moral behaviour, but too often our self-conscious pursuit of ideals hinders us from enjoying them. Self-consciousness is asked to be creative, and habit is given the role of critic; what should be subordinate has come to rule, and its rule is a misrule. Sometimes the tension appears on the surface, and on these occasions we are aware that something is wrong. A man who fails to practise what he preaches does not greatly disturb us; we know that preaching is in terms of moral ideals and that no man can practise them perfectly. This is merely the minor tension between ideal and achievement. But when a man preaches 'social justice' (or indeed any other ideal whatsoever) and at the same time is obviously without a habit of ordinary decent behaviour (a habit that belongs to our morality but has fortunately never been idealized), the tension I speak of makes its appearance. And the fact that we are still able to recognize it is evidence that we are not wholly at the mercy of a morality of abstract ideals. Nevertheless, I do not think that anyone who has considered the matter will be disposed to deny that we are for the most part dominated by this morality. It is not our fault; we have been given little or no choice in the matter. It is, however, our misfortune. And it may be relevant, in conclusion, to consider briefly how it has come about.

On this subject, the history of European morals, I have nothing new to say; I can only direct attention to what is already well known. The form of contemporary western European morality has come to us from the distant past. It was determined in the first four centuries of the Christian era, that momentous period of our history when so much of our intellectual and emotional outlook began to emerge. It would, of course, be absurd to suggest that European morality sprang from some new species of seed first sown in that period; what, if anything, was new at that time was the mixture of seed which was at the disposal of those generations, to be sown, cultivated and sown once more until its characteristic fruit became fixed. It was an age of moral change. In that Greco-Roman world the old habits of moral behaviour had lost their vitality. There were, no doubt, men who were good neighbours, faithful friends and pious citizens, whose confidence in the customs that determined their conduct was still unshaken; but, in general, the impetus of moral habit of behaviour seems to have been spent – illustrating, perhaps, the defect of a form of morality too securely insulated from the criticism of ideals. It was, in consequence, an age of intense moral self-consciousness, an age of moral reformers who, unavoidably, preached a morality of the pursuit of ideals and taught a variety of dogmatic moral ideologies. The intellectual energy of the time was directed towards the deter-mination of an ideal, and the moral energy towards the translation of that ideal into practice.[1] Moral self-consciousness itself became a virtue;[2] genuine morality was identified with the 'practice of philo-sophy'.[3] And it was thought that for the achievement of a good life it was necessary that a man should submit to an artificial moral training, a moral gymnastic, ἄσκησις; learning and discipline must be added to 'nature'. The age, of course, was able to distin-guish between a man who attained to a merely intellectual appre-ciation of moral ideals and one who was successful in the enterprise of translating ideal into conduct, but it was common ground that the moral life was to be achieved only, as Philo said, 'by reading, by meditation and by the calling to mind of noble ideals'. In short, what the Greco-Roman world of this period had to offer was a morality in which the self-conscious pursuit of moral ideals was pre-eminent.

And our inheritance from that other great source of our moral inspiration, from early Christianity, was of a similar character: indeed it is not an inheritance which in this matter can be securely separated from that of the ancient world as a whole. In the earliest days, to be a Christian was to be a member of a community animated by a faith and sustained by a hope – faith in a person and hope for a coming event. The morality of these communities was a custom of behaviour appropriate to the character of the faith and to the nature of the

[1] Epictetus, *Diss.*, i, 4 and 30.   [2] *Ibid.*, 2, 10.   [3] *Dio Chrysostom*, ii, 239.

expectation. It was a way of living distinguished in its place and time by the absence from it of a formulated moral ideal; and it was a way of living departure from which alone involved the penalty of exclusion from the community. And further, it was a way of living which admitted, but did not demand, extremes of behaviour, counsels of perfection. The nearest thing to a moral ideal known to these communities was the ideal of charity; the nearest thing to a moral rule was the precept to love God and one's neighbour. It was a morality which found its characteristic verbal expression in the phrase, τοὺς τρόπους κυρίου, the custom of the Lord. But over these earliest Christian communities, in the course of two centuries, there came a great change. The habit of moral behaviour was converted into the self-conscious pursuit of formulated moral ideals – a conversion parallel to the change from faith in a person to belief in a collection of abstract propositions, a creed. This change sprang from a variety of sources; from a change in the circumstances of the Christian's life, from the pressure of the alien intellectual world in which the Christian was set down, from the desire to 'give a reason for the hope' that animated him, from the necessity of translating the Christian way of life into a form in which it could be appreciated by those who had never shared the original inspiration and who, having to learn their Christianity as a foreign language, needed a grammar. The urge to speculate, to abstract and to define, which overtook Christianity as a religion, infected also Christianity as a way of moral life. But, whatever was the impulse of the change, it appears that by the middle of the third century there existed a Christian morality in the familiar form of the self-conscious pursuit of moral ideals, and by the time of St Ambrose the *form* of this morality had become indistinguishable from that of the morality of the surrounding world, a morality of virtues and vices and of the translation of ideals into actions. A Christian morality in the form of a way of life did not, of course, perish, and it has never completely disappeared. But from this time in the history of Christendom a Christian habit of moral behaviour (which had sprung from the circumstances of Christian life) was swamped by a Christian moral ideology, and the perception of the poetic character of human conduct was lost.

I do not wish to suggest that either the self-conscious morality of the Greco-Roman world at the beginning of our era, or the change which overtook Christian morality in the second and third centuries, was avoidable. The one was merely the filling of the vacuum left by the collapse of a traditional morality, and as for the other – perhaps, in order to convert the world, a morality must be reduced to the easily translatable prose of a moral ideal, must be defined and made intellectually coherent, even though the price is a loss of spontaneity and confidence and the approach of the danger of obsession. The fact, however, remains that the moral inheritance of western Europe, both from the classical culture of the ancient world and from Christianity, was not the gift of a morality of habitual behaviour, but of a moral ideology. It is true that, in the course of centuries, this moral form went some way towards being reconverted into a morality of habit of behaviour. Such a conversion is certainly possible when moral ideals become familiar and, finding expression in customs and institutions which exert a direct pressure upon conduct, cease to be mere ideals. And it is true, also, that the invading barbarians contributed a morality of custom rather than of idea. Nevertheless, modern European morality has never been able to divest itself of the form in which it first emerged. And having once committed the indiscretion of formulating itself in the abstract terms of moral ideals, it was only to be expected that its critics (who have never for long been silent) should seize upon these, and that in defending them against attack they should become rigid and exaggerated. Every significant attack upon Christian morality (that of Nietzsche, for example) has been mistaken for an attack upon the particular moral ideals of Christian life, whereas whatever force it possessed derived from the fact that the object of attack was a morality of ideals which had never succeeded in becoming a morality of habit of behaviour.

The history of European morals, then, is in part the history of the maintenance and extension of a morality whose form has, from the beginning, been dominated by the pursuit of moral ideals. In so far as this is an unhappy form of morality, prone to obsession and at war with itself, it is a misfortune to be deplored; in so far as it cannot now readily be avoided, it is a misfortune to be made the best of. And if a morality of ideals is now all, or at least the best, of what we have, it might seem an injudicious moment to dwell upon its defects. But in order to make the best of an unavoidable situation, we need to know its defects as well as feel its necessity. And what at the present time stands between us and the opportunity (such as it is) of surmounting our misfortune is not our sense of the difficulty of doing so, but an erroneous inference we have drawn from our situation – the belief, which has slowly settled upon us, encouraged by almost all the intellectual tendencies of recent centuries, that it is no misfortune at all, but a situation to be welcomed. For the remarkable thing about contemporary European morality is not merely that its form is dominated by the self-conscious pursuit of ideals, but that this form is generally thought to be better and higher than any other. A morality of habit of behaviour is dismissed as primitive and obsolete; the pursuit of moral ideals (whatever discontent there may be with the ideals themselves) is identified with moral enlightenment. And further, it is prized (and has been particularly prized on this account since the seventeenth century) because it appears to hold out the possibility of that most sought-after consummation – a 'scientific' morality. It is to be feared, however, that in both these appearances we are sadly deceived. The pursuit of moral ideals has proved itself (as might be expected) an untrustworthy form of morality, the spring neither of a practical nor of a 'scientific' moral life.

The predicament of Western morals, as I read it, is first that our moral life has come to be dominated by the pursuit of ideals, a dominance ruinous to a settled habit of behaviour; and, secondly, that we have come to think of this dominance as a benefit for which we should be grateful or an achievement of which we should be proud. And the only purpose to be served by this investigation of our predicament is to disclose the corrupt consciousness, the self-deception which reconciles us to our misfortune.

1948

Rational Conduct

The word *rational* has been strangely abused of late times.

COLERIDGE, *Aids to Reflection*

The word *Reason*, and the epithets connected with it – *Rational* and *Reasonable* – have enjoyed a long history which has bequeathed to them a legacy of ambiguity and confusion. Like mirrors, they have reflected the changing notions of the world and of human faculty which have flowed over our civilization in the last two thousand years; image superimposed upon image has left us with a cloudy residue. Any man may be excused when he is puzzled by the question how he ought to use these words, and in particular how he ought to use them in relation to human conduct and to politics; for, in the first place, these words come before us as attributes of 'argument', and what is puzzling is the analogy in which they are applied to 'conduct'. The philosopher may succeed in disentangling the confusion which springs from merely crooked thinking, and the historian in telling the story of the ambiguity and in making sense of it without the help of those adventitious aids, the categories of truth and error. My purpose here is to seek a satisfactory way of using the word *Rational* in connection with conduct, and to explore some of the territory which opens up in the process: the impulse is both philosophical and historical.

I

I will begin with the assumption that when we speak of human behaviour and the management of our affairs as 'rational', we mean to commend it. 'Rational conduct' is something no man is required to be ashamed of. It is usually held that something more than 'rationality' is required in order to make conduct either endearing or saintly, or to make the management of affairs a dazzling success; but, generally speaking, it belongs to our tradition to find 'rationality' a laudable quality, or, at least, to find irrationality something proper to be avoided. We are, then, to consider an idea which in relation to human conduct implies commendation. Our civilization, it is true, has acquired a parallel vocabulary in which 'rational' is a word of denigration, but the spring of this rebound was an opposition to a narrowing of human sympathies, a restriction of what was thought admirable and proper to be done which had become reflected in the word, rather than a denial of all standards of propriety.

Secondly, I shall assume that the word 'rational', when used in connection with human conduct, refers, in the first place, to a manner of behaving and only derivatively to an action in respect of what it achieves or of the success with which it accomplishes what was intended. Thus, to behave 'rationally' is to behave 'intelligently', and whether such behaviour is pragmatically successful will depend upon circumstances other than its 'rationality'. This, again, coincides with usage; a 'lunatic', whose behaviour we recognize as 'irrational', is not always unsuccessful in achieving his designs, and we know that, even in argument, a correct conclusion may be reached in spite of false reasoning.

Ever since the eighteenth century we have had presented to us a variety of forms of behaviour or projects of activity, each recommended on account of its 'rationality'. There have been 'rational education', 'rational agriculture', 'rational diet', 'rational dress', to say nothing of 'rational religion', and 'rational spelling'. The segregation of the sexes in education, eating meat and drinking intoxicants were, for example, held to be 'irrational'. One famous protagonist of rational dress asserted that a shirt-collar which did not leave space for the insertion of a loaf of bread was irrationally restrictive of the flow of air to the body; and the wearing of a hat has frequently been said to be 'irrational'. But the expression 'rational dress' was applied, in particular, in Victorian times, to an extraordinary garment affected by girls on bicycles, and to be observed in the illustrations of the *Punch* of the period. Bloomers were asserted to be the 'rational dress' for girl cyclists. And as a means to putting straight our own ideas of 'rationality' we could do worse than to consider what was being thought by those who asserted the 'rationality' of this garment.[1]

---

[1] Whether Mrs Bloomer herself made this assertion, or whether it was made by others on behalf of her invention, I do not know.

There is little doubt about what they were thinking of in the first place. They were concentrating their attention upon the activity of *propelling* a bicycle. The things to be considered, and to be related to one another, were a bicycle of a certain general design and the structure of the human body. All considerations other than these were dismissed because they were believed to be of no account in determining the 'rationality' of the dress to be designed. And, in particular, the designers were decided not to take account of current prejudice, convention or folklore, concerning feminine dress; from the standpoint of 'rationality' these must be considered only as limiting circumstances. Consequently, the first step in the project of designing a 'rational' dress for this purpose must be a certain empty- ing of the mind, a conscious effort to get rid of preconceptions. Of course knowledge of a certain sort would be required – knowledge of mechanics and anatomy – but the greater part of a man's thoughts would appear as an encumbrance in this enterprise, as a distraction from which it was necessary to avert the attention. If one were an investor anxious to employ a designer on this project, one might do well to consider a Chinese, for example, rather than an Englishman, because he would be less distracted by irrelevant considerations; just as the South American republics applied to Bentham for a 'rational' constitution. The 'rationality' sought by these Victorian designers was, then, an eternal and a universal quality; something rescued from the world of mere opinion and set in a world of certainty. They might make mistakes; and if they were not mistakes in mechanics and anatomy (which would be unlikely), they would be the mistakes of a mind not firmly enough insulated from preconception, a mind not yet set free. Indeed, they did make a mistake; impeded by preju- dice, their minds paused at bloomers instead of running on to 'shorts' – clearly so much more complete a solution of their chosen problem. Or was it a mistake? Perhaps it was, instead, some dim recognition of a more profound understanding of 'rationality' which made them stop there. We must consider the possibility later on.

Now, the questions we may ask ourselves are, why were bloomers thought to be a 'rational' form of dress for girl cyclists? And why was this way of going about things considered to be pre-eminently 'rational'? In general the answers to these questions are, first,

Because they were adapted to circumstances – bloomers were a successful solution of the specific problem set; if the bicycle to be propelled had been of a different design (if, for example, arms and not legs had been the propelling limb) the clothing considered 'rational' would have been of a different design. And secondly, Because the solution sprang (or seemed to spring) solely from the reflective consideration of the problem set – bloomers were a 'rational' form of dress because the act of designing them (or the act of wearing them) sprang from an antecedent act of independent reflective effort, undistracted by 'irrelevant' considerations. Here, in short, was an example of the much advertised 'rational method' in action.

2

The view we are to consider[1] takes *purpose* as the distinctive mark of 'rationality' in conduct: 'rational' activity is behaviour in which an independently premeditated end is pursued and which is determined solely by that end. This end may be an external result to be achieved, or it may be the enjoyment of the activity itself. To play a game in order to win (and perhaps to win a prize), and to play it for its own sake, for the enjoyment of it, are both purposive activities. Further, 'rational' conduct is behaviour *deliberately* directed to the achievement of a *formulated* purpose and is governed solely by that purpose. There may be other, perhaps unavoidable, consequences or results springing from the conduct, but these must be regarded as extraneous, fortuitous and 'irrational' because they are unwanted and no part of the design. Bloomers were not designed to shock Victorian sensibility, to amuse or to distract, but to provide a form of dress precisely suitable for cycling. The designers did not say to themselves, 'Let us invent something amusing'; nor, on the other hand, did they think that the 'absurdity' of their creation was in any degree a qualification of its 'rationality': indeed, 'absurdity' is so much a common feature of all the works of designers inspired by this notion of 'rationality' that it could normally be taken as a sign of success. 'Rational' conduct will, then, usually, have not only a specific end,

[1] Professor Ginsberg in *Reason and Unreason in Society* gives an account of the view I am considering here.

but also a simple end; for when the end is in fact complex, activity can be efficiently directed towards its achievement only when, either the complexity is presented as a series of simple ends (the achievement of one leading on to the achievement of the next and so to the final end), or where the simple components of the complex end are seen to be related to the specific components of the activity. Hence, in 'rational behaviour', the necessity of a strict formulation of the end to be pursued; the decision of the designer of bloomers to confine his attention to mechanics and anatomy and to neglect all other considerations. 'Rational' activity is activity in search of a certain, a conclusive answer to a question, and consequently the question must be formulated in such a way that it admits of such an answer.

Now, the deliberate direction of activity to the achievement of a specific end can be successful only when the necessary means are available or procurable and when the power exists of detecting and appropriating from the means which are available those which are necessary. Consequently, there will be in 'rational' conduct, not only a premeditated purpose to be achieved, but also a separately premeditated selection of the means to be employed. And all this requires reflection and a high degree of detachment. The calculated choice of end and means both involves and provides a resistance to the indiscriminate flow of circumstance. One step at a time is the rule here; and each step is taken in ignorance of what the next is to be. The 'rationality' of conduct, then, on this view of it, springs from something that we do *before* we act; and activity is 'rational' on account of its being generated in a certain manner.

A further determination of this so-called 'rational' conduct may be found in the kinds of behaviour it excludes or opposes itself to. First, merely capricious conduct will be excluded; conduct, that is, which has no end settled in advance. Secondly, it will oppose itself to merely impulsive conduct – conduct from which there is absent the necessary element of reflective choice of means to achieve the desired end. Thirdly, this 'rational' conduct is in permanent opposition to conduct which is not governed by some deliberately accepted rule or principle or canon and which does not spring from the explicit observance of a formulated principle. Further, it excludes conduct which springs from the unexamined authority of a tradition, a custom or a habit of behaviour. For, although achievement of a purpose may be embedded in a merely traditional mode of conduct, the purpose itself is not disentangled, and a man may remain true to the tradition while being wholly ignorant of any propositional formulation of the end pursued. For example, certain procedures in the House of Commons may, in fact, achieve certain specific purposes, but since they were not expressly designed to achieve these purposes their character as means to ends often remains hidden and unformulated. And lastly, I think that activity in pursuit of an end for which the necessary means are known to be absent may fairly be said to be excluded; behaviour of this sort is not 'rational'.

Let us explore the matter a little more deeply. But it must be made clear, before we begin, that what we are considering is presented to us as, taken by itself, a possible (and a valuable) *mode of conduct*, a manner of behaviour, and not merely a manner of thinking about behaviour. It may be admitted that human beings do not often achieve this mode of conduct; and it may be agreed, without detriment to the view we are considering, that the usual behaviour of the major part of mankind does not appear to be of this character, but is something very much less disciplined. But the view we are to investigate is that this is a possible mode of conduct, that concrete activity can spring up in this manner and that on account of it springing up in this manner it may be called 'rational'. What, then, we may inquire, are the assumptions of this view, and what is the validity of these assumptions?

It would appear that the first assumption is that men have a power of reasoning about things, of contemplating propositions about activities, and of putting these propositions in order and making them coherent. And it is assumed, further, that this is a power independent of any other powers a man may have, and something from which his activity can *begin*. And activity is said to be 'rational' (or 'intelligent') on account of being preceded by the exercise of this power, on account of a man having 'thought' in a certain manner before he acted. 'Rational' conduct is conduct springing from an antecedent process of 'reasoning'. In order that a man's conduct should be wholly 'rational', he must be supposed to have the power of first imagining and choosing a purpose to pursue, of defining that purpose clearly and of selecting fit means to achieve it; and this power must be wholly independent, not only of tradition and of the uncontrolled relics of his fortuitous experience of the world, but also of the activity itself to which it is a preliminary. And for a number of men to enjoy wholly 'rational' conduct together, it must be supposed that they have in common a power of this sort and that the exercise of it will lead them all to the same conclusions and issue in the same form of activity.

There are, of course, various well-known but crude formulations of this supposition but we need not concern ourselves with them. The power in question has been hypostatized and given a name; it is called 'Reason'. And it has been supposed that the human mind must contain in its composition a native faculty of 'Reason', a light whose brightness is dimmed only by education, a piece of mistake-proof apparatus, an oracle whose magic word is truth. But if this is going further than is either wise or necessary, what does seem unavoidable (if there is to be this power) is the supposition that a man's mind can be separated from its contents and its activities. What needs to be assumed is the mind as a neutral instrument, as a piece of apparatus. Long and intensive training may be necessary in order to make the best use of this piece of machinery; it is an engine which must be nursed and kept in trim. Nevertheless, it is an independent instrument, and 'rational' conduct springs from the exercise of it.

The mind, according to this hypothesis, is an independent instrument capable of dealing with experience. Beliefs, ideas, knowledge, the contents of the mind, and above all the activities of men in the world, are not regarded as themselves mind, or as entering into the composition of mind, but as adventitious, posterior acquisitions of the mind, the results of mental activity which the mind might or might not have possessed or undertaken. The mind may acquire knowledge or cause bodily activity, but it is something that may exist destitute of all knowledge, and in the absence of any activity; and where it has acquired knowledge or provoked activity, it remains independent of its acquisition or its expression in activity. It is steady and permanent, while its filling of knowledge is fluctuating and often fortuitous. Further, it is supposed that this permanent mental instrument, though it exists from birth, is capable of being trained. But what is called a 'trained mind' is, like the schoolboy's tears over a proposition in Euclid, a *consequence* of learning and activity, and is not a *conclusion* from it. Hence, mental training may take the form either of a purely functional exercise (like gymnastics), or of an exercise which incidentally gets us somewhere, like running to catch a bus. The mind may be trained by 'pelmanism' or by learning Latin grammar. Lastly, it is supposed that the mind will be most successful in dealing with experience when it is least prejudiced with already acquired dispositions or knowledge: the open, empty or free mind, the mind without disposition, is an instrument which attracts truth, repels superstition and is alone the spring of 'rational' judgment and 'rational' conduct. Consequently, the purely formal exercise of the mind will normally be considered a superior sort of training to the mixed exercise which involves a particular 'knowledge how' and unavoidably leaves behind some relic of acquired disposition. And the first training of a mind already infected with a disposition will be a process of purification, of getting rid of accumulated special knowledge and skill – a process of re-establishing virginal detachment. Childhood is, unfortunately, a period during which, from the lack of a trained mind, we give admittance to a whole miscellany of beliefs, dispositions, knowledge not in the form of propositions; the first business of the adult is to disencumber his mental apparatus of these prejudices. This, then, is 'intelligence', the 'rational' part of a man; and human activity is to be counted 'rational' if and when it is preceded and caused by the exercise of this 'intelligence'.

3

Now, it may appear that what I am describing is a fanciful view of things, held only by a few eccentrics who need not be taken seriously and whose assertions should not be taken *au pied de la lettre*. But this is not so. It is a view, a theory, which has a respectable place in the history of philosophy; and philosophers have done much to encourage the ordinary man to think in this manner. It is true that many who speak in a way which leads us to suppose that they hold some such theory would disclaim the theory while preserving the manner of speech; but these should be asked to explain what they mean. As a point of view this is common enough; it is shared, for example, by all the cruder advocates of mental training in place of education. It gives meaning to the common assertion that such and such an action or measure is 'logical', and that because it is 'logical' it should be performed or set on foot. To this view belongs the principle of *la carrière ouverte aux talents*, the notion that the members of the Civil Service should 'have no qualifications other than their personal abilities', and the suggestion that we should teach children how to use the English language but without encumbering their minds with English literature.[1] The view we are considering is not, I think, an invention of my own; it has adherents in every department of life. It sees 'rationality' in conduct as the product of a determinate, independent instrument, and asserts that the 'rational' way of going about things is to go about them under the sole guidance of this instrument.

The appearance which conduct would tend to assume if it conformed to this notion of 'rationality' is not in any doubt. Activity would be. bent towards the performance of actions in pursuit of preconceived and formulated ends, actions determined wholly by the ends sought and from which fortuitous and unwanted consequences had, so far as possible, been excluded. Its aim would be, first, to establish a proposition, to determine a purpose to be pursued, secondly, to determine the means to be employed to achieve that (and no other) end, and, thirdly, to act. Human behaviour would appear to be broken up into a series of problems to be solved, purposes to be achieved and a series of individual actions performed in pursuit of these ends. The unprejudiced consideration of every project would take place of policy, precedent and prescription would be avoided (so far as possible) in determining enterprise, and the man who had a formula would come to oust the man who had none.

Now, it is necessary to be guarded in speaking of the sort of activity which might be supposed to spring up in response to the ideal of 'rational' conduct we have before us, because what we are considering is not, in fact, a way of behaving, but a theory of behaviour. And since, as I hope to show, it is an erroneous theory, a misdescription of human behaviour, it is impossible to produce any

[1] C. D. Darlington, *The Conflict of Science and Society*.

clear and genuine example of behaviour which fits it. If this is 'rational' behaviour, then it is not merely undesirable; it is in fact impossible. Men do not behave in this way, because they cannot. No doubt those who have held this theory have thought that they were describing a possible form of behaviour; and by calling it 'rational', they recommended it as desirable: but they were under an illusion. No doubt, also, wherever this theory is current, behaviour will *tend* to conform to the pattern it suggests; but it will not succeed. The practical danger of an erroneous theory is not that it may persuade people to act in an undesirable manner, but that it may confuse activity by putting it on a false scent. But it is with the theory itself that we are concerned.

4

It is no secret that this view of 'rationality' in conduct leaves something to be desired. Criticism has fastened upon many of the details, and some of it has been cogent enough to make necessary extensive repairs to the theory. I do not myself wish to direct attention to defect in detail, but to what seems to me to be the main short-coming. And I believe that when the precise character of the theory is perceived, it will be seen to collapse under the weight of its own imperfections. My view is that this is not a satisfactory notion of *rational* conduct because it is not a satisfactory account of any sort of conduct.

Let us begin with the idea of 'the mind' or 'intelligence' which is at the centre of this theory. The notion is: that first there is something called 'the mind', that this mind acquires beliefs, knowledge, prejudices – in short, a filling – which remain nevertheless a mere appendage to it, that it causes bodily activities, and that it works best when it is unencumbered by an acquired disposition of any sort. Now, this mind I believe to be a fiction; it is nothing more than an hypostatized activity. Mind as we know it is the offspring of knowledge and activity; it is composed entirely of thoughts. You do not first have a mind, which acquires a filling of ideas and then makes distinctions between true and false, right and wrong, reasonable and unreasonable, and then, as a third step, causes activity. Properly speaking the mind has no existence apart from, or in advance of, these and other distinctions. These and other distinctions are not acquisitions; they are constitutive of the mind. Extinguish in a man's mind these and other distinctions, and what is extinguished is not merely a man's 'knowledge' (or part of it), but the mind itself. What is left is not a neutral, unprejudiced instrument, a pure intelligence, but nothing at all. The whole notion of the mind as an apparatus for thinking is, I believe, an error; and it is the error at the root of this particular view of the nature of 'rationality' in conduct. Remove that, and the whole conception collapses.

But further, and following from this, it is an error to suppose that conduct could ever have its spring in the sort of activity which is misdescribed by hypostatizing a 'mind' of this sort; that is, from the power of considering abstract propositions about conduct. That such a power exists is not to be doubted; but its prerequisite is conduct itself. This activity is not something that can exist in advance of conduct; it is the result of reflection upon conduct, the creature of a subsequent analysis of conduct. And this goes, not only for conduct in the narrow sense, but for activity of every sort, for the activity of the scientist, for example, or of the craftsman, no less than for the activity in politics and in the ordinary conduct of life. And consequently it is preposterous, in the strict meaning of the word, to maintain that activity can derive from this kind of thinking, and it is unwise to recommend that it should do so by calling activity 'rational' only when it appears to have this spring. *Doing* anything both depends upon and exhibits knowing how to do it; and though part (but never the whole) of knowing how to do it can subsequently be reduced to knowledge in the form of propositions (and possibly to ends, rules and principles), these propositions are neither the spring of the activity nor are they in any direct sense regulative of the activity.

The characteristic of the carpenter, the scientist, the painter, the judge, the cook, and of any man in the ordinary conduct of life, and in his relations with other people and with the world around him, is a knowledge, not of certain propositions about themselves, their tools, and the materials in which they work, but a knowledge of how to decide certain questions; and this knowledge is the condition of the exercise of the power to construct such propositions. Consequently, if 'rationality' is to represent a desirable quality of an activity, it

cannot be the quality of having independently premeditated propositions about the activity before it begins. And this applies to propositions about the end or purpose of an activity no less than to any
other kind of proposition. It is an error to call an activity 'rational'
on account of its end having been specifically determined in advance
and in respect of its achieving that end to the exclusion of all others,
because there is in fact no way of determining an end for activity in
advance of the activity itself; and if there were, the spring of activity
would still remain in knowing how to act in pursuit of that end and
not in the mere fact of having formulated an end to pursue. A cook is
not a man who first has a vision of a pie and then tries to make it; he is a
man skilled in cookery, and both his projects and his achievements
spring from that skill. 'Good' English is not something that exists in
advance of how English is written (that is to say, English literature);
and the knowledge that such and such is a sloppy, ambiguous construction, or is 'bad grammar', is not something that can be known independently and in advance of knowing how to write the language.

My view is, then, that this project of finding a mode of conduct
which, in this sense, is 'rational' is misconceived. The instrumental
mind does not exist, and if it did it would always lack the power to
be the spring of any concrete activity whatever.

Nevertheless, it is undeniable that men for long enough have
deliberately tried to behave in this sense 'rationally'. They have
believed that 'rational' conduct of this sort has a pre-eminent virtue.
They have been conscious often of a failure to divest themselves of
the encumbrance of other springs of action, but they have been
pleased with themselves whenever they have believed that they had
attended only to the voice of this 'reason'. And I think, perhaps, what
helps to explain the illusion is the false but plausible theory of education which makes it seem not an illusion. We may be agreed that it
is preposterous to suppose an activity can spring from the premeditation of propositions about the activity, but we are apt to believe that
in order to teach an activity it is necessary to have converted our
knowledge of it into a set of propositions – the grammar of a language, the rules of research, the principles of experiment and verification, the canons of good workmanship – and that in order to learn
an activity we must begin with such propositions. It would be

foolish, of course, to deny that this device has a pedagogic value. But it must be observed that, not only are these rules, etc., these propositions about the activity, an abridgment of the teacher's concrete knowledge of the activity (and therefore posterior to the activity itself), but learning them is never more than the meanest part of education in an activity. They can be taught, but they are not the only things that can be learned from a teacher. To work along-side a practised scientist or craftsman is an opportunity not only to learn the rules, but to acquire also a direct knowledge of how he sets about his business (and, among other things, a knowledge of how and when to apply the rules); and until this is acquired nothing of great value has been learned. But it is only when we think of this as of no account in comparison with the learning of the rules themselves, or when we reject it as not teaching in the proper sense, or not properly knowledge, that the character of learning an activity seems to sup-port the view that activity itself can spring from independently premeditating propositions about it.

But anyone who attempts to explain the lure of this 'rationality' must venture deep into the hidden history of European mental dispositions, particularly in the last four centuries. No doubt it is idle to fix upon specific causes, but I think it will be found that three circumstances have contributed greatly to the attraction which this 'rationality' has for us. First, there has been a laudable conviction that mental honesty, disinterestedness, absence of prejudice, are intellectual virtues of the highest value. But this conviction has unfortunately been combined, in a strange confusion of mind, with the belief that disinterestedness is possible only to a mind which is wholly self-moved[1] – that is, a mind devoid of acquired disposition. To value intellectual honesty and at the same time to identify it with activity specifically determined to be 'honest', and not to recognize it as an acquired skill of which there are various idioms each with its appropriate circumstances, is the first step towards this un-fortunate ideal of 'rationality'.

Secondly, there has been a passionate desire for certainty – about matters of belief and conduct – which has been combined with the

[1] It would be difficult to find a more persuasive account of this doctrine than that contained in Spinoza's *Ethics*.

conviction that certainty is possible only in respect of something we have been 'given', and not in respect of anything we have ascertained, that certainty is a gift of grace, not a reward of work. Certainty, it seemed, must be something with which we must *begin*; and only propositional knowledge, independent of activity, seemed to offer it. The craving for this sort of mistake-proof certainty is not, I think, so creditable as the desire for intellectual honesty: indeed, I think the instrumental mind may be regarded as, in some respects, the relic of a belief in magic.

And thirdly, there has been in many departments of life, and particularly in politics, a growing ignorance of how to go about things and a more frequent appearance of situations which, because they seem to be 'new', find us unprepared with a ready means of dealing with them. When in politics you do not know how to behave, you will tend to cry down the value and necessity of this sort of knowledge, and to cry up the value and necessity of a free and open mind supposed to be endowed with the capacity of knowing in advance of activity. An example of this is to be found in the French political reformers of the time of Louis XIV. The state of France, they were convinced, was desperate; but there, hidden in the traditions of French government, were institutions, ways of doing things, long fallen into desuetude, to which the reformers could and did appeal. They possessed a knowledge of how affairs had been conducted, and this knowledge determined their proposals. The state of Europe, also, was desperate. But here such knowledge was absent; Europe, so far as they knew, never had been organized. And since what was needed had to be invented (as they thought) *de novo*, their plans for European peace were presented as creatures of pure intelligence. The difference between the plans of the Abbé de St Pierre for France and his plans for Europe is remarkable. Knowledge of how to behave, of course, is never wholly absent; at this time of day (or even at that) the human race has something to call upon, and in fact calls upon it. There is no danger that anyone will succeed in achieving a purely 'rational' politics in this sense. But the resort of mankind to such genuine knowledge as it has, is often hindered by this unhappy attachment to a false ideal of freedom of mind and an abstract and attenuated 'rationality'. And politics is a field of activity peculiarly subject to the lure of this 'rational' ideal. If you start being merely 'intelligent' about a boiler or an electrical generator you are likely to be pulled up short by an explosion; but in politics all that happens is war and chaos, which you do not immediately connect with your error. The doctrinaire in politics is not a man, the spring of whose activity is independent propositional knowledge about an end to be pursued, but a man who fails to recognize what the true spring is. Usually he is a man who, having rejected as worthless the current knowledge of how to behave in politics, falls back upon his know-ledge of how to behave in other activities (which is not always a good guide) while erroneously supposing that he has fallen back upon knowledge independent of any activity and provided by some potentially infallible 'intelligence'.

To the firm believer in this idea of 'rationality', the spectacle of human behaviour (in himself and in others) departing from its norm may be expected to confirm his suspicion that 'rational' conduct of this sort is difficult, but not to shake his faith in its possibility and desirability. He will deplore the unregulated conduct which, because it is externally unregulated, he will think of as 'irrational'. But it will always be difficult for him to entertain the notion that what he identified as 'rational' conduct is in fact impossible, not because it is liable to be swamped by 'insane and irrational springs of wickedness in most men', but because it involves a misrepresentation of the nature of human conduct. He will readily admit that he has been the victim of an illusion; but the exact character of the illusion will elude him. An interesting example of this is afforded by J. M. Keynes's essay, *My Early Beliefs*,[1] where a candid attempt to super-sede what he detected as a too narrow idea of 'rationality' in behavi-our is ruined by a failure to carry out a similar reform in the idea of 'irrationality'. In the end, Keynes still retains the idea of 'rational' conduct as that which springs from an independently premeditated purpose, and he modifies his original exclusive attachment to such conduct by admitting that much of what it excludes (which he identifies as 'vulgar passions', 'volcanic and even wicked impulses', 'spontaneous outbursts') is valuable while nevertheless remaining 'irrational'. This is a confused position; and from confusion of this

[1] J. M. Keynes, *Two Memoirs*.

sort a fresh attempt to determine the meaning of 'rationality' in conduct is not likely to spring. Both this, and the current despair of the possibility of rational conduct (the current 'irrationalism'), must be put on one side if we are to make any advance.

5

Let us return to the activity of the designers of Victorian 'rational dress', and to the activity of those who wore it because they believed themselves to be behaving 'rationally' by doing so. We have supposed (not without some grounds) that what they *thought* they were doing was to design a garment suited to a particular purpose, the purpose of *propelling* a bicycle. They premeditated their purpose, and they selected a precise and narrow purpose in order to premeditate it without distraction; and they applauded their activity as 'rational' because of the manner in which they went about their enterprise. The result was 'rational' because it achieved a set and premeditated purpose and because it sprang from this prior act of theorizing. But we have observed that there were elements in the situation which might lead us to doubt whether what they *thought* they were doing (and on account of which they attributed 'rationality' to their conduct) properly coincided with what they were in fact doing. Why did their enterprise pause at 'bloomers' and not pass on to 'shorts'? The answer that they merely made a mistake, that this stopping-place represents a failure of 'rationality', is too easy. Their invention may be taken to indicate, not that they failed in their chosen enterprise, but that they were guided in fact by considerations which they believed themselves to have escaped and on account of this escape were behaving 'rationally'. Bloomers are not the answer to the question, What garment is best adapted to the activity of *propelling* a bicycle of a certain design? but to the question, What garment combines within itself the qualities of being well adapted to the activity of propelling a bicycle and of being suitable, all things considered, for an English girl to be seen in when riding a bicycle in 1880? And, unknown to themselves, it was the project of answering this question which moved the designers. But if we credit them with a belief in the idea of 'rationality' which we have found to be unsatisfactory, then we may suppose that they would regard activity in pursuit of this purpose as wanting in 'rationality'. It is true that the activity would spring from a premeditated end, and consequently would have some flavour of 'rationality' about it; but it would be a very different sort of activity from what they were accustomed to call 'rational'. It would be an activity in principle indistinguishable from that of *any* dress designer. In the first place, this is a question that *clearly* could not be answered by 'pure intelligence'; it demands something more than the instrumental mind. This, of course, is true also of the first question, the question we supposed to be actually in the mind of the designer; but its truth was obscured because it seemed that in order to answer this first question the operation called for was primarily an emptying of the mind. Here, however, something much more positive is required. No capitalist with any sense would think of entrusting the enterprise to a Chinese; his ignorance of English taste, tradition, folklore and prejudice in respect of women's clothing would be a hopeless handicap. And though there is, here, a premeditated end to be pursued, it is an exceedingly complex end; there is a tension within the purpose itself – anatomical and mechanical principles pulling one way, perhaps, and social custom another. It is a question which admits of no *certain* answer, because it involves an assessment of opinion; and it is one which cannot be answered once and for all, because the problem is tied to place and time. In short, this is hardly a 'rational' question in the sense of 'rationality' we have so far been considering. And yet, I think it is the question which the designers of 'rational dress' were, in fact, trying to answer, and which they succeeded in answering when they produced bloomers.[1]

[1] Readers of Tolstoy's *Anna Karenina* will remember the discussion between Levin and Sviajsky about 'rational' agriculture. For Sviajsky 'rational' agriculture consists wholly in the introduction of machinery, proper methods of accounting, etc. But Levin sees at once that something has been forgotten: it is not 'rational' to give complicated machinery for the use of peasants who do not know how to use it and who have a contempt for it. What is 'rational' in Germany is not 'rational' in Russia. You must educate your peasant and adapt the level of your technical improvements to the level of his education. Levin knows (but he does not know how to explain) that an activity consists in knowing how to behave; Sviajsky does not know this, and represents a typical 'rationalist' position. *Anna Karenina*, Pt. III, Chs. 27, 28; Pt. IV, Ch. 3.

Here we have reached something more like a piece of concrete human activity, and our question must be, In what respect can this be considered 'rational' activity? The unregenerate believer in the idea of 'rationality' which we have seen fit to reject, will reply that it is 'rational' because it is activity springing from a premeditated purpose, though the purpose here is neither simple nor capable of being premeditated by mere 'intelligence'; its independence of the activity is at least doubtful. He will contend that nothing has yet been said which destroys the old criterion; this is 'rational' activity because it is premeditated, 'reasoned' activity. And, although our original supposition was that the end achieved by the dress-designers was not in fact premeditated by them (what they set themselves was something much narrower than what they achieved), it would be wise to give him his point, because there seems, so far, no reason why it should not have been premeditated. But the point is good only because we have not yet achieved a concrete view of human activity; we are still dealing with abstractions, though not with such narrow abstractions as the high and dry believer in the instrumental mind.

6

Now, if we consider the concrete activity of an historian, a cook, a scientist, a politician or any man in the ordinary conduct of life, we may observe that each is engaged upon answering questions of a certain sort, and that his characteristic is that he knows (or thinks he knows) the way to go about finding the answer to that sort of question. But the questions which he knows to belong to his sort of activity are not known to be such in advance of the activity of trying to answer them: in pursuing these questions, and not others, he is not obeying a rule or following a principle which comes from outside the activity, he is pursuing an activity which, in general, he knows how to pursue. It is the activity itself which defines the questions as well as the manner in which they are answered. It is, of course, not impossible to formulate certain principles which may seem to give precise definition to the kind of question a particular sort of activity is concerned with; but such principles are derived from the activity and not the activity from the principles. And even if a man has some such propositional knowledge about his activity, his knowledge of his activity always goes far beyond what is contained in these propositions. It is clear, then, that the activity of these men (and I would say all other activity also) is something that comes first, and is something into which each one gradually finds his way: at no time is he wholly ignorant of it; there is no identifiable beginning. Of course, the activity in general does not exist in advance of the activities which compose it; it consists wholly in knowing how to tackle problems of a certain sort. But it does exist in advance of the specific engagement a particular scientist or cook may have undertaken. How, then (if this is as clear as I think it is), do we get the illusion that the activity of these and other men could spring from and be governed by an end, a purpose or by rules independent of the activity itself and capable of being reflected upon in advance, with the possible corollary that, in respect of this spring and government, it should be called 'rational'.

Each man engaged in a certain kind of activity selects a particular question and engages himself to answer this question. He has before him a particular project: to determine the weight of the moon, to bake a sponge cake, to paint a portrait, to disclose the mediations which comprise the story of the Peninsular War, to come to an agreement with a foreign power, to educate his son – or whatever it may be. And, with the normal neglect with which a man engaged upon a particular task treats what is not immediately before him, he supposes that his activity springs from and is governed solely by his project. No man engaged in a particular task has in the forefront of his attention the whole context and implications of that engagement. Activity is broken up into actions, and actions come to have a false appearance of independence. And further, this abstraction of view is normally increased when what we observe is somebody else's activity. Every trade but our own seems to be comprised wholly of tricks and abridgments. There is, then, no mystery how it can come to be supposed that an activity may spring from an independently determined purpose to be pursued: the mistake arises from endowing a whole activity with the character of a single action when it is abstracted from the activity to which it belongs, from endowing, for example, the activity of cooking with the character of making a particular pie when the maker is assumed not to be a cook.

But if our cook or scientific practitioner were to consider the implications of his particular actions he would rapidly reach two conclusions. First, he would observe that, in pursuing his particular project, his actions were being determined not solely by his premeditated end, but by what may be called the traditions of the activity to which his project belonged. It is because he knows how to tackle problems of this sort that he is able to tackle this particular problem. He would observe, in other words, that the spring and government of his actions lay in his *skill*, his knowledge of how to go about his business, his participation in the concrete activity in relation to which his particular engagement is an abstraction. And though his participation in this concrete activity (the activity of being a cook or a scientist) may on some occasions appear to take the form of the application of a rule or the pursuit of a purpose, he would see at once that this rule or this purpose derived from the activity and not vice versa, and that the activity itself could never as a whole be reduced to the pursuit of an end or the application of a rule determined in advance of the activity.

But if his first observation is that, whatever the appearances to the contrary, no actual engagement can ever spring from or be governed by an independently premeditated end – the problems put down for solution or the project selected for pursuit – and that if this were all there was, his particular activity could never begin, his second observation will be more radical: he will observe that it is impossible even to project a purpose for activity in advance of the activity itself. Not only is his participation in the concrete activity which is involved in the solution of this sort of problem the source of his power to *solve* his particular problem and is the spring of the activity which goes to solve it, but also it is his participation in this concrete activity which presents the problem itself. Both the problems and the course of investigation leading up to their solution are already hidden in the activity, and are drawn out only by a process of abstraction. It is necessary to possess a knowledge of how to go about it (that is, to be already within an activity) before you embark upon a particular project, but it is equally necessary to have the same sort of knowledge in order to formulate a project. A particular action, in short, never begins in its particularity, but always in an idiom or a tradition of activity. A man who is not already a scientist cannot even formulate a scientific problem; what he will formulate is a problem which a connoisseur will at once recognize *not* to be a 'scientific' problem because it is incapable of being considered in a 'scientific' manner. Similarly, a connoisseur in historical inquiry will at once recognize that a question such as, Was the French Revolution a mistake? is a non-historical question.

We have come back, then, to the conclusions we reached earlier on, but in a more radical form. Activity springing from and governed by an independently premeditated purpose is impossible; the power of premeditating purpose, of formulating rules of conduct and standards of behaviour in advance of the conduct and activity itself is not available to us. To represent the spring and government of activity thus is to misrepresent it. To suggest that activity ought to be of this character and to try to force it into this pattern, is to corrupt it without being able to endow it with the desired character. To speak of such conduct as 'rational' conduct is meaningless because it is not conduct at all but only an emaciated shadow of conduct. And it may be remarked also that if we agree it to be foolish to call conduct 'rational' on account of its being wholly determined by an independently premeditated purpose, we must agree further that it should not be called 'rational' in respect of it achieving its purpose, in respect (that is) of its *success*. The achievement of a desired result is not the mark of 'rationality' in conduct because, as we have seen, it is only by a process of neglect and abstraction that conduct can be supposed to spring from the desire to achieve a specific result.

7

So far our conclusions appear to be mainly negative, but the process of exploration has I think disclosed what I take to be a more profitable view of 'rationality' in conduct. If the 'rationality' of conduct does not lie in something that has taken place in advance of the conduct – in the independent premeditation of a purpose or of a rule to be applied – if the 'rationality' of conduct is not something contributed to the conduct from some source outside the idiom of the conduct concerned, it would appear that it must be a quality or a characteristic of the conduct itself.

All actual conduct, all specific activity springs up within an already existing idiom of activity. And by an 'idiom of activity' I mean a knowledge of how to behave appropriately in the circumstances. Scientific activity is the exploration of the knowledge scientists have of how to go about asking and answering scientific questions; moral activity is the exploration of the knowledge we have of how to behave well. The questions and the problems in each case spring from the knowledge we have of how to solve them, spring from the activity itself. And we come to penetrate an idiom of activity in no other way than by practising the activity; for it is only in the practice of an activity that we can acquire the knowledge of how to practise it. We begin with what we *know* – as scientists, with what we know of how a scientist works; as moral beings, with what we know about how to behave well – and if we knew nothing we could never begin. Gradually, and by a variety of means, we improve and extend our first knowledge of how to pursue the activity. Among such means (though in a subordinate position, because it obviously depends upon the achievement of a certain level in our knowledge of how to pursue the activity) is the analysis of the activity, the definition of the rules and principles which seem to inhere in it and in reflection upon these rules and principles. But these rules and principles are mere abridgments of the activity itself; they do not exist in advance of the activity, they cannot properly be said to govern it and they cannot provide the impetus of the activity. A complete mastery of these principles may exist alongside a complete inability to pursue the activity to which they refer. For the pursuit of the activity does not consist in the application of these principles; and even if it did, the knowledge of how to apply them (the knowledge actually involved in pursuing the activity) is not given in a knowledge of them.

If, then, it is agreed that the only significant way of using the word 'rational' in relation to conduct is when we mean to indicate a quality or characteristic (and perhaps a desirable quality or characteristic) of the activity itself, then it would appear that the quality concerned is not mere 'intelligence', but *faithfulness to the knowledge*

we have of how to conduct the specific activity we are engaged in.
'Rational' conduct is acting in such a w~y that the coherence of the
idiom of activity to which the conduct belongs is preserved and
possibly enhanced. This, of course, is something different from
faithfulness to the principles or rules or purposes (if any have been
discovered) of the activity; principles, rules and purposes are mere
abridgments of the coherence of the activity, and we may easily be
faithful to them while losing touch with the activity itself. And it
must be observed that the faithfulness which characterizes 'rationality'
is not faithfulness to something fixed and finished (for knowledge of
how to pursue an activity is always in motion); it is a faithfulness
which itself contributes to (and not merely illustrates) the coherence
of the activity. And the implications of this view are: first, that no
conduct, no action or series of actions, can be 'rational' or 'irrational'
out of relation to the idiom of activity to which they belong;
secondly, that 'rationality' is something that lies always *ahead*, and
not *behind*, but yet it does not lie in the success with which a desired
result or a premeditated end is achieved; and thirdly, that an activity
as a whole (science, cooking, historical investigation, politics or
poetry) cannot be said either to be 'rational' or 'irrational' unless we
conceive all idioms of activity to be embraced in a single universe of
activity. Let us consider where this view gets us.

8

How does it apply to the activity we call 'science'? Scientific activity
is not the pursuit of a predetermined end; nobody knows where it
will reach. There is no achievement, prefigured in our minds, which
we can set up as a criterion by which to judge current achievements
or in relation to which current engagements are a means. Its coherence does not spring from there being an over-all purpose which can
be premeditated. Individual investigators may, and usually do, premeditate particular purposes, set themselves particular problems.
Nevertheless, as we have seen, their activity does not spring from
these purposes and is not governed by them: they arise as abstractions out of knowing how to conduct a scientific inquiry, and are
never *independently* premeditated. Nor does the coherence of scientific activity lie in a body of principles or rules to be observed by the

scientist, a 'scientific method'; such principles and rules no doubt exist, but they also are only abridgments of the activity which at all points goes beyond them, and goes beyond them, in particular, in the connoisseurship of knowing how and when to apply them. Its coherence lies nowhere but in the way the scientist goes about his investigation, in the traditions of scientific inquiry. These traditions are not fixed and finished, and they are not to be identified with merely current scientific opinion, or with an identifiable 'method'; they are the guide in every piece of scientific investigation and at the same time they are being extended and enlarged wherever scientists are at work. And because these traditions are not a finished achievement which can be completely prefigured in the mind of the scientist before he begins his activity (such as a 'method' might be supposed to be), conformity with them cannot properly be spoken of as itself the over-all purpose in science.

Now, the view I am recommending is that the conduct of a scientist may properly be called 'rational' in respect of its faithfulness to the traditions of scientific inquiry. And the 'irrational' scientist is not the man whose activity springs from some source other than the independent premeditation of a purpose (no man's activity could spring from this source), nor is he the man whose activity is ungoverned by pre-established rules and principles (for there are no such rules and principles), nor again is he the man who makes no observations, who achieves no results, who has nothing to show for his activity: the 'irrational' scientist is in fact, the scientific crank and the eccentric. And he is identified not by his departure from merely current scientific opinion, but by his unfaithfulness to the whole tradition of scientific inquiry, by his ignorance of how to set about a scientific investigation – an ignorance which is displayed not in the results of his activity, but in the course of his activity itself, in the questions he asks as well as in the sort of answers he is satisfied to give. And if we consider the matter I think we shall find that this, as often as not, is how we are accustomed to use the word 'rational' in this connection, though we are not always as clear as we should be about what we have excluded when we do use it in this manner.

9

Now, some people in general sympathy with this view of the matter will nevertheless suspect that scientific activity is a special case and that what may be true there is not true elsewhere. Consequently, in conclusion, I must try to show the relevance of this view of things to what may be called the general moral or social conduct of human beings: for I do not admit that scientific activity is, in this respect, a special case. And if there is an appearance of dogmatism in what I have not to say, that is because I have already disclosed the arguments which have persuaded me.

Human conduct, in its most general character, is energy; it is not caused by energy, it does not express or display energy, it is energy. As energy, it may appear as appetite or desire – not, of course, as undifferentiated want, but as a certain mode of want. But here again, desire is not the cause of activity; desire is being active in a certain manner. A man, that is, does not first have 'a desire' which then causes him to become active or which manifests itself in activity: to say that he has a desire for something is only another way of saying that he is being active in a certain manner – e.g. the manner of activity involved in reaching out his hand to turn off the hot water, in making a request (such as, 'Please pass me the Dictionary' or 'Which is the way to the National Gallery?'), in looking up the times of the trains to Scotland, in contemplating with pleasure a meeting with a friend. These activities are not activities which presuppose and express or exhibit or give evidence of an antecedent state of desire; they are themselves the characteristic activities of desiring.

Now, activities of desiring are not separate and detached from one another, and the objects upon which desire is centred do not come and go at random or follow one another fortuitously. To say that a man has a character or a disposition is to say, among other things, that his activities of desiring compose a more or less coherent whole. A fresh activity of desiring appears nowhere except within an already organized whole; it does not come from the outside with the present- ation of an object, but is a differentiation within an existing idiom of activity. And our knowledge of that idiom is, in the first place, our skill in managing the activity of desiring. We do not first have a desire and then set about discovering how to satisfy it; the objects of our desires are known to us in the activity of seeking them.

Social life – the life of human beings – is to know that some directions of the activity of desiring are approved and others disapproved, that some are right and others wrong. That there may be principles, or even rules, which may be seen to underlie this approval and disapproval, is not improbable; the searching intellect will always find principles. But this approval and disapproval does not spring from these principles or from a knowledge of them. They are merely abridgments, abstract definitions, of the coherence which approvals and disapprovals themselves exhibit. Nor may approval and disapproval be thought of as an additional activity, governed by an independently predetermined end to be achieved. An independently predetermined end has no more place in moral activity than it has in scientific. Approval and disapproval, that is, is not a separate activity which supervenes upon the activity of desiring, introducing norms of conduct from some external source; they are inseparable from the activity of desiring itself. Approval and disapproval are only an abstract and imperfect way of describing our unbroken knowledge of how to manage the activity of desiring, of how to behave. In short, moral judgment is not something we pronounce either before, or after, but in our moral activity.

Human activity, then, is always activity with a pattern; not a superimposed pattern, but a pattern inherent in the activity itself. Elements of this pattern occasionally stand out with a relatively firm outline; and we call these elements, customs, traditions, institutions, laws, etc. They are not, properly speaking, *expressions* of the coherence of activity, or expressions of approval and disapproval, or of our knowledge of how to behave – they *are* the coherence, they are the substance of our knowledge of how to behave. We do not first decide that certain behaviour is right or desirable and then express our approval of it in an institution; our knowledge of how to behave well is, at this point, the institution. And it is because we are not always as clear about this as we should be that we sometimes make the mistake of supposing that institutions (particularly political institutions) can be moved around from place to place as if they were pieces of machinery instead of idioms of conduct.

Now, it might be supposed that the positive problem of social conduct (that is, human conduct) is how to secure the satisfaction of approved desires; and this, indeed, is a more reasonable way of describing it than the usual negative manner – how to prevent activity taking undesirable directions. Nevertheless, this again is not a separate problem. We do not first have a desire, then approve it, and then seek out a way of adjusting it to other approved desires and a way of satisfying it. This would make sense only if we imagined that in approval and disapproval and in finding out means of satisfaction we already had a desire fully before us and were calling upon some authority outside the activity itself to settle the question of its propriety; but to imagine this is to imagine an error. What is here set down as a linear process is in fact a single whole which is never wanting of any of its parts.

So far I have emphasized the coherence of moral activity, and it is proper to do this first because moral activity begins (if it can be said to begin anywhere) in coherence. We begin with a knowledge of how to behave – not, of course, a perfect knowledge, or a knowledge which is an endowment from another world, but a knowledge which is coeval with the activity of desiring. And what I have attributed to the activity is a set in a certain direction, a current, something that may be called a prevailing sympathy. The movement in the activity does not spring from the application of some external force, and the direction is not determined by a pre-established end; it is necessary to have recourse to such ideas as these only if we have fallen into the initial error of supposing, first, an activity which begins from rest (a 'knowledge' which springs from sheer ignorance), and secondly, an activity with no direction in particular (a 'knowledge' in which truth and error, or right and wrong, are still waiting to be distinguished). But it is time to consider the things which may clog the movement or compromise the direction; to consider our ignorance of how to behave.

That moral activity should play upon the margins of current moral achievement, appealing from contemporary incoherence to the coherence of a whole moral tradition, is as normal as the activity which merely gyrates around the pivot of contemporary coherence; they are alike exhibitions of a knowledge of how to behave. In neither is the movement clogged or the direction of the movement compromised. But a genuine clog and compromise is not impossible, and it is a sufficiently common occurrence to merit being taken into account in considering the nature of moral activity. The condition may be described comprehensively as a loss of confidence in the traditional direction of moral activity, which carries with it a failure of impetus in the activity itself, and is both a symptom and a condition of a breakdown in the effectiveness of moral education (the handing on of knowledge of how to behave).[1] It is unnecessary to investigate the possible occasions of the emergence of this condition; though it is remarkable how trivial are some of the apparent causes – an earthquake, a plague, a war, or a mechanical invention, each appears to have had the power of disrupting (more or less seriously) the current of moral activity, to have had the power of dispersing it into fortuitous eddies and of leading it to lose itself in random inundations of the countryside. But it is worth noting that this is a circumstance which has no exact parallel in the history of scientific activity – though in principle there is nothing in science which makes it immune from such a malady, and it may even now be sickening for an attack.

In general, the remedy for such a condition must, of course, be treatment which will result in a revival of confidence and a renewal of impetus. And, in general again, such treatment must make use of what is still unimpaired in the sufferer. The notion that a knowledge of how to behave can be permanently replaced by something else just as good, and the notion that the patient must be allowed (or even encouraged) to die in order that he may start life again on new and firmer foundations, will be entertained only by those who are wholly ignorant of the nature of moral activity. The remedy usually favoured in these cases is a transfusion of a specially rich mixture of ideals, principles, rules and purposes. And there are two conditions in which this remedy may have the desired result: first, if the ideals, principles, etc., are themselves drawn from the ailing moral tradition, or (shall we say) from the same blood-group as the patient; and secondly, if the patient can assimilate the transfusion and transform it in his own arteries from a knowledge of propositions about good

[1] It seems that it was for a situation of this sort that Mencius prescribed.

behaviour into a knowledge of how to behave. The first of these conditions is easily satisfied: the only principles and ideals available are in fact abridgments of the lost knowledge of how to behave. They may be presented as something more imposing – as gifts straight from the gods – and a superstitious reverence may be accorded them on account of this appearance; but it is doubtful whether this indulgence in illusion will increase the chances of the cure being effective. The second condition is more difficult to satisfy. To turn the dry bones of a morality into a living thing is by no means easy – indeed, it is utterly impossible if the sum total of our knowledge is anatomical. There is, in fact, no way in which a knowledge of how to behave can be made to spring solely from a knowledge of propositions about good behaviour. In the end, the cure depends upon the native strength of the patient; it depends upon the unimpaired relics of his knowledge of how to behave.

We have considered briefly moral activity in health and in disease: our question now is, Where in all this is 'rational' conduct? It is commonly believed (as we have seen) that there is something pre-eminently 'rational' in conduct which springs (or appears to spring) from the independent premeditation of a purpose or a rule of behaviour, and that it is 'rational' on account of the antecedent process of premeditation and on account of the success with which the purpose is achieved. And if we were to accept this view it would appear that moral conduct would be pre-eminently 'rational' when it was being treated for a diseased condition. But even this is rather more than may properly be concluded; the most that may, in fact, be claimed is that conduct is specially 'rational' when it is being cured of a disease and when the success of the treatment depends upon the illusion that the curative property of the substance injected derives from its being uncontaminated with the character of the diseased moral tradition – an illusion similar to that of the man who thinks he has found a new and independent way of living when he is really only spending his inherited capital. Of course, reflection upon the principles and ends in conduct may serve other than remedial purposes; it has a pedagogic and perhaps even a prophylactic use: the important point, however, is that it is never more than a device.

But we have seen fit to reject this whole view of the matter. This conduct may be 'rational', but if so the marks of its 'rationality' have been misconceived. Everywhere we come back to the conclusion that concrete activity is knowing how to act; and that if 'rationality' is to be properly attributed to conduct, it must be a quality of the conduct itself. On this principle, practical human conduct may be counted 'rational' in respect of its faithfulness to a knowledge of how to behave well, in respect of its faithfulness to its tradition of moral activity. No action is by itself 'rational', or is 'rational' on account of something that has gone on before; what makes it 'rational' is its place in a flow of sympathy, a current of moral activity. And there is no ground here upon which we may exclude *a priori* any type of action. An impulsive action, a 'spontaneous outburst', activity in obedience to a custom or to a rule, and an action which is preceded by a long reflective process may, alike, be 'rational'. But it is neither 'rational' nor 'irrational' on account of these or in default of these or of any similar characteristics. 'Rationality' is the certificate we give to any conduct which can maintain a place in the flow of sympathy, the coherence of activity, which composes a way of living. This coherence is not the work of a faculty called 'Reason' or of a faculty called 'Sympathy', it springs neither from a separately inspired moral sense nor from an instrumental conscience. There is, in fact, no external harmonizing power, insulated from the elements enjoying and in search of harmony. What establishes harmony and detects disharmony, is the concrete mind, a mind composed wholly of activities in search of harmony and throughout implicated in every achieved level of harmony.

And here again, it may be pointed out that this is how we are accustomed to use the word 'rational', though we do not always perceive the implications of using it in this way. When a court of law has to decide whether on a particular occasion a man used 'reasonable care', what the court is concerned with is not some abstractly 'rational' amount of care, the same in all circumstances and on all occasions, nor is it inquiring into the length and cogency of a process of reflection which may have gone on in the recesses of the man's mind before he acted – it is concerned to come to a conclusion about the action itself, to decide whether the man on the occasion used the knowledge of how to behave which he could be supposed to possess.

And the decision is reached only by considering what the man actually did, and not what he may have thought before he acted. 'Reasonable care' is not something that can be known in advance and with certainty. It is the degree of care which an English jury (or judge) would expect to be exercised in given circumstances by an Englishman of ordinary knowledge, foresight and alertness. The jury or the judge is on this occasion the voice of the current of moral activity. They represent something; but they do not represent anything beyond the knowledge of how to behave well which belongs to our way of living. In short, human conduct may be said to be 'rational' when it exhibits the sort of 'intelligence' appropriate to the idiom of activity concerned.

1950

Political Education[1]

The two former occupants of this Chair, Graham Wallas and
Harold Laski, were both men of great distinction; to follow them is
an undertaking for which I am ill-prepared. In the first of them,
experience and reflection were happily combined to give a reading
of politics at once practical and profound; a thinker without a
system whose thoughts were nevertheless firmly held together by a
thread of honest, patient inquiry; a man who brought his powers of
intellect to bear upon the inconsequence of human behaviour and to
whom the reasons of the head and of the heart were alike familiar. In
the second, the dry light of intellect was matched with a warm
enthusiasm; to the humour of a scholar was joined the temperament
of a reformer. It seems but an hour ago that he was dazzling us with
the range and readiness of his learning, winning our sympathy by the
fearlessness of his advocacy and endearing himself to us by his
generosity. In their several ways, ways in which their successor cannot hope to compete with them, these two men left their mark upon
the political education of England. They were both great teachers,
devoted, tireless, and with sure confidence in what they had to teach.
And it seems perhaps a little ungrateful that they should be followed
by a sceptic; one who would do better if only he knew how. But no
one could wish for more exacting or more sympathetic witnesses of
his activities than these two men. And the subject I have chosen to

[1] First delivered as an Inaugural Lecture at the London School of Economics, this piece was commented upon from various points of view. The notes
I have now added, and a few changes I have made in the text, are designed
to remove some of the misunderstandings it provoked. But, in general, the
reader is advised to remember that it is concerned with understanding or
explaining political activity which, in my view, is the proper object of
political education. What people project in political activity, and different
styles of political conduct, are considered here, first merely because they
sometimes reveal the way in which political activity is being understood, and
secondly because it is commonly (though I think wrongly) supposed that
explanations are warrants for conduct.

speak about today is one which would have their approval.

I

The expression 'political education' has fallen on evil days; in the wilful and disingenuous corruption of language which is characteristic of our time it has acquired a sinister meaning. In places other than this, it is associated with that softening of the mind, by force, by alarm, or by the hypnotism of the endless repetition of what was scarcely worth saying once, by means of which whole populations have been reduced to submission. It is, therefore, an enterprise worth undertaking to consider again, in a quiet moment, how we should understand this expression, which joins together two laudable activities, and in doing so play a small part in rescuing it from abuse.

Politics I take to be the activity of attending to the general arrangements of a set of people whom chance or choice have brought together. In this sense, families, clubs, and learned societies have their 'politics'. But the communities in which this manner of activity is pre-eminent are the hereditary co-operative groups, many of them of ancient lineage, all of them aware of a past, a present, and a future, which we call 'states'. For most people, political activity is a secondary activity – that is to say, they have something else to do besides attending to these arrangements. But, as we have come to understand it, the activity is one in which every member of the group who is neither a child nor a lunatic has some part and some responsibility. With us it is, at one level or another, a universal activity.

I speak of this activity as 'attending to arrangements', rather than as 'making arrangements', because in these hereditary co-operative groups the activity is never offered the blank sheet of infinite possibility. In any generation, even the most revolutionary, the arrangements which are enjoyed always far exceed those which are recognized to stand in need of attention, and those which are being prepared for enjoyment are few in comparison with those which receive amendment: the new is an insignificant proportion of the whole. There are some people, of course, who allow themselves to speak

As if arrangements were intended
For nothing else but to be mended,

but, for most of us, our determination to improve our conduct does not prevent us from recognizing that the greater part of what we have is not a burden to be carried or an incubus to be thrown off, but an inheritance to be enjoyed. And a certain degree of shabbiness is joined with every real convenience.

Now, attending to the arrangements of a society is an activity which, like every other, has to be learned. Politics make a call upon knowledge. Consequently, it is not irrelevant to inquire into the kind of knowledge which is involved, and to investigate the nature of political education. I do not, however, propose to ask what information we should equip ourselves with before we begin to be politically active, or what we need to know in order to be successful politicians, but to inquire into the kind of knowledge we unavoidably call upon whenever we are engaged in political activity and to get from this an understanding of the nature of political education.

Our thoughts on political education, then, might be supposed to spring from our understanding of political activity and the kind of knowledge it involves. And it would appear that what is wanted at this point is a definition of political activity from which to draw some conclusions. But this, I think, would be a mistaken way of going about our business. What we require is not so much a definition of politics from which to deduce the character of political education, as an understanding of political activity which includes a recognition of the sort of education it involves. For, to understand an activity is to know it as a concrete whole; it is to recognize the activity as having the source of its movement within itself. An understanding which leaves the activity in debt to something outside itself is, for that reason, an inadequate understanding. And if political activity is impossible without a certain kind of knowledge and a certain sort of education, then this knowledge and education are not mere appendages to the activity but are part of the activity itself and must be incorporated in our understanding of it. We should not, therefore, seek a definition of politics in order to deduce from it the character of political knowledge and education, but rather observe the kind of knowledge and education which is inherent in any understanding of political activity, and use this observation as a means of improving our understanding of politics.

My proposal, then, is to consider the adequacy of two current understandings of politics, together with the sort of knowledge and kind of education they imply, and by improving upon them to reach what may perhaps be a more adequate understanding at once of political activity itself and the knowledge and education which belongs to it.

2

In the understanding of some people, politics are what may be called an empirical activity. Attending to the arrangements of a society is waking up each morning and considering, 'What would I like to do?' or 'What would somebody else (whom I desire to please) like to see done?', and doing it. This understanding of political activity may be called politics without a policy. On the briefest inspection it will appear a concept of politics difficult to substantiate; it does not look like a possible manner of activity at all. But a near approach to it is, perhaps, to be detected in the politics of the pro-verbial oriental despot, or in the politics of the wall-scribbler and the vote-catcher. And the result may be supposed to be chaos modi-fied by whatever consistency is allowed to creep into caprice. They are the politics attributed to the first Lord Liverpool, of whom Acton said, 'The secret of his policy was that he had none', and of whom a Frenchman remarked that if he had been present at the creation of the world he would have said, '*Mon Dieu, conservons le chaos*'. It seems, then, that a concrete activity, which may be des-cribed as an approximation to empirical politics, is possible. But it is clear that, although knowledge of a sort belongs to this style of political activity (knowledge, as the French say, not of ourselves but only of our appetites), the only kind of education appropriate to it would be an education in lunacy – learning to be ruled solely by passing desires. And this reveals the important point; namely, that to understand politics as a purely empirical activity is to misunder-stand it, because empiricism by itself is not a concrete manner of activity at all, and can become a partner in a concrete manner of activity only when it is joined with something else – in science, for example, when it is joined with hypothesis. What is significant about this understanding of politics is not that some sort of approach to it can appear, but that it mistakes for a concrete, self-moved manner of activity what is never more than an abstract moment in any manner of being active. Of course, politics are the pursuit of what is desired and of what is desired at the moment; but precisely because they are this, they can never be the pursuit of merely what recommends itself from moment to moment. The activity of desiring does not take this course; caprice is never absolute. From a practical point of view, then, we may decry the *style* of politics which approximates to pure empiricism because we can observe in it an approach to lunacy. But from a theoretical point of view, purely empirical politics are not something difficult to achieve or proper to be avoided, they are merely impossible; the product of a misunderstanding.

3

The understanding of politics as an empirical activity is, then, inadequate because it fails to reveal a concrete manner of activity at all. And it has the incidental defect of seeming to encourage the thoughtless to pursue a *style* of attending to the arrangements of their society which is likely to have unfortunate results; to try to do something which is inherently impossible is always a corrupting enterprise. We must, if we can, improve upon it. And the impulse to improve may be given a direction by asking, 'What is it that this understanding of politics has neglected to observe?' What (to put it crudely) has it left out which, if added in, would compose an understanding in which politics are revealed as a self-moved (or concrete) manner of activity? And the answer to the question is, or seems to be, available as soon as the question is formulated. It would appear that what this understanding of politics lacks is something to set empiricism to work, something to correspond with specific hypothesis in science, an end to be pursued more extensive than a merely instant desire. And this, it should be observed, is not merely a good companion for empiricism; it is something without which empiricism in action is impossible. Let us explore this suggestion, and in order to bring it to a point I will state it in the form of a proposition: that politics appear as a self-moved manner of activity when empiricism is preceded and guided by an ideological activity. I am not concerned with the so-called ideological *style* of politics as a desirable or undesirable manner of attending to the arrangements of a society; I am concerned only with the contention that when to the ineluctable element of empiricism (doing what one wants to do) is added a political ideology, a self-moved manner of activity appears, and that consequently this may be regarded in principle as an adequate understanding of political activity.

As I understand it, a political ideology purports to be an abstract principle, or set of related abstract principles, which has been independently premeditated. It supplies in advance of the activity of attending to the arrangements of a society a formulated end to be pursued, and in so doing it provides a means of distinguishing between those desires which ought to be encouraged and those which ought to be suppressed or redirected.

The simplest sort of political ideology is a single abstract idea, such as Freedom, Equality, Maximum Productivity, Racial Purity, or Happiness. And in that case political activity is understood as the enterprise of seeing that the arrangements of a society conform to or reflect the chosen abstract idea. It is usual, however, to recognize the need for a complex scheme of related ideas, rather than a single idea, and the examples pointed to will be such systems of ideas as: 'the principles of 1789', 'Liberalism', 'Democracy', 'Marxism', or the Atlantic Charter. These principles need not be considered absolute or immune from change (though they are frequently so considered), but their value lies in their having been premeditated. They compose an understanding of *what* is to be pursued independent of *how* it is to be pursued. A political ideology purports to supply in advance knowledge of what 'Freedom' or 'Democracy' or 'Justice' is, and in this manner sets empiricism to work. Such a set of principles is, of course, capable of being argued about and reflected upon; it is something that men compose for themselves, and they may later remember it or write it down. But the condition upon which it can perform the service assigned to it is that it owes nothing to the activity it controls. 'To know the true good of the community is what constitutes the science of legislation,' said Bentham; 'the art consists in finding the means to realize that good.' The contention we have before us, then, is that empiricism can be set to work (and a concrete, self-moved

manner of activity appear) when there is added to it a guide of this
sort: desire and something not generated by desire.

Now, there is no doubt about the sort of knowledge which
political activity, understood in this manner, calls upon. What is
required, in the first place, is knowledge of the chosen political
ideology – a knowledge of the ends to be pursued, a knowledge of
what we want to do. Of course, if we are to be successful in pursuing
these ends we shall need knowledge of another sort also – a knowledge, shall we say, of economics and psychology. But the common
characteristic of all the kinds of knowledge required is that they may
be, and should be, gathered in advance of the activity of attending to
the arrangements of a society. Moreover, the appropriate sort of
education will be an education in which the chosen political ideology
is taught and learned, in which the techniques necessary for success
are acquired, and (if we are so unfortunate as to find ourselves
empty-handed in the matter of an ideology) an education in the
skill of abstract thought and premeditation necessary to compose one
for ourselves. The education we shall need is one which enables us
to expound, defend, implement, and possibly invent a political
ideology.

In casting around for some convincing demonstration that this
understanding of politics reveals a self-moved manner of activity,
we should no doubt consider ourselves rewarded if we could find
an example of politics being conducted precisely in this manner.
This at least would constitute a sign that we were on the right track.
The defect, it will be remembered, of the understanding of politics
as a purely empirical activity was that it revealed, not a manner of
activity at all, but an abstraction; and this defect made itself manifest
in our inability to find a *style* of politics which was anything more
than an approximation to it. How does the understanding of politics
as empiricism joined with an ideology fare in this respect? And without being over-confident, we may perhaps think that this is where
we wade ashore. For we would appear to be in no difficulty whatever
in finding an example of political activity which corresponds to this
understanding of it: half the world, at a conservative estimate, seems
to conduct its affairs in precisely this manner. And further, is it not so
manifestly a possible style of politics that, even if we disagree with a

particular ideology, we find nothing technically absurd in the writings of those who urge it upon us as an admirable style of politics? At least its advocates seem to know what they are talking about: they understand not only the manner of the activity but also the sort of knowledge and the kind of education it involves. 'Every schoolboy in Russia,' wrote Sir Norman Angel, 'is familiar with the doctrine of Marx and can recite its catechism. How many British schoolboys have any corresponding knowledge of the principles enunciated by Mill in his incomparable essay on Liberty?' 'Few people,' says Mr E. H. Carr, 'any longer contest the thesis that the child should be educated *in* the official ideology of his country.' In short, if we are looking for a sign to indicate that the understanding of politics as empirical activity preceded by ideological activity is an adequate understanding, we can scarcely be mistaken in supposing that we have it to hand.

And yet there is perhaps room for doubt: doubt first of all whether in principle this understanding of politics reveals a self-moved manner of activity; and doubt, consequentially, whether what have been identified as examples of a *style* of politics corresponding exactly to this understanding have been properly identified.

The contention we are investigating is that attending to the arrangements of a society can begin with a premeditated ideology, can begin with independently acquired knowledge of the ends to be pursued.[1] It is supposed that a political ideology is the product of intellectual premeditation and that, because it is a body of principles not itself in debt to the activity of attending to the arrangements of a society, it is able to determine and guide the direction of that activity. If, however, we consider more closely the character of a political ideology, we find at once that this supposition is falsified. So far from a political ideology being the quasi-divine parent of political activity, it turns out to be its earthly stepchild. Instead of an independently premeditated scheme of ends to be pursued, it is a system of ideas abstracted from the manner in which people have been accustomed to go about the business of attending to the arrangements of their

[1] This is the case, for example, with Natural Law; whether it is taken to be an explanation of political activity or (improperly) as a guide to political conduct.

societies. The pedigree of every political ideology shows it to be the creature, not of premeditation in advance of political activity, but of meditation upon a manner of politics. In short, political activity comes first and a political ideology follows after; and the understanding of politics we are investigating has the disadvantage of being, in the strict sense, preposterous.

Let us consider the matter first in relation to scientific hypothesis, which I have taken to play a role in scientific activity in some respects similar to that of an ideology in politics. If a scientific hypothesis were a self-generated bright idea which owed nothing to scientific activity, then empiricism governed by hypothesis could be considered to compose a self-contained manner of activity; but this certainly is not its character. The truth is that only a man who is already a scientist can formulate a scientific hypothesis; that is, an hypothesis is not an independent invention capable of guiding scientific inquiry, but a dependent supposition which arises as an abstraction from within already existing scientific activity. Moreover, even when the specific hypothesis has in this manner been formulated, it is inoperative as a guide to research without constant reference to the traditions of scientific inquiry from which it was abstracted. The concrete situation does not appear until the specific hypothesis, which is the occasion of empiricism being set to work, is recognized as itself the creature of knowing how to conduct a scientific inquiry.

Or consider the example of cookery. It might be supposed that an ignorant man, some edible materials, and a cookery book compose together the necessities of a self-moved (or concrete) activity called cooking. But nothing is further from the truth. The cookery book is not an independently generated beginning from which cooking can spring; it is nothing more than an abstract of somebody's knowledge of how to cook: it is the stepchild, not the parent of the activity. The book, in its turn, may help to set a man on to dressing a dinner, but if it were his sole guide he could never, in fact, begin: the book speaks only to those who know already the kind of thing to expect from it and consequently how to interpret it.

Now, just as a cookery book presupposes somebody who knows how to cook, and its use presupposes somebody who already knows how to use it, and just as a scientific hypothesis springs from a knowledge of how to conduct a scientific investigation and separated from that knowledge is powerless to set empiricism profitably to work, so a political ideology must be understood, not as an independently premeditated beginning for political activity, but as knowledge (abstract and generalized) of a concrete manner of attending to the arrangements of a society. The catechism which sets out the purposes to be pursued merely abridges a concrete manner of behaviour in which those purposes are already hidden. It does not exist in advance of political activity, and by itself it is always an insufficient guide. Political enterprises, the ends to be pursued, the arrangements to be established (all the normal ingredients of a political ideology), cannot be premeditated in advance of a manner of attending to the arrangements of a society; *what* we do, and moreover what we want to do, is the creature of *how* we are accustomed to conduct our affairs. Indeed, it often reflects no more than a discovered ability to do something which is then translated into an authority to do it.

On August 4, 1789, for the complex and bankrupt social and political system of France was substituted the Rights of Man. Reading this document we come to the conclusion that somebody has done some thinking. Here, displayed in a few sentences, is a political ideology: a system of rights and duties, a scheme of ends – justice, freedom, equality, security, property, and the rest – ready and waiting to be put into practice for the first time. 'For the first time?' Not a bit of it. This ideology no more existed in advance of political practice than a cookery book exists in advance of knowing how to cook. Certainly it was the product of somebody's reflection, but it was not the product of reflection in advance of political activity. For here, in fact, are disclosed, abstracted and abridged, the common law rights of Englishmen, the gift not of independent premeditation or divine munificence, but of centuries of the day-to-day attending to the arrangements of an historic society. Or consider Locke's *Second Treatise of Civil Government*, read in America and in France in the eighteenth century as a statement of abstract principles to be put into practice, regarded there as a preface to political activity. But so far from being a preface, it has all the marks of a postscript, and its power to guide derived from its roots in actual political experience. Here, set down in abstract terms, is a brief conspectus of the manner in which Englishmen were accustomed to go about the business of attending to their arrangements – a brilliant abridgment of the political habits of Englishmen. Or consider this passage from a contemporary continental writer: 'Freedom keeps Europeans in unrest and movement. They wish to have freedom, and at the same time they know they have not got it. They know also that freedom belongs to man as a human right.' And having established the end to be pursued, political activity is represented as the realization of this end. But the 'freedom' which can be pursued is not an independently premeditated 'ideal' or a dream; like scientific hypothesis, it is something which is already intimated in a concrete manner of behaving. Freedom, like a recipe for game pie, is not a bright idea; it is not a 'human right' to be deduced from some speculative concept of human nature. The freedom which we enjoy is nothing more than arrangements, procedures of a certain kind: the freedom of an Englishman is not something exemplified in the procedure of *habeas corpus*, it *is*, at that point, the availability of that procedure. And the freedom which we wish to enjoy is not an 'ideal' which we premeditate independently of our political experience, it is what is already intimated in that experience.[1]

On this reading, then, the systems of abstract ideas we call 'ideologies' are abstracts of some kind of concrete activity. Most political ideologies, and certainly the most useful of them (because they unquestionably have their use), are abstracts of the political traditions of some society. But it sometimes happens that an ideology is offered as a guide to politics which is an abstract, not of political experience, but of some other manner of activity – war, religion, or the conduct of industry, for example. And here the model we are shown is not only abstract, but is also inappropriate on account of the irrelevance of the activity from which it has been abstracted. This, I think, is one of the defects of the model provided by the Marxist ideology. But the important point is that, at most, an ideology is an abbreviation of some manner of concrete activity.

[1] Cf. 'Substantive law has the first look of being gradually secreted in the interstices of procedure.' Maine, *Early Law and Customs*, p. 389.

We are now, perhaps, in a position to perceive more accurately the character of what may be called the ideological *style* of politics, and to observe that its existence offers no ground for supposing that the understanding of political activity as empiricism guided solely by an ideology is an adequate understanding. The ideological style of politics is a confused style. Properly speaking, it is a traditional manner of attending to the arrangements of a society which has been abridged into a doctrine of ends to be pursued, the abridgment (together with the necessary technical knowledge) being erroneously regarded as the sole guide relied upon. In certain circumstances an abridgment of this kind may be valuable; it gives sharpness of outline and precision to a political tradition which the occasion may make seem appropriate. When a manner of attending to arrangements is to be transplanted from the society in which it has grown up into another society (always a questionable enterprise), the simplification of an ideology may appear as an asset. If, for example, the English manner of politics is to be planted elsewhere in the world, it is perhaps appropriate that it should first be abridged into something called 'democracy' before it is packed up and shipped abroad. There is, of course, an alternative method: the method by which what is exported is the detail and not the abridgment of the tradition and the workmen travel with the tools – the method which made the British Empire. But it is a slow and costly method. And, particularly with men in a hurry, *l'homme à programme* with his abridgment wins every time; his slogans enchant, while the resident magistrate is seen only as a sign of servility. But whatever the apparent appropriateness on occasion of the ideological style of politics, the defect of the explanation of political activity connected with it becomes apparent when we consider the sort of knowledge and the kind of education it encourages us to believe is sufficient for understanding the activity of attending to the arrangements of a society. For it suggests that a knowledge of the chosen political ideology can take the place of understanding a tradition of political behaviour. The wand and the book come to be regarded as themselves potent, and not merely the symbols of potency. The arrangements of a society are made to appear, not as manners of behaviour, but as pieces of machinery to be transported about the world indiscriminately. The complexities of the tradition which have been squeezed out in the process of abridgment are taken to be unimportant: the 'rights of man' are understood to exist insulated from a manner of attending to arrangements. And because, in practice, the abridgment is never by itself a sufficient guide, we are encouraged to fill it out, not with our suspect political experience, but with experience drawn from other (often irrelevant) concretely understood activities, such as war, the conduct of industry, or Trade Union negotiation.

4

The understanding of politics as the activity of attending to the arrangements of a society under the guidance of an independently premeditated ideology is, then, no less a misunderstanding than the understanding of it as a purely empirical activity. Wherever else politics may begin, they cannot begin in ideological activity. And in an attempt to improve upon this understanding of politics, we have already observed in principle what needs to be recognized in order to have an intelligible concept. Just as scientific hypothesis cannot appear, and is impossible to operate, except within an already existing tradition of scientific investigation, so a scheme of ends for political activity appears within, and can be evaluated only when it is related to, an already existing tradition of how to attend to our arrangements. In politics, the only concrete manner of activity detectable is one in which empiricism and the ends to be pursued are recognized as dependent, alike for their existence and their operation, upon a traditional manner of behaviour.

Politics is the activity of attending to the general arrangements of a collection of people who, in respect of their common recognition of a manner of attending to its arrangements, compose a single community. To suppose a collection of people without recognized traditions of behaviour, or one which enjoyed arrangements which intimated no direction for change and needed no attention,[1] is to suppose a people incapable of politics. This activity, then, springs neither from instant desires, nor from general principles, but from the existing traditions of behaviour themselves. And the form it

[1] E.g. a society in which law was believed to be a divine gift.

takes, because it can take no other, is the amendment of existing arrangements by exploring and pursuing what is intimated in them. The arrangements which constitute a society capable of political activity, whether they are customs or institutions or laws or diplomatic decisions, are at once coherent and incoherent; they compose a pattern and at the same time they intimate a sympathy for what does not fully appear. Political activity is the exploration of that sympathy; and consequently, relevant political reasoning will be the convincing exposure of a sympathy, present but not yet followed up, and the convincing demonstration that now is the appropriate moment for recognizing it. For example, the legal status of women in our society was for a long time (and perhaps still is) in comparative confusion, because the rights and duties which composed it intimated rights and duties which were nevertheless not recognized. And, on the view of things I am suggesting, the only cogent reason to be advanced for the technical 'enfranchisement' of women was that in all or most other important respects they had already been enfranchised. Arguments drawn from abstract natural right, from 'justice', or from some general concept of feminine personality, must be regarded as either irrelevant, or as unfortunately disguised forms of the one valid argument; namely, that there was an incoherence in the arrangements of the society which pressed convincingly for remedy. In politics, then, every enterprise is a consequential enterprise, the pursuit, not of a dream, or of a general principle, but of an intimation.[1] What we have to do with is something less imposing than logical implications or necessary consequences: but if the intimations of a tradition of behaviour are less dignified or more elusive than these, they are not on that account less important. Of course, there is no piece of mistake-proof apparatus by means of which we can elicit the intimation most worth while pursuing; and not only do we often make gross errors of judgment in this matter, but also the total effect of a desire satisfied is so little to be forecast, that our activity of amendment is often found to lead us where we would not go. Moreover, the whole enterprise is liable at any moment to be perverted by the incursion of an approximation to empiricism in the pursuit of power. These are features which can never be eliminated;

[1] See terminal note, p.133.

they belong to the character of political activity. But it may be believed that our mistakes of understanding will be less frequent and less disastrous if we escape the illusion that politics is ever anything more than the pursuit of intimations; a conversation, not an argument.

Now, every society which is intellectually alive is liable, from time to time, to abridge its tradition of behaviour into a scheme of abstract ideas; and on occasion political discussion will be concerned, not (like the debates in the *Iliad*) with isolated transactions, nor (like the speeches in Thucydides) with policies and traditions of activity, but with general principles. And in this there is no harm; perhaps even some positive benefit. It is possible that the distorting mirror of an ideology will reveal important hidden passages in the tradition, as a caricature reveals the potentialities of a face; and if this is so, the intellectual enterprise of seeing what a tradition looks like when it is reduced to an ideology will be a useful part of political education. But to make use of abridgment as a technique for exploring the intimations of a political tradition, to use it, that is, as a scientist uses hypothesis, is one thing; it is something different, and something inappropriate, to understand political activity itself as the activity of amending the arrangements of a society so as to make them agree with the provisions of an ideology. For then a character has been attributed to an ideology which it is unable to sustain, and we may find ourselves, in practice, directed by a false and a misleading guide: false, because in the abridgment, however skilfully it has been performed, a single intimation is apt to be exaggerated and proposed for unconditional pursuit and the benefit to be had from observing what the distortion reveals is lost when the distortion itself is given the office of a criterion; misleading, because the abridgment itself never, in fact, provides the whole of the knowledge used in political activity.

There will be some people who, though in general agreement with this understanding of political activity, will suspect that it confuses what is, perhaps, normal with what is necessary, and that important exceptions (of great contemporary relevance) have been lost in a hazy generality. It is all very well, it may be said, to observe in politics the activity of exploring and pursuing the intimations of a tradition of behaviour, but what light does this throw upon a political crisis such as the Norman Conquest of England, or the establishment of the Soviet *régime* in Russia? It would be foolish, of course, to deny the possibility of serious political crisis. But if we exclude (as we must) a genuine cataclysm which for the time being made an end of politics by altogether obliterating a current tradition of behaviour (which is *not* what happened in Anglo-Saxon England or in Russia),[1] there is little to support the view that even the most serious political upheaval carries us outside this understanding of politics. A tradition of behaviour is not a fixed and inflexible manner of doing things; it is a flow of sympathy. It may be temporarily disrupted by the incursion of a foreign influence, it may be diverted, restricted, arrested, or become dried-up, and it may reveal so deep-seated an incoherence that (even without foreign assistance) a crisis appears. And if, in order to meet these crises, there were some steady, unchanging, independent guide to which a society might resort, it would no doubt be well advised to do so. But no such guide exists; we have no resources outside the fragments, the vestiges, the relics of its own tradition of behaviour which the crisis has left untouched. For even the help we may get from the traditions of another society (or from a tradition of a vaguer sort which is shared by a number of societies) is conditional upon our being able to assimilate them to our own arrangements and our own manner of attending to our arrangements. The hungry and helpless man is mistaken if he supposes that he overcomes the crisis by means of a tin-opener: what saves him is somebody else's knowledge of how to cook, which he can make use of only because he is not himself entirely ignorant. In short, political crisis (even when it seems to be imposed upon a society by changes beyond its control) always appears *within* a tradition of political activity; and 'salvation' comes from the unimpaired resources of the tradition itself. Those societies which retain, in changing circumstances, a lively sense of their own identity and continuity (which are without that hatred of their own

---

[1] Cf. the passage from Maitland quoted on p. 157. The Russian Revolution (what actually happened in Russia) was not the implementation of an abstract design worked out by Lenin and others in Switzerland: it was a modification of *Russian* circumstances. And the French Revolution was far more closely connected with the *ancien régime* than with Locke or America.

experience which makes them desire to efface it) are to be counted fortunate, not because they possess what others lack, but because they have already mobilized what none is without and all, in fact, rely upon.

In political activity, then, men sail a boundless and bottomless sea; there is neither harbour for shelter nor floor for anchorage, neither starting-place nor appointed destination. The enterprise is to keep afloat on an even keel; the sea is both friend and enemy; and the seamanship consists in using the resources of a traditional manner of behaviour in order to make a friend of every hostile occasion.[1]

A depressing doctrine, it will be said – even by those who do not make the mistake of adding in an element of crude determinism which, in fact, it has no place for. A tradition of behaviour is not a groove within which we are destined to grind out our helpless and unsatisfying lives: Spartam nactus es; hanc *exorna*. But in the main the depression springs from the exclusion of hopes that were false and the discovery that guides, reputed to be of superhuman wisdom and skill, are, in fact, of a somewhat different character. If the doctrine deprives us of a model laid up in heaven to which we should approximate our behaviour, at least is does not lead us into a morass where every choice is equally good or equally to be deplored. And if it suggests that politics are *nur für die Schwindelfreie*, that should depress only those who have lost their nerve.

5

The sin of the academic is that he takes so long in coming to the point. Nevertheless, there is some virtue in his dilatoriness; what he

[1] To those who seem to themselves to have a clear view of an immediate destination (that is, of a condition of human circumstance to be achieved), and who are confident that this condition is proper to be imposed upon everybody, this will seem an unduly sceptical understanding of political activity; but they may be asked where they have got it from, and whether they imagine that 'political activity' will come to an end with the achievement of this condition? And if they agree that some more distant destination may then be expected to disclose itself, does not this situation entail an understanding of politics as an open-ended activity such as I have described? Or do they understand politics as making the necessary arrangements for a set of castaways who have always in reserve the thought that they are going to be 'rescued'?

has to offer may, in the end, be no great matter, but at least it is not unripe fruit, and to pluck it is the work of a moment. We set out to consider the kind of knowledge involved in political activity and the appropriate sort of education. And if the understanding of politics I have recommended is not a misunderstanding, there is little doubt about the kind of knowledge and the sort of education which belongs to it. It is knowledge, as profound as we can make it, of our tradition of political behaviour. Other knowledge, certainly, is desirable in addition; but this is the knowledge without which we cannot make use of whatever else we may have learned.

Now, a tradition of behaviour is a tricky thing to get to know. Indeed, it may even appear to be essentially unintelligible. It is neither fixed nor finished; it has no changeless centre to which understanding can anchor itself; there is no sovereign purpose to be perceived or invariable direction to be detected; there is no model to be copied, idea to be realized, or rule to be followed. Some parts of it may change more slowly than others, but none is immune from change. Everything is temporary. Nevertheless, though a tradition of behaviour is flimsy and elusive, it is not without identity, and what makes it a possible object of knowledge is the fact that all its parts do not change at the same time and that the changes it undergoes are potential within it. Its principle is a principle of *continuity*: authority is diffused between past, present, and future; between the old, the new, and what is to come. It is steady because, though it moves, it is never wholly in motion; and though it is tranquil, it is never wholly at rest.[1] Nothing that ever belonged to it is completely lost; we are always swerving back to recover and make something topical out of even its remotest moments: and nothing for long remains unmodified. Everything is temporary, but nothing is arbitrary. Everything figures by comparison, not with what stands next to it, but with the whole. And since a tradition of behaviour is not susceptible of the distinction between essence and accident, knowledge of it is unavoid-

[1] The critic who found 'some mystical qualities' in this passage leaves me puzzled: it seems to me an exceedingly matter-of-fact description of the characteristics of any tradition – the Common Law of England, for example, the so-called British Constitution, the Christian religion, modern physics, the game of cricket, shipbuilding.

ably knowledge of its detail: to know only the gist is to know nothing. What has to be learned is not an abstract idea, or a set of
tricks, not even a ritual, but a concrete, coherent manner of living
in all its intricateness.

It is clear, then, that we must not entertain the hope of acquiring
this difficult understanding by easy methods. Though the knowledge
we seek is municipal, not universal, there is no short cut to it. Moreover, political education is not merely a matter of coming to understand a tradition, it is learning how to participate in a conversation:
it is at once initiation into an inheritance in which we have a life
interest, and the exploration of its intimations. There will always
remain something of a mystery about how a tradition of political
behaviour is learned, and perhaps the only certainty is that there is
no point at which learning it can properly be said to begin. The
politics of a community are not less individual (and not more so) than
its language, and they are learned and practised in the same manner.
We do not begin to learn our native language by learning the alpha-
bet, or by learning its grammar; we do not begin by learning words,
but words in use; we do not begin (as we begin in reading) with what
is easy and go on to what is more difficult; we do not begin at
school, but in the cradle; and what we say springs always from our
manner of speaking. And this is true also of our political education;
it begins in the enjoyment of a tradition, in the observation and
imitation of the behaviour of our elders, and there is little or nothing
in the world which comes before us as we open our eyes which does
not contribute to it. We are aware of a past and a future as soon as we
are aware of a present. Long before we are of an age to take interest
in a book about our politics we are acquiring that complex and
intricate knowledge of our political tradition without which we could
not make sense of a book when we come to open it. And the projects
we entertain are the creatures of our tradition. The greater part, then
– perhaps the most important part – of our political education we
acquire haphazard in finding our way about the natural-artificial
world into which we are born, and there is no other way of acquiring it. There will, of course, be more to acquire, and it will be more
readily acquired, if we have the good fortune to be born into a rich
and lively political tradition and among those who are well educated

politically; the lineaments of *political* activity will earlier become distinct: but even the most needy society and the most cramped surroundings have some political education to offer, and we take what we can get.

But if this is the manner of our beginning, there are deeper recesses to explore. Politics are a proper subject for academic study; there is something to think about and it is important that we should think about the appropriate things. Here also, and everywhere, the governing consideration is that what we are learning to understand is a political tradition, a concrete manner of behaviour. And for this reason it is proper that, at the academic level, the study of politics should be an historical study – not, in the first place, because it is proper to be concerned with the past, but because we need to be concerned with the detail of the concrete. It is true that nothing appears on the present surface of a tradition of political activity which has not its roots deep in the past, and that not to observe it coming into being is often to be denied the clue to its significance; and for this reason genuine historical study is an indispensable part of a political education. But what is equally important is not what happened, here or there, but what people have thought and said about what happened: the history, not of political ideas, but of the manner of our political thinking. Every society, by the underlinings it makes in the book of its history, constructs a legend of its own fortunes which it keeps up to date and in which is hidden its own understanding of its politics; and the historical investigation of this legend – not to expose its errors but to understand its prejudices – must be a pre-eminent part of a political education. It is, then, in the study of genuine history, and of this quasi-history which reveals in its backward glances the tendencies which are afoot, that we may hope to escape one of the most insidious current misunderstandings of political activity – the misunderstanding in which institutions and procedures appear as pieces of machinery designed to achieve a purpose settled in advance, instead of as manners of behaviour which are meaningless when separated from their context: the misunderstanding, for example, in which Mill convinced himself that something called 'Representative Government' was a 'form' of politics which could be regarded as proper to any society which had reached a certain level of what he called 'civilization'; in short, the misunderstanding in which we regard our arrangements and institutions as something more significant than the footprints of thinkers and statesmen who knew which way to turn their feet without knowing anything about a final destination.

Nevertheless, to be concerned only with one's own tradition of political activity is not enough. A political education worth the name must embrace, also, knowledge of the politics of other contemporary societies. It must do this because some at least of our political activity is related to that of other people's, and not to know how they go about attending to their own arrangements is not to know the course they will pursue and not to know what resources to call upon in our own tradition; and because to know only one's own tradition is not to know even that. But here again two observations must be made. We did not begin yesterday to have relations with our neighbours; and we do not require constantly to be hunting outside the tradition of our politics to find some special formula or some merely *ad hoc* expedient to direct those relations. It is only when wilfully or negligently we forget the resources of understanding and initiative which belongs to our tradition that, like actors who have forgotten their part, we are obliged to gag. And secondly, the only knowledge worth having about the politics of another society is the same kind of knowledge as we seek of our own tradition. Here also, *la verité reste dans les nuances*; and a comparative study of institutions, for example, which obscured this would provide only an illusory sense of having understood what nevertheless remains a secret. The study of another people's politics, like the study of our own, should be an oecological study of a tradition of behaviour, not an anatomical study of mechanical devices or the investigation of an ideology. And only when our study is of this sort shall we find ourselves in the way of being stimulated, but not intoxicated, by the manners of others. To range the world in order to select the 'best' of the practices and purposes of others (as the eclectic Zeuxis is said to have tried to compose a figure more beautiful than Helen's by putting together features each notable for its perfection) is a corrupting enterprise and one of the surest ways of losing one's political balance; but to investigate the concrete manner in which another people goes about the business of attending to its arrangements may reveal significant passages in our own tradition which might otherwise remain hidden.

There is a third department in the academic study of politics which must be considered – what, for want of a better name, I shall call a philosophical study. Reflection on political activity may take place at various levels: we may consider what resources our political tradition offers for dealing with a certain situation, or we may abridge our political experience into a doctrine, which may be used, as a scientist uses hypothesis, to explore its intimations. But beyond these, and other manners of political thinking, there is a range of reflection the object of which is to consider the place of political activity itself on the map of our total experience. Reflection of this sort has gone on in every society which is politically conscious and intellectually alive; and so far as European societies are concerned, the inquiry has uncovered a variety of intellectual problems which each generation has formulated in its own way and has tackled with the technical resources at its disposal. And because political philosophy is not what may be called a 'progressive' science, accumulating solid results and reaching conclusions upon which further investigation may be based with confidence, its history is specially important: indeed, in a sense, it has nothing but a history, which is a history of the incoherencies philosophers have detected in common ways of thinking and the manner of solution they have proposed, rather than a history of doctrines and systems. The study of this history may be supposed to have a considerable place in a political education, and the enterprise of understanding the turn which contemporary reflection has given to it, an even more considerable place. Political philosophy cannot be expected to increase our ability to be successful in political activity. It will not help us to distinguish between good and bad political projects; it has no power to guide or to direct us in the enterprise of pursuing the intimations of our tradition. But the patient analysis of the general ideas which have come to be connected with political activity – ideas such as nature, artifice, reason, will, law, authority, obligation, etc. – in so far as it succeeds in removing some of the crookedness from our thinking and leads to a more economical use of concepts, is an activity neither to be overrated nor despised. But it must be understood as an explanatory, not a practical, activity, and if we pursue it, we may hope only to be less often cheated by ambiguous statement and irrelevant argument.

Abeunt studia in mores. The fruits of a political education will appear in the manner in which we think and speak about politics and perhaps in the manner in which we conduct our political activity. To select items from this prospective harvest must always be hazardous, and opinions will differ about what is most important. But for myself I should hope for two things. The more profound our understanding of political activity, the less we shall be at the mercy of plausible but mistaken analogy, the less we shall be tempted by a false or irrelevant model. And the more thoroughly we understand our own political tradition, the more readily its whole resources are available to us, the less likely we shall be to embrace the illusions which wait for the ignorant and the unwary: the illusion that in politics we can get on without a tradition of behaviour, the illusion that the abridgment of a tradition is itself a sufficient guide, and the illusion that in politics there is anywhere a safe harbour, a destination to be reached or even a detectable strand of progress. 'The world is the best of all possible worlds, and *everything* in it is a necessary evil.'
1951

THE PURSUIT OF INTIMATIONS

(1) This expression, as I hoped I had made clear, was intended as a description of what political activity actually is in the circumstances indicated, namely, in the 'hereditary, co-operative groups, many of them of ancient lineage, all of them aware of a past, a present, and a future, which we call "states"'. Critics who find this to be so special-ized a description that it fails altogether to account for some of the most significant passages in modern political history are, of course, making a relevant comment. But those who find this expression to be meaningless in respect of every so-called 'revolutionary' situation and every essay in so-called 'idealistic' politics may be asked to think again, remembering that it is neither intended as a description of the motives of politicians nor of what they believe themselves to be doing, but of what they actually succeed in doing.

I connected with this understanding of political activity two further propositions: first, that if true, it must be supposed to have some bearing upon how we study politics, that is, upon political education; secondly, that if true, it may be supposed to have some bearing upon how we conduct ourselves in political activity – there being, perhaps, some advantage in thinking and speaking and arguing in a manner consonant with what we are really doing. The second of these propositions I do not think to be very important.

(2) It has been concluded that this understanding of political activity reduces it to 'acting on hunches', 'following intuitions' and that it 'discourages argument of any sort'. Nothing I have said warrants this conclusion. The conclusion I myself drew in this connection was that, if this understanding of political activity were true, certain forms of argument (e.g. arguments designed to determine the correspondence of a political proposal with Natural Law or with abstract 'justice') must be considered either irrelevant or as clumsy formulations of other and relevant inquiries, and must be understood to have a merely rhetorical or persuasive value.

(3) It has been suggested that this understanding of political activity provides no standard or criterion for distinguishing between good and bad political projects or for deciding to do one thing rather than another. This, again, is an unfortunate misreading of what I said: 'everything figures, not with what stands next to it, but with the whole'. Those who are accustomed to judge everything in relation to 'justice', or 'solidarity', or 'welfare' or some other abstract 'principle', and know no other way of thinking and speaking, may perhaps be asked to consider how, in fact, a barrister in a Court of Appeal argues the inadequacy of the damages awarded to his client. Does he say, 'This is a glaring injustice', and leave it at that? Or may he be expected to say that the damages awarded are 'out of line with the general level of damages currently being awarded in libel actions'? And if he says this, or something like it, is he to be properly accused of not engaging in argument of any sort, or of having no standard or criterion, or of merely referring to 'what was done last time'? (Cf. Aristotle, *Analytica Priora*, II. 23.) Again, is Mr N. A. Swanson all at sea when he argues in this fashion about the revolutionary proposal that the bowler in cricket should be allowed to 'throw 'the ball: 'the present bowling action has evolved as a sequence, from underarm by way of round-arm to over-arm, by successive legislation of

unorthodox actions. Now, I maintain that the "throw" has no place in this sequence . . .'? Or, is Mr G. H. Fender arguing without a standard or criterion, or is he merely expressing a 'hunch', when he contends that the 'throw' *has* a place in this sequence and should be permitted? And is it so far-fetched to describe what is being done here and elsewhere as 'exploring the intimations' of the total situation? And, whatever we like to say in order to bolster up our self-esteem, is not this the manner in which changes take place in the design of anything, furniture, clothes, motor-cars and societies capable of political activity? Does it all become much more intelligible if we exclude circumstance and translate it into the idiom of 'principles', the bowler, perhaps, arguing his 'natural right' to throw? And, even then, can we exclude circumstance: would there ever be a question of the right to throw if the right to bowl over-arm had not already been conceded? At all events, I may perhaps be allowed to reiterate my view that moral and political 'principles' are abridgments of traditional manners of behaviour, and to refer specific conduct to 'principles' is not what it is made to appear (*viz.* referring it to a criterion which is reliable because it is devoid of contingency, like a so-called 'just price').

(4) It has been asserted that in politics there is no 'total situation': 'why should we presuppose that, inside the territory we call Britain . . . there is only one society, with one tradition? Why should not there be two societies . . . each with its own way of life?' In the understanding of a more profound critic this might be a philosophical question which would require something more than a short answer. But in the circumstances it is perhaps enough to say: first, that the absence of homogeneity does not necessarily destroy singleness; secondly, what we are considering here is a legally organized society and we are considering the manner in which its legal structure (which in spite of its incoherencies cannot be supposed to have a competitor) is reformed and amended; and thirdly, I stated (on p.123) what I meant by a 'single community' and my reasons for making this my starting-place.

(5) Lastly, it has been said that, since I reject 'general principles', I provide no means for detecting incoherencies and for determining what shall be on the agenda of reform. 'How do we discover what a

society [*sic*] intimates?' But to this I can only reply: 'Do you want to be told that in politics there is, what certainly exists nowhere else, a mistake-proof manner of deciding what should be done?' How does a scientist, with the current condition of physics before him, decide upon a direction of profitable advance? What considerations passed through the minds of medieval builders when they detected the inappropriateness of building in stone as if they were building in wood? How does a critic arrive at the judgment that a picture is incoherent, that the artist's treatment of some passages is inconsistent with his treatment of others?

J. S. Mill (*Autobiography*, OUP pp. 136-7, 144-5), when he abandoned reference to general principle either as a reliable guide in political activity or as a satisfactory explanatory device, put in its place a 'theory of human progress' and what he called a 'philosophy of history'. The view I have expressed in this essay may be taken to represent a further stage in this intellectual pilgrimage, a stage reached when neither 'principle' (on account of what it turns out to be: a mere index of concrete behaviour) nor any general theory about the character and direction of social change seem to supply an adequate reference for explanation or for practical conduct.

The Activity of being an Historian

Activities emerge naïvely, like games that children invent for themselves. Each appears, first, not in response to a premeditated achievement, but as a direction of attention pursued without premonition of what it will lead to. How should our artless ancestor have known what (as it has turned out) it is to be an astronomer, an accountant, or an historian? And yet it was he who, in play, set our feet on the paths that have led to these now narrowly specified activities.[1] For, a direction of attention, as it is pursued, may hollow out a character for itself and become specified in a 'practice'; and a participant in the activity comes to be recognized not by the results he achieves but by his disposition to observe the manners of the 'practice'. Moreover, when an activity has acquired a certain firmness of character, it may present itself as a puzzle, and thus provoke reflection; for, there may come a point at which we not only wish to acquire and exercise the skill which constitutes the activity, but may wish also to discern the logic of the relation of this activity (as it has come to be specified) to others and to ascertain its place on the map of human activity.

What we now understand as the activity of being an historian was generated in this manner. Beginning in a direction of attention naïvely pursued, it has achieved the condition of a specific activity whose participants are known by their faithfulness to the 'practice' that has emerged. And during the last two hundred years or so this activity has been much reflected upon.

Reflection has taken two directions. First, what has been sought is a satisfactory general description of the activity of being an historian as it has come to establish itself. The assumption here is that the activity is itself an historical emergence and that the degree of

[1] Cf. Plato, *Laws*, 672B.

specification it has now achieved is sufficient to identify it as a coherent manner of thinking about the world. And the fruits of such an inquiry would be the disclosure of the kind of intelligibility that historical thinking, in its present condition, imparts to the world, and the manner in which this activity can be distinguished from others which (in the process of emergence) it has succeeded in separating itself from. This, no doubt, is a difficult inquiry; but it is one that seems capable of yielding some conclusions.

The second direction of inquiry may be said to spring (but not necessarily) from the first. Assuming a satisfactory description of the current condition of the activity of being an historian has been achieved, the questions asked are: Does this condition intimate (or, must we not on general grounds assume) the possibility of further specification which would not merely modify in detail the present specification of the activity but would generate its definitive character? And if so, what is this character? And since I propose to concern myself very little with this line of inquiry, I should, perhaps, say a word about it before putting it on one side. Briefly, the notion appears to be this: the activity of being an historian is that of understanding the past; but, since the current manner of doing this leaves the past incompletely intelligible, there must (in principle) be another manner of understanding the past which, because it is free from this defect, may be regarded as the consummation to which 'history' in its present condition points. And, although there may be others yet unproposed, the most favoured candidate has, for some time, been an inquiry designed to make past events intelligible by revealing them as examples of general laws. I do not myself understand how this line of thought could lead to profitable conclusions; but at least it is clear that it rests upon far from self-evidently true presuppositions, and whether or not it may turn out to be profitable will depend upon our satisfying ourselves that they are warranted. Moreover, it should be observed that what is being sought here is not merely a demonstration that historical thinking in its present condition must, in principle, leave the past incompletely intelligible, but a manner of thinking about the past which is at once superior to 'history' in its present condition and is capable of taking its place.

2

I propose, then, to consider the manner and achievements of current reflection about the present condition of the activity of being an historian; the reflection, that is, which seeks a general description of the activity as it has come to establish itself, and to determine the kind of intelligibility it imparts to the world.

The historian is understood, in the first place, to be distinguished on account of the direction of his attention; he is concerned with the past. He is interested in the world around him considered as evidence for a world that is no longer present; and we recognize his activity as one of inquiring into 'the past' and making statements about it. Nevertheless, we recognize, also, that to inquire into the past and to make statements about it is an exceedingly commonplace activity and one that we engage in every day of our lives: it is represented, for example, in the activity of remembering, and in so simple an inquiry as, 'Where did you get that hat?' Consequently, if we are interested, we cast around in order to discern some special characteristics which will serve to distinguish the activity of an historian from that of others who share with him an interest in 'the past'. And many who have reflected upon this subject have reached a conclusion something like this:

Whoever pays attention to the past and asks questions or makes statements about it must be understood to be participating in some measure in the activity which is the pre-eminent concern of an historian. All statements about the past are, in some sense, 'historical' statements. But an historian is distinguished by reason of the care he takes to verify his statements. 'History' emerges as a specific activity out of a general and unspecified interest in the past whenever there is a genuine concern for 'truth'; and an 'historical' event is any happening which we are warranted in believing (in virtue of its being a conclusion to a certain method of inquiry) took place in the manner described.[1] Thus, the activity of inquiring into and making statements about the past appears as a hierarchy of attitudes towards the past. At

[1] Thus, Cicero distinguished the 'historical' from the 'imagined' past, the one being concerned with 'truth' and the other with 'pleasure'.

the head of this scale of attitudes stands 'the historian', specified by his care for 'truth', his technical skill in eliciting 'truth', and perhaps also by a propensity to regard some observations about the past, and some events, as more significant than others. In this manner his activity is differentiated, not only from the informal inquiries about the past which every man from time to time, in the course of business or pleasure, engages in, but also from the activity (for example) of an annalist or a chronicler, whose utterances spring from inquiries recognized to be less extended and less critical than those of an historian.

This general account of the matter has much to commend it. At least, it recognizes 'the historian' (in virtue of a 'practice') to be engaged in a specific activity. No doubt it is an incomplete account; and no doubt, also, it is philosophically naïve. But it has the virtue of not forbidding further investigation: indeed, it may be observed to point to two directions of further inquiry. For its incompleteness and philosophical naïvety lie, not in the formulation of the problem as one of ascertaining the *differentia* of 'historical' research, but only in the conclusions reached.

It urges us, first, to be more exact in our understanding of the details of the 'practice' of 'the historian'. And in response to this suggestion, attempts have been made to elicit a heuristic of historical investigation and to reduce the 'practice' of 'the historian' to a set of rules. But, as reflection might have warned us would be the case, this has not turned out a very profitable enterprise. And I do not propose to pursue it here.

There is, however, another direction of inquiry which this formulation of the problem suggests: it provokes us to consider whether the activity of being an historian may be more exactly specified in terms of the *kind* of question he asks and the *kind* of statement he makes about the past. And since in this direction of inquiry there remains a yet unfulfilled promise of profit, I propose to consider where it has led us and what further conclusions it is capable of yielding.

Investigators who have followed this path have already reached certain conclusions. They have observed, for example, that inquiry into the past may take the form of asking what *must* have happened, or what *might* have happened, or what *did* happen; and, for the most part, they have concluded that an *historian* is distinguished by an exclusive concern with what *did* happen. Or, again, a distinction has been drawn between the 'natural' world and the 'human' world; and it has been concluded that the events with which an historian is concerned are those which may be imputed to human actions and those which (though they belong to the 'natural' world, like earthquakes and climatic changes) we are warranted in believing to have conditioned or determined specific human conduct. And, as a refinement of this, Collingwood considered that the *res gestae* of 'history' are not *any* human actions, but only 'reflective' actions; that is, actions which spring from a purpose pursued. Further, it has been suggested that an attitude towards the past which provokes an inquiry into the 'origins' of some feature of the present world is an attitude foreign to an historian. In the same manner, the very recent past has been considered inappropriate for 'historical' investigation. And (a last example) some inquirers into the activity of the 'historian' have concluded that he is not concerned with the moral rightness and wrongness of human actions and that statements of moral approval or disapproval, of praise or condemnation, are out of place in his writings.

Now, all these suggestions may be recognized as attempts to determine more exactly the *kind* of questions it is appropriate for 'the historian' to ask, and the *kind* of statements it is appropriate for him to make about the past. They are attempts to distinguish a specifically 'historical' attitude towards 'the past' from other current or possible attitudes and thus to specify more precisely the activity of being an historian. Each suggestion is supported by some show of reasoning. The questions excluded from the concern of 'the historian' are identified either as questions inherently impossible to answer, or as questions which his evidence or his technique does not equip 'the historian' to answer; or they are excluded for some other reason. And, so far, there is much to be said for this manner of gradually elucidating the activity of 'the historian'; it has the virtues of moderation and empiricism.

Nevertheless, there remains something unsatisfactory about this procedure of piecemeal exclusion. Even if the reasoning which supports each exclusion were more cogent than it often is, the absence of attachment to a comprehensive view of the situation gives to each the indelible appearance of arbitrariness. Each remains a separate exclusion (or prohibition), supported by *ad hoc* reasoning which is apt to be either misconceived or inadequate because it is unrelated to any conspectus of the *kind* of inquiry and the *kind* of utterance appropriate to an 'historical' investigation of the past. In short, the current manner of exploring the activity of 'the historian' sets us a task: to discern the logic of these piecemeal attempts to delineate the field of historical inquiry.

The imperfectly considered assumptions of the current view appear to be something like this. It is believed that among the different kinds of statement that may be made about the past, it is possible to detect and to specify certain kinds, or even a certain kind which it is the peculiar province of 'the historian' to make. It is believed that there are many statements we, quite properly, make about the past which (even though they cannot be denied to be in some sense 'true') are, nevertheless, not 'historical' statements. It is believed that an 'historical' event is not any happening which we have warrant for thinking took place, but a happening of a peculiar sort which reveals itself in answer to a certain kind of question. Our task is to elucidate these assumptions so that the view of the activity of 'the historian' which they entail may be more fully disclosed and perhaps more firmly based.

3

It is proper to begin with our attitudes towards the world around us, because inquiring into 'the past' is the exhibition of a certain attitude towards the components of this world. Every happening that we see taking place before our eyes, if we attend to it at all, arouses a response. And every happening is capable of arousing a variety of responses. For example, I may observe the demolition of an old building, and my response may be merely a movement of self-preservation – to get out of the way of the débris. It may, however, be a more complicated response. I may recognize what is happening as an act of vandalism, and suffer anger or depression; or I may understand it as evidence of progress, and be elated on that account; or indeed, the whole scene may be contemplated without *arrière pensée*, as a picture, an image whose design is a delight to the eyes. In short, to attend to what is happening before us is always to make something of it for ourselves. Seeing is recognizing what we see as *this* or *that*. And if I have a companion I may make a statement about what I am seeing whose idiom reveals the manner in which I am attending to it and understanding it.

Everything that goes on before our eyes is, then, eligible for a vast variety of interpretations. But, in general, it seems that our responses to the world are of two kinds. Either we may regard the world in a manner which does not allow us to consider anything but what is immediately before our eyes and does not provoke us to any conclusions; or we may look upon what is going on before us as evidence for what does not itself appear, considering, for example, its causes or its effects. The first of these responses is simple and unvarying; and I shall call it the response of *contemplation*. It is pre-eminently the response of the artist and the poet, for whom the world is composed, not of events recognized as signs or portents, but of causeless 'images' of delight which provoke neither approval nor disapproval, and to which the categories 'real' and 'fictitious' are alike inapplicable. The second response, however, is capable of internal variety; and in it two main idioms may be distinguished, which I shall call, respectively, the *practical* and the *scientific* response.

First, we may recognize what is happening in respect of its relation to ourselves, our fortunes, desires and activities. This is the commonest kind of response; we absolve ourselves from it with difficulty, and relapse into it easily. I call it a *practical* response, and its partner is the perception of a *practical* event.

From birth we are active; not to be active is not to be alive. And what concerns us first about the world is its habitableness, its friend-liness or hostility to our desires and enterprises. We want to be at home in the world, and (in part) this consists in being able to detect how happenings will affect ourselves and in having some control over their effects.

This service is performed, in the first place, by our senses. In 'seeing', 'hearing', 'tasting', 'touching', we become acquainted with what is happening: and, at the same time, we place a certain interval between ourselves and what is happening, giving ourselves an opportunity to act in what we judge to be an appropriate manner. 'Seeing' places the greatest space-time interval between ourselves and events; 'hearing', a smaller, but still useful interval; in 'tasting' the interval is further contracted; and in 'touching' it is reduced to almost nothing at all.

But in order to understand the world in relation to ourselves we make use of certain conceptual distinctions. We recognize events as friendly or hostile, things as edible or poisonous, useful or useless, cheap or expensive, and so on, And most, if not all, these distinctions are examples of the recognition, in practical life, of what may be called 'cause' and 'effect'. For, in practical life, to recognize an event as a 'cause' is to understand it as a sign or signal that other events are likely to follow: to understand an event as friendly is to expect it to be followed by other events of a certain kind; to recognize a commodity as 'cheap' is to recognize it as a signal of other events to come. And the ability to recognize events as, in this sense, 'causes' at once gives us a greatly enhanced mastery over the world; it enables us to anticipate events that have not yet taken place and thus gives us an added opportunity of controlling their impact upon ourselves.

Moreover, it is to this practical attitude towards the world that our judgments of approval and disapproval and our moral appraisals and imputations belong. The categories of 'right' and 'wrong', 'good' and 'bad', 'justice' and 'injustice' etc. relate to the organization and understanding of the world in respect of its relationship to ourselves, in respect (that is) of its habitableness. 'Hero' and 'villain' may be crude categories, but their place is in the world of practical activity. And in condemning 'vice' and applauding 'virtue' we express our beliefs about what is desirable and what is undesirable in human conduct and character.

The practical attitude, then, admits us to a world of discourse; but it is not the only world of discourse available to us. It has a partner and an alternative in what I have called the *scientific* attitude. In this, we are concerned, not with happenings in their relation to ourselves

and to the habitableness of the world, but in respect of their independence of ourselves. In short, the attitude here is what we vulgarly
call an 'objective' attitude; and this 'objectivity' is reflected in the
idiom of the statements we make about the happenings we observe.
While the hunter recognizes animals as dangerous or friendly
(denoting some as specifically 'man-eating'), while the house-wife
distinguishes commodities in respect of their price, while the cook
knows things in respect of their taste, and while the moralist expresses himself in statements of approval or disapproval, the categories of the scientist arrange things in a different manner – not
at all as they affect him or his fortunes,˙ but as they are in their
independence of himself.

The general character of the scientist's concern with the world
appears in his notion of 'cause' and 'effect'. When the practical man
recognizes an event as a 'cause' he recognizes it as a *sign* that some
other event may be expected to follow; and the ground of his recognition is his experience of the world in relation to himself. For the
scientist, on the other hand, 'cause' is a much more precise and more
restricted notion; and 'cause' in his sense is so difficult to determine
that it lacks practical usefulness. It is the necessary and sufficient
conditions of a hypothetical situation. 'Cause' and 'effect', that is,
denote general and necessary relations and not merely a relation
which it has proved practically useful to observe.

The contrast between the practical and the scientific responses to
the world may be illustrated as follows: When we are concerned
with things in their relation to ourselves and to the habitableness of
the world, it is appropriate to say that 'seeing' puts things at a
greater distance from ourselves than 'hearing'. And consequently
we recognize that it is a greater handicap to be blind than to be deaf.
But when we are concerned with things in respect of their independence of ourselves, we say, instead, that the speed of light is greater
than the speed of sound. 'Light' and 'sound' are, so to speak, the
'scientific' equivalents of the practical activities of 'seeing' and 'hearing'.

Or again, if I say: 'I am hot,' I shall be recognized to be speaking
in the idiom of practice. I am making a statement about the world in
relation to myself, and the manner in which it is made will certainly

convey either satisfaction or dissatisfaction. If I say: 'It is a hot day', I am still making a statement about the world in relation to myself. Its reference is more extended, but the remark is unmistakably in the practical idiom. If I say: 'The thermometer on the roof of the Air Ministry stood at 90°F. at 12 noon G.M.T.' I may not have emancipated myself completely from the practical attitude, but at least I am capable of being suspected of making a statement, not about the world in relation to myself but about the world in respect of its independence of myself. And when, finally, I say: 'The boiling point of water is 100° Centigrade', I am making a statement which may be recognized to have achieved the idiom of 'science'. The situation described is hypothetical, and the observation is not about the world in relation to myself.

In both the practical and the scientific responses, then, the world appears as a world of 'facts'; 'truth' and 'error' are relevant categories, though in the one case it is 'practical' truth and in the other 'scientific'. And in both these attitudes we are provoked to look for what is not present: events are the 'effects' of 'causes' and the portents of events to come. On the other hand, the attitude of contemplation discloses to us a world of mere 'images' which provoke neither inquiry nor speculation about the occasion and conditions of their appearance, but only delight in their having appeared.

4

We have been considering events as they take place before our eyes; and we have concluded that these are capable of a variety of interpretation, and what we see is relative to how we look. And, further, we have agreed that the historian is concerned with 'the past'. What we must now observe is that 'the past' is a construction we make for ourselves out of the events which take place before our eyes. Just as the 'future' appears when we understand the present events as evidence for what is about to happen, so what we call 'the past' appears when we understand current happenings as evidence for what has already happened. In short (to confine ourselves to our immediate concern) 'the past' is a consequence of understanding the present world in a particular manner.

Consider: what we have before us is a building, a piece of furniture, a coin, a picture, a passage in a book, a legal document, an inscription on stone, a current manner of behaviour or a memory. Each of these is a present event. And one response (though not of course the only possible response) to these events is to understand them as evidence for events that have already taken place. There is, indeed, nothing in the present world which is incapable of being regarded in this manner; but also there is nothing which can be regarded *only* in this manner.

'The past', then, is a certain way of reading 'the present'. But in addition to its being a reading of the world in which present events are understood as evidence for events that have already taken place, it is a reading which may denote a variety of attitudes towards these past events. And (if we are to be guided by the utterance of those who have spoken and written about past events) the three most important attitudes available to us may be called the *practical*, the *scientific* and the *contemplative*. And there is a manner of speaking about past events which is appropriate to each of these attitudes.

First, if we understand a past event merely in relation to ourselves and our own current activities, our attitude may be said to be a 'practical' attitude.

This, for example, is the attitude of a practising lawyer to a past event which he concludes to have taken place by understanding a present event (a legal document before him) as evidence for something that has already happened. He considers the past event solely in relation to its present consequences and he says to his client: 'under this will you may expect to inherit £1,000'; or, 'we must take Counsel's opinion on the validity of this contract'. And further, of course, he is interested only in past events which *have* present practical consequences.

Now, just as our commonest attitude towards what we see taking place before us is a practical attitude, so our commonest attitude to what we conclude (on the evidence of a present experience) to have already taken place is a practical attitude. Usually, we interpret these past happenings in relation to ourselves and to our current activities. We read the past backwards from the present or from the more recent past, we look in it for the 'origins' of what we perceive around us, we make moral judgments about past conduct, we call upon the past to speak to us in utterance related to the present; and what appears is a practical past. And the questions we ask, and the statements we make about the past, are those that are appropriate to our practical attitude. They are statements such as these:

> You are looking very well: where did you go for your holiday?
> The summer of 1920 was the finest in my experience.
> He died too soon.
> King John was a bad King.
> The death of William the Conqueror was accidental.
> It would have been better if the French Revolution had never taken place.
> He dissipated his resources in a series of useless wars.
> The Pope's intervention changed the course of events.
> The evolution of Parliament.
> The development of industrial society in Great Britain.
> The Factory Acts of the early nineteenth century culminated in the Welfare State of the twentieth century.
> The loss of markets for British goods on the Continent was the most serious consequence of the Napoleonic Wars.
> The effect of the Boer War was to make clear the necessity for radical reform in the British Army.
> The next day the Liberator addressed a large meeting in Dublin.

Here, in each of these statements, the idiom is that of practice.

Secondly, our attitude to what we conclude to have happened in the past may be, generally speaking, what I have called a 'scientific' attitude. Here, we are concerned, not with past events in relation to ourselves and to the habitableness of the world, but in respect of their independence of ourselves. The practical response is the response of a partisan, of one sort or another; in the scientific response what appears is the past unassimilated to ourselves, the past for its own sake.

But while the word 'scientific' may properly be used, in a general way, to denote an interest in past events in respect of their independence of ourselves, it is necessary to make two qualifications. First, the concern of 'the scientist' with necessary and sufficient conditions will be reflected in the idiom in which he speaks about the past. And a model of the kind of statement he will be disposed to make is to be found in this sentence from Valery: 'all the revolutions of the nineteenth century had as their necessary and sufficient conditions the centralized constitutions of power, thanks to which . . . a minimum strength and duration of effort can deliver an entire nation at a single stroke to whoever undertakes the adventure.' In short, if we give a stricter meaning to the word 'science', what appears is not merely statements in which the past remains unassimilated to the present, but also statements in which events are understood to exemplify general laws. And secondly, if we speak still more strictly, there can in fact be no 'scientific' attitude towards the past, for the world as it appears in scientific theory is a timeless world, a world, not of actual events, but of hypothetical situations.

Lastly, our attitude – and consequently the manner in which we recognize past happenings and the utterances we make about them – may be what I have called a 'contemplative' attitude. This is illustrated in the work of a so-called 'historical' novelist, for whom the past is neither practical nor scientific 'fact', but a storehouse of mere images. For example, in Tolstoy's *War and Peace* Napoleon is an image about whom it is as irrelevant to ask: Where was he born? Was he really like that? Did he in fact do this, or say that? Where was he in the intervals when he was not on the stage? as it would be to ask similar questions about Shakespeare's Orsino, Duke of Illyria in *Twelfth Night*. But here a qualification is necessary. Since 'the past', as such, cannot appear in 'contemplation' (this attitude being one in which we do not look for what does not immediately appear), to 'contemplate' past events is, properly speaking, a dependent activity in which what is contemplated are not past events but present events which (on account of some *other* attitude towards the present) have been concluded to have taken place. To remember, and to contemplate a memory, are two different experiences; in the one past and present are distinguished, in the other no such distinction is made. In short, just as when an object of use (a ship or a spade) is 'contemplated' its usefulness is neglected, so when what in another attitude would be recognized as a past event is 'contemplated', its pastness is ignored.

What we call 'past events' are, then, the product of understanding (or having understood) present occurrences as evidence for happenings that have already taken place. The past, in whatever manner it appears, is a certain sort of reading of the present. Whatever attitudes present events are capable of provoking in us may also be provoked by events which appear when we regard present events as evidence for other events – that is, by what we call 'past' events. In short, there is not one past because there is not one present: there is a 'practical' past, a 'scientific' past and a (specious) 'contemplative' past, each a universe of discourse logically different from either of the others.

5

Now, among those who regard present events as evidence for events that have already taken place, 'the historian' is taken to be supreme. And properly so. For, although the practical man often finds it useful to take this attitude towards the present, and although both the scientist (in a general way) and the poet are each capable of doing so (or of making use of the results of others having done so), 'the historian' never does anything else. The activity of the historian is pre-eminently that of understanding present events – the things that are before him – as evidence for past happenings. His attitude towards the present is one in which the past *always* appears. But in order to understand his activity fully, the question we must ask ourselves is: Can we discern in the attitude of 'historians' towards the past and in the kind of statements they are accustomed to make about it, any characteristics that warrant us to conclude that, besides a 'practical' past, a 'scientific' past and a (specious) 'contemplative' past, there is a specifically 'historial' past?

There is one difficulty which seems to stand in the way of our inquiry, but which may be disposed of at once; it is, in fact, a fictitious difficulty. The practical manner of understanding the past is as old as the human race. To understand everything (including what we believe to have happened in the past) in relation to ourselves is the simplest and least sophisticated manner of understanding the world. And the contemplative attitude towards what are otherwise recognized as past events is, also, generally speaking, primordial and universal. Circumstances may hinder it; and even in people accustomed to it, it may get over-laid and pushed aside in favour of some other attitude. But the great poetic sagas of European and Eastern peoples show that from very early times what in other idioms of observation are known as past events have been recognized not as 'facts' but as 'images' of contemplation. The questions that are appropriate and those that are inappropriate to be asked about Jude the Obscure are the same as those that are respectively appropriate and inappropriate to be asked about Homer's Ulysses or Roland and Oliver. In short, when we consider the kind of statements men have been accustomed to make about the past, there is no doubt that the vast bulk of them is in the practical or the artistic idiom. Consequently, if we go to writers who have been labelled 'historians' (because they have displayed a sustained interest in past events) and ask, what kind of statement are they accustomed to make about the past, we shall find a great preponderance of practical and contemplative statements. And this observation seems to take the wind out of the sails of our inquiry. For where, it will be asked, are we to go to find out what it is to be an historian but to the practice of those who have displayed a sustained interest in the past? And if we go there, the answer ready for us seems to be: History is a miscellany of utterances about the past in which the practical and the contemplative idiom is predominant. And unless we are prepared to erect an imaginary character called, for no good reason, 'the historian', there remains nothing more to be said.

However, this difficulty need not disconcert us. There are, indeed, two considerations which enable us to avert this collapse of our inquiry. First, it must be remembered that in considering 'history' we are considering an activity which (like many others) has emerged gradually and has only recently begun to acquire a specific character. We easily recognize that the activity of being an astronomer, and the statements we expect from those whom we understand to be engaged in astronomy, are in many respects different from what they were when the activity was less exactly specified than it now is. We do not regard all the different kinds of statement (or even all the different kinds of 'true' statement) that have been made about the stars as proper to be made by the man whom we recognize to be 'an astronomer'; indeed, we exclude many of these statements as clearly foreign to what we now recognize as the activity of being an astronomer. And although we have been more hesitant in applying the same reasoning to the activity of being an historian, the two activities are, in this respect, similar to one another. Moreover, inquiry has disclosed in considerable detail the process in which the activity of being an historian has become specified. It is a process (similar to that in which the 'natural scientist' as we now understand him emerged) in which new techniques for the critical treatment of sources of information have been developed, and in which general organizing concepts have been generated, criticized, experimented with and rejected or reformulated.[1] And in neither of these respects has there been unbroken progress; valuable achievements have often been forgotten or allowed to lapse, only to be recovered again when a turn in the fortunes of historiography has recalled them. And again, the activity of being an historian has been dispersed over a variety of circumstantially separated fields of study, and often a closer specification of the activity has been achieved in some fields before it has appeared (often by a process of diffusion) in others. Thus, it is generally true to say that the pioneers of specification have been biblical and ecclesiastical historians, and advances made in these fields have gradually spread to others. And, for example, the rapid and remarkable achievements of historians of the Middle Ages during the last eighty years were often made possible only by the application of the earlier technical achievements of the historians of the ancient world. In short, although we may hope to discern in it some special characteristics, we are not looking for the necessary and sufficient conditions of the activity of being an historian. The activity is what it has become and our present analysis begins and ends with what has been achieved.

---

[1] In one of his notebooks (Add. 5436, 62), quoted in H. Butterfield, *Man on His Past* (p. 98), Acton observes: 'Expressions like: the growth of language, physiology of the State, national psychology, the mind of the Church, the development of Platonism, the continuity of law – questions which occupy half the mental activity of our age – were unintelligible to the eighteenth century – to Hume, Johnson, Smith, Diderot.' But it is not less true to say that the last eighty years have seen the rejection of most, if not all, of these concepts; they have again become unintelligible.

And secondly, if we study the utterances of those who have displayed a sustained interest in the past, especially those of recent writers, we shall find, in addition to practical and contemplative statements, statements in what appears to be another idiom. And since this other kind of statement is, generally speaking, found *only* in the writings of those whom we are now accustomed to recognize as 'historians' we may think it profitable to consider whether they do not provide a hint of an attitude towards the past which, being neither specifically practical, nor scientific, nor contemplative, may properly be called 'historical'.

6

Now, with these considerations in mind we are perhaps in a better position to tackle the question, what is the activity of being an historian? with greater expectation of reaching a reasoned conclusion.

We have observed, first, that 'the historian' is one who understands the events of the world before him as evidence for events that have already taken place. Other sorts of inquiries do this also; 'the historian' is unique in never doing any else. But, what sort of statements does he make about the past thus revealed? What is the character of these statements about the past which 'historians' (but not other kinds of writer about the past) sometimes (but not always) make?

Their first characteristic is that they are *not* designed to assimilate the past to a present, either of fact or desire: the attitude towards the past is *not* what I have called a practical attitude.

The practical man reads the past backwards. He is interested in and recognizes only those past events which he can relate to present activities. He looks to the past in order to explain his present world, to justify it, or to make it a more habitable and a less mysterious place. The past consists of happenings recognized to be contributory or non-contributory to a subsequent condition of things, or to be friendly or hostile to a desired condition of things. Like the gardener, the practical man distinguishes, in past happenings, between weeds and permissible growths; like the lawyer, he distinguishes between legitimate and illegitimate children. If he is a politician, he approves whatever in the past appears to support his political predilections and denounces whatever is hostile to them. If he is a moralist he imposes upon the past a moral structure, distinguishing virtue and vice in human character, right and wrong in human action, approving the one and condemning the other. If his point of observation gives him a wide view, he perceives in the more profound movements of events those that are malign and those that are beneficent. If he is governed by a favourite project, the past appears as a conflict of events and actions relative to that project. In short, he treats the past as he treats the present, and the statements he is disposed to make about past actions and persons are of the same kind as those he is disposed to make about a contemporary situation in which he is involved.

But in the specifically 'historical' attitude (as represented in the kind of statements about the past I have in mind as peculiar to historical writers), the past is *not* viewed in relation to the present, and is *not* treated as if it were the present. Everything that the evidence reveals or points to is recognized to have its place; nothing is excluded, nothing is regarded as 'non-contributory'. The place of an event is not determined by its relation to subsequent events.[1] What is being sought here is neither a justification, nor a criticism nor an explanation of a subsequent or present condition of things. In 'history' no man dies too soon or by 'accident'; there are no successes and no failures and no illegitimate children. Nothing is approved, there being no desired condition of things in relation to which approval can operate; and nothing is denounced. This past is without the moral, the political or the social structure which the practical man transfers from *his* present to *his* past. The Pope's intervention did not change the course of events, it *was* the course of events, and consequently his action was not an 'intervention'. X did not die 'too soon'; he died when he did. Y did not dissipate his resources in a series of useless wars: the wars belong to the actual course of events, not some imaginary illegitimate course of events. It was not 'the Liberator' who addressed the meeting in Dublin; it was Daniel O'Connell. In short, there is to be found an attitude towards the past which is discernibly different from the 'practical' attitude; and since this attitude is characteristic (though, of course,

[1] Compare Maitland's attitude to a legal document with that of the practising lawyer.

with some qualifications) of those whom we are accustomed to call 'historians' because of their sustained and exclusive interest in the past, its counterpart may be called the specifically 'historical' past. And further, on this reading of the situation, statements in the practical idiom about the past must be recognized, not as 'untrue' statements (because there is nothing to exclude them from being true within their own universe of discourse: if anyone died 'accidentally', William the Conqueror certainly did; and, so far as Charles V's policy was concerned, the Pope *did* intervene), but merely as 'non-historical' statements about the past.

This distinction between the 'practical' and the 'historical' past may be re-enforced by a further observation. The attention of the practical man is directed to the past by the miscellany of present happenings which, on account of his current interests, ambitions and directions of activity, are important to him, or by the present happenings which chance puts in his way or in which the vicissitudes of his life happen to involve him. That is to say, the materials of which he may ask the question, What evidence does it supply about the past? come to him either by chance or in an uncriticized choice. In short, his evidence, what he begins with, is something he merely accepts from the happenings around him; he neither looks for it, nor rejects anything that is offered. But with the historian this is not so. His inquiry into the past is not determined by chance encounters with current happenings. He collects for himself a world of present experiences (documents etc.), which is determined by considerations of appropriateness and completeness. It is from *this* world of present experiences that the 'historical' past springs.

In this reading of it, then, the activity of 'the historian' may be said (in virtue of its emancipation from a practical interest in the past) to represent an interest in past events for their own sake, or in respect of their independence of subsequent or present events. In short, it may be recognized as what I have called, in a general sense, a 'scientific' attitude towards the past. And on this account we are not surprised to observe that what, generally speaking, may be called a 'scientific' attitude towards the world, and an 'historical' attitude towards the past, have emerged together, and with some interdependence, in modern Europe. For, the specification of the activity of being a 'scientist' and the specification of the activity of being an 'historian' were both achieved in a process of emancipation from the primordial and once almost exclusive practical attitude of mankind. Nor, again, is it surprising that, for example, an inquiry into the stars emancipated from a practical interest and partnered by statements about them in the 'scientific' idiom and not the practical idiom,[1] should have appeared somewhat in advance of a similar emancipation in respect of inquiry into the past. The past choices and actions of mankind are so supremely eligible to be regarded and spoken about as if they were present, and the past is so important a component in practical activity, that to free oneself from this attitude must be recognized as an immensely difficult achievement – far more difficult than the parallel achievements of not *always* understanding the world before us only in relation to our current desires and enterprises.

Nevertheless, the observation of this general affinity between a 'scientific' attitude towards the world and an 'historical' attitude towards the past has been an occasion of stumbling. It provoked a disposition to think it proper that wherever the activity of being a scientist led (as that activity became more narrowly specified), the activity of being an historian should follow. And, in particular, the concern of the scientist with general causes and with necessary and sufficient conditions was taken as a model which 'the historian' should follow as best he could. What was forgotten was that the condition of these concerns of the 'scientist' was their application to hypothetical situations, a condition which should at once have been recognized as separating his activity from any that could be properly attributed to an 'historian'. However, the intoxication of the historian with the more specific (as distinct from the general) concerns of the scientist, was short lived; it lasted little more than a hundred years. And, paradoxically, it must be regarded as a belated intrusion of a

---

[1] By a 'scientific' inquiry into the stars I do not, of course, mean either an inquiry unprovoked by a desire for useful information (in connection with navigation, for example), or an inquiry by its character excluded from providing such information; I mean an inquiry in which the stars are not regarded (as they once were) as interesting on account of their power to determine or reveal human destiny. Indeed, an attitude towards the stars in which they are understood in respect of their independence of ourselves is a condition of any inquiry which could produce useful information (e.g. in navigation).

practical attitude into an activity which was already in process of specifying itself by means of an emancipation from this interest. For the enterprise of distinguishing general causes in respect of past events is now to be recognized as an attempt to assimilate once more (but in a new and apparently more profitable manner) the past to the present and the future, an attempt to make the past speak to the present, and consequently as a relapse in the direction of practice.

In the 'historian's' understanding of events, just as none is 'accidental', so none is 'necessary' or 'inevitable'. What we can observe him doing in his characteristic inquiries and utterances is, not extricating general causes or necessary and sufficient conditions, but setting before us the events (in so far as they can be ascertained) which mediate one circumstance to another. A scientist may detect a set of conditions which compose the necessary and sufficient conditions of a hypothetical situation denoted by the expression 'combustion' or 'oxidation'; when these are present, and nothing else is present to hinder their operation, combustion takes place. But 'the historian', although he sometimes writes of the outbreak of war as a 'conflagration', nevertheless leaves us in no doubt that he knows of no set of conditions which may properly be called the necessary and sufficient conditions of war. He knows only a set of happenings which, when fully set out, make the outbreak of *this* war seem neither an 'accident', nor a 'miracle', nor a necessary event, but merely an intelligible occurrence. This, for example, is what de Tocqueville does in *L'Ancien Régime*: the French Revolution is come upon, and its character is exhibited, not as the necessary and inevitable consequence of preceding events, but as an intelligible convergence of human choices and actions.

Or, consider this passage from Maitland:

The theory that land in the last resort is held of the King becomes the theory of our law at the Norman Conquest. It is assumed in Doomsday Book . . . quietly assumed as the basis of the survey. On the other hand we can say with certainty that before the Conquest this was not the theory of English law. Towards such a theory English law had been tending for a long while past, very possibly the time was fast approaching when the logic of the facts

would have generated this idea; the facts, the actual legal relationships, were such that the wide principle 'all land held in the last
resort of the King' would not greatly disturb them. Still this principle had not been evolved. It came to us from abroad; but it
came in the guise of a quiet assumption; no law forced it upon the
conquered country; no law was necessary; in Normandy lands
were held of the Duke, the Duke again held of the King; of
course it was the same in England; no other system was conceivable. The process of confiscation gave the Conqueror abun-
dant opportunity for making the theory true in fact; the followers
whom he rewarded with forfeited lands would of course hold of
him; the great English landowners, whose lands were restored to
them, would of course hold of him. As to the smaller people, when
looked at from a point of view natural to a Norman, they were
already tenants of the great people, and when the great people forfeited their rights, there was but a change of lords. This assumption was sometimes true enough, perhaps in other cases quite false;
in many cases it would seem but the introduction of a new and
simpler terminology; he who formerly was a *landowner* personally
bound to a lord, became a land tenant holding land of a lord.
There was no legislation, and I believe no chronicler refers to the
introduction of this new theory. As to the later lawyers, Glanvil
and Bracton, they never put it into words. They never state as a
noteworthy fact that all land is held of the King: *of course* it is.

Here what is being disclosed is a process of change. Maitland is not
concerned with general causes or with necessary and sufficient conditions. He shows us a happening (in this case, a manner of thinking
about land); and in order to make it intelligible he shows us how
events converged to provoke this happening.

Briefly, then, and without supposing it to be the last word on this
difficult subject, it seems that there is an attitude towards the past,
which has emerged gradually and in the face of many hindrances, in
which past events are understood as 'facts' and not mere 'images',
are understood in respect of their independence of subsequent events
or present circumstances or desires, and are understood as having no
necessary and sufficient conditions. That is, there is an attitude

towards the past, which provokes a specific kind of inquiry and utterance, but is neither a practical, nor a scientific, nor a contemplative attitude. There may be few inquirers into the past who persevere in this attitude without any relapse into other attitudes; but when we find this attitude adhered to consistently we recognize it as a noteworthy achievement. And the propriety of denoting it as a specifically 'historical' attitude rests upon two observations. First, although this attitude is not *always* exhibited in the inquiries and utterances of writers we are accustomed to call 'historians', it is exhibited *only* by such writers. And secondly, the activity of being an historian is not a gift bestowed suddenly upon the human race, but an achievement. It has emerged gradually from a miscellany of activities in which present events are understood as evidence for past happenings; and what seems to have been thrown up in this process of specification is an attitude of the kind I have described.

Nevertheless, it must be acknowledged that it imparts to the past, and so to the world, a peculiarly tentative and intermediate kind of intelligibility, and we may find ourselves provoked to look beyond it. It exhibits an elementary 'scientific' character, and thus often seems to point to a more comprehensively 'scientific' understanding of the world in which past events are recognized as examples of general laws. But while the pursuit of this more strictly 'scientific' understanding is enticing, and might (for a while) divert attention from what we now recognize as the enterprise in 'historical' understanding, the difficulties it would encounter (both in making its conceptual structure coherent and in the acquisition of appropriate information) would be great; and it is not easy to see how (even if it achieved conclusions of some sort) the one could ever be shown to supersede the other.

7

My contention has been that, in current reflection, the enterprise of specifying more exactly the character of 'history' has taken the course of excluding 'the historian' from certain kinds of inquiry and certain kinds of utterance, but that, in default of a concerted understanding of what at present it is to be an historian, we are unable to judge the cogency of these exclusions or the appropriateness of the reasoning with which each is supported. And, whatever the defects of the view of the activity of an historian I have put before you, it at least has the merit of allowing us to do what we were not able to do before. (Whether it enables us to do it correctly is, of course, another matter.) For it now appears that most, if not all, the exclusions which current reflection has suggested are designed to insulate the activity of 'the historian' more conclusively from what I have called a 'practical' attitude towards past events; indeed, this has been the effect of nearly all the technical achievements of historiography during the last two hundred years. And because, in the piecemeal method of determining the character of 'historical' inquiry, this has been lost sight of (or has never properly appeared), the exclusions have often been imperfectly specified and have often been supported by irrelevant reasoning.

For example, the suspicion we have of the notion of historical inquiry as an inquiry into 'origins' turns out to be a proper suspicion, but not for the reasons usually given. 'The historian' is disposed to decline the search for 'origins', not because the expression 'origin' is ambiguous (opening the door to a confusion between a 'cause' and a 'beginning'), or because 'origins' are beyond the reach of discovery, or because they are of insignificant interest, but because to inquire into 'origins' is to read the past backwards and thus assimilate it to subsequent or present events. It is an inquiry which looks to the past to supply information about the 'cause' or the 'beginning' of an already specified situation. And governed by this restricted purpose, it recognizes the past only in so far as it is represented in this situation, and imposes upon past events an arbitrary teleological structure. It is, for example, the practising lawyer, and not Maitland, who is disposed to regard inquiry into the past as a search for 'origins'. In short, such expressions as 'the origins of the French Revolution', 'the origins of Christianity', or 'the origins of the Tory Party' denote a backward reading of the past and the incursion of a practical attitude into what purports to be an 'historical' inquiry. Instead of provoking the inquirer to discover the manner in which one concrete situation is mediated into another, it provokes him merely to an abstract view of the past, the counterpart of the abstraction he has chosen to investigate.

Further, we have been warned to be sceptical about the possibility of genuine historical inquiry into the events of the recent past; and we have been warned of the qualified 'historical' character that we should expect of 'official' inquiries into the past. Here also, the view of 'history' I have suggested reinforces these warnings; indeed it extends their scope. But at the same time it transforms, rather than merely confirms, the reasoning with which they are usually supported. A variety of reasons is given for believing that inquiring into the recent past, and 'official' inquiry into the past, cannot be expected to achieve the status of 'historical' investigation. It is said that recent events are particularly difficult to get into focus, that the survival of prejudice hinders detachment and that the evidence to be mastered is at once vast in bulk and at the same time often frustratingly incomplete. And it is said that 'official' inquiring into the past is liable to be qualified by the presence of interests other than that of the discovery of the 'truth'. And all this is well observed. But the real ground of our scepticism is the observation that the past always comes to us, in the first place, in the idiom of practice and has to be translated into the idiom of 'history', and that it is specially difficult for 'the historian' to perform his task of translation when change of circumstances, the passage of time, or the intrusion of indifference has done little or nothing to assist him. Just as it is easier to 'contemplate' an object which uselessness and irrelevance to current enterprises insulates and puts a frame round, and just as it is easier to see the joke when it is not against oneself, so it will be easier (other things being equal) to make 'history' out of a past which does not positively provoke a non-historical attitude.

Moreover, this reading of the situation not only puts our scepticism upon firmer ground; it also enlarges its scope in two directions. First, it becomes clear that a wide sympathy for all the persons and interests engaged in a situation (that is to say, mere absence of bias) can never, by itself, turn a 'practical' account of the situation into an 'historical' account: we are dealing here with two discrete universes of discourse. And secondly, it appears that it is not only the recent past that it is difficult to see 'historically'; it is any period or situation that circumstantially provokes a practical interest. Not so long ago what are called 'the middle ages' of Europe were pre-eminent in provoking a practical attitude; it was exceedingly difficult not to assimilate the events of those times, in one way or another, to later times and to the present. Indeed, the expression 'middle ages' (like the expressions 'ancient', 'modern', 'renaissance', 'enlightened', 'gothic', etc.) began life as 'practical' not 'historical' expressions, and have only recently begun to acquire a limited 'historical' usefulness.[1] The study of the middle ages began under the shadow of the political destruction of the institutions of feudal society, and it was a long time before it escaped from this shadow. And there is much to be said for the belief that the seventeenth century past of England, and perhaps the Norman past of Ireland, are, at the present time, less easy for us to insulate from a practical (political or religious) attitude, and more difficult for us to view 'historically', than almost any other period of our past. An 'historical' attitude towards the Duke of Alva is, even now, difficult to achieve in Belgium; and it is still not easy for Spanish writers to translate the Iberian civilization of the Moors into the idiom of 'history'; that is to say, not to write about it as if it were an intrusion, illegitimate and regrettable. In short, when the true ground of the difficulty of writing near-contemporary 'history' is made to appear, it reveals itself as the ground of a much wider field of difficulties in the 'historical' investigation of the past.[2]

But the recommendation to the historian to exclude moral judgment (not, of course, the description of conduct in, generally speaking,

---

[1] It is worth recalling Huisinga's observation that these and similar expressions (e.g. 'Carolingian', 'feudal', 'christian', 'humanist') in historical writing are not to be regarded as hypotheses to be proved or foundations upon which large structures may be built, but as terms to be used lightly for whatever particle of intelligibility or illumination they may contain.

[2] 'The fact that the political struggles, so to call them, of modern history being part of the same in which we are ourselves engaged, affects the value of the history both ways. It increases our concern, while at the same time it blinds and distorts our view. To what an extent it is likely to do this latter may be concluded from the fact that, even as regards ancient history and times long past, if there is any resemblance between the politics then and now, we seem scarcely able to look fairly at them. A certain degree of remoteness, then, in the objects of history is desirable, though not always effective against prejudice similar to our prejudice now, and quite necessary against the actual mixture of our present prejudiced views of things with the history: we want it for every reason to stand well off from us.' John Grote, in *Cambridge Essays*, 1856, p. 111.

moral terms) from his utterance affords the best example both of
the usefulness and the defects of our current manner of specifying
the activity of 'the historian'. On the view of the activity I have
suggested, the exclusion of expressions of moral approval and condemnation and of expressions which purport to determine the moral
value of conduct in the past, is confirmed; but the reasoning with
which this exclusion is usually supported is seen to be, for the most
part, misconceived or irrelevant. Various reasons are given. We are
told that the moral assessment of past conduct involves the application either of absolute moral standards (about which nevertheless
there is no agreement), or of the standards current when and where
the actions were performed (and in this case the inquirer is merely
concerned to elicit what a moralist of the time *would* have said;
whereas he would be much better employed in eliciting what was in
fact said, and thus make his inquiry a 'history' of moral opinions), or
of the standards of some other place and time, the present time, for
example (and 'historically' there seems no more reason to choose one
time and place as our point of reference rather than another, and the
whole activity is revealed as arbitrary and redundant). And we are
told, further, that since the moral goodness and badness of conduct
relates to the motives of actions and since motives are always hidden
in the recesses of the soul, evidence will always be lacking to pronounce moral judgments of this sort about either past or present
conduct. But this argument would only exclude moral imputations,
not moral appraisals, from the writings of 'the historian'; whereas
the intention was to exclude both. The truth is, however, that the
ground for excluding moral judgment from 'historical' inquiry and
utterance is not the difficulty of agreeing upon a standard to apply,
nor the alleged absence of evidence, but the observation that to pronounce upon the moral value of conduct, and the imposition of a
moral structure upon the past, represents the incursion of a practical
interest into the investigation of the past. And, as we have seen, when
this interest intrudes there is room for no other. The investigator of
the past who appears as an advocate in the cause of good behaviour
succeeds only in setting before us a practical past. When we judge
the *moral* value of past conduct, just as when we judge the value or
usefulness of past conduct from any other point of view ('useless'

wars, for example), we are treating it as if it were present; and no other reason than this need be given for the exclusion of moral judgment from the activity of 'the historian'. In short, to inquire into the moral value of past conduct is to relapse into a practical attitude towards the past, and if relapse were allowed at this point, it could not properly be disallowed at any other.

It seems, then, that our current manner of specifying the activity of 'the historian' has resulted in a number of observations which, taken together, have gone some way towards delineating the activity. But when the logic of these separate observations is considered, it not only provides a means of confirming or rejecting them, but it also suggests modifications and extensions which put our specification on firmer ground.

8

There are many conclusions which seem to follow from this reading of the activity of being an historian. It would appear that the task of 'the historian' cannot properly be described as that of recalling or of re-enacting the past; that, in an important sense, an 'historical' event is something that never happened and an 'historical' action something never performed; that an 'historical' character is one that never lived. The idiom of happening is always that of practice, and the record of happening is usually in the idiom of practice; and 'practice' and 'history' are two logically distinct universes of discourse. The task of 'the historian' is, thus, to create by a process of translation; to understand past conduct and happening in a manner in which they were never understood at the time; to translate action and event from their practical idiom into an historical idiom. But, instead of pursuing any of these conclusions of detail, I wish to end with a more general observation on the present difficulty of being an historian.

We have come to believe that (in the same manner as other activities) the activity of being an historian has now achieved some measure of specification; and perhaps this is so. But while we have learnt to recognize some of the enemies of the 'historical' attitude towards the past, we have still far to go in defeating them. If I interpret correctly current reflection on this subject, we consider ourselves (in an intellectual effort spread over nearly a hundred years) to have struggled out of the *cul de sac* into which historical inquiry wandered under the guidance of 'science'; and we have come to recognize what I have called the 'practical' attitude to the past as the chief undefeated enemy of 'history' (although there is still both hesitation and confusion about this). But we recognize, also, that it is a very difficult enemy to defeat. In this engagement, one of our difficulties springs from our perception that a practical attitude towards the past, and the use of a practical idiom in speaking about the past, certainly cannot be dismissed as merely illegitimate. Who are we to forbid it? On what grounds should the primordial activity of making ourselves at home in the world by assimilating *our* past to *our* present be proscribed? This, perhaps, is no great difficulty; it is surmounted when we recognize that the practical past (including moral judgments about past conduct) is not the enemy of mankind, but only the enemy of 'the historian'. But we are left with the more serious difficulty that springs from the fact that the practical idiom has imposed itself for so long upon *all* inquiry into the past that its hold cannot readily be loosened, and the fact that we live in an intellectual world which, because of its addiction to 'practice', is notably hostile to 'history'.

Nor should we encourage ourselves with false hopes; with the belief that an 'historical' attitude towards the past is now more common than it used to be, the belief (as it is said) that this is in some relevant sense a peculiarly historically-minded age. This, I think, is an illusion. Certainly the disposition of our time is to regard the events that take place before our eyes as evidence for past events, to understand them as 'effects' and to turn to the past to discover their 'causes'; but this disposition is joined with another no less strong, the propensity to assimilate the past to the present. Our predominant interest is not in 'history' but only in retrospective politics. And the past is now more than ever a field in which we exercise our moral and political opinions, like whippets in a meadow on Sunday afternoon. And even our theorists (from whom something better might have been expected) are bent rather upon elucidating the tie between past and present than upon pointing out that what matters is the *kind* of 'present', and that it is precisely the task of 'the historian' to loosen the tie between the past and the 'practical' present.

The 'historian' adores the past; but the world today has perhaps less place for those who love the past than ever before. Indeed, it is determined not to allow events to remove themselves securely into the past; it is determined to keep them alive by a process of artificial respiration or (if need be) to recall them from the dead so that they may deliver their messages. For it wishes only to learn from the past and it constructs a 'living past' which repeats with spurious authority the utterances put into its mouth. But to the 'historian' this is a piece of obscene necromancy: the past he adores is dead. The world has neither love nor respect for what is dead, wishing only to recall it to life again. It deals with the past as with a man, expecting it to talk sense and have something to say apposite to its plebeian 'causes' and engagements. But for the 'historian', for whom the past is dead and irreproachable, the past is feminine. He loves it as a mistress of whom he never tires and whom he never expects to talk sense. Once it was religion which stood in the way of the appearance of the 'historical' past; now it is politics; but always it is this practical disposition.

'History', then, is the product of a severe and sophisticated manner of thinking about the world which has recently emerged from the naïve interest in what surrounds us on account of its intimations of what is no longer present. It represents neither an aesthetic enjoyment, nor a 'scientific' recognition, nor a practical understanding. Like these, it is a dream; but it is a dream of another sort. There is a past, that of legend and saga, which is a drama from which all that is casual, secondary and unresolved has been excluded; it has a clear outline, a unity of feeling and in it everything is exact except place and time. There is a past in which contingencies have been resolved by being recognized as products of necessary and sufficient conditions and as examples of the operation of general laws, And there is a past in which every component is known and is intelligible in respect of its relation to a favoured present. But the 'historical' past is of another sort than these. It is a complicated world, without unity of feeling or clear outline: in it events have no over-all pattern or purpose, lead nowhere, point to no favoured condition of the world and support no practical conclusions. It is a world composed wholly of contingencies and in which contingencies are intelligible, not because they have been resolved, but on account of the circumstantial relations which have been established between them: the historian's concern is not with causes but with occasions. It is a picture drawn on many different scales, and each genuine piece of historical writing has a scale of its own and is to be recognized as an independent example of historical thinking. The activity of being an historian is not that of contributing to the elucidation of a single ideal coherence of events which may be called 'true' to the exclusion of all others; it is an activity in which a writer, concerned with the past for its own sake and working to a chosen scale, elicits a coherence in a group of contingencies of similar magnitudes. And if in so new and so delicate an enterprise he finds himself tempted into making concessions to the idiom of legend, that perhaps is less damaging than other divergencies.

1955

On being Conservative

The common belief that it is impossible (or, if not impossible, then so unpromising as to be not worth while attempting) to elicit explanatory general principles from what is recognized to be conservative conduct is not one that I share. It may be true that conservative conduct does not readily provoke articulation in the idiom of general ideas, and that consequently there has been a certain reluctance to undertake this kind of elucidation; but it is not to be presumed that conservative conduct is less eligible than any other for this sort oi interpretation, for what it is worth. Nevertheless, this is not the enterprise I propose to engage in here. My theme is not a creed or a doctrine, but a disposition. To be conservative is to be disposed to think and behave in certain manners; it is to prefer certain kinds of conduct and certain conditions of human circumstances to others; it is to be disposed to make certain kinds of choices. And my design here is to construe this disposition as it appears in contemporary character, rather than to transpose it into the idiom of general principles.

The general characteristics of this disposition are not difficult to discern, although they have often been mistaken. They centre upon a propensity to use and to enjoy what is available rather than to wish for or to look for something else; to delight in what is present rather than what was or what may be. Reflection may bring to light an appropriate gratefulness for what is available, and consequently the acknowledgment of a gift or an inheritance from the past; but there is no mere idolizing of what is past and gone. What is esteemed is the present; and it is esteemed not on account of its connections with a remote antiquity, nor because it is recognized to be more admirable than any possible alternative, but on account of its familiarity: not, *Verweile doch, du bist so schön*, but, *Stay with me because I am attached to you.*

If the present is arid, offering little or nothing to be used or enjoyed, then this inclination will be weak or absent; if the present is remarkably unsettled, it will display itself in a search for a firmer foothold and consequently in a recourse to and an exploration of the past; but it asserts itself characteristically when there is much to be enjoyed, and it will be strongest when this is combined with evident risk of loss. In short, it is a disposition appropriate to a man who is acutely aware of having something to lose which he has learned to care for; a man in some degree rich in opportunities for enjoyment, but not so rich that he can afford to be indifferent to loss. It will appear more naturally in the old than in the young, not because the old are more sensitive to loss but because they are apt to be more fully aware of the resources of their world and therefore less likely to find them inadequate. In some people this disposition is weak merely because they are ignorant of what their world has to offer them: the present appears to them only as a residue of inopportunities.

To be conservative, then, is to prefer the familiar to the unknown, to prefer the tried to the untried, fact to mystery, the actual to the possible, the limited to the unbounded, the near to the distant, the sufficient to the superabundant, the convenient to the perfect, present laughter to utopian bliss. Familiar relationships and loyalties will be preferred to the allure of more profitable attachments; to acquire and to enlarge will be less important than to keep, to cultivate and to enjoy; the grief of loss will be more acute than the excitement of novelty or promise. It is to be equal to one's own fortune, to live at the level of one's own means, to be content with the want of greater perfection which belongs alike to oneself and one's circumstances. With some people this is itself a choice; in others it is a disposition which appears, frequently or less frequently, in their preferences and aversions, and is not itself chosen or specifically cultivated.

Now, all this is represented in a certain attitude towards change and innovation; change denoting alterations we have to suffer and innovation those we design and execute.

Changes are circumstances to which we have to accommodate ourselves, and the disposition to be conservative is both the emblem of our difficulty in doing so and our resort in the attempts we make to do so. Changes are without effect only upon those who notice nothing, who are ignorant of what they possess and apathetic to their circumstances; and they can be welcomed indiscriminately only by those who esteem nothing, whose attachments are fleeting and who are strangers to love and affection. The conservative disposition provokes neither of these conditions: the inclination to enjoy what is present and available is the opposite of ignorance and apathy and it breeds attachment and affection. Consequently, it is averse from change, which appears always, in the first place, as deprivation. A storm which sweeps away a copse and transforms a favourite view, the death of friends, the sleep of friendship, the desuetude of customs of behaviour, the retirement of a favourite clown, involuntary exile, reversals of fortune, the loss of abilities enjoyed and their replacement by others – these are changes, none perhaps without its compensations, which the man of conservative temperament unavoidably regrets. But he has difficulty in reconciling himself to them, not because what he has lost in them was intrinsically better than any alternative might have been or was incapable of improvement, nor because what takes its place is inherently incapable of being enjoyed, but because what he has lost was something he actually enjoyed and had learned how to enjoy and what takes its place is something to which he has acquired no attachment. Consequently, he will find small and slow changes more tolerable than large and sudden; and he will value highly every appearance of continuity. Some changes, indeed, will present no difficulty; but, again, this is not because they are manifest improvements but merely because they are easily assimilated: the changes of the seasons are mediated by their recurrence and the growing up of children by its continuousness. And, in general, he will accommodate himself more readily to changes which do not offend expectation than to the destruction of what seems to have no ground of dissolution within itself.

Moreover, to be conservative is not merely to be averse from change (which may be an idiosyncrasy); it is also a manner of accommodating ourselves to changes, an activity imposed upon all men. For, change is a threat to identity, and every change is an emblem of extinction. But a man's identity (or that of a community) is nothing more than an unbroken rehearsal of contingencies, each at the mercy of circumstance and each significant in proportion to its familiarity. It is not a fortress into which we may retire, and the only means we have of defending it (that is, ourselves) against the hostile forces of change is in the open field of our experience; by throwing our weight upon the foot which for the time being is most firmly placed, by cleaving to whatever familiarities are not immediately threatened and thus assimilating what is new without becoming unrecognizable to ourselves. The Masai, when they were moved from their old country to the present Masai reserve in Kenya, took with them the names of their hills and plains and rivers and gave them to the hills and plains and rivers of the new country. And it is by some such subterfuge of conservatism that every man or people compelled to suffer a notable change avoids the shame of extinction.

Changes, then, have to be suffered; and a man of conservative temperament (that is, one strongly disposed to preserve his identity) cannot be indifferent to them. In the main, he judges them by the disturbance they entail and, like everyone else, deploys his resources to meet them. The idea of innovation, on the other hand, is improvement. Nevertheless, a man of this temperament will not himself be an ardent innovator. In the first place, he is not inclined to think that nothing is happening unless great changes are afoot and therefore he is not worried by the absence of innovation: the use and enjoyment of things as they are occupies most of his attention. Further, he is aware that not all innovation is, in fact, improvement; and he will think that to innovate without improving is either designed or inadvertent folly. Moreover, even when an innovation commends itself as a convincing improvement, he will look twice at its claims before accepting them. From his point of view, because every improvement involves change, the disruption entailed has always to be set against the benefit anticipated. But when he has satisfied himself about this, there will be other considerations to be taken into the account. Innovating is always an equivocal enterprise, in which gain and loss (even excluding the loss of familiarity) are so closely interwoven that it is exceedingly difficult to forecast the final up-shot: there is no such thing as an unqualified improvement. For, innovating is an activity which generates not only the 'improvement' sought, but a new and complex situation of which this is only one of the components. The total change is always more extensive than the change designed; and the whole of what is entailed can neither be foreseen nor circumscribed. Thus, whenever there is innovation there is the certainty that the change will be greater than was intended, that there will be loss as well as gain and that the loss and the gain will not be equally distributed among the people affected; there is the chance that the benefits derived will be greater than those which were designed; and there is the risk that they will be off-set by changes for the worse.

From all this the man of conservative temperament draws some appropriate conclusions. First, innovation entails certain loss and possible gain, therefore, the onus of proof, to show that the proposed change may be expected to be on the whole beneficial, rests with the would-be innovator. Secondly, he believes that the more closely an innovation resembles growth (that is, the more clearly it is intimated in and not merely imposed upon the situation) the less likely it is to result in a preponderance of loss. Thirdly, he thinks that an innovation which is a response to some specific defect, one designed to redress some specific disequilibrium, is more desirable than one which springs from a notion of a generally improved condition of human circumstances, and is far more desirable than one generated by a vision of perfection. Consequently, he prefers small and limited innovations to large and indefinite. Fourthly, he favours a slow rather than a rapid pace, and pauses to observe current consequences and make appropriate adjustments. And lastly, he believes the occasion to be important; and, other things being equal, he considers the most favourable occasion for innovation to be when the projected change is most likely to be limited to what is intended and least likely to be corrupted by undesired and unmanageable consequences

The disposition to be conservative is, then, warm and positive in respect of enjoyment, and correspondingly cool and critical in respect of change and innovation: these two inclinations support and elucidate one another. The man of conservative temperament believes that a known good is not lightly to be surrendered for an unknown better. He is not in love with what is dangerous and difficult; he is unadventurous; he has no impulse to sail uncharted seas; for him there is no magic in being lost, bewildered or shipwrecked. If he is forced to navigate the unknown, he sees virtue in heaving the lead every inch of the way. What others plausibly identify as timidity, he recognizes in himself as rational prudence; what others interpret as inactivity, he recognizes as a disposition to enjoy rather than to exploit. He is cautious, and he is disposed to indicate his assent or dissent, not in absolute, but in graduated terms. He eyes the situation in terms of its propensity to disrupt the familiarity of the features of his world.

2

It is commonly believed that this conservative disposition is pretty deeply rooted in what is called 'human nature'. Change is tiring, innovation calls for effort, and human beings (it is said) are more apt to be lazy than energetic. If they have found a not unsatisfactory way of getting along in the world, they are not disposed to go looking for trouble. They are naturally apprehensive of the unknown and prefer safety to danger. They are reluctant innovators, and they accept change not because they like it but (as Rochefoucauld says they accept death) because it is inescapable. Change generates sadness rather than exhilaration: heaven is the dream of a changeless no less than of a perfect world. Of course, those who read 'human nature' in this way agree that this disposition does not stand alone; they merely contend that it is an exceedingly strong, perhaps the strongest, of human propensities. And, so far as it goes, there is something to be said for this belief: human circumstances would certainly be very different from what they are if there were not a large ingredient of conservatism in human preferences. Primitive peoples are said to cling to what is familiar and to be averse from change; ancient myth is full of warnings against innovation; our folklore and proverbial wisdom about the conduct of life abounds in conservative precepts; and how many tears are shed by children in their unwilling accommodation to change. Indeed, wherever a firm identity has been achieved, and wherever identity is felt to be precariously balanced, a conservative disposition is likely to prevail. On the other hand, the disposition of adolescence is often predominantly adventurous and experimental: when we are young, nothing seems more desirable than to take a chance; *pas de risque, pas de plaisir*. And while some peoples, over long stretches of time, appear successfully to have avoided change, the history of others displays periods of intense and intrepid innovation. There is, indeed, not much profit to be had from general speculation about 'human nature', which is no steadier than anything else in our acquaintance. What is more to the point is to consider current human nature, to consider ourselves.

With us, I think, the disposition to be conservative is far from being notably strong. Indeed, if he were to judge by our conduct during the last five centuries or so, an unprejudiced stranger might plausibly suppose us to be in love with change, to have an appetite only for innovation and to be either so out of sympathy with ourselves or so careless of our identity as not to be disposed to give it any consideration. In general, the fascination of what is new is felt far more keenly than the comfort of what is familiar. We are disposed to think that nothing important is happening unless great innovations are afoot, and that what is not being improved must be deteriorating. There is a positive prejudice in favour of the yet untried. We readily presume that all change is, somehow, for the better, and we are easily persuaded that all the consequences of our innovating activity are either themselves improvements or at least a reasonable price to pay for getting what we want. While the conservative, if he were forced to gamble, would bet on the field, we are disposed to back our individual fancies with little calculation and no apprehension of loss. We are acquisitive to the point of greed; ready to drop the bone we have for its reflection magnified in the mirror of the future. Nothing is made to outlast probable improvement in a world where everything is undergoing incessant improvement: the expectation of life of everything except human beings themselves continuously declines. Pieties are fleeting, loyalties evanescent, and the pace of change warns us against too deep attachments. We are willing to try anything once, regardless of the consequences. One activity vies with another in being 'up-to-date': discarded motor-cars and television sets have their counterparts in discarded moral and religious beliefs: the eye is ever on the new model. To see is to imagine what might be in the place of what is; to touch is to transform. Whatever the shape or quality of the world, it is not for long as we want it. And those in the van of movement infect those behind with their energy and enterprise. *Omnes eodem cogemur*: when we are no longer light-footed we find a place for ourselves in the band.[1]

Of course, our character has other ingredients besides this lust for change (we are not devoid of the impulse to cherish and preserve), but there can be little doubt about its pre-eminence. And, in these circumstances, it seems appropriate that a conservative disposition should appear, not as an intelligible (or even plausible) alternative to our mainly 'progressive' habit of mind, but either as an unfortunate hindrance to the movement afoot, or as the custodian of the museum in which quaint examples of superseded achievement are preserved for children to gape at, and as the guardian of what from time to time is considered not yet ripe for destruction, which we call (ironically enough) the amenities of life.

Here our account of the disposition to be conservative and its current fortunes might be expected to end, with the man in whom this disposition is strong last seen swimming against the tide, disregarded not because what he has to say is necessarily false but because it has become irrelevant; outmanoeuvred, not on account of any intrinsic demerit but merely by the flow of circumstance; a faded, timid, nostalgic character, provoking pity as an outcast and contempt as a reactionary. Nevertheless, I think there is something more to be said. Even in these circumstances, when a conservative disposition in respect of things in general is unmistakably at a discount, there are occasions when this disposition remains not only appropriate, but supremely so; and there are connections in which we are unavoidably disposed in a conservative direction.

In the first place, there is a certain kind of activity (not yet extinct) which can be engaged in only in virtue of a disposition to be conservative, namely, activities where what is sought is present enjoyment and not a profit, a reward, a prize or a result in addition to the experience itself. And when these activities are recognized as the emblems

[1] 'Which of us,' asks a contemporary (not without some equivocation), 'would not settle, at whatever cost in nervous anxiety, for a febrile and creative rather than a static society?'

of this disposition, to be conservative is disclosed, not as prejudiced hostility to a 'progressive' attitude capable of embracing the whole range of human conduct, but as a disposition exclusively appropriate in a large and significant field of human activity. And the man in whom this disposition is pre-eminent appears as one who prefers to engage in activities where to be conservative is uniquely appropriate, and not as a man inclined to impose his conservatism indiscriminately upon all human activity. In short, if we find ourselves (as most of us do) inclined to reject conservatism as a disposition appropriate in respect of human conduct in general, there still remains a certain kind of human conduct for which this disposition is not merely appropriate but a necessary condition.

There are, of course, numerous human relationships in which a disposition to be conservative, a disposition merely to enjoy what they offer for its own sake, is not particularly appropriate: master and servant, owner and bailiff, buyer and seller, principal and agent. In these, each participant seeks some service or some recompense for service. A customer who finds a shopkeeper unable to supply his wants either persuades him to enlarge his stock or goes elsewhere; and a shopkeeper unable to meet the desires of a customer tries to impose upon him others which he can satisfy. A principal ill-served by his agent, looks for another. A servant ill-recompensed for his service, asks for a rise; and one dissatisfied with his conditions of work, seeks a change. In short, these are all relationships in which some result is sought; each party is concerned with the ability of the other to provide it. If what is sought is lacking, it is to be expected that the relationship will lapse or be terminated. To be conservative in such relationships, to enjoy what is present and available regardless of its failure to satisfy any want and merely because it has struck our fancy and become familiar, is conduct which discloses a *jusqu'-aubutiste* conservatism, an irrational inclination to refuse all relationships which call for the exercise of any other disposition. Though even these relationships seem to lack something appropriate to them when they are confined to a nexus of supply and demand and allow no room for the intrusion of the loyalties and attachments which spring from familiarity.

But there are relationships of another kind in which no result is

sought and which are engaged in for their own sake and enjoyed for
what they are and not for what they provide. This is so of friendship.
Here, attachment springs from an intimation of familiarity and sub-
sists in a mutual sharing of personalities. To go on changing one's
butcher until one gets the meat one likes, to go on educating one's
agent until he does what is required of him, is conduct not inappropriate to the relationship concerned; but to discard friends because
they do not behave as we expected and refuse to be educated to our
requirements is the conduct of a man who has altogether mistaken the
character of friendship. Friends are not concerned with what might
be made of one another, but only with the enjoyment of one another;
and the condition of this enjoyment is a ready acceptance of what is
and the absence of any desire to change or to improve. A friend is
not somebody one trusts to behave in a certain manner, who supplies
certain wants, who has certain useful abilities, who possesses certain
merely agreeable qualities, or who holds certain acceptable opinions;
he is somebody who engages the imagination, who excites contemplation, who provokes interest, sympathy, delight and loyalty simply
on account of the relationship entered into. One friend cannot
replace another; there is all the difference in the world between the
death of a friend and the retirement of one's tailor from business.
The relationship of friend to friend is dramatic, not utilitarian; the
tie is one of familiarity, not usefulness; the disposition engaged is
conservative, not 'progressive'. And what is true of friendship is not
less true of other experiences – of patriotism, for example, and of
conversation – each of which demands a conservative disposition as
a condition of its enjoyment.

But further, there are activities, not involving human relationships,
that may be engaged in, not for a prize, but for the enjoyment they
generate, and for which the only appropriate disposition is the disposition to be conservative. Consider fishing. If your project is
merely to catch fish it would be foolish to be unduly conservative.
You will seek out the best tackle, you will discard practices which
prove unsuccessful, you will not be bound by unprofitable attachments to particular localities, pieties will be fleeting, loyalties evanescent; you may even be wise to try anything once in the hope of
improvement. But fishing is an activity that may be engaged in, not

for the profit of a catch, but for its own sake; and the fisherman may return home in the evening not less content for being empty-handed. Where this is so, the activity has become a ritual and a conservative disposition is appropriate. Why worry about the best gear if you do not care whether or not you make a catch? What matters is the enjoyment of exercising skill (or, perhaps, merely passing the time),[1] and this is to be had with any tackle, so long as it is familiar and is not grotesquely inappropriate.

All activities, then, where what is sought is enjoyment springing, not from the success of the enterprise but from the familiarity of the engagement, are emblems of the disposition to be conservative. And there are many of them. Fox placed gambling among them when he said that it gave two supreme pleasures, the pleasure of winning and the pleasure of losing. Indeed, I can think of only one activity of this kind which seems to call for a disposition other than conservative: the love of fashion, that is, wanton delight in change for its own sake no matter what it generates.

But, besides the not inconsiderable class of activities which we can engage in only in virtue of a disposition to be conservative, there are occasions in the conduct of other activities when this is the most appropriate disposition; indeed there are few activites which do not, at some point or other, make a call upon it. Whenever stability is more profitable than improvement, whenever certainty is more valuable than speculation, whenever familiarity is more desirable than perfection, whenever agreed error is superior to controversial truth, whenever the disease is more sufferable than the cure, whenever the satisfaction of expectations is more important than the 'justice' of the expectations themselves, whenever a rule of some sort is better than the risk of having no rule at all, a disposition to be conservative will be more appropriate than any other; and on any reading of human conduct these cover a not negligible range of

---

[1] When Prince Wen Wang was on a tour of inspection in Tsang, he saw an old man fishing. But his fishing was not real fishing, for he did not fish in order to catch fish, but to amuse himself. So Wen Wang wished to employ him in the administration of government, but he feared his own ministers, uncles and brothers might object. On the other hand, if he let the old man go, he could not bear to think of the people being deprived of his influence. *Chuang Tzu.*

circumstances. Those who see the man of conservative disposition (even in what is vulgarly called a 'progressive' society) as a lonely swimmer battling against the overwhelming current of circumstance must be thought to have adjusted their binoculars to exclude a large field of human occasion.

In most activities not engaged in for their own sake a distinction appears, at a certain level of observation, between the project undertaken and the means employed, between the enterprise and the tools used for its achievement. This is not, of course, an absolute distinction; projects are often provoked and governed by the tools available, and on rarer occasions the tools are designed to fit a particular project. And what on one occasion is a project, on another is a tool. Moreover there is at least one significant exception: the activity of being a poet. It is, however, a relative distinction of some usefulness because it calls our attention to an appropriate difference of attitude towards the two components of the situation.

In general, it may be said that our disposition in respect of tools is appropriately more conservative than our attitude towards projects; or, in other words, tools are less subject to innovation than projects because, except on rare occasions, tools are not designed to fit a particular project and then thrown aside, they are designed to fit a whole class of projects. And this is intelligible because most tools call for skill in use and skill is inseparable from practice and familiarity: a skilled man, whether he is a sailor, a cook or an accountant, is a man familiar with a certain stock of tools. Indeed, a carpenter is usually more skilful in handling his own tools than in handling other examples of the kind of tools commonly used by carpenters; and the solicitor can use his own (annotated) copy of Pollock on *Partnership* or Jarman on *Wills* more readily than any other. Familiarity is the essence of tool using; and in so far as man is a tool using animal he is disposed to be conservative.

Many of the tools in common use have remained unchanged for generations; the design of others has undergone considerable modification; and our stock of tools is always being enlarged by new inventions and improved by new designs. Kitchens, factories, workshops, building sites and offices disclose a characteristic mixture of long-tried and newly invented equipment. But, be that how it may, when business of any kind is afoot, when a particular project has been engaged in – whether it is baking a pie or shoeing a horse, floating a loan or a company, selling fish or insurance to a customer, building a ship or a suit of clothes, sowing wheat or lifting potatoes, laying down port or putting up a barrage – we recognize it to be an occasion when it is particularly appropriate to be conservative about the tools we employ. If it is a large project, we put it in charge of a man who has the requisite knowledge, and we expect him to engage subordinates who know their own business and are skilled in the use of certain stocks of tools. At some point in this hierarchy of tool-users the suggestion may be made that in order to do this particular job an addition or modification is required in the available stock of tools. Such a suggestion is likely to come from somewhere about the middle of the hierarchy: we do not expect a designer to say 'I must go away and do some fundamental research which will take me five years before I can go on with the job' (his bag of tools is a body of knowledge and we expect him to have it handy and to know his way about it); and we do not expect the man at the bottom to have a stock of tools inadequate for the needs of his particular part. But even if such a suggestion is made and is followed up, it will not disrupt the appropriateness of a conservative disposition in respect of the whole stock of tools being used. Indeed, it is clear enough that no job would ever get done, no piece of business could ever be transacted if, on the occasion, our disposition in respect of our tools were not, generally speaking, conservative. And since doing business of one sort or another occupies most of our time and little can be done without tools of some kind, the disposition to be conservative occupies an unavoidably large place in our character.

The carpenter comes to do a job, perhaps one the exact like of which he has never before tackled; but he comes with his bag of familiar tools and his only chance of doing the job lies in the skill with which he uses what he has at his disposal. When the plumber goes to fetch his tools he would be away even longer than is usually the case if his purpose were to invent new or to improve old ones. Nobody questions the value of money in the market place. No business would ever get done if, before a pound of cheese were weighed or a pint of beer drawn, the relative usefulness of these particular scales of weight and measurement as compared with others were threshed out. The surgeon does not pause in the middle of an operation to redesign his instruments. The MCC does not authorize a new width of bat, a new weight of ball or a new length of wicket in the middle of a Test Match, or even in the middle of a cricket season. When your house is on fire you do not get in touch with a fire-prevention research station to design a new appliance; as Disraeli pointed out, unless you are a lunatic, you send for the parish fire-engine. A musician may improvise music, but he would think himself hardly done-by if, at the same time, he were expected to improvise an instrument. Indeed, when a particularly tricky job is to be done, the workman will often prefer to use a tool that he is thoroughly familiar with rather than another he has in his bag, of new design, but which he has not yet mastered the use of. No doubt there is a time and a place to be radical about such things, for promoting innovation and carrying out improvements in the tools we employ, but these are clearly occasions for the exercise of a conservative disposition.

Now, what is true about tools in general, as distinct from projects, is even more obviously true about a certain kind of tool in common use, namely, general rules of conduct. If the familiarity that springs from relative immunity from change is appropriate to hammers and pincers and to bats and balls, it is supremely appropriate, for example, to an office routine. Routines, no doubt, are susceptible of improvement; but the more familiar they become, the more useful they are. Not to have a conservative disposition in respect of a routine is obvious folly. Of course, exceptional occasions occur which may call for a dispensation; but an inclination to be conservative rather than reformist about a routine is unquestionably appropriate. Consider the conduct of a public meeting, the rules of debate in the House of Commons or the procedure of a court of law. The chief virtue of these arrangements is that they are fixed and familiar; they establish and satisfy certain expectations, they allow to be said in a convenient order whatever is relevant, they prevent extraneous collisions and they conserve human energy. They are typical tools – instruments eligible for use in a variety of different but similar jobs. They are the product of reflection and choice, there is nothing

sacrosanct about them, they are susceptible of change and improvement; but if our disposition in respect of them were not, generally
speaking, conservative, if we were disposed to argue about them and
change them on every occasion, they would rapidly lose their value.
And while there may be rare occasions when it is useful to suspend
them, it is pre-eminently appropriate that they should not be inno-
vated upon or improved while they are in operation. Or again, consider the rules of a game. These, also, are the product of reflection
and choice, and there are occasions when it is appropriate to recon-
sider them in the light of current experience; but it is inappropriate
to have anything but a conservative disposition towards them or to
consider putting them all together at one time into the melting-pot;
and it is supremely inappropriate to change or improve upon them
in the heat and confusion of play. Indeed, the more eager each side is
to win, the more valuable is an inflexible set of rules. Players in the
course of play may devise new tactics, they may improvise new
methods of attack and defence, they may do anything they choose
to defeat the expectations of their opponents, except invent new
rules. That is an activity to be indulged sparingly and then only in
the off-season.

There is much more that might be said about the relevance of the
disposition to be conservative and its appropriateness even in a
character, such as ours, chiefly disposed in the opposite direction. I
have said nothing of morals, nothing of religion; but perhaps I have
said enough to show that, even if to be conservative on all occasions
and in all connections is so remote from our habit of thought as to
be almost unintelligible, there are, nevertheless, few of our activities
which do not on all occasions call into partnership a disposition to
be conservative and on some occasions recognize it as the senior
partner; and there are some activities where it is properly master.

3

How, then, are we to construe the disposition to be conservative in
respect of politics? And in making this inquiry what I am interested
in is not merely the intelligibility of this disposition in any set of
circumstances, but its intelligibility in our own contemporary
circumstances.

Writers who have considered this question commonly direct our attention to beliefs about the world in general, about human beings in general, about associations in general and even about the universe; and they tell us that a conservative disposition in politics can be correctly construed only when we understand it as a reflection of certain beliefs of these kinds. It is said, for example, that conservatism in politics is the appropriate counterpart of a generally conservative disposition in respect of human conduct: to be reformist in business, in morals or in religion and to be conservative in politics is represented as being inconsistent. It is said that the conservative in politics is so by virtue of holding certain religious beliefs; a belief, for example, in a natural law to be gathered from human experience, and in a providential order reflecting a divine purpose in nature and in human history to which it is the duty of mankind to conform its conduct and departure from which spells injustice and calamity. Further, it is said that a disposition to be conservative in politics reflects what is called an 'organic' theory of human society; that it is tied up with a belief in the absolute value of human personality, and with a belief in a primordial propensity of human beings to sin. And the 'conservatism' of an Englishman has even been connected with Royalism and Anglicanism.

Now, setting aside the minor complaints one might be moved to make about this account of the situation, it seems to me to suffer from one large defect. It is true that many of these beliefs have been held by people disposed to be conservative in political activity, and it may be true that these people have also believed their disposition to be in some way confirmed by them, or even to be founded upon them; but, as I understand it, a disposition to be conservative in politics does not entail either that we should hold these beliefs to be true or even that we should suppose them to be true. Indeed, I do not think it is necessarily connected with any particular beliefs about the universe, about the world in general or about human conduct in general. What it is tied to is certain beliefs about the activity of governing and the instruments of government, and it is in terms of beliefs on these topics, and not on others, that it can be made to appear intelligible. And, to state my view briefly before elaborating it, what makes a conservative disposition in politics intelligible is nothing to do with a natural law or a providential order, nothing to do with morals or religion; it is the observation of our current manner of living combined with the belief (which from our point of view need be regarded as no more than an hypothesis) that governing is a specific and limited activity, namely the provision and custody of general rules of conduct, which are understood, not as plans for imposing substantive activities, but as instruments enabling people to pursue the activities of their own choice with the minimum frustration, and therefore something which it is appropriate to be conservative about.

Let us begin at what I believe to be the proper starting-place; not in the empyrean, but with ourselves as we have come to be. I and my neighbours, my associates, my compatriots, my friends, my enemies and those who I am indifferent about, are people engaged in a great variety of activities. We are apt to entertain a multiplicity of opinions on every conceivable subject and are disposed to change these beliefs as we grow tired of them or as they prove unserviceable. Each of us is pursuing a course of his own; and there is no project so unlikely that somebody will not be found to engage in it, no enterprise so foolish that somebody will not undertake it. There are those who spend their lives trying to sell copies of the Anglican Catechism to the Jews. And one half of the world is engaged in trying to make the other half want what it has hitherto never felt the lack of. We are all inclined to be passionate about our own concerns, whether it is making things or selling them, whether it is business or sport, religion or learning, poetry, drink or drugs. Each of us has preferences of his own. For some, the opportunities of making choices (which are numerous) are invitations readily accepted; others welcome them less eagerly or even find them burdensome. Some dream dreams of new and better worlds: others are more inclined to move in familiar paths or even to be idle. Some are apt to deplore the rapidity of change, others delight in it; all recognize it. At times we grow tired and fall asleep: it is a blessed relief to gaze in a shop window and see nothing we want; we are grateful for ugliness merely because it repels attention. But, for the most part, we pursue happiness by seeking the satisfaction of desires which spring from one another inexhaustably. We enter into relationships of interest and of emotion, of competition, partnership, guardianship, love, friendship, jealousy and hatred, some of which are more durable than others. We make agreements with one another; we have expectations about one another's conduct; we approve, we are indifferent and we disapprove. This multiplicity of activity and variety of opinion is apt to produce collisions: we pursue courses which cut across those of others, and we do not all approve the same sort of conduct. But, in the main, we get along with one another, sometimes by giving way, sometimes by standing fast, sometimes in a compromise. Our conduct consists of activity assimilated to that of others in small, and for the most part unconsidered and unobtrusive, adjustments.

Why all this should be so, does not matter. It is not necessarily so. A different condition of human circumstance can easily be imagined, and we know that elsewhere and at other times activity is, or has been, far less multifarious and changeful and opinion far less diverse and far less likely to provoke collision; but, by and large, we recognize this to be our condition. It is an acquired condition, though nobody designed or specifically chose it in preference to all others. It is the product, not of 'human nature' let loose, but of human beings impelled by an acquired love of making choices for themselves. And we know as little and as much about where it is leading us as we know about the fashion in hats of twenty years' time or the design of motor-cars.

Surveying the scene, some people are provoked by the absence of order and coherence which appears to them to be its dominant feature; its wastefulness, its frustration, its dissipation of human energy, its lack not merely of a premeditated destination but even of any discernible direction of movement. It provides an excitement similar to that of a stock-car race; but it has none of the satisfaction of a well-conducted business enterprise. Such people are apt to exaggerate the current disorder; the absence of plan is so conspicuous that the small adjustments, and even the more massive arrangements, which restrain the chaos seem to them nugatory; they have no feeling for the warmth of untidiness but only for its inconvenience. But what is significant is not the limitations of their powers of observation, but the turn of their thoughts. They feel that there ought to be something that ought to be done to convert this so-called chaos into order, for this is no way for rational human beings to be spending their lives. Like Apollo when he saw Daphne with her hair hung carelessly about her neck, they sigh and say to themselves: 'What if it were properly arranged.' Moreover, they tell us that they have seen in a dream the glorious, collisionless manner of living proper to all mankind, and this dream they understand as their warrant for seeking to remove the diversities and occasions of conflict which distinguish our current manner of living. Of course, their dreams are not all exactly alike; but they have this in common: each is a vision of a condition of human circumstance from which the occasion of conflict has been removed, a vision of human activity co-ordinated and set going in a single direction and of every resource being used to the full. And such people appropriately understand the office of government to be the imposition upon its subjects of the condition of human circumstances of their dream. To govern is to turn a private dream into a public and compulsory manner of living. Thus, politics becomes an encounter of dreams and the activity in which government is held to this understanding of its office and provided with the appropriate instruments.

I do not propose to criticize this jump to glory style of politics in which governing is understood as a perpetual take-over bid for the purchase of the resources of human energy in order to concentrate them in a single direction; it is not at all unintelligible, and there is much in our circumstances to provoke it. My purpose is merely to point out that there is another quite different understanding of government, and that it is no less intelligible and in some respects perhaps more appropriate to our circumstances.

The spring of this other disposition in respect of governing and the instruments of government – a conservative disposition – is to be found in the acceptance of the current condition of human circumstances as I have described it: the propensity to make our own choices and to find happiness in doing so, the variety of enterprises each pursued with passion, the diversity of beliefs each held with the conviction of its exclusive truth; the inventiveness, the changefulness and the absence of any large design; the excess, the over-activity and the informal compromise. And the office of government is not to impose other beliefs and activities upon its subjects, not to tutor or to educate them, not to make them better or happier in another way, not to direct them, to galvanize them into action, to lead them or to co-ordinate their activities so that no occasion of conflict shall occur; the office of government is merely to rule. This is a specific and limited activity, easily corrupted when it is combined with any other, and, in the circumstances, indispensable. The image of the ruler is the umpire whose business is to administer the rules of the game, or the chairman who governs the debate according to known rules but does not himself participate in it.

Now people of this disposition commonly defend their belief that the proper attitude of government towards the current condition of human circumstance is one of acceptance by appealing to certain general ideas. They contend that there is absolute value in the free play of human choice, that private property (the emblem of choice) is a natural right, that it is only in the enjoyment of diversity of opinion and activity that true belief and good conduct can be expec-ted to disclose themselves. But I do not think that this disposition requires these or any similar beliefs in order to make it intelligible. Something much smaller and less pretentious will do: the obser-vation that this condition of human circumstance is, in fact, current, and that we have learned to enjoy it and how to manage it; that we are not children *in statu pupillari* but adults who do not consider themselves under any obligation to justify their preference for making their own choices; and that it is beyond human experience to suppose that those who rule are endowed with a superior wisdom which discloses to them a better range of beliefs and activities and which gives them authority to impose upon their subjects a quite different manner of life. In short, if the man of this disposition is asked: Why ought governments to accept the current diversity of opinion and activity in preference to imposing upon their subjects a dream of their own? it is enough for him to reply: Why not? Their dreams are no different from those of anyone else; and if it is boring to have to listen to dreams of others being recounted, it is insuffer-able to be forced to re-enact them. We tolerate monomaniacs, it is our habit to do so; but why should we be *ruled* by them? Is it not (the man of conservative disposition asks) an intelligible task for a government to protect its subjects against the nuisance of those who spend their energy and their wealth in the service of some pet indignation, endeavouring to impose it upon everybody, not by suppressing their activities in favour of others of a similar kind, but by setting a limit to the amount of noise anyone may emit?

Nevertheless, if this acceptance is the spring of the conservative's disposition in respect of government, he does not suppose that the office of government is to do nothing. As he understands it, there is work to be done which can be done only in virtue of a genuine acceptance of current beliefs simply because they are current and current activities simply because they are afoot. And, briefly, the office he attributes to government is to resolve some of the collisions which this variety of beliefs and activities generates; to preserve peace, not by placing an interdict upon choice and upon the diversity that springs from the exercise of preference, not by imposing substantive uniformity, but by enforcing general rules of procedure upon all subjects alike.

Government, then, as the conservative in this matter understands it, does not begin with a vision of another, different and better world, but with the observation of the self-government practised even by men of passion in the conduct of their enterprises; it begins in the informal adjustments of interests to one another which are designed to release those who are apt to collide from the mutual frustration of a collision. Sometimes these adjustments are no more than agreements between two parties to keep out of each other's way; sometimes they are of wider application and more durable character, such as the International Rules for the prevention of collisions at sea. In short, the intimations of government are to be found in ritual, not in religion or philosophy; in the enjoyment of orderly and peaceable behaviour, not in the search for truth or perfection.

But the self-government of men of passionate belief and enterprise is apt to break down when it is most needed. It often suffices to resolve minor collisions of interest, but beyond these it is not to be relied upon. A more precise and a less easily corrupted ritual is required to resolve the massive collisions which our manner of living is apt to generate and to release us from the massive frustrations in which we are apt to become locked. The custodian of this ritual is 'the government', and the rules it imposes are 'the law'. One may imagine a government engaged in the activity of an arbiter in cases of collisions of interest but doing its business without the aid of laws, just as one may imagine a game without rules and an umpire who was appealed to in cases of dispute and who on each occasion merely used his judgment to devise *ad hoc* a way of releasing the disputants from their mutual frustration. But the diseconomy of such an arrangement is so obvious that it could only be expected to occur to those inclined to believe the ruler to be supernaturally inspired and to those disposed to attribute to him a quite different office – that of leader, or tutor, or manager. At all events the disposition to be conservative in respect of government is rooted in the belief that where government rests upon the acceptance of the current activities and beliefs of its subjects, the only appropriate manner of ruling is by making and enforcing rules of conduct. In short, to be conservative about government is a reflection of the conservatism we have recognized to be appropriate in respect of rules of conduct.

To govern, then, as the conservative understands it, is to provide a *vinculum juris* for those manners of conduct which, in the circumstances, are least likely to result in a frustrating collision of interests; to provide redress and means of compensation for those who suffer from others behaving in a contrary manner; sometimes to provide punishment for those who pursue their own interests regardless of the rules; and, of course, to provide a sufficient force to maintain the authority of an arbiter of this kind. Thus, governing is recognized as a specific and limited activity; not the management of an enterprise, but the rule of those engaged in a great diversity of self-chosen enterprises. It is not concerned with concrete persons, but with activities; and with activities only in respect of their propensity to collide with one another. It is not concerned with moral right and wrong, it is not designed to make men good or even better; it is not indispensable on account of 'the natural depravity of mankind' but merely because of their current disposition to be extravagant; its business is to keep its subjects at peace with one another in the activities in which they have chosen to seek their happiness. And if there is any general idea entailed in this view, it is, perhaps, that a government which does not sustain the loyalty of its subjects is worthless; and that while one which (in the old puritan phrase) 'commands for truth' is incapable of doing so (because some of its subjects will believe its 'truth' to be error), one which is indifferent to 'truth' and 'error' alike, and merely pursues peace, presents no obstacle to the necessary loyalty.

Now, it is intelligible enough that any man who thinks in this manner about government should be averse from innovation: government is providing rules of conduct, and familiarity is a supremely important virtue in a rule. Nevertheless, he has room for other thoughts. The current condition of human circumstances is one in which new activities (often springing from new inventions) are constantly appearing and rapidly extend themselves, and in which beliefs are perpetually being modified or discarded; and for the rules to be inappropriate to the current activities and beliefs is as unprofitable as for them to be unfamiliar. For example, a variety of inventions and considerable changes in the conduct of business, seem now to have made the current law of copyright inadequate. And it may be thought that neither the newspaper nor the motor-car nor the aeroplane have yet received proper recognition in the law of England; they have all created nuisances that call out to be abated. Or again, at the end of the last century our governments engaged in an extensive codification of large parts of our law and in this manner both brought it into closer relationship with current beliefs and manners of activity and insulated it from the small adjustments to circumstances which are characteristic of the operation of our common law. But many of these Statutes are now hopelessly out of date. And there are older Acts of Parliament (such as the Merchant Shipping Act), governing large and important departments of activity, which are even more inappropriate to current circumstances. Innovation, then, is called for if the rules are to remain appropriate to the activities they govern. But, as the conservative understands it, modification of the rules should always reflect, and never impose, a change in the activities and beliefs of those who are subject to them, and should never on any occasion be so great as to destroy the *ensemble*. Consequently, the conservative will have nothing to do with innovations designed to meet merely hypothetical situations; he will prefer to enforce a

rule he has got rather than invent a new one; he will think it appropriate to delay a modification of the rules until it is clear that the
change of circumstance it is designed to reflect has come to stay for a
while; he will be suspicious of proposals for change in excess of what
the situation calls for, of rulers who demand extra-ordinary powers
in order to make great changes and whose utterances are tied to
generalities like 'the public good' or 'social justice', and of Saviours
of Society who buckle on armour and seek dragons to slay; he will
think it proper to consider the occasion of the innovation with care;
in short, he will be disposed to regard politics as an activity in
which a valuable set of tools is renovated from time to time and
kept in trim rather than as an opportunity for perpetual re-equip-
ment.

All this may help to make intelligible the disposition to be
conservative in respect of government; and the detail might be
elaborated to show, for example, how a man of this disposition
understands the other great business of a government, the conduct
of a foreign policy; to show why he places so high a value upon the
complicated set of arrangements we call 'the institution of private
property'; to show the appropriateness of his rejection of the view
that politics is a shadow thrown by economics; to show why he
believes that the main (perhaps the only) specifically economic
activity appropriate to government is the maintenance of a stable
currency. But, on this occasion, I think there is something else to be
said.

To some people, 'government' appears as a vast reservoir of
power which inspires them to dream of what use might be made of
it. They have favourite projects, of various dimensions, which they
sincerely believe are for the benefit of mankind, and to capture this
source of power, if necessary to increase it, and to use it for imposing
their favourite projects upon their fellows is what they understand
as the adventure of governing men. They are, thus, disposed to
recognize government as an instrument of passion; the art of politics
is to inflame and direct desire. In short, governing is understood to
be just like any other activity – making and selling a brand of soap,
exploiting the resources of a locality, or developing a housing estate
– only the power here is (for the most part) already mobilized, and

the enterprise is remarkable only because it aims at monopoly and because of its promise of success once the source of power has been captured. Of course a private enterprise politician of this sort would get nowhere in these days unless there were people with wants so vague that they can be prompted to ask for what he has to offer, or with wants so servile that they prefer the promise of a provided abundance to the opportunity of choice and activity on their own account. And it is not all as plain sailing as it might appear: often a politician of this sort misjudges the situation; and then, briefly, even in democratic politics, we become aware of what the camel thinks of the camel driver.

Now, the disposition to be conservative in respect of politics reflects a quite different view of the activity of governing. The man of this disposition understands it to be the business of a government not to inflame passion and give it new objects to feed upon, but to inject into the activities of already too passionate men an ingredient of moderation; to restrain, to deflate, to pacify and to reconcile; not to stoke the fires of desire, but to damp them down. And all this, not because passion is vice and moderation virtue, but because moderation is indispensable if passionate men are to escape being locked in an encounter of mutual frustration. A government of this sort does not need to be regarded as the agent of a benign providence, as the custodian of a moral law, or as the emblem of a divine order. What it provides is something that its subjects (if they are such people as we are) can easily recognize to be valuable; indeed, it is something that, to some extent, they do for themselves in the ordinary course of business or pleasure. They scarcely need to be reminded of its indispensability, as Sextus Empiricus tells us the ancient Persians were accustomed periodically to remind themselves by setting aside all laws for five hair-raising days on the death of a king. Generally speaking, they are not averse from paying the modest cost of this service; and they recognize that the appropriate attitude to a government of this sort is loyalty (sometimes a confident loyalty, at others perhaps the heavy-hearted loyalty of Sidney Godolphin), respect and some suspicion, not love or devotion or affection. Thus, governing is understood to be a secondary activity; but it is recognized also to be a specific activity, not easily to be combined with any other, because all other activities (except the mere contemplation of the scene) entail taking sides and the surrender of the indifference appropriate (on this view of things) not only to the judge but also to the legislator, who is understood to occupy a judicial office. The subjects of such a government require that it shall be strong, alert, resolute, economical and neither capricious nor over-active: they have no use for a referee who does not govern the game according to the rules, who takes sides, who plays a game of his own, or who is always blowing his whistle; after all, the game's the thing, and in playing the game we neither need to be, nor at present are disposed to be, conservative.

But there is something more to be observed in this style of governing than merely the restraint imposed by familiar and appropriate rules. Of course, it will not countenance government by suggestion or cajolery or by any other means than by law; an avuncular Home Secretary or a threatening Chancellor of the Exchequer. But the spectacle of its indifference to the beliefs and substantive activities of its subjects may itself be expected to provoke a habit of restraint. Into the heat of our engagements, into the passionate clash of beliefs, into our enthusiasm for saving the souls of our neighbours or of all mankind, a government of this sort injects an ingredient, not of reason (how should we expect that?) but of the irony that is prepared to counteract one vice by another, of the raillery that deflates extravagance without itself pretending to wisdom, of the mockery that disperses tension, of inertia and of scepticism: indeed, it might be said that we keep a government of this sort to do for us the scepticism we have neither the time nor the inclination to do for ourselves. It is like the cool touch of the mountain that one feels in the plain even on the hottest summer day. Or, to leave metaphor behind, it is like the 'governor' which, by controlling the speed at which its parts move, keeps an engine from racketing itself to pieces.

It is not, then, mere stupid prejudice which disposes a conservative to take this view of the activity of governing; nor are any highfalutin metaphysical beliefs necessary to provoke it or make it intelligible. It is connected merely with the observation that where activity is bent upon enterprise the indispensable counterpart is another order of activity, bent upon restraint, which is unavoidably corrupted (indeed, altogether abrogated) when the power assigned to it is used for advancing favourite projects. An 'umpire' who at the same time is one of the players is no umpire; 'rules' about which we are not disposed to be conservative are not rules but incitements to disorder; the conjunction of dreaming and ruling generates tyranny.

4

Political conservatism is, then, not at all unintelligible in a people disposed to be adventurous and enterprising, a people in love with change and apt to rationalize their affections in terms of 'progress'.[1] And one does not need to think that the belief in 'progress' is the most cruel and unprofitable of all beliefs, arousing cupidity without satisfying it, in order to think it inappropriate for a government to be conspicuously 'progressive'. Indeed, a disposition to be conservative in respect of government would seem to be pre-eminently appropriate to men who have something to do and something to think about on their own account, who have a skill to practise or an intellectual fortune to make, to people whose passions do not need to be inflamed, whose desires do not need to be provoked and whose dreams of a better world need no prompting. Such people know the value of a rule which imposes orderliness without directing enterprise, a rule which concentrates duty so that room is left for delight. They might even be prepared to suffer a legally established ecclesiastical order; but it would not be because they believed it to represent some unassailable religious truth, but merely because it restrained the indecent competition of sects and (as Hume said) moderated 'the plague of a too diligent clergy'.

Now, whether or not these beliefs recommend themselves as reasonable and appropriate to our circumstances and to the abilities we are likely to find in those who rule us, they and their like are in my view what make intelligible a conservative disposition in respect of politics. What would be the appropriateness of this disposition in circumstances other than our own, whether to be conservative in

---

[1] I have not forgotten to ask myself the question: Why, then, have we so neglected what is appropriate to our circumstances as to make the activist dreamer the stereotype of the modern politician? And I have tried to answer it elsewhere.

respect of government would have the same relevance in the circumstances of an unadventurous, a slothful or a spiritless people, is a
question we need not try to answer: we are concerned with ourselves
as we are. I myself think that it would occupy an important place in
any set of circumstances. But what I hope I have made clear is that it is
not at all inconsistent to be conservative in respect of government
and radical in respect of almost every other activity. And, in my
opinion, there is more to be learnt about this disposition from
Montaigne, Pascal, Hobbes and Hume than from Burke or Bentham.

Of the many entailments of this view of things that might be
pointed to, I will notice one, namely, that politics is an activity
unsuited to the young, not on account of their vices but on account
of what I at least consider to be their virtues.

Nobody pretends that it is easy to acquire or to sustain the mood
of indifference which this manner of politics calls for. To rein-in
one's own beliefs and desires, to acknowledge the current shape of
things, to feel the balance of things in one's hand, to tolerate what
is abominable, to distinguish between crime and sin, to respect
formality even when it appears to be leading to error, these are
difficult achievements; and they are achievements not to be looked
for in the young.

Everybody's young days are a dream, a delightful insanity, a
sweet solipsism. Nothing in them has a fixed shape, nothing a fixed
price; everything is a possibility, and we live happily on credit.
There are no obligations to be observed; there are no accounts to be
kept. Nothing is specified in advance; everything is what can be made
of it. The world is a mirror in which we seek the reflection of our
own desires. The allure of violent emotions is irresistible. When we
are young we are not disposed to make concessions to the world; we
never feel the balance of a thing in our hands – unless it be a cricket
bat. We are not apt to distinguish between our liking and our esteem;
urgency is our criterion of importance; and we do not easily understand that what is humdrum need not be despicable. We are impatient of restraint; and we readily believe, like Shelley, that to have
contracted a habit is to have failed. These, in my opinion, are among
our virtues when we are young; but how remote they are from the
disposition appropriate for participating in the style of government

I have been describing. Since life is a dream, we argue (with plausible but erroneous logic) that politics must be an encounter of dreams, in which we hope to impose our own. Some unfortunate people, like Pitt (laughably called 'the Younger'), are born old, and are eligible to engage in politics almost in their cradles; others, perhaps more fortunate, belie the saying that one is young only once, they never grow up. But these are exceptions. For most there is what Conrad called the 'shadow line' which, when we pass it, discloses a solid world of things, each with its fixed shape, each with its own point of balance, each with its price; a world of fact, not poetic image, in which what we have spent on one thing we cannot spend on another; a world inhabited by others besides ourselves who cannot be reduced to mere reflections of our own emotions. And coming to be at home in this commonplace world qualifies us (as no knowledge of 'political science' can ever qualify us), if we are so inclined and have nothing better to think about, to engage in what the man of conservative disposition understands to be political activity.

1956

The Voice of Poetry in the Conversation of Mankind

I

There are philosophers who assure us that all human utterance is in one mode. They recognize a certain variety of expression, they are able to distinguish different tones of utterance, but they hear only one authentic voice. And there might be something to be said for this view if we were considering some primordial condition of the race when death was close, when leisure was scarce, and when every utterance (even religious rites and magical spells) may be supposed to have had a practical bearing. But it is now long since mankind has invented for itself other modes of speaking. The voice of practical activity may be the commonest to be heard, but it is partnered by others whose utterance is in a different idiom. The most notable of these are the voices of 'poetry' and of 'science'; but it would seem that, more recently, 'history' also has acquired, or has begun to acquire, an authentic voice and idiom of its own. In these circumstances the task of discerning a singleness in human utterance has become more difficult. Nevertheless, the view dies hard that Babel was the occasion of a curse being laid upon mankind from which it is the business of the philosophers to deliver us, and a disposition remains to impose a single character upon significant human speech. We are urged, for example, to regard all utterances as contributions (of different but comparable merit) to an inquiry, or a debate among inquirers, about ourselves and the world we inhabit. But this understanding of human activity and intercourse as an inquiry, while appearing to accommodate a variety of voices, in fact recognizes only one, namely, the voice of argumentative discourse, the voice of 'science', and all others are acknowledged merely in respect of their aptitude to imitate this voice. Yet, it may be supposed that the

diverse idioms of utterance which make up current human intercourse have some meeting-place and compose a manifold of some
sort. And, as I understand it, the image of this meeting-place is not
an inquiry or an argument, but a conversation.

In a conversation the participants are not engaged in an inquiry
or a debate; there is no 'truth' to be discovered, no proposition to
be proved, no conclusion sought. They are not concerned to inform,
to persuade, or to refute one another, and therefore the cogency of
their utterances does not depend upon their all speaking in the same
idiom; they may differ without disagreeing. Of course, a conversation may have passages of argument and a speaker is not forbidden
to be demonstrative; but reasoning is neither sovereign nor alone,
and the conversation itself does not compose an argument. A girl, in
order to escape a conclusion, may utter what appears to be an out-
rageously irrelevant remark, but what in fact she is doing is turning
an argument she finds tiresome into a conversation she is more at
home in. In conversation, 'facts' appear only to be resolved once
more into the possibilities from which they were made; 'certainties'
are shown to be combustible, not by being brought in contact with
other 'certainties' or with doubts, but by being kindled by the
presence of ideas of another order; approximations are revealed
between notions normally remote from one another. Thoughts of
different species take wing and play round one another, responding
to each other's movements and provoking one another to fresh
exertions. Nobody asks where they have come from or on what
authority they are present; nobody cares what will become of them
when they have played their part. There is no symposiarch or
arbiter; not even a doorkeeper to examine credentials. Every entrant
is taken at its face-value and everything is permitted which can get
itself accepted into the flow of speculation. And voices which speak
in conversation do not compose a hierarchy. Conversation is not an
enterprise designed to yield an extrinsic profit, a contest where a winner gets a prize, not is it an activity of exegesis; it is an unrehearsed
intellectual adventure. It is with conversation as with gambling, its
significance lies neither in winning nor in losing, but in wagering.
Properly speaking, it is impossible in the absence of a diversity of
voices: in it different universes of discourse meet, acknowledge each

other and enjoy an oblique relationship which neither requires nor forecasts their being assimilated to one another.

This, I believe, is the appropriate image of human intercourse – appropriate because it recognizes the qualities, the diversities, and the proper relationships of human utterances. As civilized human beings, we are the inheritors, neither of an inquiry about ourselves and the world, nor of an accumulating body of information, but of a conversation, begun in the primeval forests and extended and made more articulate in the course of centuries. It is a conversation which goes on both in public and within each of ourselves. Of course there is argument and inquiry and information, but wherever these are profitable they are to be recognized as passages in this conversation, and perhaps they are not the most captivating of the passages. It is the ability to participate in this conversation, and not the ability to reason cogently, to make discoveries about the world, or to contrive a better world, which distinguishes the human being from the animal and the civilized man from the barbarian. Indeed, it seems not improbable that it was the engagement in this conversation (where talk is without a conclusion) that gave us our present appearance, man being descended from a race of apes who sat in talk so long and so late that they wore out their tails. Education, properly speaking, is an initiation into the skill and partnership of this conversation in which we learn to recognize the voices, to distinguish the proper occasions of utterance, and in which we acquire the intellectual and moral habits appropriate to conversation. And it is this conversation which, in the end, gives place and character to every human activity and utterance. I say, 'in the end', because, of course, the immediate field of moral activity is the world of practical enterprise, and intellectual achievement appears, in the first place, within each of the various universes of discourse; but good behaviour is what it is with us because practical enterprise is recognized not as an isolated activity but as a partner in a conversation, and the final measure of intellectual achievement is in terms of its contribution to the conversation in which all universes of discourse meet.

Each voice is the reflection of a human activity, begun without premonition of where it would lead, but acquiring for itself in the course of the engagement a specific character and a manner of speaking of its own: and within each mode of utterance further modulation is discernible. There is, then, no fixed number to the voices which engage in this conversation, but the most familiar are those of practical activity, of 'science' and of 'poetry'. Philosophy, the impulse to study the quality and style of each voice, and to reflect upon the relationship of one voice to another, must be counted a parasitic activity; it springs from the conversation, because this is what the philosopher reflects upon, but it makes no specific contribution to it.

This conversation is not only the greatest but also the most hardly sustained of all the accomplishments of mankind. Men have never been wanting who have had this understanding of human activity and intercourse, but few have embraced it without reserve and without misgiving, and on this account it is proper to mention the most notable of those who have done so: Michel de Montaigne. For the most part, however, the conversation has survived in spite of our notions about the education of the young which seem to become more and more remote from this understanding of human activity and intercourse.[1] Moreover, in some of the voices there are innate tendencies towards barbarism which make it difficult to sustain.

Each voice is at once a manner of speaking and a determinate utterance. As a manner of speaking, each is wholly conversable. But the defect to which some of the voices are liable is a loosening (even a detachment) of what is said from the manner of its utterance, and when this takes place the voice appears as a body of conclusions reached ($\delta\delta\gamma\mu\alpha\tau\alpha$), and thus, becoming eristic, loses its conver-

---

[1] Here is a passage from the reflections of an Eton master (William Cory) who understood education as a preparation for participation in conversation: At school 'you are not engaged so much in acquiring knowledge as in making mental efforts under criticism. . . . A certain amount of knowledge you can indeed with average faculties acquire so as to retain; nor need you regret the hours you spend on much that is forgotten, for the shadow of lost knowledge at least protects you from many illusions. But you go to a great school not so much for knowledge as for arts and habits; for the habit of attention, for the art of expression, for the art of assuming at a moment's notice, a new intellectual position, for the art of entering quickly into another person's thoughts, for the habit of submitting to censure and refutation, for the art of indicating assent or dissent in graduated terms, for the habit of regarding minute points of accuracy, for the art of working out what is possible in a given time, for taste, discrimination, for mental courage and mental soberness. And above all you go to a great school for self-knowledge.'

sability. 'Science', for example, is a manner of thinking and speaking represented (and always on the verge of being misrepresented) in an encyclopaedia of knowledge. The voice of philosophy, on the other hand, is unusually conversable. There is no body of philosophical 'knowledge' to become detached from the activity of philosophizing: hence Hume's perception of the supremely civilizing quality of philosophical reflection, and hence the difficulty which both men of science and of business have in understanding what philosophy is about and their frequent attempts to transform it into something more familiar to themselves. But further, the conversation may not only be destroyed by the intrusion of the eristic tendencies of the voices; it may suffer damage, or even for a time come to be suspended, by the bad manners of one or more of the participants. For each voice is prone to *superbia*, that is, an exclusive concern with its own utterance, which may result in its identifying the conversation with itself and its speaking as if it were speaking only to itself. And when this happens, barbarism may be observed to have supervened.

The image of human activity and intercourse as a conversation will, perhaps, appear both frivolous and unduly sceptical. This understanding of activity as composed, in the last resort, of inconsequent adventures, often put by for another day but never concluded, and of the participants as playfellows moved, not by a belief in the evanescence of error and imperfection but only by their loyalty and affection for one another, may seem to neglect the passion and the seriousness with which, for example, both scientific and practical enterprises are often pursued and the memorable achievements they have yielded. And the denial of a hierarchical order among the voices is not only a departure from one of the most notable traditions of European thought (in which all activity was judged in relation to the *vita contemplativa*), but will seem also to reinforce the scepticism. But, although a degree of scepticism cannot be denied, the appearance of frivolity is due, I think, to a misconception about conversation. As I understand it, the excellence of this conversation (as of others) springs from a tension between seriousness and playfulness. Each voice represents a serious engagement (though it is serious not merely in respect of its being pursued for the conclusions it promises); and without this seriousness the conversation would lack impetus. But in its participation in the conversation each voice learns to be playful, learns to understand itself conversationally and to recognize itself as a voice among voices. As with children, who are great conversationists, the playfulness is serious and the serious-ness in the end is only play.

In recent centuries the conversation, both in public and within ourselves, has become boring because it has been engrossed by two voices, the voice of practical activity and the voice of 'science': to know and to contrive are our pre-eminent occupations. There have, of course, been ups and downs in this respect; but what transformed the situation was the appearance in the seventeenth century of an unmistakable disposition in favour of a division of the intellectual world between these two masters, a disposition which has since asserted itself more and more unmistakably. And on many occasions all that there is to be heard is the eristic tones of the voice of science in conference with that modulation of the voice of practical activity *we* call 'politics'.[1] But for a conversation to be appropriated by one or two voices is an insidious vice because in the passage of time it takes on the appearance of a virtue. All utterance should be relevant; but relevance in conversation is determined by the course of the conver-sation itself, it owes nothing to an external standard. Consequently an established monopoly will not only make it difficult for another voice to be heard, but it will also make it seem proper that it should not be heard: it is convicted in advance of irrelevance. And there is no easy escape from this *impasse*. An excluded voice may take wing against the wind, but it will do so at the risk of turning the conversation into a dispute. Or it may gain a hearing by imitating the voices of the monopolists; but it will be a hearing for only a counterfeit utterance.

To rescue the conversation from the bog into which it has fallen and to restore to it some of its lost freedom of movement would

---

[1] The assimilation of 'politics' to practical activity is characteristic (though not exclusively so) of the history of modern Europe, and during the last four centuries it has become increasingly complete. But in ancient Greece (particularly in Athens) 'politics' was understood as a 'poetic' activity in which speaking (not merely to persuade but to compose memorable verbal images) was pre-eminent and in which action was for the achievement of 'glory' and 'greatness' – a view of things which is reflected in the pages of Machiavelli.

require a philosophy more profound than anything I have to offer. But there is another, more modest, undertaking which is perhaps worth pursuing. My proposal is to consider again the voice of poetry; to consider it as it speaks in the conversation. That this is an opportune enterprise no one interested in the conversation will doubt. It is true that the voice of poetry has never been wholly excluded; but it is often expected to provide no more than an entertainment to fill in the intervals of a more serious discussion, and the fact that it has fallen to imitating the voices of politics and science may be taken as a sign of the difficulty it now has in getting a hearing in its own character. And if what is now needed is some relief from the monotony of a conversation too long appropriated by politics and science, it may be supposed that an inquiry into the quality and significance of the voice of poetry may do something in this interest. But it is not merely opportune, it is also 'philosophical': for, the consideration of poetry becomes philosophical when poetic imagining is shown to have, not a necessary place, but a specific place in the manifold of human activities. At all events, anyone fond of reflection who has found delight in listening to the voice of poetry is unprotected against the inclination to meditate upon the nature of that delight; and if he gives way to the impulse to put his meditations in order, he is only doing his best to understand the quality of the voice and its relationship to the other voices. And if that best is good enough, he may say something worthwhile on behalf of poetry.

Yet expectations should be limited. Neither the poet nor the critic of poetry will find very much to his purpose in what I have to say. The poet is, of course, sovereign over himself and his own activity. And the concern of the critic is to quicken the hearing we give to the voice of poetry and to explore the qualities of a poem. In this it is not a bad thing to be something of a philosopher; philosophic reflection may perhaps hinder the critic from asking irrelevant questions and from thinking and speaking about poems in an inappropriate manner, and this (though it does not carry us very far) is something not to be despised.[1] But he requires other qualifications,

---

[1] The connoisseurship of the poetic with which philosophical reflection has endowed some critics (Coleridge, for example, or Geoffrey Scott in *The Architecture of Humanism*), in others appears as an unreflective (but, of course,

and the critic who swims too strongly in this sea is apt soon to find himself out of sight of his object. For philosophy here is concerned merely with the domain of the poetic and with enlarging our understanding of the voice of poetry as it speaks in a conversation which it may from time to time command but in which it is never alone.

2

As I understand it, the real world is a world of experience within which self and not-self divulge themselves to reflection. No doubt this distinction is ambiguous and unstable: it is difficult (if not impossible) to find anything which, in principle, belongs exclusively to either side of the partnership. But on any occasion, although uncertainty may remain at the edges, we do not hesitate to make this distinction. And what on any occasion is recognized as self is recognized on account of its separating itself from a present not-self: self and not-self generate one another.

The self appears as activity. It is not a 'thing' or a 'substance' capable of being active; it is activity. And this activity is primordial; there is nothing antecedent to it. It may display varying degrees of strength or weakness; it may be lively or lethargic, attentive or wandering; it may be educated or relatively naïve; but there is no condition of rest or passivity to be overcome before it can begin. Thus, it is inappropriate to think of this self as a room, either furnished, or empty, or on the way to being furnished; properly speaking, it is only skilful or clumsy, wakeful or sluggish. Further, on every occasion this activity is a specific mode of activity; to be active but with no activity in particular, to be skilful but with no particular skill, is as impossible to the self as not to be active at all.

I shall call this activity 'imagining': the self making and recognizing images, and moving about among them in manners appropriate to their characters and with various degrees of aptitude. Thus, sensing, perceiving, feeling, desiring, thinking, believing, contemplating, supposing, knowing, preferring, approving, laughing,

---

not unacquired) habit and aptitude of thinking and saying the appropriate kind of things about works of art. Max Beerbohm's dramatic criticism is an example of this.

crying, dancing, loving, singing, making hay, devising mathematical demonstrations, and so on, each is, or has its place in, an identifiable mode of imagining and moving about in an appropriate manner among images of a certain kind. And although we may not be always (or even often) aware of the universe of discourse to which our imagining on any occasion belongs, imagining is never unspecific (though it may in fact be confused) because it is always governed by the considerabilities which belong to a particular skill.

The not-self, then, is composed of images. But these images are not 'given' or 'presented' to the self; they are not independent existences caught as they swim by in the net of an expectant or an indifferent self. And they are not this because they are not anything at all out of relation to a self: and self is activity. Images are made. Nevertheless, self and not-self, imagining and image, are neither cause and consequent nor consciousness and its contents: the self is constituted in the activity of making and moving among images. Further, these images are not made out of some other, less-defined material (impressions or *sensa*), for no such material is available. Nor are they representations of other existences, images of 'things'; for example: what we call a 'thing' is merely a certain sort of image recognized as such because it behaves in a certain manner and responds to our questioning appropriately. Again, although images may often be vague and indefinite in appearance, they are always specific in character; that is, they correspond to a specific mode of imagining which may be discerned (if we wish to discern it) by ascertaining what sort of questions are relevant to be asked about its images: there is no image eligible to have all sorts of inquiries relevantly made about it. And finally, an image is never isolated and alone; it belongs to the world or field of images which on any occasion constitutes the not-self.

This activity of imagining, then, is neither the φαντασία of Aristotle, nor is it the 'original fancy' of Hobbes, nor is it what Coleridge called 'primary imagination', nor is it the 'blind but indispensable link' between sensation and thought which Kant calls imagination. It is not generic activity, preceding and providing the materials for special activities; in all its appearances it is governed by specific and ascertainable considerabilities. It is not a condition of thought; in one of its modes it is thought.

3

What I have called the conversation of mankind is, then, the meeting-place of various modes of imagining; and in this conversation there is, therefore, no voice without an idiom of its own: the voices are not divergencies from some ideal, non-idiomatic manner of speaking, they diverge only from one another. Consequently, to specify the idiom of one is to discern how it is distinguished from, and how it is related to the others. And since the most familiar partners to the voice of poetry are the voices of practical activity and of 'science', I should begin by saying something about these.

Practical activity is the commonest manner of imagining; we absolve ourselves from it with difficulty and we easily relapse into it. In it the self is making, recognizing, and moving about among images of a certain sort. And the aspect of practical imagining which calls first for our attention is its character as desire and aversion: the world of practice is the world *sub species voluntatis*, and its constituents are images of pleasure and pain.[1] Desiring, of course, is not the cause of activity in a hitherto inactive self; we do not first 'have a desire' which causes us to move from a condition of rest to one of movement: desiring is merely being active in a particular manner, reaching out one's hand to pick a flower, or feeling in one's pocket for a coin. Nor do we first have a desire and then set about finding the means to satisfy it: our desires are known only in the activity of desiring, and to desire is to seek a satisfaction. Much of the time, no doubt, we act like automatons, imagining not by making specific choices but by habit; but in practical activity these habits are habits of desire and aversion. The enterprise, so far, in practical activity is to fill our world with images of pleasure.

But further, what is sought in desiring is not merely images of pleasure, but images of pleasure recognized to be 'facts'; and this presupposes a distinction between 'fact' and 'not-fact'. Even a world

---

[1] My view is not that practical activity appears *first* as desire and aversion, or that it can ever be identified with desire and aversion, but merely that desire and aversion are always present.

of make-believe images presupposes this distinction, for make-believe is attaching the character of 'fact' to what is nevertheless recognized to be 'not-fact' in order to enjoy the pleasure which this ideal attachment affords. Nor are 'not-facts' to be identified as illusions; illusion is mistaking 'fact' for 'not-fact', or 'not-fact' for 'fact'.

As I understand it, the distinction between 'fact' and 'not-fact' is a distinction between different kinds of images and not a distinction between something that is not an image and a mere image. And consequently we are sometimes uncertain whether or not to recognize an image as 'fact', and when we are doubtful we have questions we are accustomed to ask ourselves in order to reach a conclusion. Nevertheless, a reflective decision of this sort is often unnecessary, and it would indeed be impossible were we not familiar with a world of images in which 'fact' and 'not-fact' were already recognized. The self does not awake to a world of undetermined images and then begin to distinguish some of them as 'facts'; the recognition of 'fact' is not an activity which, in general, supervenes upon a more primitive image-making activity, it is one which has no specified beginning, one in which we are constantly engaging without much reflection, and, though we may educate ourselves in this respect, we never lack the equipment for the engagement. Moreover, images recognized as 'facts' are not all recognized as the same sort of 'fact'. And the determinants of 'practical fact' are, generally speaking, pragmatic: image is 'fact' if by regarding it as 'fact' (pleasurable or painful) the desiring self is preserved for further activity. Death, the cessation of desire, is the emblem of all aversion. In short, there is *scientia* in practical activity, but it is *scientia propter potentiam*.

In practical activity, then, every image is the reflection of a desiring self engaged in constructing its world and in continuing to reconstruct it in such a manner as to afford it pleasure. The world here consists of what is good to eat and what is poisonous, what is friendly and what is hostile, what is amenable to control and what resists it. And each image is recognized as something to be made use of or exploited. 'We must have spent three hours,' says a writer, recalling a visit to the Owen Falls, Lake Victoria, 'watching the waters and revolving plans to harness and bridle them. So much power running to waste, such a coign of vantage unoccupied, such a

lever to control the natural forces of Africa ungripped cannot but
vex and stimulate the imagination.' This is not a poetic image such
as Keats imagined –

> *The moving waters at their priest-like task*
> *Of pure ablution round earth's human shores –*

nor is it a 'scientific' image; it is a practical image.

But to be practically active is to be a self among selves (*inter
homines esse*). Nevertheless, the relationship of selves to images
recognized as other selves is not, in the first place, different from
their relationship to images recognized as 'things' – though it is more
difficult to manage. Another self is known as the consumer of what I
produce, the producer of what I consume, one way or another the
assistant in my projects, the servant of my pleasure. That is to say,
the desiring self admits the 'fact' of other selves, but refuses to
recognize them as selves, refuses to recognize their subjectivity:
activity is acknowledged only in respect of the use that may be made
of it. Each self inhabits a world of its own, a world of images related
to its own desires; solitariness, the consequence of its inability in this
activity to recognize other selves as such, is intrinsic, not accidental.
The relations between such selves is an unavoidable *bellum omnium
contra omnes.*

The skill in desire and aversion is knowing how to preserve the
practical self from dissolution, the skill in which 'fact' at the appropriate level is recognized, illusion is escaped, and pleasure rather than
pain experienced. And it belongs to this skill to seek to accomplish
its object with the least possible expenditure of energy: to be economical in this respect is itself to place a greater distance between the
desiring self and death, and therefore to conserve energy is not a
work of supererogation. The mere expenditure of energy (for the
enjoyment of it) is foreign to the desiring self, which recognizes only
the satisfaction of accomplishment or the mortification of failure. But
if this economy is appropriate on all occasions, it will be pre-eminently so when the desiring self encounters another self. For, of all
practical images, another self is the least tractable and offers the
greatest opportunity for wasted energy and the most conspicuous

occasion for defeat. To bind another self to one's desires calls for exceptional skill. Force or peremptory command may in some circumstances suffice to convert another self to my purposes, but this will rarely be the most certain or the most economical manner of achieving my ends. It will more often happen that failure is avoided only by an acknowledgment of the subjectivity of the other self which involves taking into alliance what refuses to be treated as a slave; that is, by offering a *quid pro quo* which is itself a recognition of subjectivity.[1] Such an alliance may be of short duration, or it may have the greater degree of permanence which belongs to a settled manner of behaviour or an instituted procedure friendly to a common measure of self-maintenance in the activity of desiring.

There should, however, be no misunderstanding about the limits of this alliance, limits set, not circumstantially, but by the character of the desiring selves. It rests upon a merely *de facto* admission of the subjectivity of the selves concerned; not to make this admission is a form of illusion which may hinder successful activity. The desiring selves enter into no obligation, recognize no right; they admit the subjectivity of other selves only in order to make use of it for their own ends. It is, therefore, a disingenuous recognition of subjectivity; the *bellum omnium contra omnes* carried on by other means.

But the world of practical activity is not only the world *sub specie voluntatis*, it is also the world *sub specie moris*: it is composed not merely of images of desire and aversion but also of images of approval and disapproval.

Approving is not the same activity as desiring, and disapproval is not to be identified with aversion. For example, death is the emblem of all aversion, but not of all disapproval: we must always be averse from our own death, but there are circumstances in which we may not disapprove of it and we may act accordingly. Nevertheless, practical activity without the recognition of both these dimensions remains an abstraction. One may indeed suppose a man able, perhaps, to perceive in the activity of others the operation of these moral categories but regarding them as no more than a guide to the help or hindrance he may expect from such selves in the satisfaction of his

[1] An image recognized merely as a 'thing' neither demands nor requires a *quid pro quo* for its use.

own desires;[1] but it is an image which remains a mere image and refuses to qualify as 'fact'. Sometimes approving seems to coincide with the activity of desiring: the spectator at the Owen Falls (although he says nothing about it) clearly entertained no doubt at all about the propriety of his images of desire. On other occasions approval and disapproval are apt to appear as critics of desire and aversion, operative in an *actus secundus*. But however they appear, images of approved or disapproved desire or aversion are known only in the activities of approving or disapproving. And when the dimensions of approval and disapproval are acknowledged, practical imagining is recognized as an activity whose object is to fill our world with images both desired and approved.

This moral attitude is concerned with the relations between selves engaged in practical activities. The merely desiring self can go no further than a disingenuous recognition of other selves; in the world *sub specie moris*, on the other hand, there is a genuine and unqualified recognition of other selves. All other selves are acknowledged to be ends and not merely means to our own ends: I may employ their skill, but it is also recognized to be proper (not merely necessary) that I should pay for it. And, as Hobbes observed, a man achieves this moral attitude if 'when weighing the actions of other men with his own, they seem too heavy, to put them in the other part of the balance, and his own in their place, that his own passions and self-love, may add nothing to the weight'.[2] In other words, selves in moral activity are equal members of a community of selves: and approval and disapproval are activities which belong to them as members of this community. The moral skill in practical activity, the *ars bene beatique vivendi*, is knowing how to behave in relation to selves ingenuously recognized as such.

In general, then, moral activity may be said to be the observation of a balance of accommodation between the demands of desiring selves each recognized by the others to be an end and not a mere slave of somebody else's desires. But this general character appears

---

[1] The character of the revolutionary as he appears in Bakunin's *The Catechism of a Revolutionary* is an attempt to portray such a man; but even here what appears is not a man divested of morality but one whose approvals and disapprovals are rather eccentric.

[2] *Leviathan*, Chapter 15.

always as a particular balance, and one 'morality' differs from another in respect of the level at which this balance is struck and in respect of the quality of the equilibrium. In a 'puritan' morality, for example, the level of the autonomy of selves and the quality of the equilibrium appears in a readiness to be scandalized, a refusal to deviate a hair's breadth from the settled point of balance and an exclusion of any disposition to allow the range of sympathy to extend itself.

The utterances of the self in practical activity are, for the most part, actions; it reveals itself in conduct. But in the course of moving about among the images of the practical world we also speak words, sometimes by way of commentary on what we are doing, sometimes to add force or a more precise definition to what we are doing or looking for others to do. The character and purport of this speech is appropriate to the needs of the practical self. It is the means by which we engage the attention of other selves; it allows us to identify and describe images of desire and approval, to explain, argue, instruct and negotiate; to advise, exhort, threaten and command; to pacify, encourage, comfort and console. By means of this language we communicate our desires, aversions, preferences, choices, requests, approvals and disapprovals; we make promises and acknowledge duties; we confess hopes and fears; we signify forgiveness and penitence.

The language in which the business of practical life is conducted is a symbolic language. Its words and expressions are so many agreed signs which, because they have relatively fixed and precise usages, and because they are non-resonant, serve as a medium for confident communication. It is a language that has to be learned by imitation. In themselves, the sound (the manner in which they are pronounced) and the shape (the manner in which they are spelled) of these words are insignificant so long as they are recognizable. On many occasions other signs, gestures or movements may be substituted for words, and words have the advantage over these signs only in the finer distinctions they may express. Moreover, these other signs (nodding, smiling, frowning, beckoning, shrugging the shoulders, etc.) are themselves symbols; they also have to be learnt, and they may have different significations in different societies. In using these words and signs, then, we do not seek to enlarge their meaning, or to set going a procession of linguistic reverberations; indeed, this language is like a coinage, the more fixed and invariable the value of its components, the more useful it is as a medium of exchange. In short, speaking here is expressing or conveying images and is not itself image-making. If I say, 'I am sad', I am not seeking to add a fresh *nuance* to the word 'sad'; I expect the word to be understood without quibble or difficulty, and I expect as a reply not, 'What do you mean?', but 'What's happened?' or, 'Cheer up'. If I say, 'Put it in the bucket', my remark may puzzle a child who does not know what the word 'bucket' signifies; but an adult, practised in this symbolic language, may be expected to reply, for example, 'Where is the bucket?' A conjunction of such symbols is insignificant when they stand for images which do not cohere – like, 'boiling ice', or 'liquid trees'; and if I want to deceive somebody in this language I do so by using the wrong word. The *clichés* of the business-man's letter are unobjectionable, indeed they are to be preferred to elegance because they are familiar and more genuinely symbolic. So far as this sort of language is concerned there would be an unquestionable advantage if a single set of symbols were current throughout the world: a 'basic' language of this sort, understood by all, is both possible and desirable. And again, it is not unreasonable that rulers should regard it their duty to see that goods offered for sale are not wrongly described: at least, from the nature of the language, it is a duty possible to be performed, for every word has its proper reference or signification.

This, then, is practical activity, and this is the nature of practical language, and the idiom of the voice of practice. Its talk is not only of bullocks; it may convey endearments as well as information; it may argue as well as command: and it may move alike among conceptional and visual images. But the discourse of practice – the discourse which takes place between selves in practical activity and which the voice of practice brings to the conversation – is always conditioned by its concern with images of desire and aversion, approval and disapproval, and by the particular level of 'fact' and 'not-fact' it recognizes.

4

On our first encounter with it, as school-boys, 'science' appears as an encyclopaedia conveying information about the world fascinatingly different from what we would otherwise suppose to be the case. The image of a stationary earth is replaced by that of a stationary sun, iron dissolves into arrangements of electrons and protons, water is revealed to be a combination of gases and the concept of undulations in the air of various dimensions takes the place of the images of sounds. And we are introduced to other images which have no counterparts in our familiar world, the concepts (for example) of velocity, of inertia, and of latent heat. These are the 'wonders of science'. And with them we enter a world whose images are not images of desire and aversion and provoke neither approval nor disapproval, a world where 'fact' and 'not-fact' are distinguished, but on some other principle than the pragmatic principle of the world of practical activity. *Scientia*, the recognition of 'fact' and 'not-fact', we were already acquainted with, but hitherto it had been *scientia propter potentiam* – knowing how to get what we want, how to contrive a world of approved and pleasure-giving images. This, on the other hand, appeared to be a different kind of *scientia*: the world understood in respect of its independence of our hopes and desires, preferences and ambitions, a world of images which some other creature, differently constituted, with different desires, dwelling in a different part of the universe (an inhabitant of Mars, for example), could share with us if his attention were given the same sort of twist and came to be governed by the same considerabilities; and a world which a blind man could enter as easily and move about in as freely as one who could see. Moreover, this world of 'science' was revealed not only to be composed of images independent of our practical concerns but also to be a system of conceptional images related to one another consequentially and claiming universal acceptance as a rational account of the world we live in. Thus, *scientia* came to be understood, not as an array of marvellous discoveries, nor as a settled doctrine about the world, but as a universe of discourse, a way of imagining and moving about among images, an activity, an inquiry not specified by its current achievements but by the manner in which it was conducted. And its voice was heard to be not (as we had first supposed) the didactic voice of an encyclopaedia, but a conversable voice, one speaking in an idiom of its own but capable of participating in the conversation.

Scientific investigation, the activity of being a scientist, is mankind in search of the intellectual satisfaction which comes from constructing and exploring a rational world of related concepts in which every image recognized to be relevant 'fact' in the idiom of this inquiry is given a place and an interpretation. Its impulse is not to make a world, each of whose component images is welcome on account of the pleasure it gives or the moral approval it evokes, but to make a rational world of consequentially arranged conceptual images. The 'natural world' of the scientist is an artefact no less than the world of practical activity; but it is an artefact constructed on a different principle and in response to a different impulse. And, properly speaking, *scientia* is what happens when we surrender ourselves to this impulse for rational understanding: it exists only where this impulse is cultivated for its own sake unhindered by the intrusion of desire for power and prosperity, and only the shadow of it appears where the products of this engagement (the discoveries about the world) are what is valued, and are valued only for what can be contrived from them. Of course, desire and approval and even the expectation of pleasure have their place in the generation of this activity, but they do not enter into the structure of this universe of discourse as they do into the structure of the practical universe: pleasure is not the warrant of valid achievement, it is not even the *ratio cognoscendi* of valid achievement, but only the self-congratulation which comes with the belief that one has been successful in this intellectual undertaking.

It is not to be supposed that the self in scientific activity begins with a premeditated purpose, a ready-made method of inquiry, or even with a given set of problems. The so-called 'methods' of scientific investigation emerge in the course of the activity and they never take account of all that belongs to a scientific inquiry; and in advance of scientific thought there are no scientific problems. Even the principle of the 'rationality of nature' is not a genuine presupposition; it is merely another way of describing the impulse from which *scientia* springs. All that exists in advance of scientific inquiries is the urge to achieve an intellectually satisfying world of images. Thinking *becomes* scientific in a process similar to that in which some universities, which began as seminaries for training would-be teachers of an already settled doctrine, deserted their original sectarian character and became societies of scholars distinguished not by a doctrine held in common but by their manner of engaging in learning and teaching. But the emancipation which specifies *scientia* is not an emancipation from a dogma; it is an emancipation from the authority of practical imagining. It is a false theory of scientific knowledge which understands it as the most economical arrangement of the images of practical imagining – not because economy of concepts is a vice in scientific theory, but because its images are not those of the world of practice. The mark of the scientist is, then, his power of moving freely within current scientific theory (for this is where he begins), of perceiving the ambiguities and incoherencies which reveal its irrationality, of speculating upon and making guesses about directions of profitable advance, of distinguishing what is important from what is trivial and of pursuing his conjectures in such a manner as to produce significant and unambiguous conclusions. And in this respect, every detailed piece of scientific investigation is a microcosm of the manner in which the grander and more general scientific theories are explored and elucidated.

In practical activity each self seeks its own pleasure: *chacun est un tout à soi-même, car, lui mort, le tout est mort pour soi.*[1] But this pursuit of pleasure involves accommodation to other selves, and consequently practical activity is at least intermittently co-operative and calls for a certain level of communication between selves. *Scientia*, on the other hand, is essentially a co-operative enterprise. All who participate in the construction of this rational world of conceptual images invoking universal acceptance are as if they were one man, and exactness of communication between them is a necessity. Indeed, *scientia* may be said to be itself the mutual understanding of one another enjoyed by those who know how to participate in the construction of this world of images. Scientists do their cumulative best to inform us about the world, but *scientia* is the activity, not the information, and the principle of this activity is the exclusion of whatever is private, esoteric, or ambiguous. And in response to this requirement of exactness of communication images become measurements according to agreed scales, relationships are mathematical

[1] Pascal, *Pensées,* 457.

ratios, and positions are indicated by numerical co-ordinates: the world of science is recognized as the world *sub specie quantitatis*.

The voice of science, then, is not essentially didactic; it is a conversable voice, but the language it speaks is a more severely symbolic language even than that of practice, and the range of its utterance is both narrower and more precise. Whereas words in practical activity are often only slightly more subtle and more easily transmissible alternatives to gestures (words and gestures being alike symbolic) and may be legitimately used both to proclaim and to conceal thoughts, words in scientific utterance are more precisely symbolic, and when they can be refined no further, they give place not to gestures but to technical expressions, to signs and mathematical symbols which can be more exactly assembled and are more exactly related to one another because they have been purged of the last vestiges of ambiguity. Symbols are like chess-men: they stand for what can be done with them according to known rules, and the rules which govern the use of mathematical symbols are more strict than those which govern the use of words; indeed, some statements made in mathematical symbols are incapable of being translated into words. The idiom of scientific utterance has superficial similarities and correspondences to that of practical utterance: both, for example, recognize a distinction between 'fact' and 'not-fact'; in neither is speaking itself image-making; whereas the one must be argumentative, the other may be so; and in both, knowledge, opinion, conjecture, and supposition are severally recognized. But the similarities are only superficial. 'Fact' and 'not-fact' are, in each activity, differently determined; and *scientia* is conditioned throughout by its impulse to construct a rational world of consequentially related conceptual images, an impulse which constitutes a different universe of discourse from that of practice.

5

By 'poetry' I mean the activity of making images of a certain kind and moving about among them in a manner appropriate to their character. Painting, sculpting, acting, dancing, singing, literary and musical composition are different kinds of poetic activity. Of course, not everyone who lays paint upon canvas, who chisels stone, or moves his limbs rhythmically, or opens his mouth in song, or puts pen to paper in verse or prose, speaks in the idiom of poetry, but only those who engage in these and similar operations in a certain manner.[1] The voice of poetry is one which speaks in the idiom of this activity. How shall we specify it?

Let me recall a manner of being active different from that in either practice or science, but nevertheless not unfamiliar. I will call it 'contemplating', or 'delighting'. This activity, like every other, is making images of a certain sort and moving among them in an appropriate manner. But these images, in the first place, are recognized to be mere images; that is to say, they are not recognized either as 'fact' or as 'not-fact', as 'events' (for example) to have taken place or not to have taken place. To recognize an image as 'fact', or to ask oneself the question: Is this 'fact' or 'not-fact'?, is to announce oneself to be engaged in some other manner of activity than contemplation – a practical, a scientific, or an historical manner. Nor is it enough to say: 'This image may or may not be "fact", but in contemplating it I ignore the possibility of its factual character.' For images are never neutral, eligible to be considered in this or that manner: they cannot divest themselves of the considerabilities which determine their character and they are always the partners of a specific kind of imagining. Where imagining is 'contemplating', then, 'fact' and 'not-fact' do not appear. And consequently these images cannot be recognized as either 'possible' or 'probable', as illusions or as makebelieve images, because all these categories look back to a distinction between 'fact' and 'not-fact'.

Further, images in contemplation are merely present; they provoke neither speculation nor inquiry about the occasion or conditions of their appearing but only delight in their having appeared. They have no antecedents or consequents; they are not recognized as causes or conditions or signs of some other image to follow, or as the products or effects of one that went before; they are not instances of a kind, nor are they means to an end; they are neither 'useful' nor 'useless'. Contemplative images may have connections with one another, but they have no history: if they had a history they would be historical images. In practical activity an image may be

[1] Aristotle, *Poetics*, i, 7–8; ix, 2.

said to be impermanent because it is always a temporary resting-place in a necessarily endless process which is concluded only in death; it is a step in the execution of a policy or a project; it is something to be made use of, to be improved or transformed. And the same is true of the conceptual images of scientific theory, which are recognized as having entailments and logical connections, which are often kept ready for use as tools of inquiry for the appropriate occasion when it arises, and are capable of improvement. The images which partner contemplation, on the other hand, have the appearance of being both permanent and unique. Contemplation does not use, or use-up or wear-out its images, or induce change in them: it rests in them, looking neither backwards nor forwards. But this appearance of being permanent is not to seem durable instead of transitory; like any other image, the image which partners contemplation may be destroyed by inattention, may be lost, or may decompose. It is permanent merely because change and destruction are not potential in it; and it is unique because no other image can fill its place.

Moreover, the image in contemplation is neither pleasurable nor painful; and it does not attract to itself either moral approval or disapproval. Pleasure and pain, approval and disapproval are characteristics of images of desire and aversion, but the partner of desire and aversion is incapable of being the partner of contemplation.

Nevertheless, it is not to be supposed that some superior 'reality' or importance may properly be attributed to the images of contemplative imagining. And in this connection I must distinguish what I mean by contemplation from another, and perhaps more familiar, notion. Some writers (whose manner of thinking has impressed itself deeply upon our intellectual habits) understand contemplation as an experience in which the self is partnered, not by a world of unique but transitory images, but by a world of permanent essences: to contemplate is to 'behold' the 'universals' of which the images of sense, emotion, and thought are mere copies. And consequently, for these writers contemplation is the enjoyment of a special and immediate access to 'reality'. It seems probable that Plato held some such view as this; Spinoza appears to have attributed this character to what he calls *scientia intuitiva*;[1] and Schopenhauer found in *Kontem-*

[1] *Ethica*, ii, 40; v, 25–38.

plation a union of the self with *species rerum*.[1] And I do not think there can be any serious doubt about how Plato, at least, arrived at this conception of contemplation (Θεωρία). Activity, both human and divine, he understood as fabrication, the activity of a craftsman; and 'to make' was to copy, reproduce, or imitate an ideal model in the transitory materials of space and time. Consequently, activity was understood to entail, as a first step, a 'vision' of the archetype to be copied; and this experience he called Θεωρία. Thus, contemplation (this immediate experience, not of images, but of the real εἶδος) emerged by supposing the activity of a craftsman to have been arrested before the work of copying had been begun. And in the Platonic conspectus the voice of Θεωρία was acknowledged to be supreme in the conversation of mankind on account of its release from the concerns of craftsmanship, which were considered to be servile because they were apt to be repetitive and in any case were understood to be those of a merely imitative image-maker.

For many centuries in the intellectual history of Europe, contemplation, understood as a purely receptive experience of real entities, occupied the highest place in the hierarchy of human experiences, scientific inquiry being recognized as, at best, preparatory to it, and practical engagements as mere distractions. In recent times, however, not only has it been demoted from this position of supremacy (by a philistine concern with useful knowledge), but it has even been called in question by the re-emergence of an understanding of activity which has no place for it. The Platonic understanding of activity as copying ideal models (and therefore entailing a 'vision' of the models to be copied) has been overshadowed by a concept of 'creative' activity[2] which, having no place for ideal models or for images recognized as mere copies of these models, has no place either for this kind of contemplation. But there are difficulties inherent in this notion of Θεωρία which this reversal of its historic fortunes only imperfectly discloses. It need not be doubted that Θεωρία reflects some observed condition of human experience, but it may be questioned whether the reflection is as faithful as it should

[1] *Die Welt als Wille und Vorstellung*, §34.
[2] Cf. M. Foster, *Mind*, October 1934.

be; and I do not myself know where to place an experience released altogether from modality or a world of 'objects' which is not a world of images and is governed by no considerabilities. Moreover, to make an experience of this sort supreme seems to entail a belief in the pre-eminence of inquiry, and of the categories of 'truth' and 'reality', a belief which I would wish to avoid. But be that how it may, this is not the notion of contemplation I am now exploring. Contemplation, as I understand it, is activity and it is image-making; and the images of contemplative imagining are distinguished from those of both scientific and practical imagining, not by reason of their 'universality', but on account of their being recognized as individuals and neither as concretions of qualities any of which might appear elsewhere (as both coal and wood may be recognized for their combustibility or two men may be compared in respect of their mastery of a particular skill), nor as signs or symbols of something else. And I am disposed to think that this is all that can, in the end, survive of the Platonic conception of Θεωρία.

Since images in contemplation are different in character from those which partner both practical and scientific activity, the organization of these images will also be different. The coherence of the images of the practical world (organized by such distinctions as pleasurableness and painfulness, approval and disapproval, 'fact' and 'not-fact', expected and unexpected, chosen and rejected) springs from their being the creatures of desire; and the world of scientific images has communicable intelligibility as the principle of its order. In what fashion are the images of contemplation organized, and in what manner does the contemplating self move among them?

The world in which the self awakes in contemplation may be dark and its images indistinct, and in so far as the activity verges upon lethargy what appears will be a mere sequence of images, one following another in lazy association, each entertained for its moment of delight but none held or explored. This, however, is the nadir of contemplation, from which the contemplative self rises when one image (because of the pre-eminent delight it offers) becomes the focus of attention and the nucleus of an activity in which it is allowed to proliferate, to call up other images and be joined with them and to take its place in a more extended and complex composition. Nevertheless, this composition is not a conclusion; it is only another image of the same sort. In this process images may generate one another, they may modify and fuse with one another, but no premeditated achievement is pursued. The activity here is clearly not inferential or argumentative. Since there is no problem to be solved, no hypothesis to be explored, no restlessness to be overcome, no desire to be satisfied, or approval to be won, there is no '*This*, therefore *That*', no passage from image to image in which each movement is a step in an elucidation or in the execution of a project. And since what is sought is not an *exit* from this labyrinth of images, a guide of any kind would be out of place. At every turn what impels the activity and gives it whatever coherence it may possess, is the delight offered and come upon in this perpetually extending partnership between the contemplating self and its images.

Contemplating, then, is a specific mode of imagining and moving about among images, different from both practical and scientific imagining. It is an activity of making and entertaining mere images. In practice and in science 'activity' is undeniable. In the one there is a need to be satisfied, a thirst to be quenched, and satiety is always followed by want; there may be weariness, but there is no rest. And in the other there is a corresponding restlessness appropriate to its idiom; every achievement in the exploration of the vision of a wholly intelligible world of images being merely a prelude to fresh activity. But since in contemplation there is neither research for what does not appear nor desire for what is not present, it has often been mistaken for inactivity. But it is more appropriate to call it (as Aristotle called it) a non-laborious activity – activity which, because it is playful and not businesslike, because it is free from care and released from both logical necessity and pragmatic requirement, seems to participate in the character of inactivity. Nevertheless, this appearance of leisureliness (σχολή) is not an emblem of lethargy; it springs from the self-sufficiency enjoyed by each engagement in the activity and by the absence of any premeditated end. At whatever point contemplation is broken off it is never incomplete. Consequently, the 'delight' which I have coupled with contemplation is not to be thought of as a reward which follows upon the activity, as wages follow work, as knowledge follows upon scientific research, as release follows death or an injection of opium; 'delighting' is only another name for 'contemplating'.

Every mode of imagining is activity in partnership with images of a specific character which cannot appear in any other universe of discourse; that is, each mode begins and ends wholly within itself. Consequently, it is an error (though a common one) to speak of a manner of imagining as the 'conversion', or ' transformation', or 'reconstruction' either of a supposed unspecified image or of an image belonging to a different universe of discourse. An unspecified image is only another name for a nonentity; and the images of one universe of discourse are not available (even as raw materials) to a different mode of imagining. For example, the word 'water' stands for a practical image; but a scientist does not first perceive 'water' and then resolve it into H_2O: *scientia* begins only when 'water' has been left behind. To speak of H_2O as 'the chemical formula for water' is to speak in a confused manner: H_2O is a symbol the rules of whose behaviour are wholly different from those which govern the symbol 'water'. And similarly, contemplative activity is never the 'conversion' of a practical or a scientific image into a contemplated image; its appearance is possible only when practical and scientific imagining have lost their authority.

Nevertheless, it is clear that one mode of imagining may give place to and supersede another, and the relationship between these different universes of discourse will be illuminated if we understand how this may come about. Of all the modes of imagining practical activity is unmistakably the commonest among adult human beings – and understandably so, for the avoidance of death is the condition of any sort of activity. Departures from this activity have always the appearance of excursions into a foreign country; and this is pre-eminently so with contemplation, which can never be expected to be more than an intermittent activity. How is the passage from practice to contemplation made? In general, it would seem that any occasion which interrupts the affirmative flow of practical activity, any lessening of the urgency of desire, any softening of the wilfulness of ambitions, or anything that blunts the edge of moral appraisal offers an invitation to contemplative activity to make its appearance. Contemplation is not itself lethargic, but it may find its opportunity when practical activity becomes lethargic. An image which the desiring self has failed to make its own (if it does not become an image of aversion) is, so to speak, ready to be superseded by an image of contemplative delight. Disenchantment, or the more permanent detachment which belongs to a practical attitude of 'fatalism', commonly induce (or perhaps are only other names for) lethargy in practice which contains an intimation of the leisureness which belongs to contemplation. Moreover, a practical image which has been circumstantially loosened from its world and is framed apart (such as a house no longer habitable, or a ship no longer sea-worthy, or unrequited love) or an image that has an ambiguously practical character (such as a loaf of bread in paint, a man in stone, a friend or a lover) constitutes a momentary interruption of practical activity, and contemplation may flow in to take its place. Indeed, any practical image which, from the unfamiliar circumstances of its appearance, induces wonder may open a door upon the world of contemplation, so long as wonder does not pass into curiosity (*scientia*). And it would seem that contemplation may supervene more easily when the practical image is a memory-image. For, in regard to experiences remembered, desire and aversion are apt to be less clamorous, approval and disapproval less insistent, and even the urge to distinguish between 'fact' and 'not-fact' is diminished; though, of course, a memory and a memory contemplated are images that belong to different universes of discourse. In short, and in general, although no image can ever survive outside its proper universe of discourse, diminished or interrupted activity in one mode may generate an opportunity for the appearance of another. And those who would enjoy the difficult delights of contemplation must be ready to enter by whatever door chance or circumstance may open to them.

6

I have recalled this manner of being active because, as I understand it, poetic imagining is contemplative activity. I do not mean that poetic imagining is one species among others of contemplative imagining; I mean that the voice of contemplation is the voice of poetry and that it has no other utterance. And just as activity in practice is desiring and obtaining, and activity iñ science is inquiring and understanding, so poetry is contemplating and delighting.[1]

That the activity in poetry is imagining, making and moving about among images, is so little to be questioned that even those who do not accept my view that *all* activity (except symbolic utterance) is imagining are not likely to deny it. But, in my view, poetry appears when imagining is contemplative imagining; that is, when images are not recognized either as 'fact' or as 'not-fact',[2] when they do not provoke either moral approval or disapproval, when they are not read as symbols, or as causes, effects, or means to ulterior ends, but are made, remade, observed, turned about, played with, meditated upon, and delighted in, and when they are composed into larger patterns which are themselves only more complex images and not conclusions. A poet arranges his images like a girl bunching flowers, considering only how they will appear together. He has to do only with images to which such arrangement is appropriate; the bunch is only another image of the same sort; and the style and diction which distinguishes him from other poets lies in the character of the images he is apt to delight in and in the manner in which he is disposed to arrange them. And it is with 'style' in this sense that the critic (as distinct from the philosopher) is concerned.

Thus, any scene, shape, pattern, pose or movement in the visible or audible world, any action, happening or event or concatenation of events, any habit or disposition exhibited in movement or speech, any thought or memory is a poetic image if the manner in which it is imagined is what I have called 'contemplating'. But certain images – scenes, shapes, poses, movements, etc. – are more readily and more

---

[1] I have said that I am inclined to think that what I mean by 'contemplation' is all that can survive in the Platonic conception of Θεωρία. This belief may now be restated as the belief that what Plato described as Θεωρία is, in fact, aesthetic experience but that he misdescribed it and attributed to it a character and a supremacy which it is unable to sustain. By understanding 'poetry' as a craft, and craft as an activity of imitating ideal models, he followed a false scent which led him to the unnecessary hypothesis of a non-image-making, 'wordless' experience, namely, that of 'beholding' the ideal models to be copied. Nevertheless, the platonic Θεωρία, if it were admitted to be image-making, would direct our attention to an activity of image-making which would not be 'copying' and whose images would not be 'representations'.

[2] And therefore neither as 'illusions' nor as images of 'make-believe'.

unmistakably recognized as poetic images because of the circumstances in which they appear: they positively provoke a contemplative attitude rather than any other because of their resistance to being read symbolically. Such images we call works of art: for example, Donatello's David, Seurat's La Grande Jatte, Mozart's *Figaro*, the nurse in *Romeo and Juliet*, Moby Dick the Whale, Anna Karenina, Lord Randall of the ballad, *Paradise Lost*, a pose or a phrase of movement of Nijinski, an entrance of Rachel, Tom Walls' leer, or verbal images such as

> *Or sea-starved hungry sea*
>
> *Earth of the slumbering and liquid trees*
>
> *And man is such a marigold*
>
> *Goe, and catche a falling starre,*
> *Get with child a mandrake roote,*
> *Tell me, where all past yeares are,*
> *Or who cleft the Divels foot . . .*

Of course, none of these and similar shapes, sounds, movements, characters, verbal constructions, etc., is incapable of being imagined in an unpoetic manner. A piece of sculpture may be considered indecent, a painting may be an object of worship, Uncle Mathew's verdict on the nurse in *Romeo and Juliet* ('dismal bitch') shows him to have been imagining in the idiom of practice, and almost any verbal construction (a metaphor, for example) may be used for its 'aptness' as an oratorical device to persuade a listener of the truth of a proposition or to embellish an otherwise commonplace statement. A work of art is merely an image which is protected in an unusual degree from being read (that is, imagined) in an unpoetic manner, a protection it derives from its quality and from the circumstantial frame within which it appears.[1] This quality is perhaps less likely to be mistaken in the images of some arts than in those of others. A musical image is more secure than a pictorial image; and the poetic character of a verbal image may sometimes be intimated by its

---

[1] The frame provided, for example, by a theatre, or a picture gallery, or a concert hall, or the covers of a book.

practical incoherence. And further, a word or a verbal construction may have a recognized home in more than one universe of discourse: 'the French Revolution' for Blake was a poetic image, for de Tocqueville it represented an historical image, for Napoleon a practical image; the word 'democracy' for some people represents a quasi-scientific image, for many it signifies a practical image (the symbol of a condition desired and to be approved), for de Tocqueville it stood for an historical image, but for Walt Whitman it was a poetic image. In short, the character of an image is revealed in its behaviour, in the sort of statements which can relevantly be made about it and in the sort of questions which can relevantly be asked about it.

Let us suppose that the activity in poetry is not 'contemplating', but is some version of practical or scientific activity. It would then be relevant to ask certain questions about an image recognized to be a poetic image: we might consider whether it was 'fact' or 'not-fact' and what sort of 'fact' or 'not-fact' it was. We might ask, in respect of Donatello's David: Was David (whoever he was) of these proportions? Was he accustomed to wearing a hat of this sort, or did he wear it only on the occasions when he was posing for the sculptor? Of Anna Karenina we might relevantly ask: Is it a fact that she said these words on this occasion, or has Tolstoy misreported what she actually said? Of Hamlet we might inquire: What was his normal bed-time? Of Marlowe's Tamburlaine we should at once be sceptical; How does he come to be speaking English, or is Marlowe translating for our benefit from the Scythian tongue? Of 'Paradise Lost' we might inquire, in respect of many passages: What part of the country is being described to us? or: What was the date of Adam's death? Of a performance of *Figaro* we might ask: How close a resemblance has the singer's voice to that of the real Barbarina? And so on.

But we need only to suppose these and other inquiries in the same idiom in order to recognize that they are misconceived. What Anna said on any occasion could not have been misreported by Tolstoy because she is incapable of speaking any words which he has not put into her mouth. Hamlet never went to bed; he exists only in the play, he is a poetic image composed of the words and actions which Shakespeare gave him, and beyond these he is nothing. Rachel did not 'imitate' the words and actions, or 'resemble' the character or appearance of a living or once living person, she divested herself of her own practical self and became (on a stage) a poetic image in which movement and speech were combined.[1] Corot could not misreport a landscape because he was not making a report at all, he was making a poetic image. Donatello's David is not an 'imitation' King David as a boy; it is not even an imitation of a model: a sculptor's model is not a person, but a pose. A photograph (if it purports to record an event) may 'lie', but a poetic image can never 'lie' because it does not affirm anything. These images – shapes, scenes, movements, characters, verbal constructions – do not belong to a universe of discourse in which 'fact' and 'not-fact' can be distinguished; they are fictions. And these stories and descriptions in paint or words or stone or the movements of dance are stories of fictitious events and scenes; they are fables. And on this account, also, they are neither illusions nor make-believe images, nor are they images made in an activity of pretending; for, illusion, make-believe, and pretence are all impossible without a reference to 'fact'. Anna was not a suicide; Othello was not a murderer; Daisy Miller was not a silly girl who died of the *perniciosa* – she was never, in that sense, alive; she is a phantom. Indeed, even to speak of these images in the past tense is to speak inappropriately about them; they do not belong to the world of practical time and space. And further, moral approval or disapproval are alike inapplicable to these images; they are not people who inhabit or who have ever inhabited the practical world of desire and enterprise, and consequently their 'conduct' cannot be either 'right' or 'wrong' nor their dispositions 'good' or 'bad'. The Cenci, according to the chronicle, was a disagreeable and ill-mannered family, but the poetic image of Beatrice in Shelley's drama is an emblem neither of good nor of bad behaviour; she is a tragic fiction, ineligible for either approval or disapproval. And the fact that we are held back from approving or disapproving of the 'conduct' and character of, for example, Anna Karenina, Lord Jim, or the Duchessa Sanseverina, as they come to us in the pages of books, is evidence of our recognition of their unmistakably poetic quality. Nor, finally, are poetic images capable of giving either pleasure or pain. Pleasure and pain are the

[1] Drama is not 'acting' or 'make-believe acting', it is 'playing at acting'.

partners of desiring, but here desire and aversion are absent: what in the practical world would be pleasurable or painful situations in poetry are alike delightful.

In short, painters, sculptors, writers, musical composers, actors, dancers, and singers, when they are poets, are not doing *two* things – observing, thinking, remembering, hearing, feeling, etc., and then 'expressing' or making analogues, imitations, or reproductions of what they have seen, heard, remembered, felt, etc., in the practical world, and doing it well or ill, correctly or incorrectly – they are doing *one* thing, imagining poetically. And the images they make behave in the manner of images which are the counterparts of contemplative imagining. There are, of course, many inquiries we may properly make about these images, inquiries designed to elicit their qualities and in the course of which we may educate ourselves in the activity of delighting; but here we are concerned only to observe that inquiries appropriate to practical, scientific or historical images are not appropriate to poetic images.

Nevertheless, there are false beliefs about poetic imagining and poetic images which die hard. Some people find poetic images unintelligible unless they can be shown to be in some sense 'true' or representations of 'truth', and the obvious difficulties which face such a requirement are circumvented by means of a concept of 'poetic truth', a special kind of 'truth' usually believed to be more profound than other manifestations of 'truth'. There is, further, a disposition to understand poetic imagining as an activity (superior to other activities) in which 'things are seen as they really are', poets being thought to have a special gift in this respect, not enjoyed by other people. Again, there are people who do not understand how poetic imagining can be anything other than 'expressing' or 'conveying' or 'representing' experiences which the poet has himself enjoyed and wishes others to enjoy also; and these 'experiences' are often thought of as 'emotions' or 'feelings'. And finally, it is commonly believed that all poetic imagining is an attempt to make images which have a special quality named 'beauty'. But all these and similar beliefs are, I think, misleading, and none of them can survive investigation; and I am certain that they must be erroneous if (as I believe) poetic imagining is what I have called 'contemplating'.

The notion of 'poetic truth' has this much to be said for it: it recognizes that whatever 'truth' a poetic image may represent, it is not practical, scientific, or historical truth. That is to say, it belongs to the view that to charge a poetic image with practical impossibility, scientific solecism, or historical anachronism is as much out of the nature of things as to accuse a cabbage of theft. But, properly speaking, 'truth' concerns propositions, and while practical statements may constitute propositions and scientific and historical statements always do so, poetic images are never of this character. And I do not myself understand how the concept 'truth' applies to poetic images such as

> O sea-starved hungry sea

> Fair maid, white and red,
> Comb me smooth, and stroke my head;
> And every hair a sheave shall be,
> And every sheave a golden tree.

or to Anna Karenina, or a movement of Nijinski on the stage, or a tune of Rossini or to Bellini's St Francis. None of these purports to be an affirmation of 'fact'; and, indeed, a world of images from which 'fact' and 'not-fact' are alike absent is not a world whose constituents are properly to be qualified by such epithets as 'true' and 'erroneous', 'veracious' or 'false' or 'mistaken'.

And when, further, it is said that poetic imagining is 'seeing things as they really are', that what distinguishes a poet is the 'precision' of his observation, we seem to have been inveigled back into a world composed, not of images but of cows and cornfields, midinettes and May mornings, graveyards and Grecian urns which may be observed with varying degrees of accuracy but which otherwise owes nothing to imagining. Or, if this is not what is intended, then it would appear that poetic imagining is being presented to us (after the manner of Plato and his followers) as insight into the 'permanent essences' of the things of a phenomenal world and is, on that account, 'seeing things as they really are'. But either way, what is being said in these invocations of 'truth' and 'reality' may perhaps be recognized either as a denial of the interdependence between the self and its images, or as a somewhat confused representation of the mistaken belief that all modes of imagining and moving about among images are properly to be understood as contributions to an inquiry into the nature of the real world. Nor are these difficulties avoided in the more modest claim that poetic imagining is seeing 'things' as they are when perception is unclouded by the preoccupations of desire, approval, curiosity, or inquiry. As I understand it, the poet is not saying anything at all about 'things'[1] (that is, about images belonging to a world of discourse other than that of poetry). He is not saying, 'This is what these persons, objects and events (the return of Ulysses, Don Juan, sunset on the Nile, the birth of Venus, the death of Mimi, modern love, a cornfield (Traherne), the French Revolution) really were or are', but 'In contemplation I have made these images, read them in their own character, and seek in them only delight'. In short, when you know what things are really like you can make no poems.

And yet, no doubt, there are still some misgivings to be allayed. Even if we agree that poetic imagining is not properly described as seeing 'things' such as May mornings and graveyards 'as they really are', there are less improbable versions of this view which ought to be considered. Are you proposing (I shall be asked) to throw overboard also the theory of poetic imagining in which it is understood to be experiencing feelings or emotions and in which poetic images are understood to be the 'expressions' of such experiences? And I must confess that my answer is: 'Yes, that is exactly what I am proposing to do, but not without consideration.'

Of course it will readily be understood that I am unable to recognize poetic imagining as a 'communication' of an emotional experience designed to evoke this experience in others, for that would give it an unequivocally practical character. And Ode to Dejection is not an attempt to excite dejection in the reader; an Ode to Duty is not an attempt to make us feel dutiful, any more than a tragic situation in a play is one designed to give us pain. Nor (without inconsistency) can I accept the view that in a poetic image an emotional experience is simply 'expressed',[2] for here also the activity would be unmistak-

[1] Nor about 'aspects' of 'things'.

[2] The other words commonly used in this connection have each a different *nuance*, but they are all alike unsatisfactory: convey, communicate, represent, exhibit, display, embody, perpetuate, describe, find an objective correlative for, incarnate, make immortal, etc. The least objectionable perhaps is the most

ably practical and not contemplative, and the image a symbol; a large part of our practical activity consists in expressing our emotions in conduct and words. But beyond these there is another and perhaps more plausible theory. It is to be found explicitly in the writings of Wordsworth,[1] but other writers (Sir Philip Sidney and Shelley) seem also to hold it, and it is among the more common current theories. It runs as follows: poetry begins with an emotional experience undergone by the poet himself (anger, for example, or love, or dejection, or loss of faith), this emotional experience is then contemplated, and from this activity of contemplation a poetic image is generated which is an 'expression' of an analogue of the original emotional experience and consequently may be expected to give us what Sidney[2] calls 'a more familiar insight' into the experience.

There are several objections to this theory, the spring of which is, I think, the belief that poetry must be supposed to provide information or instruction of some sort. It requires the poet himself to have undergone the emotional experience with which poetic imagining is said to begin. And, perhaps as a corollary, the poet is presented to us in this theory as pre-eminently a man of feeling or emotion.[3] But in order to contemplate an emotion (if the expression may be allowed to pass) it is clearly not necessary to have undergone it; indeed, it would seem that the spectator-like mood of contemplation would be more likely to establish itself if the emotion had *not* been experienced. In this respect, then, the theory makes a necessity of what is no more than an unlikely possibility. Further, the theory attributes to the poet the activity of contemplating an emotion being undergone – and this is an impossibility. An emotion is a practical image, and as such it cannot belong to the contemplative world of discourse. It is only when feelings are 'imaginary' (in the sense of not being felt) that they may become the stuff of a poetic

---

time-worn: imitate. This recognizes the fictitious character of the poetic image, but it errs in suggesting an activity of copying and the presumption of something to be copied.

[1] 'Observations prefixed to the second edition of *Lyrical Ballads*.'

[2] Sidney, *Apologie for Poetrie*.

[3] Shelley, *A Defense of Poetry*; or Wordsworth: 'poetry is the spontaneous overflow of powerful feelings'.

image.[1] And it is fair to say that some of the exponents of this theory have had misgivings on this point. In Wordsworth's account, what is contemplated is a 'recollected emotion';[2] and Sidney speaks of passions that are somehow not passions at all – not felt, but 'seen through'. But misgivings are not enough; and Wordsworth's do not carry him very far, for he insists that the poetic image appears only when contemplative tranquillity has given place to another emotion 'kindred to that which was before the subject in contemplation', and is itself the expression of an emotion which 'does actually exist in the mind'. Moreover, in this theory a distinction is made between the image generated and the experience contemplated; the one is said to 'express' the other. But, as I understand it, a poetic utterance (a work of art) is not the 'expression' of an experience, it *is* the experience and the only one there is. A poet does not do *three* things: first experience or observe or recollect an emotion, then contemplate it, and finally seek a means of expressing the results of his contemplation; he does *one* thing only, he imagines poetically. Painting a picture composing a verbal image, making a tune are themselves the activities of contemplation which constitute poetic imagining.[3] The notion that there are poets who unfortunately, because of the want of some technical accomplishment, are unable to 'express themselves', that is, write poetry or paint pictures or dance, is a false notion: there are

[1] It is a profound saying that 'all sorrows can be borne if you can put them into a story', but what it means is that all sorrows can be borne if we can succeed in substituting poetic images in their place.

[2] Memories seem to be a fruitful spring of poetic images because in remembering (if we succeed in escaping the mood of nostalgia) we are already halfway released from the practical world of desire and emotion. But even here, what can be contemplated is not an actual and recognized memory, but an abstraction – a memory not identified as 'fact' and one divorced from space and time. Poetry is not the daughter of memory but its stepdaughter. Cf. Eckermann, *Gespräche mit Goethe*, 28 March 1831.

[3] The changes poets are apt to make in their work are not, strictly speaking, 'corrections' – that is to say, attempts to improve the 'expression' of an already clear mental image; they are attempts to imagine more clearly and to delight more deeply. And the 'studies' which painters often make which later may become components of a larger and complex composition (e.g. Seurat's studies for La Grande Jatte) are not hypotheses being tried out; each is itself a snatch of poetry, an image which may or may not become part of a more complex image.

no such people. There are poets (that is, people capable of creating and moving about among poetic images), and there are people capable of recognizing a work of art in its proper character.[1]

The theory, indeed, breaks down conspicuously when set against even the most plausible example. If this were a satisfactory account of any poetic image, surely it should be so of Keat's *Ode to Melancholy*. And yet, quite clearly, this poem could have been composed by a man of sanguine temperament who never himself felt the touch of melancholy; clearly, also, it is not designed to excite melancholy in the reader (or, if that were its design, it fails signally); and it cannot be said to tell us what melancholy 'really is'. Indeed, it is only when we are misled by the title of the poem (which, in a work of art, is never of any significance;[2] poets always know poems by their first lines, and in composition they never begin with a 'subject' but always with a poetic image) that we get the misleading notion that this poem is 'about melancholy' in anything like the same sense as this essay is 'about poetry'. In fact, this poem is a complex of images made in an activity of contemplation (but not the contemplation of the emotion symbolized in the word 'melancholy'), which neither 'expresses' melancholy nor gives us 'a more familiar insight' into

[1] If these objections are not conclusive against the theory, there is another which it is, perhaps, not irrelevant to mention. It is noticeable that in respect of what are recognized to be some of the most unmistakable works of art it is anybody's guess what the emotion was that the poet sought to 'express'. What emotion is expressed in *Anna Karenina*? in Botticelli's Birth of Venus? in *Figaro*? in St Paul's Cathedral? in

> *Ah sunflower, weary of time,*
> *That countest the steps of the sun?*

Can it be that these poets, on these occasions, have been so incompetent as to leave us in doubt about what, in this view of things, was their main preoccupation?

[2] It may, however, be remarked that while the 'title' which a poet (or his editor) may give to a poem is usually to be understood merely as a means of identification and might (as often happens) be absent or be replaced by a number without loss, the titles of some poems may be recognized neither as mere identifications nor as (inevitably irrelevant) indications of what the poem is 'about', but as themselves poet images and thus as a component of the poem itself, e.g. 'Sweeney among the Nightingales'. The table of contents of a book of musical compositions often (and appropriately) consists of the opening bars of the compositions themselves.

melancholy, but which allows us an opportunity for contemplative delight.

The activity in poetic imagining, then, is not an activity in which something is 'expressed', or 'conveyed', or 'mimicked', or 'copied', or 'reproduced', or 'exhibited'; there is no undifferentiated 'primary imagination'[1] to supply it with materials, nor have other modes of imagining anything it can make use of. It is the activity of being delighted in the entertainment of its own contemplative images. The patterns which these images may make together, the eligibility to become components of a more complex image, is not determined in advance. Sequences, patterns, correspondencies may give delight when they answer expectations, but only when they are poetic expectations; and they may give delight when they surprise by running wide of expectation, but only when it is poetic surprise. Nor may poetic imagining be said, with any significance, to be the pursuit of some absolute delight potential in these images. There is no 'true', or 'proper', or 'necessary' order or concretion of images to which approximation is being sought. Every poet is like the Spanish painter Orbaneja, of whom Cervantes tells us: when a bystander asked what he was painting, he answered, 'Whatever it turns out to be'. Consequently, 'beauty' (in the vocabulary of aesthetic theory, where I think it now properly belongs) is not a word like 'truth'; it behaves in a different manner. It is a word the use of which is to describe a poetic image which we are compelled to admire, not as we admire (with approval) a noble action, nor as we admire a thing well done (such as a mathematical demonstration), but on account of the pre-eminent delight it plants in the contemplative spectator.

Poetry, then, begins and ends as a language. But in the language of poetry, words, shapes, sounds, movements are not signs with preordained significances; they are not like chessmen behaving according to known rules or like coins having an agreed current value; they are not tools with specific aptitudes and uses; they are not 'conveyances' when what is to be conveyed exists already in

[1] Coleridge, *Biographia Literaria* (Everyman ed.), p. 159. Coleridge (after Kant) was disposed to understand that all experience is 'imagining', but what he calls 'primary imagination' is, in fact, 'primary' only in the sense that it is the mode of imagining we are most apt to engage in, namely, practical imagining.

thought or emotion. Nor is this a language full of synonyms where one sign may be substituted for another if it is apt to convey the same meaning, or where some other sort of sign (a gesture instead of a word) will often do as well. In short, it is not a symbolic language. In poetry words are themselves images and not signs for other images; imagining is itself utterance, and without utterance there is no image. It is a language without a vocabulary, and consequently one that cannot be learned by imitation. But if we were to call it (as I think it might properly be called) a metaphorical language we should at once go on to recognize the difference between metaphor in poetry and metaphor in a symbolic language. In a symbolic language metaphor is and remains a symbol. It may be a rhetorical expression designed to capture attention or to relieve (or to increase) the tension of an argument, or it may even be used in the interest of greater precision; but on all occasions it merely recognizes and makes use of natural or conventional correspondencies, and the aptness of the equivalence invoked is the condition of its effectiveness. Metaphors here are like counters which may carry an attractive design upon their face but it is a design which merely indicates (and does not constitute) their value: for 'son of Adam' read 'man', for 'golden meadow' read 'sunlit field of grass', for 'plum blossom' read 'chastity'.[1] In the language of poetry, on the other hand, metaphors are themselves poetic images, and consequently they are fictions. The poet does not recognize and record natural or conventional correspondencies, or use them to 'explore reality'; he does not invoke equivalencies, he makes images. His metaphors have no settled value; they have only the value he succeeds in giving them. Of course, as verbal expressions they are not immune from the infection of symbolism; any of them (and particularly the so-called 'consecrated' or 'archetypal' images) may relapse into being coins of fixed value, but when this happens they have merely ceased to be poetic images.[2] And to shuffle symbolic metaphors about, rearranging them into different patterns, is the activity which Coleridge contrasted

---

[1] The so-called 'language of flowers' is a symbolic-metaphorical language of this sort.

[2] As in imitation period architecture, character acting or a good deal of Pre-Raphaelite poetry.

with poetic imagining and called 'fancy'.[1] As in science there is no room for ambiguity, so in poetry there is no room for stereotypical images. What, therefore, has to be 'dissolved' before poetry can appear is not the images of a 'primary', non-modal manner of imagining but the authority of the symbolic language of practical activity and of the even more precisely symbolic language of science. The enemies of poetic imagining in music and in dancing are symbolic sounds and movements; the plastic arts emerge only when the symbolism of shapes is forgotten; and the symbolic language of practical activity offers a strong and continuous resistance to the appearance of poetry. There are periods in the history of every symbolic language when the symbolism is still inchoate and is consequently less hostile to poetry, and it would seem that this was the case in sixteenth-century England.[2] But, although no practical language ever becomes perfectly symbolic, the language of the twentieth century is more exactly so than that of the sixteenth century, and therefore constitutes a greater hindrance to poetic imagining. There are, however, still happily situated peoples, like the Irish, who have ready to be turned into poetry a language whose symbolism is archaic and therefore less apt to impose itself.

For those who understand poetic imagining as a naïve and a primordial activity, there is no puzzle about the historical ancestry of the poet. They recognize that a prosaic manner of thinking and speaking, one appropriate to the communication of 'scientific' knowledge, was an historic achievement, perhaps (so far as Europe was concerned) an invention of the Greeks of the classical age. They think of this as having been imposed upon a primordial mythological manner of thinking, which they identify with the poetic. And they go on to applaud or to disparage the invention as they feel inclined. This, however, I believe to be a mistaken view, and it is one which has had some unfortunate consequences in aesthetics: it has acquired a confused counterpart in fashionable psychological interpretations of poetic imagining. No doubt a mythological manner of thinking preceded what we recognize to be

[1] Coleridge, *Biographia Literaria* (Everyman ed.), p. 160.
[2] Macaulay has some matchless pages on this subject at the beginning of his essay on Milton.

a 'scientific' manner; but its idiom was practical and religious rather than poetic, and it was something from which the poet no less than the scientist had to emancipate himself. It is only in a much later passage in European history that the effort of poetic imagination to free itself from the authority of 'scientific' thought became significant.

In ancient times two figures were recognized, each of which has his counterpart in the modern world. There was the seer, the teacher, often speaking in riddles, a figure of religious significance, a priest, a judge, perhaps a magician, whose person was sacrosanct and whose utterances were distinguished by their wisdom; and there was the entertainer, the gleeman, the singer of songs, who rehearsed familiar stories in familiar words and whose audience would tolerate no innovation. The historic progenitor of the poet has been found in each of these figures, and poetic activity has been interpreted accordingly; it has been confused with both wisdom and entertainment. But the poet whose activity I have been considering is a third person, without the wisdom of the seer and without the obligations of the entertainer. It is difficult to discern his counterpart in those ancient times: the man for whom the totem was neither an object of fear, of authority or of reverence, but an object of contemplation; the man for whom myth and magical spell and the cryptic utterances of the seer were not images of power or of wisdom but of delight. But whoever he was (perhaps the man who fashioned the totem-pole, who invented the verbal image of the spell or who translated historic event into myth), it may be supposed that his activity was as unacknowledged as that of the earliest thinkers who began to explore the entailments of a world recognized as 'natural' and not as the artifice or the avatar of a god; and certainly the mediations in which this specifically 'poetic' activity emerged from the acknowledged activities of these ancient societies are lost in obscurity.

That there have always been poets, and that there have always been 'works of art' in the sense in which I have used the expression, I see no reason to doubt; but the activity of the persons has not always been acknowledged and the character of the images as poetic images has often been obscured. And, although the general conditions of poetic imagining may be discerned in this emancipation from the authority of practical (particularly religious) imagining, the event may only rarely be detected. Properly speaking, it never took place in ancient Greece; a glimpse of it is to be found among the Romans; and subsequently in Europe it has been slowly and uncertainly achieved.[1] Here, not many centuries ago, what we may recognize as 'works of art' were recognized primarily as the servants of practical activity. Their office was understood to be decorative and illustrative, the embellishment of the kingly majesty, of religious observance and of the merchant's way of life. They were prized as expressions or evocations of piety, family pride and affection, respect for justice and deference to authority; as the means whereby the memory of notable persons and events were preserved, the faces of strangers made known to one another, true belief exhibited, and good behaviour taught. But emancipation, the recognition of these objects as images designed and fit for contemplative attention, did not spring from some new and unaccountable craving for release from the authority of practical imagining, and, of course, it did not immediately result in the production of works of an entirely different kind; it sprang from circumstantial changes which (giving a new context to what was already there) transformed it, and even provoked a disposition to make things appropriate to this context. Indeed, the mere lapse of time and ordinary forgetfulness played a considerable part in this emancipation: the survival of stories whose messages had been lost and of images whose 'meaning' had been forgotten, and the encounter with images (both verbal and plastic) from elsewhere whose symbolism was unknown. In the *Midsummer Night's Dream* and in the *Tempest*, for example, a whole world of images has been emancipated from their religious and practical significance and transformed into poetry: there are spells which do not bind, images which have lost their emotive power and figures who, having lost their place in both history and myth, acquire poetic character. And in respect of plastic invention, perhaps the most important circumstance mediating this change was the mere superabundance of works eligible to be recognized as works of art. These,

[1] Of the East I hesitate to speak. But there is a significant anecdote of Chuang Tzu about Ch'ing, the chief carpenter of the Prince of Lu, whose description of the activity of being an artist is almost entirely in terms of what he had to forget.

accumulated and deposited in the treasuries of princes, nobles, ecclesiastics, merchants, municipalities and corporations, their practical origin and occasion unknown or forgotten, were detached from whatever practical use or significance they might once have had and, in this manner, framed apart in a new context, they became capable of provoking contemplative attention – as in an earlier century the invading Romans were provoked to contemplative delight by the temples and statues of Greece because for them they had no religious-symbolic significance. And it is in similar circumstances that the poetic qualities of icons and carpets, idols, buildings and utensils, seen by eyes they were never made for or removed from their native context, have received recognition in our own times. The history of modern art, from one point of view, is the story of the manner in which human imagination has filled this context (itself the undesigned gift of historical circumstance) with appropriate images. Nor is this true only of the plastic arts; the history of European drama and of music tells the same story and displays the same combination of contingency and invention responding to one another. And whatever in our current attitude runs counter to this – our attention to the 'subject' of a poem or a picture; our disposition to seek in poetry a guide to conduct; our confusion of poetry with wisdom or with entertainment; our interest in the 'psychology' of the poet; the difficulty we have of accepting the fictitious as such, being disposed to interpret it as symbolic, or make-believe, or as illusion, and so on – may be understood as a survival from bygone times before poetry had emerged and had been recognized, or as a revulsion from what is for us, historically, a comparatively new and still imperfectly assimilated experience.

7

Every apology for poetry is an attempt to discern its place on the map of human activity; every defence attributes to poetic imagining a certain character and, in virtue of this character, a certain place on the map. And it is to be expected that anyone who believes in the pre-eminence of a particular mode of activity will be concerned to discover the office of poetry in relation to that mode. Thus, since it is now commonly believed that practical enterprise and moral endeavour are the pre-eminently proper occupations of mankind, we are not surprised when we find that the commonest apology for poetry is a vindication of it in respect of these occupations. An inquiry into the relation of art to society is understood to be an inquiry into its relation to a society of men engaged in practical activity: what is the 'function' of poetry in the social order? Some of the writers who steer this course, having no great opinion of poetic imagining, understand it to be a regrettable distraction from the proper business of living; at best it is a holiday excursion from which a man might hope to return to work rested and perhaps with renewed energy. Others, however, recognize poetry to be a profitable servant of practical endeavour, apt to perform a variety of useful tasks. The office of poetry, we are informed by these writers, is to tell us how we ought to live or to provide us with a particular kind of criticism of our conduct; it is to record and disseminate a scale of moral values; it is to give a special kind of moral education in which good emotions are not merely described and recommended but actually awakened in us; it is to promote emotional health and sanity; it is to cure a corrupt consciousness and to 'attune us to existence'; it is to reflect the structure and operation of the 'society' in which it appears;[1] it is to comfort the miserable, to strike terror into sinners, or merely to provide 'music while you work'. In a more profound view (Schiller's), the 'social value' of art is recognized to lie in the relief it offers from the uniformities and rigidities of a life narrowly concentrated upon practical endeavour. And in a notorious piece of hyperbole poets have been called 'the unacknowledged legislators of the world'.[2]

Those writers, on the other hand, who believe inquiry about ourselves and the world we inhabit to be the pre-eminently proper occupation of mankind are appropriately concerned to interpret the office of poetry in relation to *scientia*. The problem of art and society

[1] Writers who take this view recognize *Provençale* love poetry of the twelfth century, not as a new direction of contemplative attention but as a reflection of a change in human sentiment, not as an event in the history of poetry but as an event in the history of morals.

[2] Perhaps, instead of hyperbole we should recognize this as merely a reflection of the manifold character of Apollo. Cf. Bacon, *Advancement of Learning*, I; Vico, *Scienza Nuova*, II, §615.

is the problem of its place in a society of men engaged in scientific investigation. Apologists in this idiom have, perhaps, the harder task; but they have not been dilatory in undertaking it. Here again, there are writers who find in poetic imagining merely a distraction from the engagements of *scientia*, and who find in the non-symbolic language of poetry only a worthless instrument of scientific communication. These are the abolitionists: they have a notable pedigree and they have flourished among us since the seventeenth century. But they are partnered by writers who claim for poetic imagining the power of 'seeing things as they really are', who recognize poetry as a record and repository of knowledge about the world, and who understand it in such a manner as to attribute to it the power and the office of giving us 'a clear and impartial awareness of the nature of the world'. And there are even some people who discern in the very process of scientific inquiry and discovery a component which they identify as poetic imagining.

So far as I am concerned, an apology for poetry in either of these idioms is misconceived; although some of the things said in this manner may not be ill-observed or untrue.[1] Having chosen their course, those who think in this manner understand everything merely in respect of the help or hindrance it offers them in reaching their destination. Their inquiry is not concerned with ascertaining the place of poetry on the map of human activity; it is concerned only with the subordinate relation of poetry to the feature on the map which happens to interest them most. But, as I understand it, the only apology for poetry worth considering is one which seeks to discern the place and quality of the voice of poetry in the conversation of mankind – a conversation where each voice speaks in its own idiom, where from time to time one voice may speak louder than others, but where none has natural superiority, let alone primacy. The proper context in which to consider poetic utterance, and indeed every other mode of utterance, is not a 'society' engaged in practical enterprise, nor one devoted to scientific inquiry; it is this society of conversationists.

Each voice in this conversation, from one point of view, represents an emancipation from the conditions which determine the

---

[1] For example, Schiller's thoughts on the usefulness of a 'useless' activity.

idiom of each of the others. *Scientia* is an 'escape' from the *scientia propter potentiam* of practice, and practical activity is an 'escape' from scientific 'fact'. Consequently, if we speak of poetic imagining as a form of 'escape' (recognizing contemplation as an 'escape' from desiring, approving, contriving and inquiring) we are saying no more than that it moves in a universe of discourse differently constituted from that of any other kind of imagining; we are saying no more than what may properly be said of both practice and science. And the note of deprecation which obtrudes itself when poetic imagining is said to be an 'escape' merely advertises an imperfect understanding of the conversation. *Of course*, from one point of view, poetry is an 'escape'; not escape (as is sometimes supposed) from the perhaps unmanageable or frustrating practical life of a poet, but from the considerabilities of practical activity. But there is nothing sacrosanct about practical enterprise, moral endeavour, or scientific inquiry that 'escape' from them is to be deplored. Indeed, these are inherently burdensome activities from which we may properly seek release; and it is a tiresome conversation in which only these voices are heard. In poetry, then, a self which desires and suffers, which knows and contrives, is superseded by a self which contemplates, and every backward glance is an infidelity at once difficult to avoid and fatal in its consequences. Nevertheless, in order to participate in the conversation a voice must not only speak in its own idiom, it must also be capable of being understood; and we should consider how it is possible for the voice of poetry to be heard and understood in conversation with partners of so different a character.

There is, I think, no mystery in the common understanding enjoyed by the voices of science and practical activity. Although the idioms in which they speak are different, there is a counterpart in practice to many of the features of the scientific universe of discourse: the images of both practice and of science are apt to be arranged consequentially, in both activities there is a recognition of 'fact' and 'not-fact', and the language of both is a symbolic language. But, as I have described it, there would appear to be little or no possibility of common understanding between the voice of poetry and the other voices in the conversation: its utterance points to no conclusion, it recognizes neither 'fact' nor 'not-fact' and its language is not a language of signs. And this remoteness of poetic utterance no doubt accounts for the disposition to assimilate it somehow or other to the idioms of science and of practice. Most poets (even when we do not make the mistake of attributing to them the opinions they put into the mouths of their characters) have some thoughts about the world in general and about the conduct of life, and when we listen to these thoughts the voice of poetry seems to acquire an intelligibility which it otherwise lacks. Shakespeare's 'view of life' may appear to us profound, or we may find it as unsatisfactory as Johnson found it,[1] but whatever our conclusion we seem, by considering it, to have drawn the voice of poetry into the conversation and given it a place it would otherwise be without. But it is an illusion; we have caught merely what is unpoetic – the theology of Dante, the perishable religious convictions of Bunyan, the verisimilitude of Ingres, the dated 'pessimism' of Hardy, the pseudo-scientific speculations of Goethe, the patriotism of Chopin – and the poetic image itself has slipped through our net and escaped into its proper element. Or again, it may be conjectured that to be brought up (like French boys and girls) on Racine is an education in desire and approval remarkably different from that which English boys and girls derive from being brought up on Shakespeare; but, whether the difference is profound or superficial, it does not spring from the different poetic qualities of these writers. And yet, just as Plato discerned in the desiring soul a shadowy counterpart of reason (which he called 'temperance') enabling it not to behave rationally but to hear the voice of reason and to submit to its rule, we may, I think, find in practical activity itself intimations of contemplative imagining capable of responding to the voice of poetry.

In the common relationships of practical activity – those of producer and consumer, master and servant, principal and assistant – each participant seeks some service or recompense for service, and if it is not forthcoming the relationship lapses or is terminated. And this is the case also in the relationship of partners in an enterprise, and even in that of comrades where attachment is circumstantial and springs from a common occupation, interest, belief, or anxiety. In

[1] *Preface to Shakespeare.*

the world *sub specie voluntatis* we normally reject what is not to our liking; and in the world *sub specie morum* we normally reject what proves itself to be irrational or imperfect. But there are relationships, still unmistakably practical, where this is not so. It is not so, for example, in love and in friendship. Friends and lovers are not concerned with what can be made out of each other, but only with the enjoyment of one another. A friend is not somebody one trusts to behave in a certain manner, who has certain useful qualities, who holds acceptable opinions; he is somebody who evokes interest, delight, unreasoning loyalty, and who (almost) engages contemplative imagination. The relationship of friends is dramatic, not utilitarian. And again, loving is not 'doing good'; it is not a duty; it is emancipated from having to approve or to disapprove. Its object is individual and not concretion of qualities: it was for Adonis that Venus quit heaven. What is communicated and enjoyed is not an array of emotions – affection, tenderness, concern, fear, elation, etc. – but the uniqueness of a self. But while there is nobody incapable of being loved, there is nobody who singles himself out as pre-eminently proper to be loved. Neither merit nor necessity has any part in the generation of love; its progenitors are chance and choice – chance, because what cannot be identified in advance cannot be sought; and in choice the inescapable practical component of desire makes itself felt.[1] In short, the world *sub specie amoris* is unmistakably the world of practical activity; there is desire and frustration, there is moral achievement and failure, there is pleasure and pain, and death (of one kind or another) is both a possibility and is recognized as the *summum malum*. Nevertheless, the image in love and friendship (what is created in these manners of imagining) is, more than in any other engagement in practical imagining, 'whatever it turns out to be'. If these are not properly speaking contemplative activities, they are at least ambiguously practical activities which intimate contemplation and may be said to constitute a connection between the voices of poetry and practice, a channel of common understanding. And, no doubt, it is on this account that fictitious persons in fictitious love are the most familiar of all poetic images.

[1] Hence St Augustine's difficulty in understanding how God can be said to 'love' man. *De Doct. Christ*, i, 34.

Further, there is, perhaps, in 'moral goodness' (as distinguished from 'virtuous conduct', 'excellence of character', or the engagement in 'good works') a release from the deadliness of doing and a possibility of perfection, which intimates poetry. For here is a private and self-sufficient activity, not accommodated to the world, emancipated from place or condition, in which each engagement is independent of what went before and of what may come after, in which no man is ineligible to engage on account of ignorance or inexpertness in judging the probable consequences of actions, or (as Kant says) by reason of some special disfavour of destiny or by the niggardly endowment of a step-motherly Nature,[1] and in which success is entirely independent of 'usefulness' or external achievement.

Moreover, a poetic utterance (a work of art) is itself often an ambiguous image. Its place in the practical world – in respect of occupying space, being desirable, having a price, and so on – may make it liable to be misread. And there are some works of art – buildings, for example – which may be said to be intrinsically ambiguous because they demand to be considered not only as poetic images but also from the point of view of their durability and the manner in which they satisfy a practical need. But the opportunities which works of art (some more so than others) give for the neglect of their poetic character may also be an oblique means of getting themselves recognized in their poetic character. Our attention may be attracted to a work of art, in the first place, for some entirely extraneous reason – because it seems to represent something in the practical world which is familiar to us or of special interest, because it supplies us with a piece of historical information we have been seeking, because some detail catches our fancy, or merely because it is the work of a friend or an acquaintance – but having, in this manner, been lured into looking or listening, the mood of contemplation may supervene and its proper character as a poetic image may, suddenly or gradually, come to impose itself upon us. And even this entrance to the world of poetry is not to be despised.

And again, the recollections of childhood may constitute the connection sought. Everybody's young days are a dream, a delightful insanity, a miraculous confusion of poetry and practical activity

[1] *Grundlegung zur Metaphysik der Sitten*, 394.

in which nothing has a fixed shape and nothing has a fixed price. 'Fact' and 'not-fact' are still indistinct. To act is to make a bargain with events; there are obscure longings, there are desires and choices, but their objects are imperfectly discerned; everything is 'what it turns out to be'. And to speak is to make images. For, although we spend much of our early years learning the symbolic language of practical intercourse (and when we learn a foreign tongue it is always learnt as a symbolic language), this is not the language with which we begin as children. Words in everyday use are not signs with fixed and invariable usages; they are poetic images. We speak an heroic language of our own invention, not merely because we are incompetent in our handling of symbols, but because we are moved not by the desire to communicate but by the delight of utterance. And however immersed we may become in practical or scientific enterprise, anybody who recollects the confusion it was to be young will have a ready ear for the voice of poetry.

It is, then, not impossible to understand how the voice of poetry should be able to make itself heard in a conversation apt, as it now is, to be dominated by the voices of practice and of science. Nevertheless, as I understand it, poetic imagining brings to the conversation a unique utterance, not to be assimilated to any other. Its voice is pre-eminently conversable. In both scientific and practical imagining utterance and voice, *what* is said and *how* it is said, doctrine and activity, are distinguishable and may become separated from one another; in poetry this is impossible. A poetic image is not a symbol; since it 'expresses' nothing, there can be no tension between imagining and utterance. Moreover, the relationship between poetic images is itself a conversational relationship; they neither confirm nor refute one another, they merely evoke one another and join, not to compose a premeditated conclusion, but to compose another and more complex image of the same kind. Further, poetry has nothing to teach us about how to live or what we ought to approve. Practical activity is an endless battle for noble or for squalid but always for illusory ends, a struggle from which the practical self cannot escape and in which victory is impossible because desire can never be satisfied: every attainment is recognized to be imperfect, and every imperfection has value only as an incipient perfection which is itself an illusion. And even 'forgiveness' is only an emblematic break in the chain of the fatality of doing; every action, even those that are forgotten, is irreparable. Poetic activity has no part in this struggle and it has no power to control, to modify, or to terminate it. If it imitates the voice of practice its utterance is counterfeit. To listen to the voice of poetry is to enjoy, not a victory, but a momentary release, a brief enchantment. And perhaps, obliquely, it is to enjoy something more. Having an ear ready for the voice of poetry is to be disposed to choose delight rather than pleasure or virtue or know-ledge, a disposition which will reflect itself in practical life in an affection for its intimations of poetry.

Nevertheless, we must expect to listen for this voice more often than we hear it. Poetic imagining has frequently been recognized as a 'visitation'; but while this has been taken as an emblem of its superior status, even of its divine inspiration, properly understood it is testimony only of the unavoidable transience of contemplative activity:

> *All things can tempt me from this craft of verse:*
> *One time it was a woman's face, or worse —*
> *The seeming needs of my fool-driven land;*
> *Now nothing but comes readier to the hand*
> *Than this accustomed toil. When I was young,*
> *I had not given a penny for a song*
> *Did not the poet sing it with such airs*
> *That one believed he had a sword upstairs;*
> *Yet would be now, could I but have my wish,*
> *Colder and dumber and deafer than a fish.*

But it is a wish that can have only an intermittent fulfilment. In short, there is no *vita contemplativa*; there are only moments of contemplative activity abstracted and rescued from the flow of curiosity and contrivance. Poetry is a sort of truancy, a dream within the dream of life, a wild flower planted among our wheat.
1959

The Moral Life in the Writings of Thomas Hobbes

The moral life is a life *inter homines*. Even if we are disposed to look for a remote ground (such, for example, as the will of God) for our moral obligations, moral conduct concerns the relations of human beings to one another and the power they are capable of exerting over one another. This, no doubt, spills over into other relationships – those with animals, for example, or even with things – but the moral significance of these lies solely in their reflection of the dispositions of men towards one another. Further, the moral life appears only when human behaviour is free from natural necessity; that is, when there are alternatives in human conduct. It does not require that a specific choice should be made on each occasion, for moral conduct may be habit; it does not require that each occasion should find a man without a disposition to behave in a certain manner; and it does not require that on any occasion the range of choices should be unlimited. But it does require the possibility of choice, and we may perhaps suppose that specific choices of some sort (though not necessarily the choice of *this* action) have been made at some time even though they have become lost and superseded in a settled disposition. In other words, moral conduct is art, not nature: it is the exercise of an acquired skill. But the skill here is not that of knowing how to get what we want with the least expenditure of energy, but knowing how to behave as we *ought* to behave: the skill, not of desiring, but of approving and of doing what is approved.

All this is, of course, well known. Every moralist has perceived a gap between the ascertained inclinations of human beings and what ought to be done about them. But there is something else to be observed, namely, that what we ought to do is unavoidably connected with what in fact we are; and what we are is (in this connection) what we believe ourselves to be. And a moralist who fails to recognize this is apt to fall into absurdity. What Hume complained of was not the attempt to ascertain the connection between moral and factual propositions but the hasty and unsatisfactory manner in which this was done. It was the acute Vauvenargues who detected that it was only by the subterfuge of inventing a 'virtu incompatible avec la natur de l'homme' that Le Rochefoucauld was able to announce coldly that 'il n'y avait aucun virtu'. Indeed, the idioms of moral conduct which our civilization has displayed are distinguished, in the first place, not in respect of their doctrines about how we *ought* to behave, but in respect of their interpretations of what in fact we are.

There are, I believe, three such idioms, which I shall denote: first, the morality of communal ties; secondly, the morality of individuality; and thirdly, the morality of the common good.

In the morality of communal ties, human beings are recognized solely as members of a community and all activity whatsoever is understood to be communal activity. Here, separate individuals, capable of making choices for themselves and inclined to do so, are unknown, not because they have been suppressed but because the circumstances in which they might have appeared are absent. And here, good conduct is understood as appropriate participation in the unvarying activities of a community. It is as if all the choices had already been made and what ought to be done appears, not in general rules of conduct, but in a detailed ritual from which divergence is so difficult that there seems to be no visible alternative to it. What ought to be done is indistinguishable from what is done; art appears as nature. Nevertheless, this is an idiom of *moral* conduct, because the manner of this communal activity is, in fact, art and not nature; it is the product, not (of course) of design, but of numberless, long-forgotten choices.

In the morality of individuality, on the other hand, human beings are recognized (because they have come to recognize themselves in this character) as separate and sovereign individuals, associated with one another, not in the pursuit of a single common enterprise, but in an enterprise of give and take, and accommodating themselves to one another as best they can: it is the morality of self and other selves. Here individual choice is pre-eminent and a great part of happiness is connected with its exercise. Moral conduct is recognized as consisting in determinate relationships between these individuals, and the conduct approved is that which reflects the independent individuality understood to be characteristic of human beings. Morality is the art of mutual accommodation.

The morality of the common good springs from a different reading of human nature, or (what is the same thing) the emergence of a different idiom of human character. Human beings are recognized as independent centres of activity, but approval attaches itself to conduct in which this individuality is suppressed whenever it conflicts, not with the individuality of others, but with the interests of a 'society' understood to be composed of such human beings. All are engaged in a single, common enterprise. Here the lion and the ox are distinguished from one another, but there is not only one *law* for both, there is a single approved condition of circumstance for both: the lion shall eat straw like the ox. This single approved condition of human circumstance is called 'the social good', 'the good of all', and morality is the art in which this condition is achieved and maintained.

Perhaps a deeper review of the history of European morals would disclose other general moral dispositions to be added to these, and perhaps my descriptions of those I have noticed are unnaturally precise, ideal extrapolations of what has actually been felt; but I have no doubt that dispositions of these kinds have appeared, and (without ever quite superseding one another) they have followed one another during the last thousand years of our history, each in turn provoking moral reflection appropriate to itself.

2

In considering the writings of a moralist the first thing to be ascertained is, then, the understanding he has of the nature of human beings. And in Hobbes we may recognize a writer who was engaged in exploring that idiom of the moral life I have called the morality of individuality. Nor is it at all remarkable that this should be so. It is only a very poor moralist who invents for himself either virtues or a version of human nature; both precepts and his reading of human character he must take from the world around him. And, since the emergent human character of western Europe in the seventeenth century was one in which a feeling for individuality was becoming pre-eminent – the independent, enterprising man out to seek his intellectual or material fortune, and the individual human soul responsible for its own destiny – this unavoidably became for Hobbes, as it was for his contemporary moralists, the subject matter of moral reflection. For Hobbes (or for any other moralist in the seventeenth and eighteenth centuries) to have undertaken to explore either the morality of communal ties or the morality of the common good would have been an anachronism. What, then, distinguishes Hobbes from his contemporaries is not the idiom of the moral life he chose to explore, but the precise manner in which he interpreted this current sentiment for individuality and the doctrine of moral conduct he associated with it, or purported to deduce from it. And if it is the enterprise of every philosopher to translate current sentiments into the idiom of general ideas and to universalize a local version of human character by finding for it some rational ground, this enterprise was fortified in Hobbes by his notion of philosophy as the science of deducing the general causes of observed occurrences. His concern was with both men and things; but he was content to allow a certain looseness in the connection between the two,[1] and unlike Spinoza, who presents us with a universe composed of metaphysical individualities (man being only a special case of a universal condition), Hobbes's starting-point as a moralist was with unique *human* individuality; and, as he understood it, his first business was to rationalize *this* individuality by displaying its 'cause', its components and its structure.

Hobbes's complex image of human character was settled upon what he calls 'two most certain postulates of human nature', namely, the postulate of 'natural appetite' or passion, and the postulate of 'natural reason'.[2] It was an image which, in various idioms, had haunted European reflection for many centuries, and though its most familiar idiom is Christian, it is traceable in the Latin thought of pagan antiquity. It is displayed in the lines of the sixteenth century poet, Fulke Greville:

[1] *English Works* (Molesworth), II, xx.
[2] *E.W.*, II, vii.

O wearisome condition of humanity,
Born to one law and to another bound,
Vainly begot and yet forbidden vanity,
Created sick, commanded to be sound,
What meaneth nature by these diverse laws,
Passion and Reason, self-division's cause.

But, whereas the poet is content to compose an image, the philosopher's task is to resolve its incoherence and to make it intelligible.

Any abridgment of Hobbes's carefully pondered and exceedingly complicated image of human nature is hazardous, but to follow all its intricacies is impossible now. To be brief – at least as compared with Hobbes himself – he understood a human being to be a bodily structure characterized by internal movements. There is, first, what he called *vital* movement, the involuntary movement which is identified with being alive and which is exemplified in the circulation of the blood and in breathing. This bodily structure, however, exists in an environment to which it is sensitive, and its contacts with this environment are felt either to assist its vital movements or to impede them. Experiences friendly to vital movement are pleasures and are recognized as good; those which are hostile to it are pains and recognized as evil. Thus, pleasure and pain are our own introspective awareness of being alive; and we prefer pleasure to pain because we prefer life to death. Further, what we prefer we endeavour to bring about. We endeavour to experience those contacts which promote our vital movements and to avoid those which hinder them; and these endeavours are understood by Hobbes as incipient movements towards and away from the components of our environment, movements which he calls respectively appetites and aversions.

In general, for Hobbes, this account of being alive applied both to human beings and to animals, and some of it, perhaps, to other organisms also: an original endowment of vital movement stimulated or hindered by contacts with an environment, and a primordial aversion from death. But at this point Hobbes distinguished between human beings and other organisms. An animal, for example, may feel pleasure and pain, but its vital movements are affected only by an environment with which it is in immediate contact, its appetites and aversions are movements of like and dislike only in relation to what is present, and its hunger is the hunger of the moment.[1] But human beings have other endowments which amplify the range of their appetites and aversions. The chief of these are memory and imagination. Human beings are capable of storing up their experiences of pleasure and pain and of recollecting their causes at a later time; and, in addition to their inescapable environment of objects, they surround themselves with a world of imagined experiences, and they are capable of desiring what is not present except in imagination. Their appetites are inventive and self-consciously pursued, and they are capable of voluntary movements for the achievement of their imagined ends and not merely of reflex responses to whatever happens to constitute their environment. To the simple passions of desire and love, of aversion and hate and of joy and grief, are added hope and despair, courage and anger, ambition, repentance, covetousness, jealousy and revenge. They desire not only an environment presently favourable to their vital movements, but a command over that environment which will ensure its friendliness in the future; and the end they seek, Felicity, is not, properly-speaking, an end, but merely 'continual success in obtaining those things which a man from time to time desireth'.[2] They are, however, restless and ever unsatisfied, not merely because the world is continually provoking them to fresh responses, but because the appetite of an imaginative creature is essentially unsatisfiable. They have 'a restless desire for power after power which ceaseth only in death', not because they are driven to seek ever 'more intensive delights', but because they cannot be assured of the power to live well which they have at present without the acquisition of more.

Moreover, as Hobbes understood it, although men and animals are alike in their self-centredness, the characteristic difference between them lies in the competitive nature of human appetite and passion: every man wishes to out-do all other men. 'Man, whose Joy consisteth in comparing himself with other men, can relish nothing but what is eminent.'[3] Human life, consequently, is a race

[1] *Leviathan* (Pogson Smith), 82.
[2] *L*, 48.
[3] *L*, 130.

which has 'no other goal, nor other garland, but being foremost'; Felicity is 'continually to outgo the next before'.[1] Indeed, the greatest pleasure of a human being, what most of all stimulates the vital movement of his heart, is the consciousness of his own power; the spring of his natural appetite is not what the present world offers him, but his desire for precedence, his longing to be first, for glory and to be recognized and honoured[2] by other men as pre-eminent. His supreme and characteristic passion is Pride; he wishes above all else to be convinced of his own superiority. And so strong is this desire that he is apt to try to satisfy it in make-believe, if (as is usually the case) actual circumstances deny it to him. Thus, pride may degenerate into vain glory, (the mere supposition of glory 'for delight in the consequences of it'); and in the illusions of vain glory he loses ground in the race for precedence.[3]

The passion of pride has, however, a partner; namely, fear. In animals, fear may be understood as merely being affrighted, but in man it is something much more important. Any creature of imagination engaged in maintaining his superiority over others of his kind must be apprehensive of not being able to do so. Fear, here, is not merely being anxious lest the next pleasure escape him, but dread of falling behind in the race and thus being denied felicity. And every such dread is a reflection of the ultimate fear, the fear of death. But, whereas animals may fear anything which provokes aversion, with men the chief fear (before which all others are of little account) is fear of the other competitors in the race. And whereas with animals the ultimate dread is death in any manner, the ultimate fear in man is the dread of violent (or untimely)[4] death at the hand of another man; for this is dishonour, the emblem of all *human* failure. This is the fear which Hobbes said is the human passion 'to be reckoned with': its spring is not a mere desire to remain alive in adverse circumstances, nor is it a mere aversion from death, least of all from the pain of death; its spring is aversion from shameful death.

Human life is, then, a tension between pride and fear; each of

[1] *Elements of Law*, I, ix, 21.
[2] To 'honour' a man is to esteem him to be of great power. *E.W.*, IV, 257.
[3] *Elements*, I, ix, 1; *L*, 44, 77.
[4] *L*, 100.

these primary passions elucidates the character of the other, and together they define the ambivalent relationship which men enjoy with one another. They need one another, for without others there is no precedence, no recognition of superiority, no honour, no praise, no notable felicity; nevertheless every man is the enemy of every man and is engaged in a competition for superiority in which he is unavoidably apprehensive of failure.[1]

So much, then, for the postulate of 'natural appetite' and its entailments in human disposition and conduct. But there is a second postulate, that of 'natural reason'.

'Reason', 'rational' and 'reasoning' are words which, in Hobbes's vocabulary, signify various human powers, endowments and aptitudes which, though they are related to one another, are not identical. In general, they are words which stand for powers which distinguish men, not from one another, but from animals. Human beings are different from beasts in respect of having two powers which may be recognized as, at least, intimations of rationality. First, they are able to regulate their 'Traynes of Thoughts' in such a manner as, not merely to perceive the cause of what has been imagined, but, 'when imagining any thing whatsoever, [to] seek all the possible effects, that can be produced by it; that is to say, [to] imagine what [they] can do with it, when [they] have it'.[2] In other words, human processes of thinking have a scope and an orderliness denied to those of beasts because in them sensation is supplemented by reasoning. This, it seems, is a natural endowment. Secondly, human beings have the power of Speech;[3] and speech is the transference of the 'Trayne of our Thoughts into a Trayne of Words'.[4] This power is a special endowment received from God ('the first author of

---

[1] This is the 'warre of every man, against every man' (*L*, 96), understood by Hobbes to be a permanent condition of universal hostility. It is, of course, a mistake to suppose that Hobbes invented this image of 'natural' human relations (it goes back at least to Augustine, who took the story of Cain and Abel to be the emblem of it), what he did was to rationalize it in a new manner, detaching it from 'sin'. Further, Hobbes distinguished this condition from another, also called 'warre', where hostility is both intermittent and particular and which he recognized as a means by which a condition of peace (a *civitas*) might be established and defended, which the 'warre of every man against every man' could never be.

[2] *L*, 20.   [3] *L*, ch. iv.   [4] *L*, 24.

Speech') by Adam when he was taught by God how to name such creatures as were presented to his sight; and it is the condition of that uniquely human power of 'reasoning', the power of putting words together in a significant manner and of composing arguments. Nevertheless, the power of Speech has to be learned afresh by each generation, and a child becomes recognizable as a 'Reasonable Creature' only when it has 'attained the use of Speech'.[1]

The first use of words is as '*Markes*, or *Notes* of remembrance' and to register the consequences of our thoughts.[2] But they may be used also to communicate with other men; to communicate both information and desires. Beasts, it is true, have some means of communicating their desires to one another; but, not having the use of words, they are unable to communicate (what, because of the narrowness of their imaginations, they have not got), namely, those long-term, considered enterprises which in human beings are properly called 'wills and purposes'. Their power of communication, and consequently the agreement they may have with one another, is 'natural' or instinctive.[3] Among men, on the other hand, communication is by means of the artifice of words. By these means they can (among much else) 'make known to others [their] wills and purposes, that [they] may have the mutual help of one another'.[4] Speech, then, is the ground of such mutual understanding as human beings enjoy among themselves; and this mutual understanding is the ground of any agreement they may have with one another in the pursuit of their desires. Indeed, as Hobbes understands it, Speech itself (as a means of communication) is based upon agreement – agreement about the significance of words.

Generally speaking, agreement between human beings appears only in specific agreements, and these may be of three different sorts. Sometimes it happens that a man, wanting what another man has and is willing to part with if he is recompensed, an exchange may be agreed upon and concluded on the spot, as with buying and selling with ready money. This is a situation described by Hobbes as one in which the thing and the right to the thing are transferred together.[5] And however mistrustful one may be of the man with

[1] *L*, 37.   [2] *L*, 25   [3] *L*, 130 *sq.*
[4] *L*, 25.   [5] *L*, 102.

whom one makes such a bargain, the only disappointment one may suffer is the disappointment to which every buyer is liable, namely, finding that what he has bought turns out to be different from what he had expected it to be. On other occasions, however, the right may be transferred before the thing itself is handed over, as when for a sum of money paid an undertaking is given to deliver tomorrow what has been purchased, or when a man agrees to do a week's work for payment to be received at the end of the week. Such an agreement is called a Pact or Covenant, one party promising and the other performing and waiting for the promise to be fulfilled. In other words, Covenant is an agreement entailing credit. And this element of credit is supremely characteristic of the third kind of agreement; what Hobbes calls 'covenants of mutual trust'. These are Covenants in which neither party 'presently performs', but both agree to perform later. And it is in respect of these that 'reason' gives its most unmistakable warning and in which the true predicament of men in a state of nature is revealed.

Human beings, then, on account of the scope of their imaginations (embracing the future as well as the present), and on account of their powers of speech, are recognizable as contract – and – convennant-making creatures: their agreement is not 'natural' but executed in 'artificial' agreements.[1] Moreover, since agreements may be recognized as endeavours to modify the condition of suspicion and hostility which is their natural circumstance, and therefore to modify the fear that this condition entails, human beings have, in general, a sufficient motive for entering into them. But the regrettable fact is that the relief given by the otherwise most useful sort of agreement (that is, Pacts or Covenants of mutual trust) is uncertain and apt to be evanescent. For in these one party must perform first, before the other keeps his part of the bargain, and the risk of him who is to be the second performer not keeping his promise (either because it may not then be in his interest to do so, or, more probably, because 'ambition' and 'avarice' have intervened) must always be great enough to make it unreasonable for any man to consent to be the first performer. Thus, while such covenants may be entered into,

---

[1] *L*, 131. Covenants, of course, are not possible between men and beasts; but they are also impossible without an intermediary with God. *L*, 106.

reason warns us against being the first to execute them,[1] and therefore against entering into them except as second performers. In short, if 'reason' merely enabled human beings to communicate and to make convenants with one another, it must be recognized as a valuable endowment but insufficient to resolve the tension between pride and fear. This, however, is not the limit of its usefulness: these 'rational' powers also reveal the manner in which the defects of covenanted agreements may be remedied and make possible the emancipation of the human race from the frustrations of natural appetite.

'Reason', here, as Hobbes understood it, is not an arbitrary imposition upon the passionate nature of man; indeed, it is generated by the passion of fear itself. For fear, in human beings, is active and inventive; it provokes in them, not a mere disposition to retreat, but 'a certain foresight of future evil' and the impulse to 'take heed' and to provide against what is feared. 'They who travel carry their swords with them, . . . and even the strongest armies, and most accomplished for fight, [yet] sometimes parley for peace, as fearing each other's power, and lest they might be overcome.'[2] In short, fear of the mischances that may befall him in the race awakens man from his dreams of vain glory (for any belief in continuous superiority is an illusion) and forces upon his attention the true precariousness of his situation.

His first reaction is to triumph by disposing of his immediate enemy, the one next before him in the race for precedence; but 'reason' rejects this as a short-sighted triumph – there will always remain others to be disposed of and there will always remain the uncertainty of being able to dispose of them. And besides, to dispose of an enemy is to forgo recognition of one's own superiority, that is, to forgo felicity.[3] What has to be achieved is a permanent release from fear of dishonourable death; and reason, generated by fear and pronouncing for the avoidance of the threat of death as the condition of the satisfaction of any appetite, declares for an agreed modification of the race for precedence, that is, for a condition of peace. The consequence of natural appetite is pride and fear; the 'suggestion' and promise of reason is peace. And peace, the product of the mutual

[1] *L*, 131.   [2] *E.W.*, II, 6 fn.   [3] Cf. *L*, 549–50.

recognition of a common enemy (death) is to be achieved only in a condition of common subjection to an artificially created sovereign authority, that is, in the *civitas*.[1] There, under a civil law made and enforced by a Common Power authorized to do so, Covenants lose their uncertainty and become 'constant and lasting', and the war of every man against every man is brought to an end. The endeavour for peace is natural, begotten by human reason upon human fear; the condition of peace is a contrivance, designed (or discerned) by reason and executed in an agreement of 'every man with every man' in which each surrenders his 'right to govern himself' to a 'common authority'.[2]

To survive, then, is seen to be more desirable than to stand first; proud men must become tame men in order to remain alive. Yet, if we accept this as Hobbes's solution of the predicament of natural man, incoherence remains. Human life is interpreted as a tension between pride (the passion for pre-eminence and honour) and fear (the apprehension of dishonour) which reason discerns how to resolve. But there are difficulties.

First, the resolution suggested is one-sided: fear is allayed but at the cost of Felicity. And this is a situation to be desired only by a creature who fears to be dishonoured more than he desires to be honoured, a creature content to survive in a world from which both honour and dishonour have been removed – and this is not exactly the creature Hobbes had been describing to us. In the end, it appears, all that reason can teach us is the manner in which we may escape fear, but a man compact of pride will not be disposed to accept this low-grade (if gilt-edged) security as the answer to his needs, even if he believes that to refuse it entails almost inevitable dishonour. In short, either this is a solution appropriate to the character of a more commonplace creature, one who merely desires 'success in obtaining those things which a man from time to time desireth',[3] who wants to prosper in a modest sort of way and with as little hindrance and as much help as may be from his fellows, and for whom survival in this condition is more important than Joy; or Hobbes was guilty of defining human Felicity in such a manner that it is inherently impossible to be experienced by human beings as he understands them,

[1] See p.294, note. [2] *L*, 131–2. [3] *L*, 48.

guilty of the solecism of making the conditions of Felicity a bar to its attainment.

And secondly, we may, perhaps, inquire why, on Hobbes's reading of the situation, pride and fear should not be allowed to remain without any attempt to resolve the tension between them. No doubt, when reason speaks it may legitimately claim to be heard; for reason, no less than passion belongs to 'nature'. But if (as Hobbes understood it) the office of reason is that of a servant, revealing the probable causes of events, the probable consequences of actions and the probable means by which desired ends may be attained, whence comes its authority to determine a man's choice of conduct? And if no such authority may be attributed to it, are we constrained to do more than to take note of its deliverances and then choose (with our eyes open) what we shall do? A prudent man, one set upon survival, will not easily be argued out of his prudence, and he may like to support himself with the opinion that he is acting 'rationally'; but he may suddenly find his prudence deprived of its value when he sees in another (who has chosen the risky enterprise of glory) the 'Joy' he has himself foregone. He will be reminded that there is such a thing as folly; and his gilt-edged security may seem a shade less attractive, a shade less adequate to human character.[1] Perhaps, even, he may dimly discern that

> There is no pleasure in the world so sweet
> As, being wise, to fall at folly's feet.

At all events (though, as we shall see, Hobbes is unjustly accused of ignoring these considerations), we may, perhaps, suspect that in seeming here to recommend the pursuit of peace and the rejection of glory as 'rational' conduct, he was, as on some other occasions, being forgetful of his view that 'reason serves only to convince the truth (not of fact, but) of consequence'[2] and was taking improper advantage of that older meaning of 'reason' in which it was recognized to have the qualities of a master or at least of an authoritative guide.

---

[1] But against this may be set the fact that in the *civitas* there is still some opportunity for competition and taking risks; all that we are deprived of is the 'joy' of success in utterly unprotected imprudence.

[2] *L*, 292, etc.

3

As it first appears, the condition of peace is merely a conclusion of natural reason. Awakened from the make-believe of vain glory and inspired by the fear of shameful death, 'reason' not only reveals to men the connection between survival and peace, but also 'suggesteth' the means by which this condition may be achieved and discerns its structure, which Hobbes called 'the convenient articles of peace'.[1] With the first (the means of achievement) we are not now concerned, but a consideration of the second discloses what Hobbes meant by 'peace'. There are, in all, nineteen of these articles and together they outline a condition in which the struggle for precedence is superseded, not by co-operative enterprise, but by mutual forebearance. This array of articles, said Hobbes, may, however, be 'contracted into an easy sum, intelligible even to the meanest capacity, that is, *Do not to another, which thou wouldest not have done to oneself'*.[2] The negative form of the maxim reveals the idiom of the moral life which Hobbes was exploring, but he interprets it (as Confucius did before him) as an injunction to have consideration for others and to avoid partiality for onself.[3]

But a transformation has taken place. The conditions of peace, first offered to us *rational theorems* concerning the nature of shameful-death-avoiding conduct (that is, as a piece of prudential wisdom), now appear as *moral obligation*. Clearly (on Hobbes's assumptions) it would be foolish, in the circumstances, not to declare for peace and not to establish it in the only manner in which it can be established; but, somehow, it has also become a dereliction of duty not to do so. Nor is this change of idiom inadvertent. For Hobbes leaves us in no doubt that he properly understood the nature of moral conduct and the difference between it and merely prudent or necessary conduct.

It is to be observed, however, that in Hobbes's vocabulary the words 'good' and 'evil' had (as a rule) no moral connotation. 'Good' merely stood for what is desirable, that is, for whatever may be the object of human appetite; 'evil' signified whatever is the object of aversion. They are, therefore, redundant words which merely repeat what is already signified in words such as 'pleasurable' and 'painful'. When Hobbes said: 'Reason declares peace to be good,' he

[1] *L*, 98.   [2] *L*, 121; *E.W.*, IV, 107.   [3] *Analects*, xv, 23.

did not mean that all men *ought* to promote peace, but only that all sensible men will do so.[1] And when he said :'Every man desires his own good and his own good is peace', he could not conclude that every man *ought* to endeavour peace,[2] but only that a man who does not do so is 'contradicting himself'.[3] There is, it is true, something that Hobbes calls a 'precept of reason', and even a 'rule of reason' or a 'law of reason' or a 'dictate of reason', thus making it appear that what is rational is, on that account, somehow obligatory. But all the examples he gives make it clear that a 'precept of reason' is only a hypothetical precept and not the equivalent of a duty. Temperance, he says, 'is a precept of reason, because intemperance tends to sickness and death';[4] but temperance cannot be a duty unless to remain alive and well is a duty, and Hobbes is clear that these are 'rights' and therefore not duties. And when he writes of the laws of Nature in general as 'dictates of Reason' he makes clear that he means 'sayings' or 'pronouncements' of reason, and *not* 'commands'.[5]

But the word 'justice' has a moral connotation, and it was the word Hobbes most often used when he was writing in the normative idiom: to behave morally is to do just actions, and to be a virtuous man is to have a just disposition. Nevertheless, although to behave justly is to be identified with the performance of certain actions and with refraining from others, the identification calls for some subtlety. A man's duty is to have 'an unfeigned and constant endeavour'[6] to behave justly; what counts, in the first place, is the endeavour and not the external achievement. Indeed, a man may do what, on the surface, is a just action, but because it is done by chance or in pursuance of an unjust endeavour he must be considered, not to be doing justice, but merely not to be guilty; and, conversely, a man may do an injurious action, but if his endeavour is for justice, he may be technically guilty but he has not acted unjustly.[7] But it must be understood, first, that for Hobbes 'endeavour' is not the same as 'intention': to 'endeavour' is to perform actions, to make identi-

---

[1] *E.W.*, II, 48; V, 192.

[2] In Hobbes's idiom it is meaningless to say that a man ought to *desire* anything, though there are occasions when he falls into this way of speaking. Cf. *L*, 121.

[3] Cf. *L*, 101, 548; *E.W.*, II, 12, 31.　　　　[4] *E.W.*, II, 49.

[5] *L*, 122 *sq.*　　　[6] *L*, 121.　　　　[7] *E.W.*, II, 32; IV, 109.

fiable movements, and it is, therefore, possible for others to judge of a man's 'endeavour' where it might be difficult to be confident about his intention. And secondly, while it seems to me doubtful whether Hobbes held there to be an obligation to be a just man, duty is fulfilled only where a man both acts justly (that is, makes movements which constitute 'endeavouring justice') and acts guiltlessly (that is, avoids doing injury).

Now, as Hobbes understood it, the object of moral endeavour is peace; what we already know to be a rational endeavour is now declared to be the object of just endeavour. Or, to amplify this definition a little, just conduct is the unfeigned and constant endeavour to acknowledge all other men as one's equal, and when considering their actions in relation to oneself to discount one's own passion and self-love.[1] The word 'unfeigned' was, I think, intended to indicate that this endeavour is not moral endeavour unless it is pursued for its own sake and not, for example, in order to avoid punishment or to win an advantage for oneself. And the word 'endeavour' meant not only always to intend peace, but always to act in such a manner that peace is the probable consequence of our action.

The precept we have before us is, then, that 'every man *ought* to endeavour peace', and our question is, What reason or justification did Hobbes provide for this delineation of moral conduct? Why ought a man unfeignedly endeavour to keep his word, to accommodate himself to others, not to take more than his share, not to set himself up as a judge in his own cause, not display hatred and contempt towards others, to treat others as his equals, and to do everything else that pertains to peace?[2] How did Hobbes bridge the gap between men's natural inclinations and what ought to be done about them? And with this question we reach the obscure heart of Hobbes's moral theory. For, not only is an answer to it the chief thing we should look for in the writings of any moralist, who normally takes his precepts from current moral opinion and himself contributes only the reasons for believing them to be true; but also, in the case of Hobbes, it is the question which his commentators have had most trouble in discovering the answer to, though some of

[1] *L*, 118, 121.   [2] *L*, ch. xv.

them have pressed their conclusions upon us and dismissed those of others with remarkable arrogance. Hobbes was usually so much more concerned with elucidating adequate motives or 'causes' for what is alleged to be just conduct than with finding adequate reasons for calling it just, that those who seek an answer to our question are forced to use all their ingenuity.

4

There are three current readings of Hobbes's answer to this question which deserve consideration because, though none is (I believe) entirely satisfactory, each has been argued acutely and carefully and none is without plausibility.[1]

1. The first account runs something like this:[2]

Every man must either endeavour 'the preservation of his own nature', or endeavour something more than this, for example, to be first in the race. To endeavour nothing at all is impossible: 'to have no desire is to be dead'. Now every man, in all circumstances, has the right to endeavour 'the preservation of his own nature';[3] in doing so he is acting justly. And in no circumstances has any man the right to endeavour more than this (for example by indulging in useless cruelty or by desiring to be first); if he seeks what is superfluous to 'the preservation of his own nature',[4] his endeavour is unreasonable, reprehensible and unjust because it is an endeavour for his own destruction. But to endeavour to preserve his own nature, we have seen, is precisely, to endeavour peace; and to endeavour more than this is to endeavour war and self-destruction. Therefore a man is just when he endeavours peace, and unjust when he endeavours war. Every man has an obligation to be just, and (in principle) he has no other obligation but to endeavour peace. In short, duty is identified with dispositions and actions which are 'rational' in the sense of not being 'self-contradictory'. And Hobbes, it is said, found support for this position in the observation that the endeavour of a man to preserve his own nature has the approval of conscience, and the

---

[1] In all, of course, there are many more than three.
[2] L. Strauss, *The Political Philosophy of Hobbes*.
[3] *L*, 99.   [4] *E.W.*, II, 45n; *L*, 116 *sq.*

endeavour to do more than this is disapproved by conscience: the feeling of guiltlessness and of guilt attach themselves respectively to each of these endeavours. Thus, activity which springs from fear of shameful death and is designed to mitigate that fear alone has the approval of conscience and is obligatory.

Now, there can be no doubt that this is a moral doctrine in so far as it is an attempt to elucidate a distinction between natural appetite and permissible appetite; it does not assimilate right to might or duty to desire. Moreover, it is a doctrine which identifies moral conduct with prudentially rational conduct: the just man is the man who has been tamed by fear. But if Hobbes has said no more than this, he must be considered not to have said enough. And, in any case, he did say something more and something different.

In the first place, the answer given here to the question, why ought all men to endeavour peace? itself provokes a question: we want to know why every man has an obligation only to endeavour to preserve his own nature. The whole position rests upon the belief that Hobbes thought every man had an *obligation* to act in such a manner as not to risk his own destruction, whereas what Hobbes said is that every man has a *right* to preserve his own nature and that a right is neither a duty nor does it give rise to a duty of any sort.[1] Secondly, an interpretation of Hobbes which represents him as saying that dutiful conduct is rational conduct in the sense of being 'consistent' or non-self-contradictory conduct, and that it is dutiful because it is rational in this (or any other) sense, must be considered wide of the mark. There are occasions when Hobbes appealed to the principle of 'non-contradiction' in order to denote what is desirable in conduct;[2] but, it is safe to say, he distinguished clearly between merely rational conduct and obligatory conduct. On no plausible reading of Hobbes is the Law of Nature to be considered obligatory because it represents rational conduct. Thirdly, this interpretation does not recognize moral conduct as the disinterested acknowledgment of all others as one's equal which Hobbes took to be fundamental for peace; on this showing, all endeavours for peace, however interested, would be equally just. And lastly, there is in this account a confusion between the cause of conduct alleged to be just and the reason for thinking it

[1] *L*, 99.   [2] E.g. *E.W.*, II, 12, 31; *L*, 101, 548.

S

just. For the apprehension of shameful death and the aversion from it are not reasons why we have an obligation to endeavour peace; they are the causes or motives of our doing so. And if 'reason' is added (as Hobbes added it) as a mediator between fear and pride, we have still not made our escape from the realm of causes into the realm of justifications, because 'reason' for Hobbes (except where he is being unmistakably equivocal) has no prescriptive force. In short, if Hobbes said no more than this he must be considered not to have had a moral theory at all.

2. There are, however, other interpretations of Hobbes's views on this matter, which run on different lines. And we may consider next what is, perhaps, the simplest of all the current accounts. It goes as follows:

According to Hobbes, all moral obligation derives from *law*; where there is no law there is no duty and no distinction between just and unjust conduct, and where there is law in the proper sense there is an obligation to obey it upon those who come under it if there is also an adequate motive for obeying it. Now, law properly speaking (we are told) is 'the command of him, that by right hath command over others';[1] or (in a more ample description) 'law in general ,. . . is command; nor a command of any man to any man; but only of him whose command is addressed to one formerly obliged to obey him'.[2] And a law-maker in the proper sense is one who has acquired this antecedent authority to be obeyed by being given it, or by being acknowledged to have it, by those who are to be subject to his commands, 'there being no obligation on any man, which ariseth not from some act of his own'.[3] This act of authorization or acknowledgment is a necessary condition of genuine law-making authority. In other words, there can be no such thing, for Hobbes, as a 'natural', unacquired, authority to make law.[4] To this, two other conditions of

[1] *L*, 123.
[2] *L*, 203, 406; *E.W.*, II, 49.
[3] *L*, 166, 220, 317, 403, 448; *E.W.*, II, 113, 191; IV, 148.
[4] Those passages in which Hobbes seems inclined to recognize mere Omnipotence as authority to make law are not to be excluded from this condition. Omnipotence, no less than any other authoritative characteristic, is something accorded; he only is Omnipotent who is admitted or acknow-

obligation are added: law in the proper sense can issue from a 'law-maker' only when those who are obliged by it know him as the author of the law, and when they know precisely what he commands. But these conditions are, in fact, entailed in the first condition; for, no subject could know himself to be a subject without this act of authorization or acknowledgment, and it would be impossible to perform such an act and at the same time be ignorant of who the law-maker is and what he commands.

In short, it is unmistakably Hobbes's view that law is something made and that it is binding solely on account of having been made in a certain manner by a law-maker having certain characteristics; and that obligation springs only from law. Or, in other words, no command is inherently (that is, merely on account of what it commands or on account of the reasonableness of what it commands) or self-evidently binding; its obligatoriness is something to be proved or rebutted, and Hobbes told us what evidence is relevant for this proof or rebuttal. This evidence is solely concerned with whether or not the command is law in the proper sense, that is, whether or not it has been made by one who has authority to make it.

Now the proposition that the law of the *civitas* is law in the proper sense was, for Hobbes, not an empirical but an analytic proposition;[1] *civitas* is defined as an artificial condition of human life in which there are laws which are known to have been made by a law-maker who has acquired the authority to make them by being given it by those who are subject to him,[2] and in which what is commanded is known, and in which there is an authentic interpretation of what is commanded. And further, those who are subject to these laws have an adequate motive for their subjection. All the conditions for law in the proper sense are satisfied by civil law. Consequently (it is argued by those who defend this reading of Hobbes's writings) Hobbes's

ledged to be so or who has been expressly accorded unlimited power. And this is true of God (except where the name God denotes merely a First Cause) no less than of men, for 'God' is a name to which men have agreed to accord a certain significance. *L*, 282, 525.

[1] Cf. *L*, 443.

[2] This is true both in respect of sovereigns whose authority is by Acquisition and those who acquire it by Institution (*L*, 549 *sq.*). And it is taken by Hobbes to have been true also of the ancient 'Kingdom' of the Jews (*L*, ch. 35).

settled view was that civil laws are unquestionably obligatory, and their obligatoriness springs not from their being a reflection of some other 'natural' law which carries with it 'natural' duties, but solely from the character of their maker and the manner in which they have been made, promulgated and interpreted. The question, Why am I morally bound to obey the commands of the sovereign of my *civitas*? (which, for Hobbes, is the important question) requires no other answer than, Because I, in agreement with others in a similar plight to myself, and with a common disposition to make covenants, having 'authorized' him, know him indubitable to be a law-giver and know his commands as laws properly speaking.[1] Furthermore (it is argued), not only are the laws of a *civitas* laws in the proper sense, but, in a *civitas*, they are, for Hobbes, the only laws which have this character. Neither the so-called 'laws' of a church, nor the so-called Laws of Nature, are, in a *civitas*, laws in the proper sense unless and until they have been made so by being promulgated as civil laws.[2] Indeed, it is Hobbes's view that there is no law that is law properly speaking which is not a 'civil' law in the sense of being the command of a civil sovereign: God's laws are laws in the proper sense only where God is a civil sovereign exercising his sovereignty through agents. The civil sovereign does not, of course, 'make' the Laws of Nature as rational theorems about human preservation, but he does, in the strictest sense, 'make' them laws in the proper sense.[3] It may, for example, be accounted reasonable to render unto God (where God is *not* a civil sovereign) the things that are God's and unto Caesar the things that are Caesar's, but, according to Hobbes, this does not become a duty until these respective spheres are defined, and, in both cases, the definition is a matter of civil law. No doubt in a *civitas* a subject may retain the relics of a Natural Right, but a natural right, according to Hobbes, is not an obligation and has nothing whatever to do with a man's duties.

On this reading of Hobbes's thoughts on moral obligation, there remains the question whether or not he thought that men who are not subjects of a properly constituted civil sovereign and who therefore have no duties under a civil law nevertheless have duties as well

---

[1] *L*, 131, 135, 166, 220, 317.   [2] *L*, 205, 222, 405, 406, 469.
[3] *L*, 437.

as rights. And this question resolves itself into the question, Where there is no civil law, is there a law which is law in the proper sense? This is an interesting question, but for two reasons it is not a highly important question for those who read Hobbes in the manner we are now considering. First, Hobbes is understood to be writing, not for savages, but for men who belong to a *civitas*; his project is to show what *their* obligations are and whence they arise, and if he has given a reason for believing that civil law is binding and is the only law that is binding, he does not need to do more than this. And secondly (on the interpretation we are now considering) there can be no question of the obligations of civil law being derived from or being in any way connected with, another law, even if that other 'law' were found, in circumstances other than those of the *civitas*, to be law in the proper sense and to impose duties upon all mankind: in a *civitas* the *only* law in the proper sense is civil law. The core of this interpretation is the belief that, for Hobbes, the *civitas* constituted not a useful addition to human life, but a transformation of the natural conditions of human life. However, the consideration of Hobbes's thoughts on obligations imposed by a law other than civil law is more appropriate in connection with another interpretation of his moral theory for which this question is central.

In the interpretation we are now considering, then, what *causes* human beings to enter into the agreement by which the civil sovereign is constituted and authorized is their fear of destruction which has been converted into a rational endeavour for peace; but they have no obligation to do so. Their *duty* to endeavour peace begins with the appearance of civil law, a law properly so-called and the only one of its kind, commanding this endeavour.

This interpretation (like any other) depends upon a certain reading of important passages in Hobbes's writings, and without calling attention to all the relevant passages it may be noticed, first, that it relies upon what must be recognized as the only intelligible reading of the passage in *Leviathan* where Hobbes maintains what may be called the sovereignty of civil law;[1] and secondly, it entails understanding the expression 'whose command is addressed to one formerly obliged to obey him'[2] (used by Hobbes to define the law-

[1] *L*, 205.   [2] *L*, 203.

giver in the proper sense) to signify 'one who has already covenanted to set him up, or who has otherwise recognized him, or acknowledged him as a sovereign law-maker'. This, I believe, in spite of the weakening of the word 'obliged' that it involves, is the most plausible reading of this expression.[1] But this reading is not without difficulties and we shall have to consider another reading of it the acceptance of which would go far to make this interpretation of Hobbes's moral theory untenable.

To this interpretation there are three main objections. First (it is observed), if the only obligation of the subject in a *civitas* is to perform the duties imposed by the law-maker whom he has (by covenant or acknowledgment) authorized, and if it is based solely upon the fact that they are genuine duties because the civil law is undoubtedly law in the proper sense and applies to the subject in a *civitas*, what, if anything, binds him to go on observing the acknowledgment or covenant which authorizes the law-maker to make law? Has he a duty to continue this acknowledgment, in so far as it can be separated from the duty to obey the laws? If not, does not Hobbes's account of moral obligation hang suspended for want of an answer to a pertinent question? And if he has such a duty, must not there be a law in the proper sense, other than civil law, which imposes it? This must be recognized as a formidable objection, but in the view of those whose views we are now considering, it is not unanswerable; indeed, there are two possible answers. First, it may be contended that there is little in Hobbes (except what is obscure or equivocal, e.g. *L*, 110) to suggest that he held the making of the Covenant (besides being a prudent act) was also a moral obligation, and that 'keeping the covenant' and 'obeying the law' were not inseparable activities; and if there is a duty to obey the law (which there is), then there is a constructive duty to keep and protect the covenant.[2] But, secondly, if it is conceded that for there to be a duty to 'keep the covenant' there must be a law imposing this duty and it cannot be the civil law itself, then, since on this interpretation there is no such other' law in the proper sense (i.e. no law which is *not* based on the acknowledgment of the ruler by the subject) to be found in Hobbes's

[1] Cf. Pollock, *An Introduction to the History of the Science of Politics*, p. 65.
[2] Cf. *E.W.*, II, 31; *L*, 101, 548.

writings, we must conclude that for Hobbes there was no specific duty to keep the covenant. And why should there be? Neither Hobbes's moral theory nor any other is to be reckoned defective because it does not show every desirable action to be also a duty. For Hobbes duty is always (directly or indirectly) the activity of endeavouring peace, and to endeavour peace *is* a duty only when there is a law commanding it. To make and keep the covenant (or the acknowledgment) in which the *civitas* is set up are activities of endeavouring peace. But if, in this respect, they are eligible to become duties, it is not necessary for them to be duties; and, if they are not duties (for lack of a law commanding them) they are not, on that account, unintelligible. They are for Hobbes (on this reading) acts of prudence which are reasonable and desirable to be performed on condition that others perform them, or acts of 'nobility' which make no conditions. It is, of course, true that, for Hobbes, it could never be a duty to act against one's own interest (that is, to endeavour the war of all against all), but it does not follow from this that endeavouring peace must always be a duty. In short, if Hobbes is understood to have said that there is a duty to obey the law of the *civitas* because, for the subjects of a *civitas*, it is law in the proper sense, but that there is no separate duty to make and keep the covenant or acknowledgment which sets up the civil sovereign, he is not being understood to have said anything inherently absurd: he is merely being recognized to have said that there is a proper use for the word 'duty', but that what holds the *civitas* together is not 'duty' (except, for example, the duty imposed by a law against treason) but either self-interest instructed by reason, or the nobility which is too proud to calculate the possible loss entailed in obedience to a 'sovereign' who lacks power to enforce his commands.[1]

The second objection is as follows: it is alleged that, for Hobbes,

---

[1] In the Conclusion of *Leviathan* (548) Hobbes added a twentieth Law of Nature, namely, 'that every man is bound by Nature, as much as in him lieth, to protect in Warre, the Authority, by which he himself is protected in time of Peace'. And he explains that this is so because not to act in this way would be self-contradictory. But to demonstrate self-consistency, is not to demonstrate duty: and the conduct which is here asserted to be self-consistent becomes a duty only when there is a law in the proper sense imposing it, and for members of a *civitas* such a law must be a civil law.

rational behaviour is endeavouring peace, and that this becomes a duty if and when it is commanded by law in the proper sense. Further, since civil law *is* law in the proper sense and the only law in the proper sense (owing its propriety not to its being a reflection of some other, superior and equally proper law, but solely to the manner in which it has been made, published and authentically interpreted) and commands its subjects to endeavour peace, these have a duty (which persons in other circumstances have not) of 'endeavouring peace'. But (it is objected) this is not an accurate account of the situation. What, even for Hobbes, the civil law commands is not merely that a man shall 'endeavour peace' but that he shall perform specific actions and refrain from others: it is no defence for the lawbreaker to say, 'I am endeavouring peace', if he neglects to do what the law commands or does what it forbids. The answer to this objection is, however, that, for Hobbes, 'endeavouring peace' was always performing specific acts (and not merely having peaceful intentions or a generally peaceful disposition); to be disposed in a certain direction is to make movements in that direction. And, while reason acquaints all but madmen and children with the general pattern of acts which may be expected to promote a peaceful condition of human life, it is the province of law to decide what acts, in specific circumstances, are necessary to a condition of peace and to impose them as duties.[1] When 'endeavouring peace' is a *duty*, it is always the duty of obeying a law, and a law is always a set of specific commands and prohibitions. Hence, the duty of endeavouring peace is indistinguishable from the duty of performing the acts prescribed by law: a man cannot at the same time 'endeavour peace' and do what the law forbids, though he may do so by actions which the law does not require of him – by being benevolent, for example. But his *duty* to 'endeavour peace' is a duty to obey the law, that is, to be both just and guiltless.

The third objection is that Hobbes is often to be found writing about 'natural laws' and writing about them as if he considered them to be laws in the proper sense and capable of imposing a 'natural obligation' upon all men to endeavour peace, and any account of Hobbes's moral theory which ignores this is implausible. This, again,

[1] *L*, 136.

is not easily to be disposed of. It is true that Hobbes repeatedly and clearly asserted that Natural Laws are not properly speaking laws at all except where they appear as the commands of a law-giver *who owes his authority to a covenant or an acknowledgment*; apart from this, they are only 'qualities which dispose men to peace and order', 'dictates', 'conclusions' or 'theorems' of natural reason 'suggesting' the conduct which belongs to a condition of peace and therefore the rational (but not the moral) foundation of the *civitas*.[1] But these assertions are partnered by others capable of being interpreted to mean that the Laws of Nature themselves impose obligations upon all men (rulers included), and even that the obligations of the subject to obey the laws of his *civitas* derives from the duty he has under one or more of these natural laws.[2] However, since the view that Hobbes believed Natural Law to be law in the proper sense and to be the source of all moral obligation is the central theme of the third important account of Hobbes's moral theory, the force of this objection to this account will best be considered in that connection.

3. This third interpretation begins at the same place as the one we have just considered.[3] It recognizes that, for Hobbes, all moral obligation derives from a law of some sort: where there is authentic law there is, on that account, duty; where there is no law there is no duty. Consequently, endeavouring peace can be shown to be a duty upon all men if there is a valid and universally applicable law commanding it. So far, I think there can be no serious disagreement about what Hobbes thought. But it is now contended that the Law of Nature itself and without further qualification is, in Hobbes's view, a valid, universal and perpetually operative law imposing this duty upon all men. Every interpreter of Hobbes recognizes that what Hobbes called the Laws of Nature and what he called 'the convenient articles of peace' are, in respect of content, the same thing and that they are the 'suggestions' or conclusions of reason about the

---

[1] *L*, 97, 122, 205, 211, etc.; *E.W.*, II, 49–50, etc.
[2] *L*, 99, 110, 203, 121, 273, 258–9, 363; *E.W.*, II, 46, 47, 190, 200.
[3] H. Warrender, *The Political Philosophy of Hobbes*; J. M. Brown, *Political Studies*, Vol. I, No. 1; Vol. II, No. 2.

preservation of human life. What is asserted now is that Hobbes also believed them to be laws in the proper sense; namely, that their author is known and that he has acquired an antecedent right to command, that they have been published and are known, that there is an authentic interpretation of them and that those who have a duty to obey have a sufficient motive for doing so. And the conclusion suggested is that endeavouring peace was, for Hobbes, an obligation laid upon all men by a Law of Nature and that any further obligation there may be to obey the laws of the *civitas*, or to obey covenanted commands, derives from this natural and universal obligation.[1]

Now, it is not to be denied that there are expressions and passages in Hobbes's writings which appear to be designed to make us believe that this is his view, but before we accept them at their face value we must consider in detail whether Hobbes also held the beliefs which are for him certainly entailed in this view. And if we find this not to be the case, it may be thought that these passages are eligible for some other interpretation, or that we must be content to have detected what, on any reading, is a notable incoherence in his writings.

The direction of our first inquiry is unmistakable. Since, according to Hobbes, the obligation a law imposes is due not to the law itself but to its author,[2] who must not only be known as its author but known also to have a right to command, our first inquiry must be: Did Hobbes believe the Law of Nature to have an author known as such to all mankind? And if so, who did he think was its author and in what manner did he think this author was known to be the maker of this law? And, together with this, we may appropriately consider what thoughts Hobbes's writings disclose about the right

---

[1] There are further subtleties in some versions of this interpretation which I do not propose to consider here because, whether or not they can be shown to be components of Hobbes's view of things, they do not affect the main point. For example, the suggestion that the *civitas* is a condition in which the obligation to endeavour peace (already imposed by a Natural Law) is 'validated'. Clearly, this suggestion is cogent only when it is believed that, for Hobbes, the Law of Nature is law in the proper sense. Our main concern is with the question: Is the Law of Nature, by itself and without qualification of circumstances or persons, law in the proper sense and capable of imposing upon all mankind the duty of 'endeavouring peace'?

[2] E.g. *E.W.*, II, 191 *sq.*

of this author to make this law. The answer urged upon us in the interpretation we are now considering is that Hobbes unmistakably believed the Law of Nature to have an author who is naturally known to all men as such; that this author is God himself; and that his right to legislate derives, not from his having created those who should obey his commands, but from his Omnipotence.[1] The Law of Nature, it is contended, is law in the proper sense; it is binding upon all men in all circumstances because it is known to be the command of an Omnipotent God.

The first difficulty which stands in the way of our accepting this interpretation is that it must remain exceedingly doubtful (to say the least) whether Hobbes thought that our natural knowledge includes (or could possibly include) a knowledge of God as the author of imperative laws for human conduct. He reasoned thus about the word 'God': divinities appear first as projections of human fear consequent upon our frequent ignorance of the causes of the good and ill fortunes which befall us, but the notion of 'one God, Infinite and Omnipotent' derives, not from our fears, but from our curiosity about 'the causes of natural bodies, their several virtues and operations': in tracing these causes backwards we unavoidably 'come to this, that there must be one First Mover; that is a First, and Eternal cause of all things; which is that which men mean by the name of God'.[2] It is this God, then, a necessary hypothesis, of whom we may be said, in the first place, to have natural knowledge. And in virtue of the Omnipotence of this God (his 'rule' as a First Cause being inescapable and absolute) we may speak of him as 'King of all the earth', and we may speak of the earth as his natural Kingdom and everything on earth as his natural subject; but if we do speak in this manner, we must recognize that we are using the words 'King' and 'Kingdom' in only a metaphorical sense.[3]

---

[1] This excludes two otherwise possible views. First, that it is a duty to conform to the Law of Nature because it is self-evidently rational or because it is axiomatically obligatory: there is, I think, no plausible reading of Hobbes in which the Law of Nature is recognized to be obligatory except in respect of its authorship. And secondly, that the Law of Nature is obligatory on account of its authorship, but that the author is not God. For this third interpretation of Hobbes's theory, God is essential.

[2] L, 83.   [3] L, 90, 314 sq.

Nevertheless, the name God may also be used with another signification in which he may be said to be a 'King' and to have a natural Kingdom and natural subjects in the proper meaning of these expressions: he is a genuine ruler over those 'that believe that there is a God that governeth the world, and hath given Praecepts, and propounded Rewards and Punishments to Mankind'.[1] But, about this there are two observations to be made. First, these beliefs fall short of natural knowledge, which is confined (in this connection) to the necessary hypothesis of God as the Omnipotent First Cause;[2] the 'providential' God is no less a 'projection' of human thought than the God who is the First Cause, but whereas the First Cause is a projection of human reason, the providential God is a projection of human desire.[3] And secondly, since these beliefs about a 'providential' God are avowedly *not* common to all mankind,[4] God's natural subjects (i.e. those who have an obligation to obey his commands) are those only who have acknowledged a 'providential' God concerned with human conduct and who hope for his rewards and fear his punishments. (And it may be remarked here, in passing, that this circumstance qualifies the distinction Hobbes was apt to make between God's natural subjects and his subjects by covenant: the only proper understanding of the expression 'Kingdom of God' is when it is taken to signify 'a Commonwealth, instituted (by the consent of those who were to be subject thereto) for their Civil Government'.[5]) The law which the subjects of this God are bound to obey is the Law

[1] *L*, 274, 314. This is a necessary condition, but (as we shall see shortly) the necessary and sufficient condition is that they should not only 'believe' in a God of this sort, but that they should have acknowledged him as *their* ruler.

[2] According to Hobbes we have no natural knowledge of God's nature, or of a life after death. *L*, 113.

[3] *L*, 525.

[4] *L*, 275. This is not because some men are atheists. An 'atheist', according to Hobbes, is an ill-reasoner who fails to arrive at the hypothesis of a First Cause and is only inferentially a man who does not believe in a 'providential' God concerned with human conduct. Hobbes recognizes various classes of person in this respect – Atheists; those who recognize a First Cause but do not believe in a providential God; the insane and the immature; and those who recognize a First Cause and believe in a 'providential' God. It is only those who compose the last of these classes who are obliged by the Law of Nature.

[5] *L*, 317, etc. But *E.W.*, II, 206, should be noticed.

of Nature;[1] they have a duty always to endeavour peace. Others, it is true, may feel the weight of this law, may find themselves in receipt of pleasure for following its precepts or pain for not doing so, but these have no moral obligation to obey it and this pleasure is not a reward and this pain is not a punishment.

It would appear, then, that, according to Hobbes, God as the author of a law imposing the duty of endeavouring peace, is the ruler, not of all mankind, but only of those who acknowledge him in this character and therefore know him as its author; and this acknowledgment is a matter of 'belief', not of natural knowledge.[2] It is a loose way of talking to say that Hobbes anywhere said that we are obliged by the Laws of Nature because they are the Laws of God; what he said is that we would be obliged by them if they were laws in the proper sense, and that they are laws in the proper sense only if they are known to have been made by God.[3] And this means that they are laws in the proper sense only to those who know them to have been made by God. And who are these persons? Certainly not all mankind; and certainly only those of mankind who have acknowledged God to be maker of this law. The proposition, then, that Hobbes thought the Law of Nature to be law in the proper sense and to bind all mankind to an endeavour for peace, cannot seriously be entertained, whatever detached expressions (most of them ambiguous) there may be in his writings to support it.[4]

But further, if it is clear that even God's so-called 'natural subjects' can have no natural knowledge of God as the author of a universally binding precept to endeavour peace, it is clear also that Hobbes did not allow them to have any other sort of knowledge of God as the author of a Law of Nature of this kind. He expressly affirmed that if they claim to know God as the author of a law imposing the duty of endeavouring peace on all mankind by means of 'Sense Supernatural' (or 'Revelation', or 'Inspiration') their claim must be disallowed:[5] whatever else 'Sense Supernatural' might acquaint a man with, it cannot acquaint him with a universal law or with God as the author of a universal law. Nor can 'Prophecy' supply what 'natural know- ledge' and 'Sense Supernatural' have failed to supply. It is true that

[1] L. 276. [2] Cf. L, 300. [3] L, 403.
[4] E.g. L, 315, 363. [5] L, 275.

by 'Faith' a man may know God as the author of a law, but what 'Faith' can show us is not God as the author of a 'Natural Law' imposing duties on all men, but God as the author of a 'Positive Law' enjoining duties only upon those who by indirect covenant have acknowledged him as their ruler and have authorized him by their consent. In short, only where the endeavour for peace is enjoined by a positive law does it become a duty, this law alone being law in the proper sense as having a known author; and this law is binding only upon those who know its author.

The question, Did Hobbes think the Law of Nature to be law in the proper sense in respect of having a known author? resolves itself into the question, Who among mankind, because they know God as the author of a precept to endeavour peace, did Hobbes think to be bound to obey this precept? And in answering this question, we have found that Hobbes's much advertised distinction between God's 'natural subjects' and his subjects by covenant or acknowledgment is not as firmly based as we at first supposed: God's only 'Kingdom', in the proper sense, is a *civitas* in which God is owned as the author of the *civil* law. And the same conclusion appears when we consider the related question, By what authority does God impose this obligation? In the interpretation of Hobbes's writings we are now considering the authority of God over his so-called 'natural subjects' is said to derive from his Irresistible Power and consequently to be an authority to make law for all mankind.[1] But this cannot be so, whatever Hobbes seems to have said in these passages and elsewhere. Omnipotence or Irresistible Power is the characteristic of God as 'the First, and Eternal Cause of all things', but this God is not a law-maker or a 'ruler', and we have been warned that to speak of him as a 'King' and as having a 'Kingdom' is to speak metaphorically. The God who appears as, in the proper sense, a 'ruler' (the imposer of authentic obligations) is not the 'ruler' of everybody and everything in the world, but only of 'as many of mankind as acknowledge his Providence'. It is in their acknowledgment of him as their ruler that he comes to be known as the author of law properly speaking; this acknowledgment is the necessary 'act' from which all obligation 'ariseth' because it is the act without which the ruler remains

[1] *L*, 90, 276, 315, 474, 551; *E.W.*, II, 209; VI, 170.

unknown.[1] Not Omnipotence, then, but a covenant or an acknowledgment is the spring of God's authority to make laws in the proper sense.

Now, besides having a known author, the Law of Nature, if it is to be law in the proper sense, must have two other characteristics; namely, it must be known or knowable by those who are obliged to obey it (that is, it must have been in some manner 'published' or 'declared'), and there must be an 'authentique interpretation' of it. Did Hobbes think that the Law of Nature has these characteristics?

In regard to the first, the interpretation of Hobbes we are now considering appears to be in no difficulty: it relies upon Hobbes's statements that the Law of Nature is declared by God to his natural subjects in the 'Dictates of Natural Reason' or of 'Right Reason'; that it is known in this manner 'without other word of God'; and that a sufficient knowledge of it is available even to those whose power of reasoning is not very conspicuous.[2] But, it may be asked, how can a man know 'by the Dictates of Right Reason' that the endeavour for peace is a command emanating from a proper authority, and therefore imposing upon him a duty to obey, when 'Reason' (being, according to Hobbes, the power of discerning the probable causes of given occurrences or the probable effects of given actions or movements serving 'to convince the truth (not of fact, but) of consequence')[3] can neither itself supply, nor be the means of ascertaining, categorical injunctions? How can God 'declare his laws' (as *laws* and not merely as theorems) to mankind in 'the Dictates of Natural Reason'? And the answer to these inquiries is clear: nobody holding Hobbes's views about the nature of 'reason' could possibly hold God to be able to do anything of the sort. And if God cannot do this, then the whole idea of the Law of Nature being law in the proper sense and imposing duties on all mankind because it is known and known to be the law of God, collapses. No doubt there are occasions when Hobbes encourages us to think that he thought the Law of Nature was naturally known, *as a law in the proper sense imposing upon all mankind the duty of endeavouring peace*; he was not above speaking of 'natural duties'[4] (though he refused to recog-

---

[1] *L*, 97, 166, 317.
[2] *L*, 225, 275, 277, 554.
[3] *L*, 292; *E.W.*, I, 3.
[4] *L*, 277.

nize the expression 'natural justice'),[1] and we shall have to consider later why he encourages us to think in this manner. But there is also no doubt that, according to his own understanding of 'Reason', all that he may legitimately think is that the Law of Nature *as a set of theorems about human preservation* is known to all mankind in this manner.[2] In default, then, of evidence from the writings of Hobbes other than these unmistakably equivocal references to 'natural reason', we must conclude that the Law of Nature is not law in the proper sense, and that the duty to endeavour peace is not naturally known either to all mankind or even to God's so-called 'natural subjects'. What *is* known is the duty to endeavour peace when it is recognized as imposed by the positive law of God upon those who by indirect covenant have acknowledged his authority to impose this duty; it is known to them because it has been published to them either in the 'propheticall' word of God, or in the positive law of the *civitas*; and in the *civitas* 'prophecy' and the command of the Sovereign are not to be distinguished, for the Civil Sovereign in 'God's prophet'.[3]

The third characteristic of law in the proper sense is the existence of an 'authentique interpretation' of its meaning;[4] and this the Law of Nature manifestly lacks unless it is supplied by some positive and acknowledged authority, such as a civil sovereign or a 'prophet' instructed by God and acknowledged by his followers:[5] God himself cannot be the interpreter of the Law of Nature any more than he can be the interpreter of his Scriptural 'word'. In short, for Hobbes, there can be no interpreter or interpretation of the Law of Nature

---

[1] *E.W.*, II, vi.

[2] *L*, 286. The expression 'Right Reason' belongs to a well-established view of things in which it was supposed that 'reason', a 'divine spark', could acquaint mankind with at least some of its moral duties, but it is a view of things which Hobbes on most occasions is concerned expressly to deny. For Hobbes 'our natural reason' is 'the undoubted word of God' (*L*, 286), but what it conveys is hypothetical information about causes and effects, not categorical information about duties; and there is even some inconsistency in his use of the expression '*our* reason' – 'reason', properly speaking, is, for him, the power of reasoning, i.e. of drawing warrantable conclusions. The appearance, then, of this expression 'Right Reason' in Hobbes's writings is a signal to the attentive reader to be on his guard and to suspect equivocation.

[3] *L*, 337.   [4] *L*, 211 *sq.*, 534; *E.W.*, II, 220.   [5] *L*, 85, 317.

which is at once 'natural 'or 'uncovenanted' and 'authentique'. It is true that the 'natural reason' or the 'conscience' of private men may be represented as interpreters of the Law of Nature,[1] but they cannot be thought to supply an 'authentique' interpretation of it as a law. When each man is his own interpreter, not only is it impossible to exclude the partiality of passion (and conscience, in the end, is only a man's good opinion of what he has done or is inclined to do), but the obligation of the law thus interpreted ceases to be a universal obligation to endeavour peace and becomes, at most, an obligation upon each man to obey his own *bona fide* version of the law – which is not enough. A law which may be different for each man under 'it' is not a law at all but merely a multiplicity of opinions about how the legislator (in this case, God) wishes us to behave.[2] There is, in fact, no law where there is no *common* authority to declare and interpret it.[3] Nor does it mend matters to suggest that each man is responsible to God for the *bona fide* character of his interpretation: this responsibility could only apply to that fraction of mankind who believed in a providential God concerned with human conduct.

The inquiry provoked by the interpretation of Hobbes's writings we are now considering has led us to the view that the question, Has the Law of Nature, according to Hobbes, the necessary and sufficient characteristics of a law in the proper sense binding all mankind to the duty of endeavouring peace? Or (in another from) Is the duty of endeavouring peace a 'natural', uncovenanted duty, binding upon all men? must be answered in the negative. But this inquiry has also suggested that perhaps the more relevant questions are, In what circumstances did Hobbes think the Law of Nature acquires these characteristics? and, To whom is the endeavour for peace not only a rational course of conduct for those intent upon survival but a morally binding injunction? For, although Hobbes said much that pushes our thoughts in another direction, it seems clear that for him the Law of Nature possessed these characteristics

---

[1] *L*, 249.
[2] Cf. *L*, 453, 531, 534. Compare Hobbes's rejection of 'writers' and 'books of Moral Philosophy' as authentic interpreters of the civil law (*L*, 212). An 'authentique' interpretation must be single and authoritative, and without an interpretation there is no known law and therefore no law and no duty.
[3] *L*, 98.

only in certain circumstances and imposed duties only upon certain persons. In general, these circumstances are those in which to endeavour peace has become a rule of positive law, human or divine; and, in general, the persons bound are those only who know the author of this law and have acknowledged his authority to make it.[1] This seems to correspond with what I take to be Hobbes's deepest conviction about moral duties; namely, that there can be 'no obligation upon any man which ariseth not from some act of his own'.[2] But the bearing of this principle is not that, for Hobbes, the choice of him who is obliged creates the duty, but that where there has been no choice (covenant or acknowledgment) there is no known law-giver and therefore no law in the proper sense and no duty. And it is a principle which seems to me to exclude the possibility of 'natural' (that is, uncovenanted) duties. The necessary 'act' may be the acknowledgment of God in the belief in a 'providential' God concerned with human conduct; but, for those who live in a *civitas*, it is the act which creates and authorizes the civil sovereign because, for such persons, there are no duties which do not reach them as the commands of this sovereign.

There may be other and more obscure thoughts to be taken into account, but it seems to me certain that Hobbes thought that, whatever may or may not belong to other conditions of human circumstance, the *civitas* is unquestionably a condition in which there is a law in the proper sense[3] (namely, the civil law), in which this law is the only law in the proper sense, and in which it is the duty of all subjects to endeavour peace. The reading of Hobbes in which this

---

[1] Hobbes, it is well known, distinguished between two classes of obligation – *in fore interno* and *in fore externo*. This distinction has been elucidated with great care and subtlety by Mr Warrender, but it will be agreed that it is subsidiary to the question we are now concerned with, namely: What, in Hobbes's view, are the necessary conditions of obligation of any sort? Consequently I do not propose to go into it here. It may, however, be remarked that Mr Warrender's view that Hobbes held that, *in the State of Nature*, the Laws of Nature bind always *in fore interno*, and *in fore externo* not always (Warrender, p. 52; *L*, 121), is not quite convincing. What Hobbes must be understood to be saying is that the Laws of Nature, *where they are laws in the proper sense*, oblige always *in fore interno* and *in fore externo* not always. Is it not going further than the text warrants to interpret 'always' as meaning 'in all conditions of human life', including the State of Nature?

[2] *L*, 314, 317, 403, 448.   [3] *L*, 443.

covenanted duty derives from a 'natural' duty, imposed antecedently upon all mankind by an independent and perpetually operative Law of Nature, ignores so many of Hobbes's conclusions about God, 'reason', human knowledge, 'the signification of words' and the conditions of moral obligation, that what it explains is little compared with what it leaves unaccounted for, and cannot be accepted as a satisfactory account. And besides these fundamental discrepancies, perhaps the most fertile source of the misunderstanding reflected in this interpretation is the confusion (for which Hobbes is responsible) between what he said about the 'Laws of Nature' as 'theorems concerning what conduceth to the conservation and defence' of mankind (namely, their availability to natural reason and their unquestionable intelligibility to even the meanest intellect) and what he said about them as morally binding injunctions – the confusion between reason which teaches and laws which enjoin.

5

It is safe to say that every interpretation of Hobbes's moral theory leaves something that Hobbes wrote imperfectly accounted for. But it is reasonable to distinguish between those interpretations which conflict with some (perhaps, many and repeated) detached statements in the writings, and those which conflict with what may, perhaps, be considered the structural principles of Hobbes's view of things, though it is difficult to decide where to draw the line. Of the interpretations we have before us, the first seems to me the least possible to accept, and the second (in which duty is understood to be an endeavour for peace according to the laws of the *civitas*) to be the most plausible because it conflicts least with what I take to be the structural principles of Hobbes's philosophy. Nevertheless, it must be acknowledged that Hobbes's statements about 'natural' duties imposed by a Natural Law (which are the central theme of the third interpretation) are not to be regarded as mere inadvertencies. It is true that they are inconsistent with some of Hobbes's most cherished principles, but they are far too numerous to be merely ignored; indeed, Mr Warrender has shown that, if they are abstracted from the whole, they are capable of composing together a tolerably complete moral theory. The situation we have on our hands (as I understand it) is, then, a set of philosophical writings in which there appear (not side by side, but almost inextricably mixed) a theory of moral obligation at once original and consistent with the other philosophical novelties to be found in them, and another account of moral obligation the vocabulary and general principles of which are conventional (though there are original touches of detail); and anyone disposed to find the one more significant than the other[1] may be expected to offer a more plausible explanation of the presence of what he finds less significant than that it springs merely from the confusion of Hobbes's thoughts. No doubt there is confusion at some points, but the presence of these two theories of obligation cannot be taken as an example of mere confusion.

Our question, in general, is: Why did Hobbes, in an enterprise designed to elucidate the ground and character of the obligations entailed in living in a *civitas*, run together two strikingly different (and at some points contradictory) accounts of moral obligation? And, in detail, our puzzle is to account for the discrepancies which appear in his writings of which the following are a brief selection.

    1. He tells us that in nature 'every man has a right to everything; even to another's body', a right to govern himself according to his own judgment, 'to do anything he liketh', and to preserve himself in any manner that he finds expedient.[2] And he tells us that in nature every man has a 'natural' obligation to endeavour peace, imposed by a Natural Law which is the command of an omnipotent God.

    2. He tells us that 'Reason' 'serves only to convince the truth (not of fact, but) of consequence',[3] that it deals only in hypothetical propositions about causes and effects, that its business in human conduct is to suggest fit means for achieving desired ends, and that nothing is obligatory on account of being reasonable; but he tells us also that the Laws of Nature, as laws and not merely as hypothetical

---

[1] Besides the other reasons I have already stated for finding less to object to in the first of these two than the second, as an interpretation of Hobbes's writings, some weight may perhaps be given to the fact that Hobbes believed what he had written on the subject of moral obligation would appear offensively eccentric to his contemporaries (e.g. *L*, 557), and he could scarcely have believed this if his theory were of the character Mr Warrender attributes to it.

  [2] *L*, 99.   [3] *L*, 292, etc.

conclusions about human preservation, are made known to us in 'the dictates of natural reason.'[1]

3. He tells us that, by means of reason, we may know God as the author of a moral law; and he tells us also that by reason we can know nothing whatever about God as the author of a moral law (or about his rewards and punishments in another life), but may know God only as a First Cause.

4. He tells that 'our obligation to civil obedience ... is before all civil law',[2] and suggests that it is a 'natural' and universal obligation and derives from it an obligation not to rebel against the civil sovereign; but elsewhere he denies the universality of this 'natural' obligation and specifies a class of person to whom it applies and makes it rest upon a covenant or an acknowledgment.

5. He asserts the independent *authority* of both Natural Law and Scripture, the one based on reason and the other on revelation, but elsewhere he tells us that, as members of a *civitas*, the *authority* of Natural Law derives from the imprimatur of the civil sovereign and that the precepts of Scripture are what the civil sovereign says they are.

6. He uses the word 'precept' of reason as an alternative to the expression 'general rule' of reason[3] to describe the first Law of Nature in an account which ends by denying that the prescriptive character of Natural Law has anything to do with its reasonableness.[4]

7. He uses the expression 'natural Laws' both when he means to denote the hypothetical conclusions of human reason about human self-preservation and to denote obligations imposed by God upon those who believe in a providential God and obligations alleged to be imposed by God upon all men except atheists(?), lunatics and children. This is a manner of speaking which is almost a confession of a design to confuse.

8. He says that a sovereign (without qualification) is obliged by the Law of Nature to 'procure the safety (and welfare) of the people' and must 'render an account thereof to God, the Author of the Law, and to none but him';[5] but, on his own showing (and apart from numerous other difficulties), this is at best true of a sovereign who

---

[1] *L*, 275, etc. [2] *E.W.*, II, 200. [3] *L*, 100.
[4] *L*, 122. [5] *L*, 258.

belongs to that class of person who believes in a providential God concerned with human conduct, a class which (in Hobbes's writings) it is exceedingly difficult to distinguish from that of Christian believers.

9. He makes great play with a distinction between 'God's natural kingdom' and his 'natural subjects', and then tells us that the word 'kingdom' and the word 'subject' are merely metaphorical expressions in default of the 'artifice' of a 'covenant'.

10. He distinguishes between 'the first Founders, and Legislators of Commonwealths among the Gentiles'[1] who, in order to promote civil obedience and peace, encourage their subjects to believe the civil law has divine sanction, and the situation (as among the ancient Jews) where 'God himself' is said to establish a kingdom by covenant; but he ignores the fact that all that he has said about God and human imagination brands the expression 'God himself' as meaningless: God 'is' what he is believed or 'dreamed' to be, and he 'does' what he is believed or 'dreamed' to do.

Some commentators have believed themselves to have satisfactorily resolved some of these examples of discrepancy without having to resort to a general explanation, and perhaps the most notable of these resolutions is that attempted by Mr Warrender in respect of *Leviathan* p.205.[2] But even that cannot be considered successful. He finds in this passage a *reductio ad absurdum* of natural-law theory which he conjectures Hobbes could not have intended, and he rejects what must be recognized as the literal meaning of the passage because he cannot bring himself to believe that Hobbes (who certainly both asserts and denies them elsewhere) could have concurred with its entailments. But whatever success or lack of success commentators have had in resolving some of the more superficial discrepancies of Hobbes's writings, there remains a core of discrepancy impervious to this kind of treatment, and we are provoked to seek a general explanation more plausible than mere native confusion of mind, careless reasoning and a propensity to exaggeration.

Hobbes's writings on civil obedience (and *Leviathan* in particular) may be taken to have a twofold purpose. It would appear that his project was to display a theory of obligation consistent with the

[1] *L*, 89-90.   [2] Warrender, p. 167.

tenets of his general philosophy and with his reading of human nature; and also to show his contemporaries where their civil duties lay and why they lay there, in order to combat the confusion and anarchical tendencies of current thought and conduct.[1] The first of these enterprises is an exercise in logic, and it is appropriately conducted in the vocabulary which Hobbes had made his own. The second, on the other hand, could not be successful unless it were framed in the idiom and the vocabulary of current political theory and thus present a doctrine whose novelties (if any) were assimilated to current prejudices about moral conduct. Now, as it turned out, these two enterprises (which in a more conventional writer might have been run together without notable discrepancy) conflicted with one another, not in matters of periferal importance but in matters of central importance. Hooker, in an earlier generation, had found it possible to expound a doctrine of civil obedience, not very unlike Hobbes's more conventional theory, by making a few adjustments in the current natural-law theory, and Hobbes may be read (in one of his moods) as attempting the same sort of enterprise, though his adjustments were more radical and did not escape giving offence. But no conceivable adjustment of this conventional natural-law doctrine could result in an account of civil obligation even remotely compatible with his general philosophy. In short, if we have to choose between an explanation of the more important discrepancies in Hobbes's writing in terms of mere confusion or an explanation in terms of artful equivocation, I think the probability lies with the latter.

And if we do settle for an explanation of this sort, which recognizes Hobbes to have two doctrines, one for the initiated (those whose heads were strong enough to withstand the giddiness

[1] If we distinguish (as we may) between an account of the dispositions and actions alleged to be morally obligatory and a doctrine designed to display the reason why whatever is believed to be obligatory is so, it may be observed, first, that, in so far as Hobbes was engaged in recommending new duties (which he is loth to do, *E.W.*, II, xxii), they were not inventions of his own but were the duties inherent in the emerging conditions of a modern State where governing is recognized as a sovereign activity; and secondly, that the two enterprises upon which Hobbes was (on this reading of him) engaged, conflict (where they do conflict) not notably in respect of the duties recognized but in respect of the reason given for their being duties.

provoked by his scepticism) and the other for the ordinary man who must be spoken to in an idiom and a vocabulary he is accustomed to, and to whom novelties (both in respect of duties and in respect of their grounds) must be made to appear commonplaces, we are not attributing a unique and hitherto unheard of character to *Leviathan*. Numerous other writers on these topics (Plato, for example, Machiavelli and even Bentham) were the authors of works which contain at once, and imperfectly distinguished from one another, an esoteric and an exoteric doctrine; and the view that matters of this sort (indeed, political questions generally) are 'mysteries' to be discussed candidly and directly only with the initiated goes back to the beginnings of political speculation and was by no means dead in the seventeenth century.

I do not suppose that this account of Hobbes's thoughts on obligation will commend itself to everyone, and in the nature of the case it cannot be demonstrated to be true. But what appears to me probable is that the discrepancies in Hobbes's writings are of a character to require some such general explanation.

6

Our study of Hobbes has reached some conclusions which most readers will find difficult to avoid. It seems clear that he believed that a rational disposition in human beings was to be indentified as an endeavour for peace. And peace meant acknowledging all others as our equal, keeping our promises, not displaying contempt and hatred and not endeavouring to out-do all others in order to have the elation of being recognized to occupy first place. This manner of living is suggested by reason, which also suggests the means by which it may be instituted and maintained: it is the *civitas*. The reward of its accomplishment is emancipation from the constant fear of violent and shameful death at the hands of other men. And, so far, the sufficient *cause* or *motive* for endeavouring peace is found in fear of shameful death: fear prompts reason and reason discloses what must be done to avoid the circumstances which generate fear.

We have looked further to find if Hobbes had anything to say in support of his view that this endeavour is, in fact, not only reasonable, but also just – that is, morally obligatory. Here, we have observed, first, that Hobbes was certainly capable of distinguishing between the sufficient causes for human conduct and the reasons which may be given in justification of it. And further, we have observed the sort of reason which Hobbes considered adequate; namely, the existence of a law in the proper sense commanding this endeavour. Beyond this, there lies a region difficult to map. And the best an explorer can do is to determine what he thinks to be its more significant features and to give his reasons for prefering these to others. And this is what I have done. But there is still something more to be said.

The morality we have seen Hobbes to be defending is the morality of the tame man. It is still true that the greatest stimulus to the vital movement of the heart is the elation generated by being continuously recognized to be superior. But this greatest good must be foregone: pride, even when it does not degenerate into vain-glory, is too dangerous a passion to be allowed, even if its suppression somewhat dims the brilliance of life.

But, in the writings of Hobbes there is another line of argument, not extensively elaborated, but enough to push our thoughts in a different direction. In this line of thought the just disposition is still recognized to be an endeavour for peace and what is sought is still emancipation from the fear of violent and shameful death at the hands of other men, but the desired condition is to be attained, not by proud man, awakened by fear, surrendering his pride and becoming (by covenant) tame man, but by the moralization of pride itself. How can this happen?

Let us suppose a man of the character Hobbes supposed all men to be: a man unavoidably his own best friend and (on account of his weakness) subject to the fear of finding himself shamed and dishonoured and even killed. But let us also suppose that the preponderant passion of this man remains pride rather than fear; that he is a man who would find greater shame in the meanness of settling for mere survival than in suffering the dishonour of being recognized a failure; a man whose disposition is to overcome fear not by reason (that is, by seeking a secure condition of external human circumstances) but by his own courage; a man not at all without imper-

fections and not deceived about himself, but who is proud enough
to be spared the sorrow of his imperfections and the illusion of his
achievements; not exactly a hero, too negligent for that, but perhaps
with a touch of careless heroism about him; a man, in short, who
(in Montaigne's phrase) 'knows how to belong to himself', and who,
if fortune turned out so, would feel no shame in the epitaph:

Par delicatesse
J'ai perdu ma vie.

Now, a man of this sort would not lack stimulus for the vital
movement of his heart, but he is in a high degree self-moved. His
endeavour is for peace; and if the peace he enjoys is largely his own
unaided achievement and is secure against the mishaps that may
befall him, it is not in any way unfriendly to the peace of other men
of a different kind. There is nothing hostile in his conduct, nothing
in it to provoke hostility, nothing censorious. What he achieves for
himself and what he contributes to a common life is a complete
alternative to what others may achieve by means of agreement
inspired by fear and dictated by reason; for, if the unavoidable
endeavour of every man is for self-preservation, and if self-preservation is interpreted (as Hobbes interprets it), not as immunity from
death but from the fear of shameful death, then this man achieves in
one manner (by courage) what others may achieve in another (by
rational calculation). And, unlike others, he not only abstains from
doing injury but is able to be indifferent to having to suffer it from
others. In short, although this character looks, at first sight, much
more like the *âme forte* of Vauvenargues than anything we might
expect to find in Hobbes, there is nothing in it which conflicts with
Hobbes's psychology, which, in fact, identifies differences between
men as differences in their preponderant passions and can accommodate the man in whom pride occupies a greater place than fear.

Indeed, it is a character which actually appears in Hobbes's
writings, and is, moreover, recognized there as just character.
'That which gives to human actions the relish of justice,' he says, 'is
a certain Nobleness or Gallantness of courage (rarely found), by
which a man scorns to be beholden for the contentment of life, to
fraud or breach of promise. This justice of Manners, is that which is

meant, where justice is called a virtue.'[1] He recognized that a man may keep his word, not merely because he fears the consequences of breaking it, but from 'a glory or pride in appearing not to need to break it'.[2] He identified magnanimity with just conduct that springs from 'contempt' of injustice, and recognized that men are sometimes prepared to lose their lives rather than suffer some sorts of shame.[3] And the only hindrance to our recognizing this as a genuinely Hobbesian character is the general assertion that Hobbes always used the word 'pride' in a derogatory sense.[4]

But this assertion is, in fact, too sweeping. It is, of course, true that Hobbes sometimes used the word 'pride' in a derogatory sense to indicate one of the three passions pre-eminent in causing strife;[5] but he also identified it with generosity, courage, nobleness, magnanimity and an endeavour for glory,[6] and he distinguished it from 'vain-glory', which is always a vice because it entails illusion and strife without the possibility of felicity.[7] In short, Hobbes (who took the conception 'pride' from the Augustinian tradition of moral and political theology) recognized the twofold meaning which the word has always carried. Pride, in that tradition, was the passion to be God-like. But it was recognized that this may be either the endeavour to put oneself in the place of God, or the endeavour to imitate God. The first is a delusive insolence in which a Satanic self-love, believing itself to be omnipotent, is not only the last analysis of every passion but the only operative motive, and conduct becomes the imposition of oneself upon the world of men and of things. This Hobbes, like every other moralist, recognized as a vice and an absolute bar to a peaceful condition of human circumstance: it is the pride which provokes a destroying nemesis, the pride which Heraclitus said should be put out even more than a fire. But, as Duns Scotus said, there is no vice but it is the shadow of a virtue; and in the second manner of being God-like, self-love appears as self-knowledge and self-respect, the delusion of power over others is replaced by the reality of self-control, and the glory of the invulnerability which comes from courage generates magnanimity and magnanimity, peace.

[1] *L*, 114. [2] *L*, 108; cf. 229. [3] *E.W.*, II, 38.
[4] Strauss, 25. [5] *L*, 57, 128, 246. [6] *L*, 96.
[7] *L*, 44, 77.

This is the *virtue* of pride whose lineage is to be traced back to the nymph Hybris, the reputed mother of Pan by Zeus; the pride which is reflected in the *megalopsychos* of Aristotle and at a lower level in the wise man of the Stoics; the *sancta superbia* which had its place in medieval moral theology; and which was recognized by Hobbes as an alternative manner to that suggested by fear and reason of preserving one's own nature and emancipating oneself from the fear of shameful death and from the strife which this fear generates.

Nor is this idiom of the character of the just man without its counterpart in the writings of other moralists of the same general disposition as Hobbes. Spinoza, considering the same problem as Hobbes, indicated two alternative escapes into peace from the competitive propensities of human nature; the one generated by fear and prudential foresight which results in the law and order of the *civitas*, and the other the escape offered by the power of the mind over the circumstances of human life. And Hume, taking pride and humility (which, like Hobbes, he identified with fear)[1] as the simple passions, equally self-centred, recognized both as generators of virtue, but 'self-esteem' as the generator of the 'shining virtues' – courage, intrepidity, magnanimity, and the endeavour for the sort of glory in which 'death loses its terrors' and human life its contentiousness. But whereas Hume found the merit of pride as the motive for just conduct not only in its 'agreeableness' (identifying it with pleasure and humility with frustration) but also in its superior 'utility',[2] the question we have to ask ourselves about Hobbes is, Why did he not pursue this line of argument further? Why did he deny utility to pride and conclude that, in the end, 'the passion to be reckoned with is fear?'

And to this question Hobbes himself provided a clear answer, an answer less fully elaborated than Spinoza's but in principle the same: it is not because pride does not provide an adequate motive for a successful endeavour for peace, but because of the dearth of noble characters. 'This,' he says, 'is a generosity too rarely to be found to be presumed, especially in pursuers of wealth, command and sensual pleasure; which are the greatest part of Mankind.'[3] In short, Hobbes

---

[1] *Elements*, I, ix, 2.
[2] *Treatise*, II, i and iii; *Enquiries*, §263; *Essays*, xvi; The Stoic.
[3] *L*, 108.

perceived that men lack passion rather than reason, and lack, above all, *this* passion. But where it is present, it is to be recognized as capable of generating an endeavour for peace more firmly based than any other and therefore (even in the *civitas*, where it is safe to be just) the surest motive for just conduct. Indeed, it seems almost to have been Hobbes's view that men of this character are a necessary cause of the *civitas*; and certainly it is only they who, having an adequate motive for doing so, may be depended upon to defend it when dissension deprives the sovereign of his power. And he saw in Sidney Godolphin the emblem of this character.[1] Nevertheless, even here Hobbes displays his disposition to be more interested in the causes or motives of just conduct than in the reasons for believing that we have an obligation to endeavour peace: 'pride' does not supply a reason, it is only a possible alternative cause.

There is, perhaps, one further observation to be made. Fear of shameful death, provoking reason to suggest the convenient articles of peace and the manner in which they may become the pattern of human life, generates the morality of the tame man, the man who has settled for safety and has no need of nobility, generosity, magnanimity or an endeavour for glory in order to move him to behave justly. And, in so far as this was Hobbes's view, he has been recognized as the philosopher of a so-called 'bourgeois' morality. But this is an idiom of the moral life which, in spite of Hobbes's individualistic reading of human nature, seems to intimate and point towards the notion of a 'common good'. It seems to suggest a single approved condition of human circumstances for all conditions of men, and morality as the art in which this condition is achieved and maintained. But there are qualifications to be noticed which tend to confirm the view that, with Kant and others, he was pre-eminently a philosopher of the morality of individuality. First, Hobbes was primarily concerned with motives for obeying civil law; he is less concerned with what a man might otherwise do with his life than with the minimum conditions in which the endeavour for peace could be the pattern of conduct for even the least well-disposed man. These minimum conditions are that there shall be one *law* for the lion and the ox and that both should have known and adequate motives for obeying it.

[1] *L*, Dedication, 548; *Vita* (1681), 240.

And this, while perhaps intimating the disposition which generated the morality of the 'common good', does not itself entail it. And secondly, Hobbes had this other mood, in which pride and self-esteem are recognized to supply an adequate motive for endeavouring peace, and in this mood he was unmistakably a philosopher of the morality of individuality. This idiom of morality is 'aristocratic'; and it is neither inappropriate nor unexpected to find it reflected in the writings of one who (though he felt constrained to write for those whose chief desire was to 'prosper') himself understood human beings as creatures more properly concerned with honour than with either survival or prosperity.

NOTE TO P.259

The precise manner in which Hobbes believed a *civitas* may be 'caused', or may be imagined to emerge, lies to one side of the subject of this essay, but it is an interesting topic, attractive if for no other reason than because of its difficulty and I propose to consider it briefly.[1]

Hobbes's position is that unless something is done to change his natural condition, no man is secure against the natural 'covetousness, lust, anger and the like' of his fellows and (consequently) has nothing better to look forward to than a nasty and brutish existence, frustrated and full of contention. Even in this state of nature, men (it is true) are capable of making contracts, agreements, covenants, etc., with one another, but these, so far from substantially modifying the condition of insecurity, are themselves infected with this insecurity. And this is specially the case with covenants of mutual trust. For in these, one of the covenanters must perform his part of the bargain first, but he who does so risks being bilked; indeed, the risk that he whose part it is to be the second performer will not keep his promise (not necessarily because it may be against his interest to do so, but because 'avarice' and 'ambition' are apt triumph over reason) must always be great enough to make it unreasonable for any man to consent to be a first performer. Thus, while in these conditions

---

[1] In the following account I have had the advantage of suggestions kindly offered me by Mr J. M. Brown, who nevertheless must not be held responsible for the blunders it may still contain.

contracts may be made and executed, and even covenants of mutual trust, they always entail a risk which no reasonable man will take and they offer no extensive or reliable modification of the war of all men against all men.

This situation, however, would be transformed if there were a 'common power' acknowledged by all men to have the authority to compel the keeping of covenants; and Hobbes's question is: How may such a 'common power' be imagined to be 'caused' and what must be its character?

The only manner in which such a 'common power' may be erected, he tells us, is for every man to covenant with every man to transfer his natural *right* to govern himself and to preserve his own nature, and to relinquish his natural *power* (such as it is) to secure the fulfilment of his own desires, to one man or an assembly of men, and to 'acknowledge himself to be the author of whatsoever he that so beareth their person, shall act, or cause to be acted, in those things which concern the common peace and safety; and therein to submit their wills, every one to his will, and their judgments, to his judgment'.

Now, accepting for the moment the conclusion, namely, that those who have put themselves in this situation will enjoy what they seek to enjoy, peace, what we have to consider is the intelligibility of the process by which it is reached. Certain difficulties appear. The covenant by means of which this common power is purported to be established is unmistakably what Hobbes calls a covenant of mutual trust, and it is made by men in a state of nature, consequently (unless we are given some cogent reason for thinking otherwise) it cannot be supposed to be exempt from the considerations which make all such covenants unreasonably risky undertakings for the first performer and therefore not to be relied upon by reasonable men. It is true that its terms are different from the terms of any other covenant of mutual trust; but how can its terms (that is, *what* is promised) transform a covenant of a kind in which it is unreasonably risky to be the first performer into one in which the risk (if any) is not unreasonable? It is true, also that it is (what not all other covenants of mutual trust are) a covenant to which many are parties; but, since there is no reason why an ordinary covenant of mutual trust should not be of this sort, and if it were so, there is no reason why it should be less reasonable to suspect non-performance on the part of at least some of the participants, the multilateral character of this covenant does not appear to distinguish it to any advantage. And further, Hobbes's words often seem to suggest that the mere entering into this covenant, the mere 'signing' of it (so to speak), generates the 'common power', and it is not easy to understand how this can be so.

But if we go again to what Hobbes wrote we may, perhaps, find him to be saying something that avoids these difficulties. This would, I think, be so if we were to interpret him as follows:

There will be 'peace' and a condition in which covenants will be lasting and constant, only if there is a Sovereign to enforce peace and to compel the keeping of covenants. This Sovereign, in order to perform his office, must have *authority* (that is, right), and he must have *power*. The only way in which he can be imagined to acquire authority is by means of a covenant of the sort already described, and in order to have authority nothing more than this covenant is needed. Therefore such a covenant (or something like it) may be recognized as a necessary 'cause' of a *civitas*. And, further, it may, perhaps, also be recognized as empirically necessary as a means of generating the *power* required by the Sovereign, because it is hardly to be imagined that a number of individuals will in fact acknowledge his authority in the acts and dispositions of obedience which constitute his power unless they have covenanted to do so. Nevertheless, the covenant by itself is not the sufficient cause of a *civitas*; it gives authority, but it merely promises power. The necessary and sufficient cause of a Sovereign possessed of the authority and the power required to establish a condition of 'peace' is a covenant of this sort combined with a sufficiently widespread disposition (displayed in overt acts) to observe its terms; for the Sovereign's power is only the counterpart of his subjects' disposition to obey. And consequently, we are provoked to look in Hobbes's account for some argument which will convince us that it is reasonable to expect that this covenant, unlike others made in the state of nature, will be kept. For, perhaps with some colour of paradox, it now appears that the power necessary to establish peace and to compel the keeping of covenants is generated not by making the covenant but only in the process of keeping it, that is, in dispositions and acts of obedience. In short, we have been convinced that it must always be unreasonable to be the first performer in an ordinary covenant of mutual trust in the state of nature, and what Hobbes has now to demonstrate to us is that it is not unreasonable for any man to be the first performer in *this* covenant of mutual trust. And it may be observed, at once, that this condition of affairs cannot be made to spring from there being a power to compel those who are to be the second performers to keep their promises, because what we are seeking is an intelligible explanation of how such a power can be 'errected'.

Now, on this question Hobbes seems to have made his position doubly secure. He undertakes to show us: first, that it is reasonable to be the first performer in this covenant even if there is no reasonable expectation that the other covenanters will keep their promises; and further, that there is in fact a reasonable expectation that a significant number of covenanters will keep their promises, and that in the case of *this* covenant (unlike that of ordinary covenants) this is enough to make it not unreasonable to be a first performer.

First, a party to this covenant is, to be sure, taking some risk if he obeys a Sovereign authority who is unable to compel the obedience of the other parties and if he has no reasonable expectation that they also will obey. Nevertheless, it is not an unreasonable risk because what he stands to lose is insignificant compared with what he stands to gain, and because, in fact, unless someone is the first performer in this covenant the 'common power' necessary to peace can never come into existence.[1] This is a cogent argument; it observes a relevant distinction between the covenant to authorize the exercise of sovereign authority and other covenants of mutual trust, and it points out the entailment of this in respect of the reasonableness of being a first performer in this covenant; but most readers of Hobbes will look for something to fortify it. And, at least without going against anything he wrote, this may be found in the following considerations.

One of the important differences between the covenant to acknow-

---

[1] Perhaps, for the generation of the *civitas*, it is necessary to assume a man, not 'reasonable', but proudly careless of the consequences of being the first for peace; if so, there is some authority in Hobbes for this assumption.

ledge the authority of a Sovereign and thus endow him with power and any other covenant of mutual trust is that it may be effectively fulfilled even if all the parties do *not* behave as they have promised to behave. In an ordinary covenant of mutual trust between two the first performer is not requited unless the other keeps his word when his time comes. And this is true, also, in an ordinary covenant of mutual trust (one concerned with goods and services) in which there are many participants; the first performer, and each other performer, is deprived of something significant unless *all* the participants perform. But in this covenant among many to obey a Sovereign authority, the first performer, and each other willing performer, loses nothing if, instead of all performing, only some do so – as long as those who do are sufficient in number to generate the power necessary to compel those who are not disposed to obey. And while it may be unreasonable to expect that ambition and avarice will distract none of the parties to this covenant from keeping their promise to obey, it is not unreasonable to expect that a sufficient number will be immune from this distraction. Thus, there is a feature in this covenant which distinguishes it from all others and makes it not unreasonable to be a first performer; and every party to it is potentially a first performer. But, since what is sought by all reasonable men and what is counted upon by a first performer in this covenant is a durable condition of peace, the position is, perhaps, better understood as one in which it is not unreasonable to be a first performer and to go on performing because it is not unreasonable to expect that enough of the other parties will themselves voluntarily perform for enough of the time to generate enough power in the sovereign to force those who on any particular occasion may not be disposed to obey. For, the reasonableness of being a first performer does not depend upon his having a reasonable expectation that there will be a permanent body of particular persons who will always be disposed to requite his trust in them; it will suffice if he has a reasonable expectation that at any particular time there will be enough who are so disposed. The clouds of avarice, ambition and the like sweep over the sky and their shadows fall now upon this man and now upon that; no single man can be depended upon to keep the covenant all the time and upon every occasion. But this is not necessary; it is enough if enough may on any occasion be reasonably depended upon to endow by their willing obedience the sovereign with enough power to terrify into obedience those who on that occasion are not disposed to obey.

The argument, then, seems to run, briefly, as follows: Natural reason warns us against being the first performer in all ordinary covenants of mutual trust; and it tells us, also, that it is in our interest to seek peace and it suggests the manner in which peace may emerge. The necessary condition of peace is a Sovereign at once authoritative and powerful. The authority of this Sovereign can derive only from a covenant of mutual trust of every man with every man in which they transfer to him their natural right to govern themselves and in which they own and acknowledge all his commands in respect of those things which concern the common peace and safety as if they were their own. But the power of this Sovereign to enforce his commands derives only from those who have thus covenanted to obey actually obeying. A start must be made somewhere, and it must be shown to be a reasonable beginning. Is it not reasonable to expect that, having been reasonable enough to have made the covenant, enough men at any one time will be reasonable enough (that is, will be free enough from avarice and ambition and the like to recognize where their interest lies) to be disposed to keep it? And if this is so, it becomes a not unreasonable risk for any man to be the first performer. And every party to this covenant is a potential first performer. 'This is the generation of that great Leviathan . . . to which we owe under the Immortal God, our peace and defence.'

It must be acknowledged, however, that this account shows not that it is undeniably reasonable to be a first performer in this covenant to set up a sovereign authority (or even that it is undeniably not unreasonable to be such), but only that the risk entailed here is far more reasonable (or far less unreasonable) than the risk entailed in an ordinary covenant of mutual trust. And since, as I understand it, what Hobbes is seeking is a demonstration of reasonableness and not merely the probability of superior reasonableness, I must suspect that this account is either faulty or incomplete. To what extent the supposition of a man (such as Hobbes understood Sidney Godolphin to have been) careless of the consequences of being bilked as the first performer in this covenant, a man of 'pride' and not of 'reason', supplies what is lacking, the reader must decide for himself.

1960

The Study of 'Politics' in a University

AN ESSAY IN APPROPRIATENESS

The shape of the education offered in a university, like everything else, is subject to change. Those changes which have been engendered within a university by the emergence of some branch of study claiming to be in a condition to take its place beside the others already being pursued by undergraduates have usually been well enough managed. Of course, mistakes have been made, and changes which were distortions have been allowed to take place, but no great damage has been suffered from this cause. The sponsors of a new 'subject' of undergraduate study (and I am not here concerned with anything else) have usually not mistaken the sort of qualities they must claim on its behalf if they were to expect to launch it successfully; and in the early stages of its voyage they have been content to heave the lead every inch of the way. It was in this manner that schools of natural science, of modern history, of modern languages, of English literature and of economics made their appearance in English universities, and studies such as international law and genetics established themselves. Their inception was sometimes eased by the benevolence of a patron content to endow what had been approved; but on every occasion what was admitted to the undergraduate curriculum was something which had already been pursued as an academic study for a generation or more before the proposal was made.

In recent times, however, the shape of university education has been modified by changes springing from a different source. Benefactors with favourite projects of their own, a persuasive and energetic body of evangelists with a patron in their pockets, a profession set upon winning the status of a university study for its *mystique*, or even a government have made proposals designed to modify this shape. And though some of these proposals have turned out to be less disastrous than might have been forecast, they have not, on the whole, been so well managed. Greed, or the desire to appear abreast of the times, have often supervened to destroy both judgment and proper inquiry, and the shape of a university education has suffered some ill-considered and some destructive changes.

'Politics' found its way into English university education in a somewhat tortuous manner, quite unlike the simple and naïve manner in which it entered American university education. Proper consideration was not altogether lacking; there seemed to be something in existing arrangements to which it could appropriately be attached; generous and opinionated benefactors were not absent; persuasive and energetic evangelists often played their part. It was supported by distinguished and sometimes scholarly sponsors; ancient (though, alas, irrelevant) precedent and continental practice (not very closely observed) was cited in its favour; the disposition of the times flattered it. The entry was effected unobtrusively and under a number of different names, which made it appear eligible for whatever interpretation its professors and teachers might be disposed to put upon it. And in these unusual circumstances it is not surprising that, alongside the engagement to teach 'politics' to undergraduates, there should be (rather late in the day) an inquiry about what is to be taught. Confidence has not been lacking, but it has often been an irrelevant confidence in political opinions or in the existence of a suitable body of information to be imparted. And the inquiry itself has not always been well-directed; it has been too easily silenced whenever a likely formula has been devised . 'Politics', we have been told, is 'the study of political behaviour', or 'the study of power in society', or 'the study of political institutions and political theory'; but there has been an ominous silence about the manner in which this study is to be conducted.

This condition of things I find to be unsatisfactory, and I propose to reopen this inquiry and to set it going in a somewhat different direction. The question I propose to consider is: What study under the plausible name of 'Politics' is an appropriate component of a university education? And I propose to explore this theme by considering first the character of a university education in general.

I

We have a small stock of ideas at our disposal on this topic. We know that university education is after-school education; and we talk of it as 'advanced' or 'further' or 'higher' or 'specialized' education, education for adults, and so on. But these are all vague ideas, and if they were all we had we might have to confess that 'university' education is not very different from any other sort of education. This, indeed, is what some people believe to be the case. They are content with the distinction between 'elementary' and 'advanced', they think that advanced studies are characterized by greater detail and the requirement of more developed mental powers, and that consequently a 6th Form in a school begins to approximate to a university, and that a technical college is something like a university.

I do not, myself, believe any of this to be the case. I believe that university education is a specific sort of education, in some ways distinguished by its *elementary* character; and that although it is not the only sort of education and cannot take the place of any other sort, it is both important and unique. And I believe, consequently, that every component of a university education is properly a component in virtue of having a certain character or propensity.

Education I will take to be the process of learning, in circumstances of direction and restraint, how to recognize and make something of ourselves. Unavoidably, it is a two-fold process in which we enjoy an initiation into what for want of a better word I will call a 'civilization', and in doing so discover our own talents and aptitudes in relation to that civilization and begin to cultivate and to use them. Learning to make something of ourselves in no context in particular is an impossibility; and the context appears not only in what is learned but also in the conditions of direction and restraint which belong to any education.

Some people think of a civilization as a stock of things like books, pictures, musical instruments and compositions, buildings, cities, landscapes, inventions, devices, machines and so on – in short, as the results of mankind having impressed itself upon a 'natural' world. But this is an unduly restricted (indeed, an exceedingly primitive) understanding of that 'second nature' (as Hegel called it) which is the context of our activity. The world into which we are initiated is composed, rather, of a stock of emotions, beliefs, images, ideas, manners of thinking, languages, skills, practices and manners of activity out of which these 'things' are generated. And consequently it is appropriate to think of it not as a stock but as a capital; that is, something known and enjoyed only in use. For none of these is fixed and finished; each is at once an achievement and a promise. This capital has been accumulated over hundreds of years. And in use it earns an interest, part of which is consumed in a current manner of living and part reinvested.

From another point of view, however, a civilization (and particularly ours) may be regarded as a conversation being carried on between a variety of human activities, each speaking with a voice, or in a language of its own; the activities (for example) represented in moral and practical endeavour, religious faith, philosophic reflection, artistic contemplation and historical or scientific inquiry and explanation. And I call the manifold which these different manners of thinking and speaking compose, a conversation, because the relations between them are not those of assertion and denial but the conversational relationships of acknowledgment and accommodation.

If, then, we recognize education as an initiation into a civilization, we may regard it as beginning to learn our way about a material, emotional, moral and intellectual inheritance, and as learning to recognize the varieties of human utterance and to participate in the conversation they compose. And if we consider education as a process in which we discover and begin to cultivate ourselves, we may regard it as learning to recognize ourselves in the mirror of this civilization.

I do not claim universality for this image of education; it is merely the image (or part of it) which belongs to our civilization. But it is impossible to escape this sort of contingency, and we must take it as the context of our inquiry if anything relevant to our situation is to be said.

This education begins in the nursery where, for the most part, a child is learning to become at home in the natural-artificial world into which it was born. Here it is learning to use and to rely upon its senses and its limbs, to control its voice, to recognize its emotions, to suffer and overcome frustrations and to accommodate itself to others. It learns to speak, to play with words and at the same time to use and to understand the symbolic language of practical life. Here everything, or almost everything, is play. The product is insignificant; it is the activity it entails that matters. What is learned is all invested in the child itself; though, of course, being a child is having the command of a capital of pleasure and pain which earns an interest in the family life. And here, also, education has no specific orientation; it is not yet significantly concerned with individual talents and aptitudes, though these may show themselves early.

During school-days this sort of nursery education continues. To begin with, reading is from books designed to teach the recognition of words; writing is an exercise in calligraphy rather than a significant composition; there is the endless repetition of playing scales and pieces designed to improve dexterity; foreign languages appear merely as saying the same things only in other words; arithmetic is an exercise in handling figures.

But gradually and imperceptibly a transformation takes place, or begins to take place; a transformation for which story-telling, singing, drawing, dancing and social intercourse (that is, activities which unavoidably have some significant product, however transitory) have paved the way. *What* is read begins to be significant and to afford an entrance into literature; instrumental music becomes less a thing of the hand and eye than of the ear; and even foreign languages begin to appear as organizations of thoughts incapable of literal translation. In short, the intellectual capital of a civilization begins to be enjoyed and even used while the dexterities by which it is known and recognized are still imperfectly acquired. Or, perhaps, we have no more than a glimpse of how it might be enjoyed or used.

However, there is so much information to be gathered from so many different sources that, in school days, the intellectual inheritance appears much more like a stock of ideas, beliefs, perceptions, images and so on, than a capital. We acquire much that we do not know how to use, and much that we never think of in terms of use, that is, of investment to generate something valuable on its own account. Learning here is borrowing raw material the possible uses of which remain concealed. Or, to put it another way, most of what is learned is immediately and automatically reinvested in the ability to learn so that it appears to have no specific communicable or shareable product.

School-education, then, is not merely early education or simple education; it has a specific character. It is learning to speak before one has anything significant to say; and what is taught must have the qualities of being able to be learned without necessarily being understood, and of not being positively hurtful or nonsensical when learned in this way. Or, it may be said, what is taught must be capable of being learned without any previous recognition of ignorance: we do not begin to learn the multiplication tables because it suddenly dawns upon us that we do not know the sum of nine 8s, nor the dates of the Kings of England because we know we do not know when Edward I came to the throne: we learn these things at school because we are told to learn them. And further, school-education is without specific orientation; it is not yet concerned with individual talents and aptitudes, and if these show themselves (as they may) the design in school-education is not to allow them to take charge. At school we are, quite properly, not permitted to follow our own inclinations.

But our 'school-days' are now a longer period than they used to be; never less than ten years and for some fourteen and fifteen years. And before they come to an end, features of 'specialization' (as it is called) have begun to make their appearance in education. This I believe to be a mistake. But one can perceive the illusion of those who have imposed this mistake upon school education, and one can discern the misapplied pressures which have encouraged it. What it entails, however, is that the area of delusive overlap between this level of education and other levels has been increased and what belongs properly to school-days is unfortunately curtailed in favour of a kind of 'specialization' which belongs neither to a vocational education nor to a university education and which stands in the way of both; namely, a 'specialization' in which the range of study is arbitrarily restricted without either an increase in depth or any specific orientation. Or, if there is an orientation, giving this school-specialization a turn in a 'vocational' direction, then it conflicts with the commendable English tradition that professional education should be seriously undertaken from its beginning and should not be preceded by a sort of pantomime: to learn a profession is to learn how to *do* something and the best preparation for this is not to learn how to act as if you were doing it.

Leaving school is, then, a momentous occasion. It is the signal for the appearance of a new attitude towards the capital we have inherited. Nevertheless, education continues, and it is apt to branch out in two different directions – which I shall call 'vocational' education and 'university' education. And these represent two different and to some extent complementary attitudes towards the capital which composes a civilization. They are two different kinds of education.

From one point of view, a civilization may be regarded as a collection of skills which together make possible and define a current manner of living. Learning one of these skills – that of a lawyer, a doctor, an accountant, an electrician, a farmer, a motor-mechanic or a commercial traveller – is borrowing an appropriate quantum of the total capital and learning to use it in such a manner that it earns an interest – an interest which, in principle, may be either expended in current consumption or reinvested to produce improvements in the skill itself. Each of these skills has an intellectual content, and many have a component of physical dexterity. A purely physical dexterity (pushing a barrow in Covent Garden comes near to this) is not a skill; it entails a negligible call upon the capital which composes a civilization, and the interest it earns (which is minimal) is all dispersed in current consumption. On the other hand, a skill with a large intellectual content is one which makes a considerable call upon capital (an emblem of which is the length of time required to learn it), and it is capable of earning a large unconsumed interest.

'Vocational' education is that in which these skills are acquired; and in this sort of education a civilization has the naïve appearance of the things known and the skills practised which are entailed in a current manner of living. This manner of living is never, of course, fixed and finished; but it has some sort of general direction of contemporary movement depending upon these skills and others which may spring from them. Nor is it ever absolutely coherent: it is composed of skills which are on their way out and those which are on their way in; with us, heraldry and the handloom lie side by side with animal genetics and the computer.

Now, in respect of what is taught and learned in this 'vocational' kind of education, some observations may be made. For most people it is an education in *one* skill. The skill may be complicated and may have a considerable intellectual content, or it may be simple and easily learned. But it is, essentially, a highly specialized education, and not only on account of its concentration upon a single skill. For, learning here means acquiring a specific body of knowledge and being able to move about within it with ease and confidence and to use it. The sort of familiarity which a carpenter or a builder may have with his tools and his materials often goes far beyond anything that is achieved, with *his* tools and materials, by an historian of the Papacy or a classical scholar; but there is a reason for this, namely, that his is a strictly circumscribed body of knowledge which does not significantly look outside itself. The design of a 'vocational' education is to be concerned with current practice and always with what is believed to be known. How it came to be known, what errors and imperfections it has left behind are no more significant than the practices of a sixteenth century printer are to a twentieth century linotype operator. The significant principle of specialization in this sort of education derives not only from the fact that most learners are concerned to acquire only one skill, but from its being concerned to impart to the learner what may be called the current achievement of a civilization in respect of a skill or practice needed in the contemporary world. In short, a 'vocational' education, while it does not absolutely forbid it, is not concerned with that level of learning at which what is learned is capable of earning an unconsumed interest: it makes no provision for teaching people how to be ignorant; knowledge here is never the recognition of something absent.

And here I want to introduce a distinction which I propose to use later on: the distinction between a 'language' (by which I mean a manner of thinking) and a 'literature' or a 'text' (by which I mean what has been said from time to time in a 'language'). It is the distinction, for example, between the 'language' of poetic imagination and a poem or a novel; or between the 'language' or manner of thinking of a scientist and a text-book of geology or what may be called the current state of our geological knowledge.

Now, what is being studied in a 'vocational' education is a

'literature' or a 'text' and not a 'language'. What is being acquired is
a knowledge of what has been authoritatively said and not a familiarity with the manner of thinking which has generated what has
been said. For example, in this sort of education what is learned is
not how to think in a scientific manner, how to recognize a scientific
problem or proposition or how to use the 'language' of science, but
how to use those products of scientific thought which contribute to
our current manner of living. Or, if this distinction seems to be too
rigid, then it may be said that in a 'vocational' education what is
learnt is not a 'living' language with a view to being able to speak it
and say new things in it, but a 'dead' language; and it is learnt merely
for the purpose of reading a 'literature' or a 'text' in order to acquire
the information it contains. The skill acquired is the skill of using
the information, not of speaking the 'language'.

Further, 'vocational' education is learning one of the skills of
current life. Generally speaking only those skills which are currently
practised are taught. This, where the skill is an ancient skill, sometimes entails drawing upon long accumulated capital; but in most
cases it means drawing only upon capital accumulated in the last
hundred years, or fifty, or even twenty: for the electrical engineer the
world began the day before yesterday. In other words, a 'vocational'
education is education to fit a man to fill a specific place in a current
manner of living, or to satisfy a current demand. And consequently,
it is not utterly far-fetched (as it would be in the case of school education and, as we shall see, of a university education) to attempt to
determine the number of persons who are needed to be trained in
any particular skill if a current manner of living is to be sustained.

Now, as I understand it, university education is something
entirely different from both school and 'vocational' education. It
differs in respect of what is taught (and the criterion for determining
what is appropriate to be taught), and in respect of how it is taught;
and where it is a specialized education (which it need not be, but a
'vocational' education must be), the principle of specialization is
different from that which is characteristic of 'vocational' education.
Or, if that seems too dogmatic, then, I may say that I think that there
is a sort of education which is clearly different from both school and
'vocational' education, and I think it is the sort which for centuries

has been the concern of what we have hitherto called universities. And, to put it briefly, a university education is unlike either a school or a 'vocational' education because it is an education in 'languages' rather than 'literatures', and because it is concerned with the use and management of explanatory languages (or modes of thought) and not prescriptive languages. While a school-boy may be a passionate reader and may acquire from some books a store of information and from others a knowledge of himself and of how to behave, at a university he will be invited to seek something different from, perhaps, these same books. And he will come to understand that some books whose information is out-of-date or whose prescriptive utterances (if any) are unreliable – Gibbon or Stubbs, Dicey, Bagehot, Clark-Maxwell, Adam Smith – and are therefore worthless in a 'vocational' education, nevertheless have something to offer appropriate to a university education.

First, a university is an association of persons, locally situated, engaged in caring for and attending to the whole intellectual capital which composes a civilization. It is concerned not merely to keep an intellectual inheritance intact, but to be continuously recovering what has been lost, restoring what has been neglected, collecting together what has been dissipated, repairing what has been corrupted, reconsidering, reshaping, reorganizing, making more intelligible, reissuing and reinvesting. In principle, it works undistracted by practical concerns; its current directions of interest are not determined by any but academic considerations; the interest it earns is all reinvested.

This engagement is not, of course, confined to universities; many who are not members of one of these associations take part in it. But nowhere else is it undertaken in the manner I have described (that is, continuously and exhaustively) except in a university. And when universities have been negligent of this engagement, there has been nothing comparable to take their place. For the essence is that it is a co-operative enterprise, in which different minds, critical of one another, are engaged; and that it concerns not merely that part of our intellectual capital which has been accumulated in the last fifty or a hundred years, and not merely those items which have some immediate and practical contemporary relevance. And consequently, in a society (such as ours) which has a high standard of practical relevance, universities have often to be defended. And the usual defence is either to show that they also contribute (as least obliquely) to the prosecution of current undertakings, or to claim for them the status of an 'amenity' – that is, a piece of costly nonsense protected by our sentimental attachment from designed and immediate destruction but not so well protected against the imposition upon them of alien directions of activity.

Secondly, in a university this intellectual capital appears not as an accumulated result, an authoritative doctrine, a reliable collection of information, or a current condition cf knowledge, but as a variety of modes of thinking or directions of intellectual activity, each speaking with a voice, or in a 'language' of its own, and related to one another conversationally – that is, not as assertion or denial, but as oblique recognition and accommodation. Science, for example, in a university, is not an encyclopaedia of information or the present state of our 'physical' knowledge: it is a current activity, an explanatory manner of thinking and speaking being explored. And the same is true of mathematics, of philosophy and of history: each is an idiom of thought, a 'language' neither dead nor used simply to convey results, but in constant process of being explored and used. Doctrines, ideas, theories, which are used elsewhere to yield practical profits or to keep going a practical manner of living (like the Mendelian theory of biological inheritance, the molecular structure of matter, or Parkinson's law), in a university are recognized as temporary achievements whose value is their reinvestment value, and reinvestment here is being used in the exploration of the 'language', the explanatory manner of thinking and speaking, to which they properly belong.

Thirdly, a university is a place, not merely of learning and research, but of education. And what distinguishes the education it offers is, first of all, the character of the place itself. To study in a university is not like studying under a learned private scholar, nor is it like being taken on the grand tour by a lively and well-informed tutor. Each of these would be an education, but neither is a university education. Nor again, is it like being given the run of a first-class library. University education is the sort of education that may be enjoyed by having the run of a place where the activities I have described are going on and are going on in the manner I have described. And this distinguishes it, at once, from any other kind of education – school-education, the education available in a place of specialized 'vocational' training, in a polytechnic where a variety of skills are taught, in a specialized research institute which offers a few places for pupils, and that provided by a private scholar, engaged in one of these activities, who takes a pupil, as Döllinger took the young Acton. To be no more than a recognized spectator is to enjoy the opportunity of a kind of education which a different sort of place does not and cannot give, and which universities have offered in varying degrees ever since medieval times when they were places of 'chivalric' disputation between Masters and Doctors and undergraduates were spectator-learners of a mystery. In short, there appears in a university what cannot (or cannot so easily) appear elsewhere, the image of a civilization as a manifold of different intellectual activities, a conversation between different modes of thinking; and this determines the character of the education it offers.

Finally, a university is an association of persons engaged in formal teaching. In this respect it is distinguished by the engagements of the teachers. As teachers, they may be either better or worse than those elsewhere; but they are different because they are themselves learners engaged in learning something other than what they undertake to teach. They are not people with a set of conclusions, facts, truths, dogmas, etc., ready to impart or with a well-tried doctrine to hand out; nor are they people who make it their main business to be familiar with what may be called 'the current state of knowledge' in their department of study: each is a person engaged in the activity of exploring a particular mode of thought in particular connections.

Nevertheless, *what* they teach is not what they themselves are in process of learning, nor is it what they may have learned or discovered yesterday. As scholars they may live on what are called the 'frontiers of knowledge', but as teachers they must be something other than frontiersmen. Nor, again, is what they teach exactly the activity in which they are themselves engaged: their pupils are not exactly apprentices to an activity. A scientist, an historian or a philosopher does not teach his pupils to be scientists, historians, or philosophers. That is to say, his engagement as a teacher is not merely to educate possible successors to himself – though some of his pupils may turn out to be this. What a university teacher has, and what (because he is not distracted by considerations of immediate useful-ness or contemporary appropriateness) he may impart, is familiarity with the modes of thought, the 'languages' which, from one point of view, compose the whole intellectual capital of a civilization. What a university has to offer is not information but practice in thinking; and not practice in thinking in no manner in particular but in specific manners each capable of reaching its own characteristic kind of conclusions. And what undergraduates may get at a university, and nowhere else in such favourable circumstances, is some understand-ing of what it is to think historically, mathematically, scientifically or philosophically, and some understanding of these not as 'subjects', but as living 'languages' and of those who explore and speak them as being engaged in explanatory enterprises of different sorts.

Going further, a university may be recognized as an association of teachers of this sort whose activity reflects some beliefs about how this sort of teaching may best be carried on. And the most important of these beliefs (now, alas, somewhat eroded) is that the proper way to impart a mode of thinking (that is, a 'language') is in conjunction with the study of an appropriate 'literature' or 'text': the belief that learning to think scientifically is best achieved by studying, not some so-called 'scientific method', but some particular branch of science; and learning to think historically is to be achieved, not by studying something called 'the historical method', but by observing and following an historian at work upon a particular piece or aspect of the past. This (but only to the unwary) may suggest an approxi-mation of university to 'vocational' education, but that this is an illusion is revealed when we observe that in a university education a 'text' is understood, not as an organization of information but as the paradigm of a 'language'. Consequently, with the recognition in a university that 'languages' may be most appropriately studied in conjunction with 'literatures' goes the recognition that some 'litera-tures' (that is, some branches of scientific study, some periods or

x

passages of history, some legal systems, some philosophical writers) are in a more appropriate condition to be studied, or offer a clearer paradigm of the 'language' concerned, and that it is these 'literatures' or 'texts', and for these reasons, that the undergraduate is encouraged to read: chemistry rather than solar physics; the history of medieval England rather than of contemporary Java; Roman Law rather than Hittite or Celtic; Aristotle, Hume or Kant rather than Democritus, Leibnitz, Rickert or Bergson. And this is a convenient and appropriate way of determining what is to be studied because it leaves room for change and it indicates a criterion by which a branch of learning is to be judged in respect of undergraduate study – a criterion which is purely paedagogic and has nothing whatever to do with vocational or other extraneous considerations, such as the current academic interest of scholars, which may be in an entirely unsuitable condition for undergraduate pursuit.

From this enterprise of teaching undergraduates something about the intellectual capital of our civilization there has emerged, in general, two marginally different manners of setting it out for undergraduate study. Two sorts of 'specialized' study have established themselves. In the one (perhaps best represented by 'Greats'), a variety of modes of thinking – e.g. historical, philosophical, poetic, legal, and perhaps scientific – are studied, but in connection with 'literatures' or 'texts' in the Greek and Latin tongues or having place in the world of classical antiquity. In the other (represented by Schools of Modern History, of Mathematics, of Natural Science etc.), a single 'language', or mode of thought, is studied in connection with whatever 'literatures' or 'texts' there may be available in a suitable condition from time to time – e.g. the Constitutional History of Medieval England, Chemistry, Physics, Geology, etc., the English Law of Property, the poetry of sixteenth-century England, and so on. What determines the choice of these 'literatures' rather than others is their appropriateness to represent modes of thought; and this is recognized to depend upon their current condition, and (of course) their appropriateness for study by undergraduates who had received a certain sort of school-education.

This, then, is what I understand by university education. It is not something nebulous or indistinct, but something clear, unmistakable and distinct from every other sort of education. To be an under-graduate is to enjoy the 'leisure' which is denoted by thinking with-out having to think in the pragmatic terms of action and talking without having to speak in terms of prescription or practical advice – the 'leisure', in short, which distinguishes the peculiar academic engagement of explanation. And the belief that it is valuable, even for those who are to pass their lives in practical occupations of one sort or another and for whom (in that connection) a 'vocational' education may also be appropriate, to spend three years in which attention (so far as their studies are concerned) is expressly abstrac-ted from prescriptive manners of thinking in order to concentrate it, not merely upon explanations, but upon the understanding of explanatory enterprises, is the belief in which the whole specific character of a university education is abridged. And anyone who wishes to impose a different character upon university education will not only be transforming the character of universities but will also have taken a decisive step in a direction which points to the removal from the scene of this kind of education.

2

Now, it may be supposed that, under the name of 'politics' (or some equivalent word), there is something appropriate to be taught and learned in each of the three kinds or levels of education I have mentioned – school, 'vocational' and university education. Politics, in fact, is talked and written about, studied and taught in a variety of manners which readily distinguish themselves from one another. We may, indeed, find that our present circumstances are not free from confusion, 'politics' being taught (for example) in universities in a manner more appropriate to some other kind of education; but (with this sketch of the respective characters of these sorts of education before us) it should not be impossible to discern the kind of political study appropriate to each.

In respect of school-education there is, I think, little difficulty in determining what in general is appropriate to be taught in this connection. It is, in the first place, something suitable to be learned by everybody, for one of the principles of school education is that it is without significant orientation. And further, it is something that may be learned without the point of learning it being evident to the learner, and something that if learned in this way is not positively harmful or nonsensical. In the thoughts of the teacher it may be either a propaedeutic (like Greek grammar to the reading of Greek poetry) or it may compose a stock of information considered to have some general usefulness on its own account; but in the thoughts of the learner it need not have any more attachment to a specific useful-ness than geometry, algebra or physical geography. In short, what is appropriate is something which offers an introduction to an aspect of a civilization (the civilization which is the pupils' inheritance) understood as a stock of ideas, beliefs, images, practices, etc., rather than as a capital. And this, surely, was the character of 'civics' as it used to be taught in schools and is the character of its successor in our school education, namely, 'current affairs': an introduction to the current activities of governments and to the relevant structures and practices with some attention to the beliefs and opinions which may be held to illuminate them. Not, perhaps, a very inspiring study, and in its more desiccated passages (e.g., the duties of a town clerk, the House of Commons at ,work, and the pronouncements of a Kennedy, a Krushchev or a Castro) unlike Greek irregular verbs in holding out no evident promise of better things to come. Never-theless, it is capable of defence as part of a school-education on the ground that, with us, politics is everybody's business; and because this sort of study is no more misleading than many other school studies (like economics and history) are bound to be. At least it is something to modify the mystery of the world as it appears in the newspapers, and it entails nothing to prohibit a more profound interest in public affairs such as occasionally (along with county cricket, space travel and church brasses) makes its appearance among school-boys. The interest it serves is an interest in public affairs.

Nor, I think, is there any greater difficulty in determining the character of what may be called a professional or 'vocational' educa-tion in politics, that is, an education designed specifically for those who are called upon or who wish to engage in political activity. A 'vocational' education (in the sense in which I am using the expres-sion) may appear when three general conditions are satisfied, and it is apt to appear, in some form or other, whenever these conditions

THE STUDY OF POLITICS IN A UNIVERSITY   317

are satisfied. First, there must be a specific skill generally recognized
to be entailed in a current manner of living; secondly, there must be
something in connection with this skill which is capable of being
taught, although it may also require practice which cannot formally
be taught before the skill itself can be effectively exercised; and
thirdly, there must be people who desire to exercise this skill and
therefore desire to be educated in it. And it may plausibly be supposed that all these conditions are satisfied in respect of what we
recognize as political activity – that is, activity concerned with
governing and the instruments of government. Politics is unmistakably one of the skills entailed in our current manner of living.
And not only are there people who engage in it professionally
(politicians, party managers, agents and their assistants), but, as in
respect of other professional skills (only more so), there are occasional participants or the servants of participants (like government
or Trade Union officials) to whom the knowledge which is the
stock-in-trade of the professional is also relevant. Indeed, the
particular style of politics which has now imposed itself upon the
world calls for and accommodates large numbers of these occasional
participants, to say nothing of the political commentators and enter-
tainers who have become a feature of our life and who require this
information in their daily business. In these circumstances a 'vocational' education in politics has to be recognized as appropriate to a
larger, more miscellaneous and consequently less precisely determined set of students than is the case in some (but not in all) other
avocations. And if we hesitate to follow those who find it to be an
appropriate 'vocational' education for every citizen in a 'democracy',
or for a sufficient number to leaven the whole, then it may perhaps be
recognized as a 'vocational' education appropriate to those who are,
or who wish to be, politically self-conscious. But this does not
entail any modification of its character as a 'vocational' education
which here, as elsewhere, is an education designed to impart a
body of reliable knowledge necessary in the successful exercise of a
more or less particularized practical activity. And if the knowledge
imparted here is used by some continuously and by others intermittently, by some professionally and by others incidentally, this
does not distinguish it from (for example) the knowledge imparted

in a professional legal education which is a necessary part of the equipment not only of those who practise the law as a profession but also of many who are engaged in many other businesses and occupations. And lastly, whatever doubts we may have about its extent, reliability and coherence (and whatever else we may think it desirable for a participator in politics to know), it would be absurdly captious to take the view that, in connection with politics, there is no information about current practices and current manners of thinking and speaking such as is the characteristic knowledge imparted in a 'vocational' education, or that this knowledge is incapable of being taught. Indeed, there is a vast quantity of this information, and much of it is so obscurely situated that it requires the persistence of a beaver to discover it and the mind of a chancery barrister to put it in order. On the face of it there is no reason why one should not undertake to teach politics as one might undertake to teach plumbing, 'home-making', librarianship, farming or how to run a bassoon factory; and this teaching is, in fact, undertaken.

And, to confirm this view, there already exists an extensive political literature (both books and periodicals), not devoid of general interest and capable of answering the curiosity of the unengaged, but satisfying the specification of a literature appropriate to a 'vocational' education. It is concerned with current practice; it is designed to convey the sort of information about the conduct of public affairs (what to do and how to do it) which anyone called upon or volunteering to participate needs to know; and the authors of it (by reason of their skill and knowledge) are frequently invited to perform the services of political architects or to act as consultants in the conduct of administration or of foreign affairs.

In this unsophisticated literature the properties of political and administrative devices such as federalism, second chambers, committees of inquiry, public corporations, taxes on capital, sumptuary laws, concentrations of power, etc., are dispassionately examined; the behaviour of voters is studied; the organization and propensities of different political parties are investigated; pressure groups, 'establishments' and *élites* are detected; policies are scrutinized in respect of their formation and consequences; the relative efficiency of different administrative areas and of the various methods of com-

munication in current use are considered; and a vast array of information about the current politics of other countries is collected and
marshalled ready for those who have to take (or who want to take)
decisions or make judgments about the conduct of foreign affairs.
And at a somewhat lower level, there are handbooks designed for
the guidance and instruction of the inferior ranks of administrators.
Of course, all this outdistances in intellectual content (and sometimes in unengaged general interest) the technical literature concerned, for example, with building houses or growing tomatoes; but
the disproportion is not overwhelming, and in design and purport all
these technical literatures are indistinguishable from one another.

Moreover, technical literatures, even those in the highest class
(like those of law or medicine), are apt to have their popular counterparts; and there seems little to stand in the way of the appearance of a
vulgar counterpart to this literature of political inquiry and instruction. A little book on *How to Restore old Cottages* may be flanked on
the bookstalls by one on *How to Restore old Monarchies*; an article on
'A face-lift for the kitchen: new and exciting materials' in a *Do It
Yourself* magazine will be followed by others on 'Dos and Don'ts in
making a Revolution', 'How to win an Election' and 'What you
should know about Public Corporations'. Indeed, writings of this
kind (with perhaps less obvious titles) have been available for more
than a century.

Now, the contemplation of all these investigations has generated
the vision of a modern 'science' of government and administration, a
growing body of what is believed to be well-tested information,
daily becoming more comprehensive, about the operation and reliability of the various processes, projects, policies, materials and
devices available in current political and administrative activity 'to
solve the political and governmental problems which confront
mankind'.

The descriptions we have of this so-called 'master science'[1] do not
present it as an enterprise in which events are understood in terms of
the operation of general laws, but (more modestly) as 'a systematic,

[1] W. A. Robson, *The University Teaching of the Social Sciences – Political
Science*, UNESCO, 1954; H. J. Blackham, *Political Discipline in a Free
Society*.

organized, teachable body of knowledge' springing from the study of political ideas, of the constitutions and processes of governments, of the structure and operation of political parties and groups, of the generation of public policy and public opinion and of the relations between states.[1] From this knowledge it is designed to elicit a 'body of rational principles' concerning political activity and the administration of public affairs. And when we consider what we are told about 'the hopes and expectations reposed in this master science', the design in collecting together this body of knowledge and the design in teaching it, we are left in no doubt that it is intended to be the material of an education in political and administrative activity. The 'authentic aims' of this science are: 'to study the moral problems of mankind in order to establish the principles of collective morality'; to formulate 'the principles which should inspire political organization and action'; 'to throw light on political ideas and political action in order that the government of man may be improved'; 'to throw some light on the great problems of our time: such as the problem of avoiding war, of increasing international peace and security, of extending freedom, of assisting the development of backward countries, of preventing the exploitation of native races, of using government as a means of raising living standards and promoting prosperity, of banishing ignorance, squalor, destitution and disease through the social services, of increasing welfare, happiness and the dignity of mankind'; 'to solve the political and governmental problems which confront mankind'; 'to assuage the maladies and struggles and conflicts of men in society'; 'to show the nations how to achieve peace and security'. And the design in teaching this science is to equip the student 'to comprehend the important political issues of the day'; 'to participate effectively in political discussion, to grasp the important questions of policy, to withstand the flattery of the demagogue, to resist the lies of the dictator or the promises of the imposter, to distinguish between propaganda and truth, to bring informed criticism to bear on public authorities, or to appreciate the criteria by which government action can be appraised'; and 'to give the voter an intelligent interest in the government of his country'

[1] This is sometimes generalized as the study of the manifestations, processes, scope, results and moral basis of 'power in society'.

without which 'democracy cannot work effectively'. In short, what is described here is unmistakably a 'vocational' education in politics; not a training appropriate only to a would-be official (though there is much here which is specially appropriate to those who engage professionally in politics or administration), but an education designed for participants in one of the skills which sustain our current manner of living, designed to improve the quality of their participation, and defended on account of 'the burning practical importance' of the problems with which this skill is concerned. It is an education with the same sort of design as that of a farmer or a medical practitioner, but (it is alleged) of unmistakably greater importance.

But avoiding flights of fancy, exaggerated expectations and a certain incoherence between what is set for study and the conclusions designed to be reached, it is difficult to disagree with the proposition that the serious inquiries I have mentioned, whose virtue is to investigate current political ideas and practices in a manner relevant to their use in political and administrative activity, intimate a body of knowledge capable of being taught and appropriate to be taught in a 'vocational' education in politics. The current state of our knowledge about voting habits, about the organization of the Conservative Party, about the President of the U.S.A., about the propensities of Trade Unions, and about the structure, control and administration of Public Corporations are as tangible pieces of information as the current state of our knowledge about the properties of the materials and devices used in domestic plumbing. And why should a voter, a political entertainer, a politician, a political agent or a local government official know less about his business than a doctor, a solicitor or a librarian?

Moreover, the other main aspect of political activity is, on the evidence, not less susceptible of similar treatment. Politics has always been three-quarters talk, and not to know how to use the current vocabulary of politics is a serious hindrance to anyone who, either as an amateur or as a professional, wishes to participate in the activity. The language of politics is the language of desire and aversion, of preference and choice, of approval and disapproval, of praise and blame, of persuasion, injunction, accusation and treat. It is the language in which we make promises, ask for support, recommend beliefs and actions, devise and commend administrative expedients and organize the beliefs and opinions of others in such a manner that policy may be effectively and economically executed: in short, it is the language of every-day, practical life. But men engaged in political activity (like others engaged in business or in the promotion of a religion), in order to make their opinions and actions more attractive, are apt to recommend them in the idiom of general ideas; and in order to make the opinions and actions of others less attractive are apt to denigrate them in terms of general ideas. In this manner (and often by appropriating words and expressions originally designed for a wholly different use) the current vocabulary of politics has made its appearance. It contains such words and expressions as these: Democratic, liberal, equal, natural, human, social, arbitrary, constitutional, planned, integrated, communist, provocative, feudal, conservative, progressive, capitalist, national, reactionary, revolutionary, fascist, privileged, private, public, socialist; open, closed, acquisitive, affluent, responsible and irresponsible societies; the international order, party, faction, welfare and amenity. It is a complicated vocabulary, and to teach its use is clearly appropriate to a 'vocational' education in politics. And here, also, there is a literature whose virtue (if not design) is to teach the use of this vocabulary. Books are produced every day which are concerned to teach us how to think politically and to provide an education for those whose business or pleasure it is to speak the current language of politics. Indeed, an expression has been invented (or seconded) to specify this literature; it is the so-called literature of 'political theory'; and 'political theories' (in this usage) are appropriately qualified by adjectives such as 'democratic', 'socialist', 'conservative', 'liberal', 'progressive' – that is, by adjectives which themselves belong to the current vocabulary of politics and are designed to indicate the political colour of the theories.

A 'vocational' education in politics, then, is not a merely imagined possibility; the skills it is designed to impart are among the most frequently (and most unskilfully) practised in our current manner of living, and the words and ideas it is designed to familiarize us with are those most frequently used in public discussion: there is unmistakably appropriate material for composing a curriculum for such an education. And whatever the limitations of the 'science' of government to be imparted in this education, I am not among those who believe that it must be nugatory because it lacks the imposing generalizations of some other sciences. It can without difficulty sustain its character as a compendium of reliable information useful for those engaged in political activity.[1] And when we consider the relative complexity of this skill, the mixture of amateurism and professionalism which political and administrative activity among us provokes, and the absence of settled professional standards, it is not at all surprising, either that the curriculum of such an education should still lack authoritative definition, or that the institutions offering such an education should (outside the USA, Russia and China) remain comparatively few.

But there is another reason why the appearance of the possibility of a 'vocational' education in politics provoked, in this country, no great efflorescence of educational institutions to exploit it. For when, at long last, observation and reflection on current political activity had generated a body of information about government and administration, and when professional political skill ceased to be the exclusive business of Kings and hereditary ruling classes, when (in short) government ceased to be a mystery, and after a suitable interval had elapsed, politics *eo nomine* began to be taught in our universities; and the manner in which it was taught was that which is appropriate to a 'vocational' education. Unsuspecting undergraduates, most of whom had no thought of becoming professional politicians or administrators, but in a few of whom there was perhaps a vague desire to be politically self-conscious coupled with an inability to do it for themselves, found imposed upon them a curriculum of study of unimaginable dreariness in which they learned the structures of the current constitutions of the world and whose anatomical studies were enlivened only by some idle political gossip and some tendentious speculation about current policy. As a 'vocational' education in

[1] This, however, is the most that can be said for it. The larger claims made on behalf of this 'master science' rest either upon the moral prejudices of those who make them (and which we cannot all be expected to share), or upon a naive ethical naturalism.

politics it was, of course, worthless; and yet the information it offered, and the manner in which it was offered, could have no conceivable interest to anyone except those whose heads were full of the enterprise of participating in political activity or to persons with the insatiable curiosity of a concierge. It merely provided a spurious academic focus for whatever political interest there might be about, and it was saved from manifest academic disgrace by the intrusion of a little genuine historical study. Together with this went the study of some notable books (like Plato's *Republic*, Hobbes's *Leviathan*, Rousseau's *du Contrat Social*, Mill's essay on *Liberty* and Bosanquet's *Philosophical Theory of the State*) and some less notable tracts, believed to be in some sense 'about politics' and therefore assumed to have a political 'ideal', or programme, or policy, or device to recommend. And the manner in which they were studied was designed to elicit and criticize this programme: they were recognized, in short, as books of 'political theory'.[1] Indeed, I can describe the manner in which these books were read only as a mixture between the manner in which one might read an out-of-date text-book on naval architecture and the manner in which one might study a current election manifesto. The result was that we were alive only to the political quaintness (or enormity) of these books, and our attention was narrowed down to listening either for the political *faux pas* or for the echos of political modernity.

Some, of course, escaped. There were individuals who never surrendered to it; those universities in which 'politics' had long had its place as an occasion for historical or philosophical study were in some degree fortified against it; and, in any case, English universities are far less deeply compromised than those in America. But this regrettable disposition – regrettable because it conflicted with the most deeply rooted traditions of university education – set a course for 'politics' in those universities in which it established itself as an independent 'subject' of undergraduate study, a course from which divergence has been difficult even where it has been desired.

[1] And we had commentaries, like Hobhouse's *Metaphysical Theory of the State* (and later Crossman on *Plato Today* and Popper on *The Open Society and its Enemies*), to encourage us in this recognition.

It was, no doubt, long ago agreed that this was a manner of studying politics (now perhaps to be found only in American textbooks) not entirely appropriate in a university; and many improvements have been made. But these improvements have, for the most part, been directed not to doing something else more appropriate in a university education, but to doing better what had been ill-done before. We have added the study of operation to the study of structure; we have added political parties, pressure groups, civil services, local authorities and public corporations to the study of the constitutions of governments; we have uncovered obscure passages in political organization; we have heard the call of political sociology; we have explored what can only be called the curiosities of politics; and we have tried to elicit information of more general interest by comparing one set of structures with another. In short, we have been neither idle nor unadventurous; but, in the main, we have continued to work at the same level of information as the pioneers of political study in universities – a level appropriate only to a 'vocational' education. And in respect of these classics of political reflection, our pupils are still encouraged to read them in order to discover the injunctions about political conduct they are believed to contain and in order to reflect upon the appropriateness to us of these injunctions; and they are still written about in this manner. The search for anything in the present teaching of 'politics' in our universities (wherever that teaching has firmly established itself) which separates it decisively and unmistakably from what is appropriate to what I have called a 'vocational' education in politics, anything which carries us beyond the study of 'literatures' as repositories of information to the study of a 'language' or a manner of thinking, is not very rewarding. Indeed, the most comprehensive recent description of the teaching of 'politics' in universities (from which I have already quoted) accepts without misgiving or apology this 'vocational' or participatory study as appropriate to a university education. No doubt, there is a certain amount of confusion, but there is little inclination to look in any other direction.

Now, I may be told I have overlooked two directions of movement both of which point to a manner of study which, it may be alleged, has gone some way to emancipate the teaching of 'politics' in a university from this 'vocational' disposition and to give it what is somewhat naïvely called a 'liberal' character. First, it will be said, we are no longer content to observe and to impart the miscellaneous results of our observation; we have out-grown political anatomy. Instead, we 'analyse' (blessed word) and teach the art of analysis, we compare (no less blessed word) and teach the science of making comparisons, we make ideal models, we construct hypotheses, we formulate the problems of the future and seek solutions. And this (or some of it) may, no doubt, be counted to us as merit: nobody can say we are simple-minded in our study of politics. But none of it has served (or is even designed) to set us on to some other questions than the essentially 'vocational' questions: How does it work? How can it be improved? Is it democratic? and so on. And much of it (because it has come to be concerned with imaginary 'systems' and 'processes', 'powers', 'establishments' and *élites*, stereotypes of one sort or another) diverts our attention from the often irregular character of political organizations and events, and thus makes our 'vocational' education less good than it might be. In short, and in spite of these complexities and subtleties which have given to our original naïvety a touch of sophistication, we are still disposed to teach 'politics' in universities as a kind of staff-duties course in politics.

But secondly, it will be said, in spite of our rather lamentable tendency to urge our pupils to acquaint themselves with the patterns and structures of current politics (that is, with the contents of political 'texts') and to provide for their needs by engaging experts on an ever increasing number of these 'texts', experts in the political 'systems' of India and Iraq, of Ghana and Indonesia, we do make a notable attempt to teach them how to use a 'language', namely, the language of politics. The difference between ourselves and the pioneers of 'politics' in universities, it will be said, is that for us the study of the dull and doubtful detail of political structures and operations is designed as a means of teaching our pupils how to think politically. In short we have begun to recognize that 'politics' in a university is appropriately concerned with the study of a 'language' and with 'literatures' only as paradigms of this 'language'. Yet, when we consider the efforts made to persuade our pupils to acquaint them-

selves with as large as possible a number of these 'texts', our disposition to recognize the 'authority' of those who are themselves
engaged in political activity (or who have retired from it) and our
recognition that there is a problem of 'bias' in teaching 'politics' in a
university (all of which can relate only to a 'vocational' political
education), we may perhaps doubt the truth of this claim. But, even
assuming this difference between ourselves and the pioneers is well
observed, something else is needed to distinguish our enterprise from
that of a 'vocational' education in politics. All that is being alleged
here is that we offer a 'vocational' education superior to that which
used to be offered.

To be brief, the difference lies in the nature of the 'languages'
concerned. To teach the language of current politics is an essential
part of a 'vocational' education in politics, because skill in using this
language, and being familiar with the manners of thinking it represents, is an essential part of political activity. But this is not a
language of the same kind as the 'languages' which I have suggested
it is the distinctive feature of a university education to put before
undergraduates. These 'languages' – the 'languages' of history, of
philosophy, of science and of mathematics – are all of them *explanatory* languages; each of them represents a specific mode of
explanation. But the language of politics is not a language of
explanation, any more than the languages of poetry or moral conduct are languages of explanation. There is no specifically 'political'
explanation of anything: the word 'politics' stands for holding certain kinds of beliefs and opinions, making certain kinds of judgments,
performing certain kinds of actions, and thinking in terms of certain
practical, not explanatory, considerabilities. If there is a manner of
thinking and speaking that can properly be called 'political', the
appropriate business of a university in respect of it is not to use it, or
to teach the use of it, but to explain it – that is, to bring to bear upon
it one or more of the recognized modes of explanation. If the expression 'political activity' stands for something which plausibly offers
itself to be understood and to be explained, the questions a teacher of
'politics' in a university should ask himself are: In what manner do I
design to explain it? Into what explanatory 'language' or 'languages'
should I translate it? What 'languages' of explanation may an under-

graduate find himself learning to use and to manage in connection with politics?

Now, I believe that, if we put behind us the alluring but inappropriate 'vocational' enterprise of teaching the use and management of the language of politics, the study of 'politics' at a university may afford an undergraduate the opportunity of acquainting himself with two different manners of understanding, two modes of thought, two explanatory 'languages', namely, the 'languages' of history and of philosophy. What falls outside these is, I think, one or other of these manners of thinking disguised in some not very elegant fancy dress. Each of these manners of thinking is a genuine mode of explanation: each operates with clear criteria of relevance; each is capable of reaching conclusions appropriate to itself; in each it may be said that this or that is an error, but also (and more significantly) that this or that is out of character; and statements made in these 'languages' do not pretend to have injunctive force. Thus, the appropriate engagement of an undergraduate student of 'politics' at a university will be to be taught and to learn something about the modes of thought and manners of speaking of an historian and a philosopher, and to do this in connection with politics, while others (in other Schools) are doing it in other connections. While one undergraduate may acquire some insight into the manner in which an historian thinks and speaks and understands and explains in connection with the English wool trade in the fifteenth century, or in connection with the Papacy in the sixteenth century (these being the chosen 'texts'), another, in a School of 'Politics', may do the same thing in connection with a political party, the House of Commons, Machiavelli's *Prince* or the Haldane Report. And while an undergraduate in a School of Philosophy may study Kant's *Critique of Pure Reason* (and if he does so in a university manner it is not merely to acquaint himself with Kant's conclusions but to understand Kant's problems and to acquire the connoisseurship which can recognize a philosophical argument), so an undergraduate in a School of 'Politics' may read Hobbes's *Leviathan* or Hegel's *Philosophy of Right* and hope to learn from his study something about the philosophical mode of thinking. And if it should turn out that politics is an appropriate occasion for acquiring a familiarity with other authentic languages of explanation, then the opportunity may properly be taken.[1] But it is only in this manner that a study of 'politics' unmistakably distinguished from a 'vocational' study, and one that can sustain a place in a specifically university kind of education, can appear.

The main hindrance to its doing so is the 'vocational' disposition with which 'politics' has come to establish itself in a university education and which it has never succeeded in throwing off. I do not think this disposition among university teachers of 'politics' is commonly the result of profound reflection, although some are held to it with a passionate attachment which they have tried their hands at defending. It springs, rather, from their being themselves primarily interested in politics in the vulgar sense and in the problems of administration, from their being impressed with the information about political and administrative activity believed to be available, and from an inability to understand why this information should not be imparted as a university education to undergraduates, or, indeed, what else there is plausibly to teach under the head of 'politics'. Their mistaken disposition, as university teachers, does not spring from the direction in which their own studies have taken them, but from their desire to teach undergraduates what they themselves are interested in, regardless of its inappropriateness.[2] They understand

[1] It is true that for more than a century the possibility of a genuinely explanatory 'science' of politics has been explored. But since nobody is likely to claim that anything in a condition even remotely suitable to be put before an undergraduate as an occasion for his acquiring a familiarity with a scientific mode of thinking has appeared, I have not thought it necessary to consider what our situation would be if this enterprise had been more fruitful. Nor (except perhaps in America) has anyone attempted to teach such a 'science' to undergraduates.

[2] It will, of course, be understood that I am not objecting to dons being concerned with politics. It is long since academics began to take an interest in the activity of governing and the instruments of government, and among the circumstances which in England (and perhaps also in America) have, in recent times, promoted this sort of interest is the fact that many academics, seconded during two wars to government offices, have found there a virgin (but not unsuspected) world and have felt the impulse to explore it. Moreover, the study of politics is not a novelty in European and American universities: it is said that the earliest European professorship in 'politics', founded at Uppsala in the seventeenth century, was the Chair of 'Statesmanship and Eloquence' (doing and talking, the inseparable components of political activity); and something called 'political science', constructed on various analogies and

their problem as university teachers to be the problem of raising the
study of politics above the level of 'current affairs' and to give it a
respectable intellectual content. But they rarely understand that this
can be done only by recognizing that the word 'politics' in a university education signifies, not a 'subject' of study, but a library of 'texts'
which, in this kind of education, is merely the occasion for learning
how to handle and manage some of the 'languages' of explanation.

And if it is said that the manner in which 'politics' is taught in
universities has not forbidden a connection with history and philosophy, the reply must be that the connection is often resented
as a diversion from the proper concerns of 'political science', and
that wherever it has been made it has been apt to be corrupting
rather than emancipating. 'History' appears, not as a mode of explanation, but merely as some conclusions of allegedly 'historical'
writers believed to account for the present structure or to forecast
the future prospects of (for example) a political party, or to provide
evidence relating to the origin or the efficiency of an administrative
device. 'History' is patronizingly admitted so long as it remains in
the 'background' (whatever that may mean). And 'philosophy'
appears, not as a manner of thinking but as a misused word to
identify what is believed to be a certain kind of interest in politics.
Merely to extend our studies backwards a little way into the past in
order to account for a piece of political conduct is not 'doing' history;
it is indulging in a piece of retrospective politics which makes certain that the historical mode of thinking never properly appears.
And when in the writings of Plato or Hobbes or Rousseau or Hegel
or Mill what is being looked for is the political disposition of these

---

offering conclusions of various degrees of abstraction, has been pursued for
more than a century. But if every don were to teach undergraduates what he
himself is interested in, and if every professorial chair were held to entail or
to authorize a counterpart to itself in undergraduate education, there would
be little in these days to distinguish a university from a mad-house. And if
the contention is that undergraduates in significant numbers want to devote
a large part of their university days learning what (it is alleged) will prepare
them for a more intelligent participation in politics, the answer is that (except
for the few who mistake a university for a place of 'vocational' education
and who want to 'go in' for politics or to become administrators) this is not
true; and in any case it is irrelevant.

writers, when expressions like 'natural law', 'general will', 'freedom', 'the rule of law', 'justice', or 'sovereignty', which, philosophically speaking, are explanatory concepts, whose explanatory value might have been explored, are turned (as the politician turns everything he touches) into prescriptive concepts, and when what is reflected upon is merely their injunctive force, all chance is lost of learning something about the philosophical mode of thought. When, in this manner, a philosophical argument is turned into a so-called 'political theory', and it is thought appropriate to give it a political label, calling it 'democratic', 'conservative', 'liberal', 'progressive', or 'reactionary', a 'vocational' education in politics may be seen to have reimposed itself; and the opportunity has been lost of understanding that a philosopher is never concerned with a condition of things but only with a manner of explanation, and of recognizing that the only thing that matters in a philosophical argument is its coherence, its intelligibility, its power to illuminate and its fertility. And when we ask our pupils to display their attainments by discussing such questions as Was Mill a democrat? or, Has the House of Lords outlived its usefulness? or, Would not Ghana do better with a Presidential system of government than a Parliamentary? or, Is Great Britain heading for a One-Party State? we may suspect that a not very high class 'vocational' education in politics is at work.

We have far to go; and having got off on the wrong foot, progress towards a proper university education connected with politics is not likely to be very rapid. But there are two precepts which, if followed, would take us in what I believe to be the proper direction.

First, in a School of 'Politics' we should never use the language of politics; we should use only the explanatory 'languages' of academic study. Of course, the words which compose our vocabulary of politics may be uttered, but only in order to inquire into their use and meaning, in order to take them to pieces and write them out in the long-hand of historical or philosophical explanation. They should never be given the appearance of being themselves explanatory words and expressions. And we should recognize that this so-called 'political theory' is itself a form of political activity, and therefore not itself to be taught, but to be explained, historically or philosophically.

And secondly, since in a university we should regard ourselves as supervising, not the study of 'texts' understood as organizations of information, but the study of the use of explanatory 'languages' in connection with appropriate 'texts', these 'texts' should be chosen with care and for the relevant (paedagogic) reasons. As things are at present, any but the proper criteria are applied. A part of the world has only to be often in the newspapers, a state has only to be new or powerful, an administrative device has only to be considered interesting or administratively important by the pundits, and its claim to be chosen as a 'text' for undergraduate study in a university is believed to be irrefutable. But these, instead of being the best reasons for choosing it, are the worst; they are political, not paedagogic reasons. For example, it appears to me that the place which the politics of contemporary Russia has come to occupy in undergraduate study is indefensible except in the irrelevant terms of a 'vocational' political education. We know incomparably less about what goes on in Russian politics than in the politics of any other country in the world, bar perhaps China. Even in a 'vocational' political education this 'text' would be suspect: to set it for study would be inviting superficial and useless learning – systems instead of realities, mechanical models in place of concrete behaviour – and it would be justified only on account of the power and political importance of the Russian state and therefore the desirability of teaching something about it, however inadequate. But in a university education these are not significant considerations; what matters there is that the material should be in a suitable condition for the enterprise of teaching undergraduates how to think historically. And this, unquestionably, is not the condition of current Russian politics. Why should a School of 'Politics' go out of its way to choose for undergraduate study particularly obscure and corrupt 'texts', 'texts' suitable only for the most skilful emandators, when well-edited 'texts', like the politics of France, or Sweden, or the USA, or Spain (to say nothing of Great Britain), are available?

An academic study appears only when an activity is isolated and when it is in a fit condition to be an occasion for explanatory modes of thought. There are large tracts of the human past – arts and literatures, laws and customs, happenings in the world, the thoughts that men have entertained, their inventions and devices – which are eligible for this kind of study. Physical and chemical operations wherever they take place, the properties of numbers, the habits and customs of remote peoples, the structure and composition of the earth, and our own moral ideas, may be disengaged from our approval and disapproval and may be studied from some other standpoint than that of usefulness in the pursuit of our own practical enterprises. Even the study of the scarce opportunities the world offers for satisfying our wants may be detached from considerations of public or private policy. Each, it is true, contains an invitation other than the invitation to explain; but it is an invitation we may easily decline. In respect of current politics (our own or that of neighbouring peoples), however, this is more difficult; it is not unmistakably promising material for the enterprise of explanation. It is too difficult for most people to turn their backs upon the enterprise of participating and of thinking in the 'vocational' idiom of participation; it is too easy to confuse injunction and explanation; it is too attractive to neglect philosophy for finding reasons for holding favourite political opinions, and to avoid doing history for ourselves in favour of making use of the convenient conclusions of historians. Politics offers the most difficult of all 'literatures', the most difficult of all collections of 'texts', in connection with which to learn to handle and manage the languages of explanation: the idiom of the material to be studied is ever ready to impose itself upon the manner in which it is studied. Nevertheless, if we recognize what we should be doing at a university, the difficulty may itself be an attraction; if we recognize that our proper business is not with politics at all but with teaching, in connection with politics, how to manage the 'languages' of history and philosophy and how to distinguish them and their different sorts of utterance.

1961